D1496090

Traditions and contexts in
the poetry of Horace

This book explores the whole range of the output of an exceptionally versatile and innovative poet, from the *Epodes* to the literary-critical *Epistles*. Distinguished scholars of diverse background and interests introduce readers to a variety of critical approaches to Horace and to Latin poetry. Close attention is paid throughout to the actual text of Horace, with many of the chapters focusing on the reading of a single poem. These close readings are then situated in a number of different political, philosophical and historical contexts. The book sheds light not only on Horace but on the general problems confronting Latinists in the study of Augustan poetry, and it will be of value to a wide range of upper-level Latin students and scholars.

TONY WOODMAN is Professor of Latin at the University of Durham. He is the author of *Velleius Paterculus: the Tiberian narrative* (1977), *Velleius Paterculus: the Caesarian and Augustan narrative* (1983), *Rhetoric in classical historiography* (1988), *Tacitus reviewed* (1998) and a translation of Tacitus' *Annals* for Hackett (2002). He has co-authored, with Ronald Martin, editions of Tacitus' *Annals* 4 for the Cambridge Greek and Latin Classics series (1989) and *Annals* 3 for the Cambridge Classical Texts and Commentaries series (1996), and, with C. S. Kraus, *Latin historians* for the *Greece and Rome* New Surveys in the Classics (1997). In addition he is the co-editor of *Quality and pleasure in Latin poetry* (1974), *Creative imitation and Latin literature* (1979), *Poetry and politics in the age of Augustus* (1984), *Past perspectives* (1986), *Author and audience in Latin literature* (1992), *Tacitus and the Tacitean tradition* (1993) and *Papers of the Leeds International Latin Seminar* (1995).

DENIS FEENEY is Giger Professor of Latin at Princeton University. He previously held the positions of Professor of Classics at the University of Wisconsin, Professor of Latin at the University of Bristol, and Fellow and Tutor in Classics at New College, Oxford. He is the author of *The gods in epic: poets and critics of the classical tradition* (1991) and *Literature and religion at Rome* (1998) and is a General Editor of the series Roman Literature and its Contexts, published by Cambridge University Press.

Traditions and contexts in the poetry of Horace

EDITED BY

TONY WOODMAN
UNIVERSITY OF DURHAM

&

DENIS FEENEY
PRINCETON UNIVERSITY

CAMBRIDGE
UNIVERSITY PRESS

PUBLISHED BY THE PRESS SYNDICATE OF THE UNIVERSITY OF CAMBRIDGE
The Pitt Building, Trumpington Street, Cambridge, United Kingdom

CAMBRIDGE UNIVERSITY PRESS
The Edinburgh Building, Cambridge CB2 2RU, UK
40 West 20th Street, New York, NY 10011-4211, USA
477 Williamstown Road, Port Melbourne, VIC 3207, Australia
Ruiz de Alarcón 13, 28014 Madrid, Spain
Dock House, The Waterfront, Cape Town 8001, South Africa

http://www.cambridge.org

First published 2002

Printed in the United Kingdom at the University Press, Cambridge

Typeface Plantin 10/12 pt.   *System* LaTeX 2$_\varepsilon$ [TB]

A catalogue record for this book is available from the British Library

Library of Congress Cataloguing in Publication data

Traditions and contexts in the poetry of Horace / edited by Tony Woodman &
Denis Feeney.
    p.   cm.
Includes bibliographical references and index.
ISBN 0 521 64246 9
1. Horace – Criticism and interpretation.   2. Epistolary poetry, Latin – History and
criticism.   3. Laudatory poetry, Latin – History and criticism.   4. Verse satire,
Latin – History and criticism.   5. Influence (Literary, artistic, etc.)   6. Rome – In
literature.   1. Woodman, A. J. (Anthony John)   11. Feeney, D. C.
PA6411 .T725   2002
874′.01 – dc21   2001052630

ISBN 0 521 64246 9

CONTENTS

vi   Contents

CONTRIBUTORS

ALESSANDRO BARCHIESI. Professor of Latin Literature at the University of Verona. Author of *La traccia del modello* (1984), *The poet and the prince* (1997), *Speaking volumes* (2001), a commentary on *Heroides* 1–3 (1993) and co-editor of *Ovidian transformations* (1999). He has written a series of recent papers on Horace.

ARNOLD BRADSHAW. Formerly Master of Van Mildert College, University of Durham, and author of articles on African languages and Greek and Latin literature.

IAN M. LE M. DU QUESNAY. Lecturer in Classics in the University of Cambridge and Senior Tutor of Jesus College. Author of numerous studies of republican and Augustan poetry.

DENIS FEENEY. Giger Professor of Latin in Princeton University. Author of *The gods in epic: poets and critics of the classical tradition* (1991) and *Literature and religion at Rome: cultures, contexts, and beliefs* (1998).

KIRK FREUDENBURG. Professor of Classics at the Ohio State University. Author of *The walking Muse: Horace on the theory of satire* (1993) and *Satires of Rome: threatening poses from Lucilius to Juvenal* (2001).

ALAN GRIFFITHS. Senior Lecturer in Greek and Latin at University College London. He is editor of *Stage directions: essays in ancient drama in honour of E. W. Handley* (1996), and has also published in the areas of archaic and Hellenistic poetry and Greek vase-painting.

MICHÈLE LOWRIE. Associate Professor of Classics at New York University. Author of *Horace's narrative Odes* (1997) and articles on Horace, Ovid and Baudelaire.

JOHN MOLES. Professor of Latin at the University of Newcastle upon Tyne. Author of *Plutarch: the Life of Cicero* (1988) and numerous articles on Greek and Latin literature and philosophy.

R. G. M. NISBET. Corpus Christi Professor of Latin in the University of Oxford from 1970 to 1992. Author of commentaries on Cicero, *In Pisonem* (1961) and (with Margaret Hubbard) on Horace, *Odes* 1 (1970) and *Odes* 2 (1978). His *Collected papers on Latin literature* appeared in 1995.

ELLEN OLIENSIS. Associate Professor of Classics at the University of California, Berkeley. Author of *Horace and the rhetoric of authority* (1998).

TONY WOODMAN. Professor of Latin in the University of Durham. Author of commentaries on Velleius Paterculus (1977, 1983) and (with Ronald Martin) on Tacitus, *Annals* 3 (1996) and *Annals* 4 (1989), and of *Rhetoric in classical historiography* (1988), *Tacitus reviewed* (1998) and (with C. S. Kraus) *Latin historians* (1997); co-editor of *Quality and pleasure in Latin poetry* (1974), *Creative imitation and Latin literature* (1979), *Poetry and politics in the age of Augustus* (1984), *Past perspectives: studies in Greek and Roman historical writing* (1986), *Author and audience in Latin literature* (1992) and *Tacitus and the Tacitean tradition* (1993).

JAMES E. G. ZETZEL. Professor of Classics and James R. Barker Professor of Contemporary Civilization at Columbia University, New York. Author of a commentary on Cicero's *De re publica* (1995) and of *Cicero: On the commonwealth and On the laws* (1999).

PROLOGUE

In compiling this volume, we sought contributors who were known to be engaged in the field of Horatian scholarship and who, between them, seemed likely to cover most of Horace's *œuvre* and to represent a variety of different approaches. We saw our editorial task as drawing conclusions in an Epilogue, highlighting the common themes of the chapters in order to draw into focus the preoccupations that contemporary Latinists bring to bear on a canonical Latin author.

Inevitably there is a degree of circularity in this procedure, since the personal preferences of individual scholars are generally well known and it is unlikely that, for example, younger scholars in one country will adopt the same approaches as a middle-aged in another. Indeed three papers, familiar from oral performance, were commissioned especially for this volume and hence were known in advance. Nevertheless one cannot make absolute predictions: it was not to be expected that two contributors would exchange topics half-way through the proceedings, and we were surprised that the final submission of another was devoted to an entirely different work of Horace's from that stipulated on the contract.

Not every invitation to contribute to this volume was accepted, and the alacrity with which some scholars accepted was in inverse proportion to the speed with which they produced their papers. Hence there have been repeated delays, for which apologies are due to all concerned. Nevertheless we believe that the resulting volume has been well worth the wait and we hope that it may stand as a fitting complement to *Homage to Horace*, edited by S. J. Harrison (1995).

April 2001   D.C.F., A.J.W.

ACKNOWLEDGEMENTS

Grateful thanks are due to Peter Heslin and Esther McGilvray for their invaluable help during the word-processing stages of this book's production.

ARNOLD BRADSHAW

1 HORACE'S BIRTHDAY AND DEATHDAY

In every human life there are two days of special significance – birthday and deathday. The first is marked with a rubric in the diary, while the second lurks unknown among all the leaves of the year. In Rome birthdays were noted and celebrated throughout life and sometimes afterwards,[1] but deathdays were less liable to leave a permanent mark, unless the deceased was an emperor or a Christian saint. Cases where an individual's precise dates are recorded are rare, and of all Latin authors up to the fifth century AD only five – apart from Caesars and saints with literary pretensions – appear to qualify.[2] Horace is one of the few, and it seems worthwhile to review the evidence for his lifespan and to examine what he himself had to say about his beginning and his end.

THE TRADITION

The dates commonly quoted in modern biographical notices are derived from the *Vita* which is ascribed with plausibility to Suetonius and which ends with the following passage (unamended):

> Natus est VI Idus Decembris L. Cotta et L. Torquato consulibus [8.12.65], decessit V Kal. Decembris C. Marcio Censorino et C. Asinio Gallo consulibus [27.11.8] post nonum et quinquagesimum annum herede Augusto palam nuncupato, cum urgente ui ualetudinis non sufficeret ad obsignandas testamenti tabulas. humatus et conditus est extremis Esquiliis iuxta Maecenatis tumulum.[3]

Centuries ago critics pointed out that the interval between birth and death amounts, not to 59, but to 57 years (counting by the *fasti*, not by the stars); they ascribed the error in the text either to Suetonius or (more often) to the copyist. How this arithmetical problem is to be resolved, whether by emendation or other means, will be considered later.

YEAR OF BIRTH

The year at least is confirmed by Horace's own statements, of which there
are three:

(a) tu uina Torquato moue consule pressa meo   (*Epod.* 13.6)
(b) O nata mecum consule Manlio   (*Carm.* 3.21.1)
(c) forte meum siquis te percontabitur aeuum
    me quater undenos sciat impleuisse Decembris
    collegam Lepidum quo duxit Lollius anno [21 BC].

             28 *v.l.* dixit
                           (*Epist.* 1.20.26–8)

The third of these, the final lines of Book 1 of the *Epistles*, signalling his
age at the point of writing, is valuable as giving an approximate date for
the publication of that book as well as an indication of when Horace, for
the first time, abandoned lyric. The other two references, in *Epod.* 13 and
Carm. 3.21, are more specifically references to his birth-year and they
merit particular attention.

The two poems were probably separated by some years, but they share
certain characteristics. First of all their excellence has been widely recognised. Epode 13 in particular is a great favourite, being often described
as the best, the most elegant, the most ode-like of the epodes.[4] Not surprisingly it has received a good measure of critical attention;[5] it has also
raised considerable controversy, in particular over its supposed relation
to early Greek lyric models and its date.[6]

A more insistent question which can hardly be ignored, however wary
we may be of 'the autobiographical fallacy', is whether the poem is related
to some episode in the author's life. The arguments threaten to be inter-
minable, but many commentators do at least agree that the storm appears
to be symbolic as well as real; that Horace and his friends[7] are dismayed
by some historical crisis; that the poem proclaims the power of wine and
song to mitigate misery. The message is given added authority by repeating it in the words of a semi-divine teacher of heroes and strengthening it
by contrast, for, if these sweet alloquies of the sick heart relieve one who
is doomed, how much more must they lighten the spirit of those whose
fortunes may yet be restored!

The lesson both in its content and expression suits Horace's role as a
poet in the sympotic tradition, but has the poem anything to do with the
events of his own life? Poets live by their imagination; they can people
their poems with invented characters taken from life or literature; they
are actors who can put on any masks and play any part they wish. But,
if *persona* and wearer are revealed as identical, it is fair to assume that

we are face to face with the real man. That is precisely what happens in line 6, for, when a character speaks of his birthday (such is the implication of *meo*) and it is the birthday of the author, pretence is at an end. It is this detail which encourages us to take Epode 13 seriously as part of Horace's life. Claims that the poem is based on a Greek model do not deprive it of personal significance, for the poet would be likely to imitate an original which matched his own experience.

If the voice is Horace's own, where is he speaking from and when? What predicament could have produced anxieties so dreadful and literally monstrous (*sollicitudinibus*) in the lives of Horace and his companions, and how could their situation be analogous to that of Achilles? The simple answers which satisfy many are: we don't know and the convivial cure is analogue enough. But there is at least one point of resemblance between Horace's company and the Homeric hero which is emphasised: youth. For the former *dumque uirent genua | et decet* (4–5) is a conventional phrase, but an adolescent Achilles is something of a novelty.[8] For all who had been brought up on Homer, Achilles was the supreme warrior and the model of bravery in battle. The Achilles of Epode 13 is nothing of the kind: he is not yet a man of war; he is a boy still under tutelage, and no school-leaver was ever given a final report with grimmer prognostics. His teacher with supernatural perception gives him no promise of glory but only the prospect of death in an unpleasant-sounding foreign land. Could this remarkable picture have any relevance to Horace and his friends? It certainly could if they were young soldiers fearful at the prospect of going into battle for the first time.[9]

Now the only military phase in Horace's career for which there is un-questionable evidence occurred when, at the age of 22, he followed his fellow-student at the Academy in Athens, Marcus Junius Brutus, and took up arms against Octavian and Antony in the campaign which ended at Philippi in 42 BC.[10] It is not surprising that since at least the sixteenth century Epode 13 has been linked with that experience.[11] Acceptance of that link does not however allow any safe conclusion about the date of composition, for the sensations of a young man going off to war do not quickly fade from his mind; he might have written the poem long after the event.

Claims have, however, been made that he may also have been involved in other military service at a later date, and, if any of these were justi-fied, we should have to consider whether the epode could relate to the action concerned. The evidence depends upon the interpretation of four passages, two identified with specific campaigns (the war against Sextus Pompeius and Actium), and two of general import. In *Carm.* 3.4.26–8 Horace says he was saved from death on three occasions: *non me Philippis uersa acies retro,* | *deuota non exstinxit arbos,* | *nec Sicula Palinurus unda.* We know about Philippi and the falling tree but the third adventure is mysterious. The explanation of Ps.-Acro is: *Promuncturium est Siciliae, non a Palinuro Aeneae gubernatore dictum, sed [ab] Hannibalis, ubi redeuntem se Horatius de Macedonia periclitatum dixit, qui est et nauibus periculosus locus.* Clearly there is confusion here between Pelorus and Palinurus (both capes and helmsmen),[12] while the statement that Horace's misadventure occurred when he was returning from Greece may be merely a guess.[13] Some commentators believe that Horace is referring to the occasion in 36 when the greater part of Octavian's fleet was destroyed in two storms off Cape Palinurus on the Lucanian coast between Velia and Buxentum. Maecenas must have been present on this occasion, as it is recorded that he was later sent back to Rome to prevent panic, and Horace, by now accepted as *comes* and *amicus,* might well have been in his patron's entourage.[14] Whether this solution is more plausible than the explanation of the scholiast is a matter of opinion.

The belief that Horace was present at Actium is based on Epode 9. This poem has generated an enormous controversy among scholars determined to extract from it all – and sometimes more than all – that it can yield because, by an unfortunate accident, it has been given a role for which it was neither intended nor suited as a contemporary historical record of a momentous battle.

Here it is best to concentrate on asking whether Horace was present, but this in turn depends on Maecenas' movements, for, if Maecenas was there, as in the case of the naval mishap in 36, Horace might have been expected to accompany him. On the likelihood of Maecenas' presence at Actium learned opinion is divided, the choice depending to some extent on the credence attached to some halting verses of dubious date, the first *Elegia in Maecenatem.*[15] Some critics have even argued that Epode 9 is a vivid eye-witness account, virtually 'a running commentary' of what the poet saw.[16] The assertion that the narrative indicates autopsy is attractive but it is open to obvious objections. First, it must be admitted that an imaginative writer is capable of picturing a scene vividly as if he had been there. Second, any description of the battle of Actium composed shortly after the event was bound to be based on the accounts of participants, for the circle in which Horace moved must have been full of men who were eager to say, 'I was there and I'll tell you all about the great deeds *quorum pars magna fui*'. More specific doubts are raised by details of the ten lines (11–20) relating to the battle. The first six of these present what is hardly the description of an eye-witness; it is more like an emotive portrayal of the enemy designed to stimulate anger and disgust. This is not a war-correspondent's snapshot but a grand dramatic painting.

Elucidation of the next four lines which contain *the only elements of action* is made difficult by the crux at the beginning of 17 and uncertainty about the precise significance of 19–20. However these problems are resolved, arguments that this short passage must have been written by a man on the spot are tendentious.

There remain the two passages of general import which have been thought to refer to Horace's military service after Philippi: *Epist.* 1.20.23 and *Carm.* 2.6.5–8.[17]

In the final epistle of Book 1 Horace proudly declares *me primis urbis belli placuisse domique*. It has been asserted that Horace is referring to his own performance in the field but would not have dared to include the tyrannicide Brutus among *primis urbis*. Unfortunately the line is doubly ambiguous and may have been intended to be so. Though it is preferable to take *belli domique* with *placuisse* it cannot be shown that it would be absolutely wrong to take it with *primis*. Even in the former case the statement that he was a favourite of leading men in wartime is not the same thing as saying he was a soldier; moreover the assumption that the Republican leaders must be excluded from *primis urbis* is questionable and historically false; the army in which Horace served was not a rabble led by a Spartacus. It is to the point that in none of his references to this episode in his life does Horace express shame or repentance for having been on the losing side.

On *Carm.* 2.6.5–8 Wistrand observed: 'Now if Horace's only personal experience of war was with Brutus' army in 43–42 BC, would it then have been possible for him to say – twenty years after he had last seen active military service – that he was now tired and wished that his military labours might finally come to an end in Tibur or Tarentum?'[18] But Horace is not talking about *now* in a matter-of-fact fashion; he is adopting a pose and using Homeric and possibly Alcaic language to imagine how he would like to end his days when he is an old man looking back on the adventures of a lifetime. We cannot extract a campaign-record from a daydream of a future state.

Finally, though arguments from silence are dubious, if Horace really did witness action on the winning side, it is astonishing that he never says so explicitly. As early as *Sat.* 1.6.48 he was ready to admit his involvement with the losers; we might have expected him to emphasise later presence in the train of Octavian, especially as he suffered from social carping until in the end he secured unquestionable pre-eminence as a poet.

To sum up, on the basis of his own testimony Horace definitely served in the campaign which ended at Philippi; if certain speculative interpretations are correct, he might also have been involved in a naval disaster of the Sicilian war and he could have been at Actium. We are left with

a certainty and two possibilities which are simply guesses. The choice
between these three occasions as the background for the epode may be
narrowed when *Carm.* 3.21 is considered.

The ode *O nata mecum consule Manlio* is a superb one (even though
Fraenkel ignores it). It is in a sense a delightful adaptation of the hymn
form (I wish to avoid the usual word 'parody', which suggests mockery of
the model and is in this case misleading). The deity ostensibly addressed
turns out to be a wine-jar: 'My dear twin-sister bottle born in 65'.[19]

The poet invites the reader to laugh at the form, not the faith: the
joke is in the structure not the content, which is sensible, even wise,
and respectful of both men and gods. It is certainly not a frivolous or
irresponsible poem. There are several serious aspects: first, it is addressed
to one of the great aristocratic commanders and orators of the Augustan
Age, M. Valerius Messalla Corvinus, and in encouraging this very distinguished man to enjoy the benefits of wine Horace recognises that he is
soaked in Plato and offers him a very serious-minded exemplar – Cato,
that paragon of severity, who is said often to have warmed his virtue with
the juice of the grape.[20] Secondly, and this is a point which commonly
goes unremarked, the end of the poem is cast in a genuinely religious
form: in the final stanza Horace brings in Bacchus, Venus, the Graces
as good companions, and Apollo to let in the light. The position of the
poem may also be significant, for it is followed by two essentially religious
and serious odes.[21]

Thirdly the wine is very special. It is Massic, which is one of the best
varieties, and this is obviously an ancient vintage. Are we to take it, then,
that emphasis on age is the main point in describing the wine-jar as coeval
with the author? In their enthusiasm to rework Norden, commentators
have tended to assume so and to hurry past the first line. But what makes
it uniquely valuable is that it is an *Horatian* wine, and now that really
means something; in the interval since Epode 13 was written 'Château
Horace' has arrived – it is one of the great brand-names and so forms
a significant part of the priceless compliment which Horace is paying to
Messalla. The word 'priceless' is apt because in *Odes* 1–3 there are hints
and in Book 4 incontrovertible evidence that Horace knew he had something enormously valuable to give – or more likely to sell – to anyone he
names: immortality.[22] The tone of this ode, however, suggests a genuine
friendship rather than commerce. Was there some personal reason for
offering Horace's birthday vintage to Messalla?

One possibility is that Messalla too was born in 65. There is general
agreement that Jerome's date for his birth, 59 (linked incidentally with
Livy), is too late, and 64 has been preferred because the similarity of
the names of the consuls of the two years provides an explanation of
the confusion in Jerome's *tumultuarium opus* – Caesar and Figulus (64)

and Caesar and Bibulus (59).[23] While a birthdate in 65 cannot be entirely excluded there are objections: the explanation for Jerome's error
disappears and the description *nata mecum* stresses the birthdate of the
author not the addressee. One thing is clear and that is that Horace begins *Carm.* 3.21 with a back-reference to his earlier poem, Epode 13.
It can hardly be accidental that these two poems contain the only two
references to the poet's year of birth and that those references are in
the form of a precious vintage. Did this have special significance for
Messalla?

Although they achieved eminence in very different fields Horace and
Messalla shared one notable experience in that both fought for the tyran-
nicides against Octavian.[24] They had been *commilitones* in the camp of
Cassius and there is at least a strong presumption that they knew each
other there and that their friendship dated from that period. If, as I
have argued, Epode 13 is linked with Philippi, there is a good case for
suggesting that, when Horace came to write *Carm.* 3.21 as a complimentary poem to his former companion in arms, he repeated the reference
to the wine of the year of the consul L. Manlius L. f. Torquatus to remind his friend of the earlier poem which poignantly expressed their
feelings at that critical moment in their lives. Horace's coeval wine is the
Massic of remembrance.[25] Like many of Horace's hints this one is subtle
and tactful and in no way compromises the public figure to whom it is
addressed.

It is of course conceivable that Messalla and Horace were together in
a later campaign – in the Sicilian War or at Actium – and that we simply
lack the evidence to connect them, in which case Epode 13 could be taken
to refer to that event, but the claim that *Carm.* 3.21 contains a reminder
is no less valid. Once again the choice is between a probable association
based on testimony and two possibilities which are purely speculative.

BIRTHDAY

Horace wrote many 'occasional' poems and he might have been expected
to use his birthday – as distinct from his birth year – as an occasion. It is
suggested here that he did exploit it in a fashion which has not hitherto
been recognised.

To approach the matter indirectly I point to one undoubted birthday
poem, the ode in Book 4 centred on Maecenas' birthday, *Carm.* 4.11,
Est mihi nonum superantis annum. It is the ode in which Horace addresses
Phyllis, the last of his loves, the girl with the irresistible singing voice, of
which the final stanza is a clear signal that his career as a lyric poet is
drawing to its ultimate close.

Like many elements in Book 4 the poem is reminiscent of earlier work, and the obvious precursor is *Carm.* 3.28, *Festo quid potius die*. This ode is short and apparently simple, but it is by no means trivial; it is a very important poem, if for no other reason than that it was the last love poem and the last religious lyric Horace intended to write – or more accurately to present to his readers, for I have no doubt that at the time he considered his lyric work to be complete.[26]

Its position points to its significance. It is enclosed between two massive odes, the first of which is the longest of the odes concerned with love and the second is the longest ode to Maecenas, the whole group being followed by the monumental final poem of the lyric collection. Place alone does not of course prove the importance of *Festo quid potius die*, for the insertion of a frivolous piece might be defended as a cushion between two heavy poems, but the prominent position invites the reader to look closely in case there is a deeper meaning beneath the smooth and glittering surface.[27]

The key has been provided by Viktor Pöschl, who pointed out that in this poem Horace is using one of the oldest poetical metaphors, which is based on the analogy between transient day and passing life and especially between evening and old age.[28] For the ageing Horace the sun is already past the zenith, and he feels a desperate urgency as his own evening approaches; prudence must be thrown to the winds and, before it is too late, the precious old wine must be snatched from store; it is time to sing the final hymns to the gods, the last ode to love, and at the end a dirge to darkness.[29] The message is plain: soon the lyre and the songs which accompany it will be heard no more.

Once the underlying meaning of the ode is seen to be a moving valediction to lyric and to life, it becomes clear that it must have been specially composed for its position at the close of the lyric corpus and was not an earlier piece placed there when the poet was arranging his poems for final publication. But why on earth did Horace choose Neptune as the god to celebrate in his last lyric party? Apart from anything else, he was the one god who had no sense of humour, hardly likely to attract Horace's devotion. Surely Phoebus, Bacchus, Venus, Mercury, or the Muses would have been more appropriate.

The usual answer is that the festival of Neptune was on 23 July, a hot time of year, so it provides an excuse for boozing – *adduxere sitim tempora*. This is weak to the point of inanity, considering the position and grave implications of the ode, for it invites us to believe that this twilight lyric arose from an incidental occasion which had no personal or political significance. Besides, Caecuban is a most precious wine, preserved for celebrating Battles of Actium and the suicide of lewd Egyptian queens; it is not lemonade for summer picnics.[30]

Why Neptune? The question is never asked because the answer given above has seemed so obvious: summer heat is at its height and Horace felt thirsty, so he calls urgently for drink in a simple sympotic-erotic piece; there were, after all, Lesbian precedents.[31] This is a case where the wrong answer has suppressed the right question. Why Neptune?

Neptune is a mysterious god in the Roman pantheon and almost nothing is known about the July festival of Neptune – rather less in fact than the notes of commentators suggest. Ovid's account of the junketings in honour of Anna Perenna have nothing to do with the case.[32] One might speculate that the reference is to another festival at which Neptune was honoured, associated perhaps with Actium or Augustus' birthday, but this is essentially a personal poem:[33] Horace is playing his own lyre not blowing the trumpet of state.

In religion above all *Graecia capta ferum uictorem cepit* and Horace is preeminent among Latin poets in avowedly writing Greek poems in Latin. His Neptune is Poseidon, and the place to look for our answer is in Greece, and particularly in Athens, where, like many educated men of means, Horace spent some time in higher studies. There is no evidence of the length of his stay at the Academy but it is probable that he was there for a considerable period, learning to *want* to distinguish true from false – *scilicet ut uellem curuo dinoscere rectum* (*Epist.* 2.2.44). He may have had a Roman diary in his luggage, but it is reasonable to assume that when in Athens he had to do as the Athenians did and used the local calendar; in which case he must have recognised that the month of the winter solstice, corresponding roughly to his birthday month of December, was called the month of Poseidon. He would also have observed that Poseidon was honoured on the eighth day of every month and, as all the surviving evidence indicates, in 'Posedeion' the festival of the god occurred on the eighth day of the month, the day of his birth.[34] It should not cause surprise that, when he came to write what he intended to be his last love lyric, the follower of Sappho and Alcaeus and the other seven Greek lyric poets of the canon, was thinking half in Greek, and mixing his drinks, so to speak – Falernian with Chian.

A birthday is a time to look back, a time to pause, a time to change. To which of Horace's birthdays should we attach this poem? I surmise his 43rd. In antiquity there were many more ways of distinguishing the ages of man than the simple threefold division of the sphinx.[35] Horace himself once described four ages (*Ars P.* 153–78), but stricter, more sophisticated systems were in vogue. Several of the most popular among Greeks, Etruscans, and Romans were based upon the number seven , the magical, sacred, astronomical number seven.[36] For example, Hippocrates, according to Censorinus, divided life into seven phases of seven years, which meant the final period of old age begins after 42.[37] Seven was of major importance too in medical and astrological theories of 'climacterics' or critical stages. In terms of human life each seven-year period ended in a climacteric; moreover when seven was combined with another potent number, three (or $3 \times 3 = 9$), crises of even greater gravity were expected at the ages of 21, 42, and above all 63.[38] That this idea was a familiar one in Horace's circle is proved by a letter of Augustus to his grandson Gaius (Gell. 15.7.3) in which he writes with satisfaction at having passed the most dangerous climacteric by completing his 63rd year.

Is there any evidence that Horace himself attached significance to seven-year periods? Two passages may be considered.

> (a) septimus octauo propior iam fugerit annus
> ex quo Maecenas me coepit habere suorum
> in numero   (*Sat.* 2.6.40–2)

> (b) ingenium sibi quod uacuas desumpsit Athenas
> et studiis annos septem dedit insenuitque
> libris et curis   (*Epist.* 2.2.81–3)

(a) Most readers assume that Horace is simply being numerically precise, but those of us who prefer to regard all Horace's autobiographical statements with a degree of scepticism may have reservations. He may simply be saying that his friendship is a long-standing one which has spanned a complete phase of life.

(b) Commentators have either passed over the reference to seven years in silence or admitted perplexity, as for example, Wickham's note: 'No reason is given for the selection of "seven". It seems to imply something much beyond the usual time allowed for an educational residence at Athens.'[39] But in terms of the seven-year system there is obvious point in *insenuit* which suggests that the scholar has devoted a whole segment of his life-span to study and so passed a climacteric, moving from youth to old age.

So it seems possible that Horace did pay regard to the hebdomadal scheme. If so, he must have been acutely conscious that in December 23 BC he had passed a critical turning-point in life and was entering a new phase – his consular year, so to speak: he had made his name and built his imperishable monument as a lyric poet.[40] He would turn, or return, to philosophy, as he explained at the beginning of the *Epistles*.

This surmise fits in with the popular hypothesis, based admittedly on tenuous evidence, that Books 1–3 of the *Odes* were published in about 23 BC.[41]

DEATHDAY

Hidden in the calendar lies a date which the individual does not know –
and may never know: the date of death. Apprehension about death and
morbid curiosity about its timing have nourished many forms of super-
stitious practice and in particular the dismal science of astrology, which,
in spite of attempts to control its practitioners, had become popular in
Rome by Horace's time.[42] On estimating the time of death, his own or
another's, Horace was unequivocal. *Carm.* 1.11 is one of the best known
odes and it contains what is certainly Horace's best known phrase – *carpe
diem*. It is a short and simple poem, but it has had a very odd effect upon
commentators. Again and again they assert that this poem proves Horace
was not interested in astrology, was too sensible to believe in astrology,
made fun of astrology. As often happens in literary criticism, what pre-
vails is not what the author said but what the critics tell the reader to
believe.

What Horace tells the simple-minded Leuconoe in *Tu ne quaesieris* is
not to try to ascertain how long he or she will live – for this is a moral and
religious offence – and not to meddle with astrological calculations. This
certainly does not imply that Horace regarded astrology as nonsense; it
could indeed signify the opposite: astrology is a hazardous craft, not a
plaything for the ignorant, and there are some secrets it is better not
to know. If someone tells a child not to play with matches, it does not
imply a contempt for fire. The analogy is not as far-fetched as it sounds,
for there is plenty of evidence that at this time astrology was regarded
as dangerous. For reasons which are not far to seek in a society where
legacy-hunting was rife (*Sat.* 2.5, *Epist.* 1.1.77–9), attempts to calculate
the expected time of death were especially suspect. What Horace declared
to be *nefas* was actually made illegal a generation later by a law repeatedly
renewed – and broken sometimes with dire consequences – for centuries.
The poet is proclaiming a contemporary official Roman attitude, not just
an Epicurean principle.[43]

A peculiar feature of this ode was pointed out by Professor Dilke: it
consists of 56 words – and Horace died at the age of 56.[44] Numerical co-
incidences are all too easily found in poetry, and many wonderful theories
have been based on them. The abuse of numerology as a mind-bending
drug goes back to antiquity, so it is just conceivable that an ancient biographer, not knowing the truth and seeking clues to Horace's date of death,
might have resorted to this desperate solution. Few critics will want to
give house room to a *larua* of this kind.

When Horace comes to speak of his own death in *Carm.* 2.6 he adopts
a light-hearted, even frivolous tone. This is a jocular, tongue-in-cheek

poem in which he calls the bluff of a younger friend who has pledged his loyalty in extravagant terms. Part of the fun is based on two obvious literary echoes, first of Catullus 11 and then of Virgil, *G.* 4.116–48. Septimius, it seems, has made the conventional loyal friend's offer to accompany Horace to the ends of the earth. In fact, says the poet, I'd like to retire in Tibur when I'm old and have completed my Odyssey; or, if the Fates are too mean to allow that (Tibur was a rich man's resort), I'll settle for a Virgilian rural idyll as a bucolic Sybarite. You must come with me and see me safely to the crematorium.

If Septimius – and we have no reason to doubt it – was the Septimius of *Epist.* 1.9 and the *Vita*, he was a young man on the make, and the last place he would want to remain for any length of time would be 300 miles from Rome. Tibur would certainly be preferable, from his as well as Horace's point of view.[45] The poet who makes such bold claims to immortality enjoys making a joke about his actual demise. He is a man who takes life as it comes, day by day, in accordance with a philosophy which he expresses seriously and with incomparable force in his penultimate ode of the main collection – *Carm.* 3.29.29–48.[46]

While *Carm.* 2.6 is a humorous poem about a friend keeping Horace company till he dies, *Carm.* 2.17 is a serious one about Horace accompanying his patron to the grave. The nature of Maecenas' complaints is obscure and is in a sense irrelevant: they merely provide the excuse for a passionate declaration. Horace makes a fervent statement of loyalty (for that is what the first four stanzas represent), adapting the *topos* which was displayed in *Carm.* 2.6 and swearing to accompany Maecenas, not to the world's end but to life's end: he will play Pylades to Maecenas' Orestes.

The poem begins with a metaphor – colloquial maybe but still powerful – *exanimas*, 'you are killing me with your complaints'. In fact the whole of the first half of the ode is a metaphorical way of saying, 'you are my patron and my friend and we are bound indissolubly together'. The language is hyperbolical and is crammed with literary echoes, but is not on that account insincere. The second half of the ode complements the first and says in effect, 'our fates are linked and we are under heaven's protection, as our lucky escapes from death prove'.

The first lines of the second half (17ff.) plunge the reader into an astrological conundrum which has bedevilled criticism. Until recently the favourite form of interpretation was to take this passage as evidence that (a) Horace did not know or care what his horoscope was and (b) he was gently mocking Maecenas as a devotee of astrology. In a paper in which he threw doubt on assumptions of Maecenas' hypochondria David West also questioned the first of these inferences and suggested two ways in which the details given here could fit a horoscope.[47] No doubt an adept could invent many more, but lines 17–20 can be interpreted in a different fashion altogether.

The stanza presents a list of signs of the zodiac – three signs in the correct order but not in uninterrupted sequence (Sagittarius comes between Scorpio and Capricorn). Horace was partial to lists, as the following examples show.

1 *Sat.* 2.1.57: three pairs of life – long/short, rich/poor, at Rome/in exile

2 *Carm.* 1.22.5–8: three wild parts of the world

3 *Carm.* 3.4.22–4: four holiday resorts

4 *Carm.* 3.21: five effects of wine

5 *Carm.* 4.2.10ff.: four kinds of Pindar's poems

6 *Epist.* 1.3.23–4: three professions

7 *Ars P.* 63ff.: three types of engineering work.

While the choices in 1 and 4 may be regarded as exhaustive, the remainder are certainly not; they are exemplary selections suggesting a wider range. The same principle may be applied to Libra, Scorpio, and Capricorn, specimen signs of the zodiac. In effect Horace is saying that whatever sign may be dominant at any time, his fortune and Maecenas' are amazingly alike, and the proof is that at a critical juncture Jupiter protected Maecenas and Faunus (= Pan, son of Mercury) saved Horace.

According to this thesis Horace could have named any signs at random. Did the three he listed have special significance? Some have suspected a reference to the horoscope of the poet or Maecenas, but there is another intriguing possibility. Two of the signs were certainly important in the horoscope of Augustus and the third may have been.[48] Octavian was born under Libra (i.e. the ascendant) and he selected Capricorn as his emblem either because the moon was in Capricorn when he was born or because at his conception (conventionally 273 days before birth and in this case coincidentally with the winter solstice) sun, moon and Mercury were in Capricorn.[49] Horace's display of *sideralis scientia* in the second half of the ode may be another metaphor meaning 'you and I, Maecenas, are both under the protection of the Princeps' (cf. *Carm.* 1.12.49–60, where an analogy is drawn between Jupiter in heaven and Caesar on earth). Be that as it may, the significance of lines 22–5 in astrological terms is plain: Maecenas passed through a critical phase in life when he was rescued from the malefic Saturn by benefic Jupiter. Here it seems necessary to point out that *uolucrisque Fati | tardauit alas* only makes sense in 'soft' astrology, the popular system of the period which combined genethlialogy with calculation of celestial conditions at a given moment.

We cannot assess the precise significance of the astrological references, but they suggest knowledge rather than ignorance. We are the ignorant ones, as can be simply illustrated by considering the obstacles to finding out the horoscope of Horace himself. We do not know the time or even the day he was born (uncertainties about intercalation make it impossible to place his birthday in the Julian calendar); even if we did, we do not have contemporary ephemerids or reliable information about the methods which contemporary astrologers might have used – and it is probable that there were nearly as many methods as there were practitioners.

Before leaving this troublesome poem we must glance at two awkward questions which have been raised by it. Is it possible that biographers, not knowing the date of Horace's death, either used the astrological details to calculate it or linked his death with that of Maecenas? The first suggestion is made in a note of Syndikus' valuable commentary, and it must be admitted that he is right in saying that the possibility cannot be completely excluded.[50] With astrology all things are possible – for a fee. But let us not waste our money on this offer. The other proposition is to be taken more seriously.

At the time it is probable that the death of Maecenas was a much more noteworthy event than the death of the poet, and it would not be surprising if a biographer lacking accurate information assumed that Horace must have fulfilled the promise made in *Carm.* 2.17 by dying at the same time as his patron to end life's journey buried by his side, as the last sentence of the *Vita* states. It is time to look more closely at Suetonius' testimony.

First, something must be said about the fault in the text. The arithmetic is wrong and the wording has been suspected. Nearly all editors and commentators have accepted Vahlen's improvement upon Reifferscheid's emendation:

> decessit V Kal. Decembris C. Marcio Censorino et C. Asinio Gallo consulibus post nonum et quinquagesimum (diem quam Maecenas obierat aetatis agens septimum et quinquagesimum) annum.[51]

Parablepsy is a well known scribal error where a word has been repeated in a narrow compass, but it is hazardous to assume that a phrase involving such a repetition has been omitted unless there are clear signs of disruption. Vahlen saw evidence of a lacuna in the expression *decessit post nonum et quinquagesimum annum* which he asserted was not even Latin, but this claim is contradicted by examples in contemporary writers.[52] He based his solution on the practice of Suetonius of giving the length of an emperor's rule in years, months, and days. Such measurements of reigns are unexceptionable, but precise calculation of the gap between the deaths of two *priuati*, however eminent, is extraordinary and unique. Are there not more likely explanations of the arithmetical mistake?

Briefly I suggest two preferable possibilities: (1) reliance on misleading *fasti* of consular years, or (2) corruption of numerical symbols.

(1) One of the disadvantages of the Roman system of dating was that one could not immediately calculate the difference between two given years; it was necessary to refer to lists of consuls, and probably these were sometimes misleading, especially when consuls changed in the course of a year. In this connection it may be significant that in the MSS of Suetonius' *De Viris Illustribus* there are errors of two years too many both in the life of Virgil and in the life of Persius. (2) Errors in copying numerals are very common in historical texts, and in this case it would have been easy to confuse *LVI* and *LIX*. A slight displacement of the right hand stroke of the *V* would transform *VI* into *IX*.

The *Vita* is not in fact the only testimony for the date of Horace's death. There are three others:

1 Jerome, *Chronica* under Olympiad 192, 4 (= 9 BC)
   Horatius LVII aetatis suae anno Romae moritur
2 Ps.-Acro in cod. Parisinus lat. 7900 *A*
   Septuagesimo aetatis anno periit
3 Ps.-Acro in codd. *M*, *f*, *j* (Keller)
   Septuagesimo septimo anno periit

The entry in Jerome is not really a separate testimony as he obviously used Suetonius' biographies when making his insertions in Eusebius' chronicle, and the fact that he is slightly adrift by one year is of no significance. Of the two other statements one may suspect that they mean no more than 'he died old', the seventy being rhetorical,[53] but that raises the difficult question why, if the precise date was recorded by Suetonius, it was not known to these scribblers in margins. Modern critics who are not slow to expose the faults of their ancient predecessors (though quick to quote them when they agree) will see here only one more proof of ignorance.

Earlier in this paper brief mention has been made of three conceivable ways in which a biographer short of facts might have guessed the date of Horace's death: (1) by counting words in *Carm.* 1.11; (2) from astrological indications in *Carm.* 2.17; (3) by the assumption that Horace died at the same time as Maecenas. Only the third of these should give us pause. A biographer who knew the date of Maecenas' death but not Horace's, recalling the promise made in *Carm.* 2.17, might have concluded that the deathday of the poet coincided with that of his patron. A brief entry in Dio (55.7) indicates that Maecenas died in 8 BC.[54] Who is to say that the date was not *V Kal. Decembris*?[55]

To sum up: Horace probably died on 27 November 8 BC, as Suetonius stated, aged 56,[56] but we cannot be as sure of this date as we can be of the poet's birthday. Even if the doubts about his death were more substantial than they are, it should not concern us. His death, though doubtless a great grief to those who knew him personally, was of no literary or historical significance, for he had already completed the work which would survive and spread as he predicted in the final poems of *Odes* 2 and 3. His birth on the other hand was one of the most important events in Graeco-Roman history; its effects have continued through two millennia and will persist far into a third.

IAN M. LE M. DU QUESNAY

2   *AMICVS CERTVS IN RE INCERTA CERNITVR*
     Epode 1

DATES, CONTEXTS AND PERSPECTIVES

The latest datable reference in the *Epodes* is the battle of Actium. In the central poem, Epode 9, Horace vividly recapitulates the main phases of the campaign, which culminated in the sea battle of 2 September 31 BC. The dramatic setting would appear to be the evening of the day of the battle, when, according to Suetonius, Caesar and his forces had spent the night at sea.[1] In 32 BC, Caesar had taken care to see that the war had been declared on Cleopatra alone and that she alone was *hostis*.[2] By omitting Antony, Caesar contrived to leave the way open for as many as possible of his supporters to transfer allegiance, and Dio has both Antony and Caesar, in their harangues to their troops immediately before the battle, dwell on the fact that Antony had not been declared *hostis*.[3] But it is clear that at some point Antony was formally declared *hostis*.[4] This would seem most probably to have happened when the many senators who had accompanied Caesar to Actium had returned to Rome: having seen Antony fight alongside the public enemy and against themselves, they would have no hesitation in now declaring him *hostis*.[5] The language of *Epodes* 9.27 (*terra marique uictus hostis*) reflects the language of the official decrees recognising Caesar's victory, according him the triumph which would be celebrated in 29 BC,[6] and sanctioning the foundation of Nicopolis on the site of Caesar's camp at Actium, where the dedication reads:

> Imperator Caesar Diui Iuli filius *uictoriam consecutus* bello quod pro re publica gessit in hac regione consul quintum imperator septimum pace parta *terra marique* Neptuno et Marti castra e quibus ad *hostem* insequendum egressus est naualibus spoliis exornata consacrauit.[7]

Most probably the Epodes were collected and published during the winter of 31/30 BC.[8] This was an extremely difficult time for Caesar, in spite of the recent victory at Actium. He had placed Maecenas in charge of affairs in Italy, although he had no official position. According to

17

Dio (51.3.1–3), the freedmen were threatening disruption in protest at the final demand for the very heavy emergency tax which had been imposed before Actium (Dio 50.10.4).[9] Caesar responded by remitting the final payment. The veterans of both his and Antony's former legions, who had served beyond their term, were sent back to Italy and dispersed. But they too threatened trouble, as they had so far received no reward for their contribution to the victory. This time Caesar felt that Maecenas would not have the authority to quell the disturbances and sent Agrippa to deal with the matter. But even that was not enough. In January of 30 BC,[10] Caesar was forced to return to Italy in person. The seas at this time of the year were normally closed to shipping and he twice encountered violent storms, which damaged his ship.[11] There could hardly be clearer evidence of the seriousness of the situation in Italy. Caesar stopped over at Brundisium and asserted his control over the situation by having the people come to him to make their petitions and to welcome him. He remained for only twenty-seven days, underlining the urgency of the unfinished business he still had with Antony and Cleopatra and the need for continuing loyal support. The event is described in some detail by Dio (51.4.4–5):

> When the Senate learned of his approach, they all went to meet him, except for the tribunes and two praetors [...]. The equestrian order, the greater part of the populace and other groups also gathered at Brundisium in large numbers, some as envoys and others spontaneously. In the face of his arrival and the enthusiasm of the majority there was no further rebellion from any quarter.

The gathering at Brundisium in January 30 BC contrasted grimly with the gathering at the same place less than a year before in preparation for the expedition against Cleopatra in the spring of 31 BC. Dio describes the scene (50.11.5–6):

> [Caesar] assembled at Brundisium all his troops [...] and all the men of influence, both senators and equestrians, wanting the soldiers to cooperate with him and also wishing to prevent the others from starting trouble, as they might if left to themselves. But most of all he wanted to show everyone that he had the largest and strongest following among the Romans in his support. From Brundisium he issued instructions that they should all, except for the soldiers, bring with them a number of servants and also their own supplies.

From the perspective of Caesar and his supporters, those whom he ordered to present themselves at Brundisium, on both occasions, were being called upon to honour the oath of allegiance they had sworn to Caesar of their own accord in the summer of 32 BC.[12]

The beginning of 30 BC is the most probable date not only for the publication of the collection but also for the composition of Epode 1. Amidst the troubles and disruption of that winter a reminder of that sense of solidarity and purpose in the previous spring would be timely.[13] Epode 9 was similarly written after the event, though probably not long after it.[14] The dramatic setting of Epode 1 is clearly, if allusively, established in the opening lines. Maecenas is about to depart in the spring or early summer of 31 BC: the setting is that described by Dio (50.11.5–6).[15] There is, however, no good reason to suppose that the composition of the poem is contemporary with its dramatic setting. In spite of the future tense (*Ibis*), the language of the opening lines really makes sense only from the perspective of one writing after the event. For, at the time of the departure, Horace could not have known that Maecenas' journey would find its climax in a sea battle, much less that the Liburnians would play such a decisive role in the victory. The outcome of the campaign was far from certain, as is well illustrated by the anecdote preserved by Macrobius about the man who had trained two ravens to hail the victor. One would say: *aue Caesar uictor imperator*, the other *aue uictor imperator Antoni*.[16]

The strongest evidence that Maecenas (and Horace) were in fact present at the battle of Actium is provided by Epodes 1 and 9.[17] Dio simply refers to his being in charge of affairs in Rome and the rest of Italy generally during this period.[18] But that does not preclude his being at Actium.[19] For Horace to imply that Maecenas went to Actium if it were not true would not only be absurd but would expose both himself and Maecenas to ridicule from the hundreds of senators and at least as large a number of equestrians who did go and would have known that they were not there.[20] These were the very people who would have constituted Horace's primary audience. This point would be decisive even if it were a matter of a poem composed earlier and simply chosen to head the collection. But, if it is accepted that Epode 1 was written after the event it purports to enact, then it becomes impossible to think of any reason why Horace should have deliberately based his poem on a palpable fiction and flown in the face of a truth in the public domain and of ancient rhetorical precept (Menander Rhetor 398.1–6):

> If you mention anything that does not apply to him and which everyone knows does not apply to him, it not only seems unconvincing, but you will make yourself suspect for other occasions and you will have an uphill struggle with your audience. One must always concur with what is commonly admitted.

THE POEM

Ibis Liburnis inter alta nauium,
    amice, propugnacula,
paratus omne Caesaris periculum
    subire, Maecenas, tuo.

In your light craft you will go, my friend, right in amongst the galleons' towering ramparts, and you are prepared to undergo every danger, Maecenas, that faces Caesar, even at risk to yourself.

The first word evokes a familiar scene and establishes the generic identity of the poem. It is a propemptikon, a farewell to a departing friend.[21] The first two couplets both implicitly and explicitly define the dangers of the journey that Maecenas is about to make.[22] Maecenas is about to go on a journey with the Liburnians.[23] These were swift, light and very manoeuvrable ships used in warfare, which came to stand for the whole of Caesar's fleet at the battle of Actium.[24] The first couplet makes a contrast between them and the much larger ships equipped with towers from which rocks and fire were hurled down onto the opposing ships.[25] Ships of the latter type were possessed by both sides at Actium, although Caesar did not have as many of the really large vessels as Antony had. The phrase *ire inter* can be used of charging into the midst of the enemy.[26] Since the battle of Actium came very quickly to be represented as the triumph of the swift light Liburnians over the massive but unwieldy ships constructed by Antony, it seems necessary to take it in that sense here.[27] The strong contrast between *Liburnis* and *alta nauium propugnacula* then has an obvious point.

The second couplet provides an explanation of why Maecenas is about to leave. The phrase *paratus omne...periculum subire* (3–4) seems to have been a standard part of the declaration of friendship and may have been specifically incorporated into the *coniuratio totius Italiae*.[28] It seems likely that Horace is here recalling the recent public affirmation of loyalty to Caesar by Maecenas along with other leading equestrians and senators. While the exact terms of the oath are not known, it can be reconstructed with some certainty because of the formulaic and repetitive nature of surviving oaths of a similar nature.[29] In taking the oath, the *coniurati* swore to consider Caesar's friends their friends and Caesar's enemies their enemies,[30] to pursue by land and by sea anyone who threatened danger to him,[31] to consider themselves and their children less dear than the safety of Caesar,[32] and to endure any danger in his service.[33] The emphatic and repeated use of *omne* is a notable linguistic feature of such oaths but that need not, in the case of *omne...periculum*, preclude a specific reference to the presence of Maecenas at Philippi and in the war against Sextus in order to emphasise that Maecenas will not shrink from the battle now in prospect, the *maximi discriminis dies* (Velleius 2.85.1).[34] The importance attached to such loyalty is well illustrated in an almost exactly contemporary letter from Caesar who commends another of his supporters by speaking of 'Seleukos my admiral who campaigned with me throughout the whole time of the war and distinguished himself in every way and furnished every proof of his goodwill and his loyalty'.[35] Additionally *subire* serves to disambiguate *Ibis inter*: the role of the Liburnians in battle was to use their speed to get in close to the enemy ships, under the range of the devices mounted on the high ramparts, and inflict what damage they could such as holing them below the water-line or breaking off their oars.[36] The verb *subire* is used precisely for this manoeuvre.[37] The *periculum* which faces Caesar, and which Maecenas will *subire*, is not here the generalised possibility that it had been at the time of the *coniuratio* in 32 BC or the unknown dangers that might be envisaged at the start of the compaign but precisely the danger constituted by the Antonian fleet, the *alta nauium propugnacula*.

The couplet ends emphatically on *tuo* [sc. *periculo*].[38] The notion that a man should be willing to risk his life for a friend is one that was approved by traditionally minded Romans, and Horace's purpose here is in part to praise the bravery of Maecenas, as is clear from comparison with Cicero, *De amicitia* 24:

> itaque, si quando aliquod officium exstitit amici in periculis aut adeundis aut communicandis, quis est qui id non maximis efferat laudibus? qui clamores tota cauea nuper in hospitis et amici mei Marci Pacuui noua fabula! cum ignorante rege uter Orestes esset, Pylades Orestem se esse diceret ut pro illo necaretur, Orestes autem ita ut erat Orestem se esse perseueraret. stantes plaudebant in re ficta: quid arbitramur in uera facturos fuisse?

Such sentiments are to be expected in a propemptikon.[39] But they have a special resonance at this time as is clear from the terms in which Caesar commends his admiral Seleukos:

> Seleukos...has served with us...under our command, has on our behalf suffered many great hardships, has faced danger without flinching from any terror in his steadfastness, has exhibited complete affection and loyalty for the Republic, has linked his own fortune to our safety, has undergone every suffering on behalf of the Republic of the People of the Romans, and in our presence and absence has been of service to us.[40]

While Maecenas in general during the thirties advertised his Epicureanism by an ostentatious devotion to *otium* and to *uoluptas*, which would subsequently incur the criticism of Seneca, that is not in any way inconsistent with his decision to share his friend's danger.[41] For Epicurus had said 'it is necessary to take risks for the sake of friendship', and even that an Epicurean 'will on occasion die for a friend'.[42]

The reader might be struck by the absence from these opening lines of the standard formula *sine me* and be wondering whether or not Maecenas has asked Horace to go with him.[43] The problem posed for friends by separation was recognised in the literature on friendship. So Cicero, *De amicitia* 75:

> nec enim, ut ad fabulas redeam, Troiam Neoptolemus capere potuisset, si Lycomedem, apud quem erat educatus, multis cum lacrimis iter suum impedientem audire uoluisset. et saepe incidunt magnae res, ut discedendum sit ab amicis; quas qui impedire uult eo quod desiderium non facile ferat, is et infirmus est mollisque natura, et ob eam ipsam causam in amicitia parum iustus.

The scene evoked by Cicero, in which a weeping Lycomedes attempts to dissuade Neoptolemus from departing for Troy, is clearly propemptic. In the normal propemptikon, the speaker remains behind and affirms his friendship by initially protesting at the decision and attempting to dissuade his departing friend from going.[44] However, the war against Cleopatra was certainly *magna res*, even though, in a way characteristic of the late thirties, this is presented as a threat to Caesar rather than to the *res publica*.[45] Horace will not in such circumstances plead with his friend to stay with him, a reaction that would reveal Horace himself to be *infirmus* and *mollis natura* and *in amicitia parum iustus*. The echoes of Cicero's language in what follows (*non mollis* (10); *firmus parum* (16)) suggest that Horace has in mind either this precise passage or perhaps the play to which Cicero alludes or both.[46] Horace will instead resort to a less common propemptic *topos* and seek to change his departing friend's mind about his decision to leave Horace behind.[47] Even more unusually he will succeed.[48]

While Horace accepts the necessity of Maecenas' departure from the start, he still has a dilemma (5–6):

> quid nos, quibus te uita sit superstite
>   iucunda, si contra, grauis?
>
> *What are we to do, for whom life, if you survive, would be congenial, but burdensome, if it were to turn out otherwise?*[49]

The question follows naturally from the opening couplets. Horace had started by pointedly addressing Maecenas as *amice*, establishing *amicitia* as the central theme of the poem.[50] The first couplet graphically evokes his concern for the dangers faced by his addressee by placing the word *amice* literally in amongst *alta nauium...propugnacula*.[51] The second couplet ends emphatically by switching the focus to the danger that faces Maecenas (*tuo* sc. *periculo*). It is commonplace to proclaim love or friendship by saying that the lover or friend is dearer than oneself or one's life and it probably found a place in the *coniuratio*.[52] The closest parallel comes from Catullus' profession of love for Lesbia (68.159–60):[53]

> et longe ante omnes, mihi quae me carior ipso est,
> lux mea, qua uiua uiuere dulce mihi est.

In response to the circumstances Horace intensifies the expression from a general declaration of affection to one of anxious concern, substituting *te...superstite* for *te uiuo*, as the condition which determines whether life is congenial or even bearable.[54] Specifically, *superstite* [sc. *huius periculi*][55] looks back to *periculum subire*, where the danger consists in being sunk by missiles hurled from the *alta nauium propugnacula*. The question is carefully articulated, as if seeking to convey the effort required by Horace to control his emotions: *quid* is echoed in *quibus*; *te...superstite* suggestively embrace and enclose Horace's *uita*; the antithetical *iucunda~grauis* frame the dimeter[56] and are separated only by the euphemistic hint at the possibility which Horace most fears and which alone for Horace can determine whether life is worth living or not.[57] The nature of the sentiment implies an intense one-to-one relationship, such as that supposed to have existed between Laelius and Scipio.[58] The pronoun *nos* cannot be a genuine plural, as this is hardly a sentiment which Horace can or would wish to express on behalf of others. Rather, the plural modestly and tactfully avoids setting up Horace in direct competition with Caesar for Maecenas' affection.[59]

Horace, as already noted, accepts the necessity and the praiseworthiness of Maecenas' decision to follow Caesar and will make no effort to persuade him to stay, as the propemptic speaker often does. But the propemptic speaker's conventional problem remains: Horace cannot bear to be separated from his friend, although this is because of, rather than in spite of, the dangers he will face. In the following lines, Horace clarifies his dilemma (7–10):

> utrumne iussi persequemur otium
> (non dulce ni tecum simul)

an hunc laborem, mente laturi decet
  qua ferre non mollis uiros?

*Shall we, as bidden, seek out a life of ease (not sweet unless spent together
with you) or this hardship and bear it with the resolution with which it
befits unwomanly men to bear it?*[60]

Maecenas has told him to stay behind and the request from a *potens amicus* is not easily rejected.[61] Although those equestrians and senators who
were to embark with Caesar were restricted in the number of followers
they could take with them, the primary inference that Horace invites is
that Maecenas was showing consideration and concern for him, as well
as knowledge of his nature, when he told him to stay behind.[62] But the
choice of words is pointed: those who had sworn *Caesaris in uerba* had
sworn *sponte sua*. By representing Maecenas as having ordered him to
stay behind, Horace emphasises the voluntary nature of his own decision.
The *coniurati* had sworn *terra marique persequi* whoever posed *periculum* to
Caesar.[63] Maecenas has told Horace by contrast *persequi otium*. Horace
protests,[64] again exploiting a commonplace of the literature on friendship,
that even *otium*, which he implies Maecenas had described as *dulce*,[65]
will not be so if he is separated from Maecenas.[66] He then goes on to
put the alternative, that he should seek *hunc laborem*. The demonstrative
hunc makes it clear that *laborem* refers to the dangers and hardship of
war evoked in his opening lines and recalled by Maecenas' implied use
of the word *persequi*: *labor* and *periculum* are a stock pair of nouns used
to characterise the life of a soldier.[67] The litotes *non mollis* implies that
Maecenas had imputed *mollities* to Horace and used that among the reasons for telling him to stay behind.[68] The point of the litotes lies in the ancient views of the etymology of *miles/militia*: *militem Aelius a mollitia* κατὰ
ἀντίφρασιν *dictum putat, eo quod nihil molle, sed potius asperum quid gerat*.[69]
  Before Maecenas can answer or object, Horace takes his own decision:

feremus et te uel per Alpium iuga
  inhospitalem et Caucasum
uel Occidentis usque ad ultimum sinum
  forti sequemur pectore.

*We shall bear it and, through Alpine ridges and the hostile Caucasus or
even to the furthest shoreline of the West, we shall follow you with bold
heart.*

The opening *feremus* answers the question implied in *laturi*.[70] The ability to bear hard labour is characteristic of the soldier: *sed illi, qui laborem in portandis ueteribus munimentis armorum ferre non possunt, detectis*

corporibus et uulnera sustinere coguntur et mortes et, quod est grauius, aut capi aut certe fuga rem publicam prodere (Vegetius, *De re militari* 1.20.9).[71] But it is also normal for friends in the Roman world to share the *militia* of their friends.[72] Horace will share the dangers and hardships of Maecenas, just as Maecenas will share those of Caesar.

Those who had sworn their allegiance had undertaken to go anywhere, using the standard polar expression *terra marique*. Horace expresses the same idea in an elaborate variation of the commonplace declaration of loyalty between friends.[73] The linkage between the Alps and the Caucusus is not immediately obvious: it is not geographic but rather based on ethnography and etymology. The Alps are a standard feature in such declarations[74] and like the Caucasus they had a reputation for barbaric ferocity.[75] Horace has also paired them because of their similar etymologies: *album...Sabini...alpum dixerunt, unde credi potest, nomen Alpium a candore niuium uocitatum*; and *pro niuium candore Caucasus nuncupatur. nam orientali lingua caucasum significat candidum, id est niuibus... candicantem. unde et eum Scythae...Croucasim uocauerunt. casim enim apud eos candor siue nix dicitur.*[76] The Caucasus marks the far Eastern extreme of the inhabited land mass, and to complete his polar expression Horace then thinks of a sea voyage to the furthest West.[77] In the closing words of his declaration, *sequemur* finally answers *persequemur*,[78] while the heroic cliché *forti...pectore*[79] picks up *feremus* and reinforces the implications of *non mollis* with a further etymological play: *fortis, quia fert aduersa uel quaecumque acciderint: siue a ferro, quod sit durus nec molliatur.*[80] Horace's decision mirrors that of Maecenas to accompany Caesar and is equally laudable. Both Horace and Maecenas have given the lie to the charges of *mollities* made against them.[81]

The reason why Horace takes such a wide geographical sweep in envisaging the distant places to which he might accompany Maecenas is not immediately obvious. Only at *Epodes* 1.24–5 (*hoc et omne militabitur | bellum*) does it become clear that Horace sees the present war, properly speaking against Cleopatra, as possibly the first of many campaigns in which he will accompany Maecenas.[82] The Alps, the Caucasus and Spain had been the source of Roman triumphs and the site of various notable campaigns during the thirties and, after the fall of Alexandria, Gaul, Spain, Syria and Egypt would be granted to Caesar Augustus as his province.[83] In the troubled times at the beginning of 30 BC, the future seemed likely to be an unending series of campaigns against far-flung enemies which would make further calls on Horace's loyalty.

Horace may have resolved the constant hesitation and qualification of his question into a highly elaborate and confident declaration of intent but he anticipates that Maecenas may still be less than convinced (15–22):

roges tuum labore quid iuuem meo
    imbellis ac firmus parum:
comes minore sum futurus in metu,
    qui maior absentis habet,
ut adsidens implumibus pullis auis
    serpentium allapsus timet,
magis relictis, non uti sit auxili
    latura plus praesentibus.

*You may ask to what extent I shall relieve your hardship by my own, seeing
that I am no warrior and not battle-ready: but as your companion I am
likely to be in less fear, since a greater fear grips those who are absent:
just as a bird, sitting on unfledged chicks, fears for them the glide-attacks
of snakes,*[84] *even more when they are left behind, not that she would be
likely to bring them more assistance if they were before her eyes.*

The anticipated objection picks up and reiterates Maecenas' concerns:
roges echoes *iussi* (7) and *labore* picks up *hunc laborem* (9), which looks
back in turn to *Caesaris periculum* (3). The pointed phrasing of *tuum
labore ... meo* echoes that of *Caesaris periculum ... tuo* and underlines the
parallel between the relationship of Caesar and Maecenas on the one hand
and that of Horace and Maecenas on the other. The verb *iuuem* picks up
iucunda (*iucundum a iuuando*[85]) with the implication that Horace will find
it *iucundum* to be with Maecenas, whatever use his presence may or may
not be to Maecenas.[86] In general friends were expected to share the hardships of their friends, and even the Epicureans agreed, while arguing that
this was to be done for the sake of one's own pleasure.[87] Maecenas is
imagined as protesting that Horace's assistance will lack *utilitas* to him.
The second line of the couplet is telling. It quotes an insult (Homeric in
origin[88]) ἀπτόλεμος καὶ ἄναλκις against Horace's heroic claim (*forti pectore*):
imbellis is a standard antithesis to *fortis*.[89] There may be the further implication that, although Horace is *iuuenis* and so ought to be able *rem
publicam in re militari iuuare*, he will make a poor soldier.[90] Finally, *firmus
parum* perhaps suggests that, while the *firmitas* of Horace's *amicitia* is not
in doubt, his readiness for war surely is.[91]

Horace makes no attempt to contradict but rather counters by reassert-
ing his friendship for Maecenas and so confirming the implication that
Maecenas' motivation in ordering him to stay behind had been consideration for his unwarlike nature. Friends, like lovers, were proverbially
anxious for the well-being of the objects of their affections: *amor omnis
[sc. est] sollicitus atque anxius.*[92] It was also proverbial that one feared
most what one could not see: *omnia ... plerumque, quae absunt, uehementius
hominum mentes perturbant.*[93] While *fortitudo* is properly marked by

absence of fear,[94] Horace uses his very timidity as a reason why Maecenas should allow him to accompany him,[95] just as in another propemptikon a wife begs to be allowed to accompany her husband (Ovid, *Metamorphoses* 11.441–2): *me quoque tolle simul! certe iactabimur una | nec nisi quae patiar metuam.*

To underline the naturalness of his feelings, Horace turns for comparison to the world of nature, again exploiting a commonplace tactic both of literature on friendship and of the propemptikon.[96] The simile, which is used to bring a sense of closure to this part of the poem,[97] belongs to a long and rich literary tradition going back to Homer.[98] The first couplet (19–20), where the word order mimetically suggests her protective spreading of her wings, stresses the fear that the mother bird constantly feels for her unfledged offspring:[99] *adsidens* corresponds to *comes*, and *minore sum futurus in metu* to *timet*. The next couplet (21–2) opens with *magis relictis*,[100] which balances *maior absentis*, and closes with *praesentibus* in deliberate contrast with both *relictis* and *absentis*: *praesens dictus quod sit prae sensibus, id est coram oculis.*[101]

In the standard propemptikon, the speaker uses his protests at his friend's proposed departure to assert his own affection.[102] He then changes his mind, admits the necessity of his friend's departure and wishes him well. Horace has played against those expectations by rather insisting on going with his friend, who has attempted to dissuade him because of the dangers he would face. In the next section of the poem, Horace makes it clear that Maecenas has dropped his opposition to Horace's proposal and Horace elaborates further on his reasons for going (23–30).

> libenter hoc et omne militabitur
>   bellum, in tuae spem gratiae,
> non ut iuuencis inligata pluribus
>   aratra nitantur mea,
> pecusue Calabris ante sidus feruidum
>   Lucana mutet pascuis,
> neque ut superni uilla candens Tusculi
>   Circaea tangat moenia.

Willingly shall I serve in this and every war, in the hope of your favour, but not so that my ploughshares might struggle on, bound to even more oxen, or that my flocks might exchange Calabrian for Lucanian pastures before the rising of the Dog Star, nor that I should have a gleaming villa tucked below the walls of Tusculum, founded by Circe's son.

The words *hoc et omne . . . bellum* resume and define *hunc laborem* (9) and *omne . . . periculum* (3): Horace will serve *pro milite* in the forthcoming campaign at Actium, like the other equestrians and senators *qui sub meis signis tum* [sc. *bello quo uici ad Actium*] *militauerint* (*Res gestae* 25.2–3). Horace's *libenter* stands highlighted by the contrast with Maecenas' instructions to stay behind (*iussi*, 7): like those who had sworn their oath to Caesar in 32 BC, Horace is going because he wishes to support his friend and entirely of his own free will.[103] As Augustus put it in his *Res Gestae* (25.2): *iurauit in mea uerba tota Italia sponte sua.*

Horace then moves on to explain his motives for going. Since the speaker normally remains behind, this is inevitably a novelty in the propemptikon. In generic terms this might be seen as a variation on the standard account of the addressee's reasons for going.[104] Alternatively the phrase *in tuae spem gratiae* is to be seen as a variation on the 'remember me' *topos*.[105] The word *gratia* lies at the heart of Roman thinking about the mutual exchange of goods and services that characterises *amicitia*. Its basic sense is 'the feeling or offering of goodwill' especially in return for a *beneficium*.[106] In spite of the fact that Horace has insisted on going with Maecenas to allay his own fears, he now decides, not without humour, to represent his *comitatus* as a *beneficium* that he has bestowed on Maecenas rather than the reverse, presumably because he is acting *libenter*.[107] It is a moral obligation for the recipient to feel gratitude, as Cicero declares (*De officiis* 1.47): *nullum enim officium referenda gratia magis necessarium est*. And that meant above all to remember the *beneficium*: so Seneca, *De beneficiis* 2.24.1: *nihil magis praestandum est, quam ut memoria nobis meritorum haereat, ... quia nec referre potest gratiam, nisi qui meminit, et, qui meminit, eam refert*.[108] But *gratia* normally implies an obligation to reciprocate, as is clear from Cicero's definition (*De inventione* 2.161): *in qua* [sc. *gratia*]*amicitiarum et officiorum alterius memoria et remunerandi uoluntas continetur*.[109] Moreover, Maecenas can be assumed to be inclined to show his gratitude in a manner appropriate to his *liberalitas*: as Cicero says (*De officiis* 2.56), *liberales autem qui suis facultatibus ... opitulantur in re quaerenda uel augenda*. For the barest moment, it seems that Horace is going to undercut the noble sentiments of the earlier part of the poem and declare that he is motivated by self-interest. Since a desire for wealth was a standard part of the ancient motivation for going to war and for showing courage,[110] even if not the most laudable,[111] it would be entirely normal and appropriate for Horace to expect some material reward for participating in the forthcoming campaign.[112] But he immediately and elaborately refutes the implication, since, as Seneca puts it (*De beneficiis* 4.20.3), *ingratus est qui in referenda gratia secundum datum uidet, qui sperat cum reddit*.[113] That would be to treat the performance of a *beneficium* within the context of friendship too much like a business transaction: so Seneca, again (*De beneficiis* 4.13.3): *non est beneficium, quod in quaestum mittitur.*

'*hoc dabo et hoc recipiam*' *auctio est.*[114] While it was clearly common practice to confer benefits on others in expectation of reciprocation, it was held to be more honourable and appropriate for the benefactor to perform his service without thought of return: so Pliny takes it as a truism that *perit gratia si reposcatur* (*Epistulae* 1.13.6).[115] Seneca too is scathing about benefactors who seek an immediate return (*De beneficiis* 2.31.2–3): *qui beneficium dat, quid proponit? prodesse ei, cui dat, et uoluptati esse. . . . non enim in uicem aliquid sibi reddi uoluit; aut non fuit beneficium, sed negotiatio. . . . sed sperauit emolumenti aliquid: non fuit hoc beneficium, cuius proprium est nihil de reditu cogitare.* He contrasts this with what is in fact a more demanding expectation (*De beneficiis* 4.21.2–3): *dicitur gratus, qui bono animo accepit beneficium, bono debet . . . atqui hic, etiam si ultra facere nil potest, gratus est: amat, debet, referre gratiam cupit; quidquid ultra desideras, non ipse deest.*

Any suggestion that Horace expects an immediate reward in the form of a grant of land or property is immediately and emphatically refuted in a series of denials in which each couplet depicts a more extravagant demand than the last. The series is structured like a reverse priamel, which typically highlights the speaker's peculiar desire (in this case Maecenas' *gratia*) against the more conventional wishes of others. In the first couplet (25–6) he simply disclaims a wish for more land, the standard reward for the discharged soldier, but the language is elevated by the ἀπὸ κοινοῦ construction, whereby *plura* is understood with *aratra* from *pluribus* and *meis* with *iuuencis* from *mea*, and by the hypallage which transfers the struggle of the oxen to the ploughs themselves.[116] It might seem particularly appropriate to reward a *iuuenis* who has chosen to assist (*iuuem*, 15) his friend, though primarily in pursuit of the *iucunditas* of his company (*iucunda*, 6), by a gift of *iuuenci*: *iuuencus iuuare qui iam ad agrum colendum posset.*[117] The next couplet (27–8) expands this to a rejection of any claim for vast *latifundia* which will facilitate the transhumance of his sheep from Calabria to Lucania in order to avoid the hottest days of summer, an image which Horace later used to illustrate the very essence of pointless wealth.[118] The couplet is enhanced by further playful allusions to ancient etymologies: *foruum est calidum: unde et feruidum.*[119] He is perhaps suggesting that Calabria (the heel of Italy in ancient times) was so called *quod est calida* (*vel sim.*: cf. *aestuosae . . . Calabriae*, *Carm.* 1.31.5),[120] while at the same time backing an etymology of Lucania *a lucis, id est a non lucendo* against its alternative: *Lucani appellati dicuntur, quod eorum regio sita est ad partem stellae luciferae.* There is also a possible allusion to an etymology of *Canis*, the Dog Star: *Canis uocatur . . . propter flammae candorem, quod eiusmodi sit ut prae ceteris lucere uidetur.*[121] This couplet does not however just amplify the claim in terms of size but adds a note of urgency. The next rising of the Dog Star (in July) is only months away. The series reaches its climax in the third couplet with the thought of a luxury villa on the slopes below Tusculum, an ancient city which could be seen from the newly constructed *turris Maecenatiana* on the Esquiline.[122] Tusculum was founded, according to legend, by Telegonus, the son of Odysseus and Circe. Once the birth-place of the elder Cato, it was now a place where the super-rich, such as Cicero and Lucullus, had their villas constructed of the light-coloured travertine limestone and white marble and set off (for *superni candens uilla Tusculi* is another example of mimetic word order) against the ancient stonework of the city walls.[123]

This emphatic rejection of wealth in the form of land might seem oddly elaborate. But in the winter of 31/30 BC, at the time the poem was written, those who had served at Actium were clamouring for their rewards: the veterans for land, the dispossessed for compensation, others for their share of the spoils of war.[124] At this time Caesar's funds were in short supply and he was forced to resort to the desperate gesture of offering for auction or exchange both his own possessions and those of his close friends. Although Maecenas cannot be shown for certain to have had a villa at Tusculum, it would not be surprising if he did and it would give added point to the climactic position of this item in Horace's list.[125] Dio notes that no one dared to take up Caesar's offer but that it provided a way to delay the implementation of his earlier promises, which would be paid in full from the booty from Alexandria.[126] Against this background, Horace's restraint can be seen as exemplary in the fullest sense. Those who had supported Caesar in the war against Cleopatra had done so, as Horace had supported Maecenas, voluntarily and in accordance with the obligations they had incurred when they swore their loyalty and friendship. They too can be assured of the *gratia* of those they supported, but should not press unreasonable demands for immediate material recompense.

The final lines pick up and confirm the implications of *pluribus* (25). Maecenas' generosity was perhaps already legendary[127] and Horace acknowledges what he has received in the past (31–4):

> satis superque me benignitas tua
>   ditauit; haud parauero
> quod aut auarus ut Chremes terra premam,
>   discinctus aut perdam nepos.

> *Enough and more has your generosity enriched me; I do not expect to acquire something either to bury in the ground, like the old miser Chremes, or to squander, like a dissolute wastrel.*[128]

The prosaic *satis superque* signals closure and marks a return to a more sober reality in contrast with the poetic elevation of the preceding lines.[129]

Now it becomes clear that his desire to accompany Maecenas is in part a proper return of the *beneficia* he has already received.[130] The war has provided him with an opportunity to offer service to his friend. There may be future reward and he feels confident of Maecenas' *gratia*, but it is in principle a service grounded in his affection for Maecenas. Cicero makes a similar point at *De amicitia* 51, where Laelius says:

> ubi enim studia nostra uiguissent, si numquam consilio, numquam opera nostra nec domi nec militiae Scipio eguisset? non igitur utilitatem amicitia, sed utilitas amicitiam secuta est.[131]

In the Roman view, *benignitas* was a significant virtue:[132] it was proper for a man to bestow such gifts upon his friends as they needed and deserved. Augustus once claimed, in a light-hearted moment, *benignitas... mea me ad caelestem gloriam efferet* (Suetonius, *Augustus* 71.3) and in more serious vein the *Res gestae* carefully records his lavish donations to the Roman people. In acknowledging and commemorating Maecenas' generosity Horace demonstrates his own *gratia* for what he has received. But *benignitas* ought not to lead a man to give beyond his means, as is clear from Cicero (*De officiis* 2.64): *habenda autem ratio est rei familiaris, quam quidem dilabi sinere flagitiosum est, sed ita ut illiberalitatis auaritiaeque absit suspicio: posse enim liberalitate uti non spoliantem se patrimonio nimirum est pecuniae fructus maximus.*[133] As we have seen, in the winter of 31/30 BC many were expecting and demanding recompense for their part in supporting Caesar at Actium. But he had insufficient means at this time to meet their demands. Horace has shown that he expects Maecenas will feel *gratia* for the support Horace will provide at Actium. His confidence is based on his past experience. The inference which Horace is inviting is clarified by the first-century pamphlet on seeking office ([Cicero] *Commentariolum petitionis* 44.1): *benignitas... quae quamquam ad multitudinem peruenire non potest, tamen ab amicis si laudatur, multitudini grata est.* Knowledge that someone treated well those close to him was pleasing to others, for it gave an assurance that he would be as generous to them as his means would allow. By giving evidence of Maecenas' past generosity, Horace is able to provide assurance for the future to those who had supported Caesar in the war against Cleopatra.

In the final lines (32–4) Horace then disavows his need for any more riches, which he could only either hoard or squander. The stereotypical figures with which he contrasts his own behaviour are taken from comedy, a genre which, like iambic poetry, held up to scorn and ridicule behaviour which violated social propriety. Chremes serves to exemplify *auaritia*: *nullum... uitium taetrius est... quam auaritia* (Cicero, *De officiis* 2.77). Although the name is commonly used of an old man in New Comedy, it is not attested of a miser like the Euclio of Plautus' *Aulularia*. On one level the adjective *auarus* (*ex eo dictus quod sit auidus auri*[134]) might serve to suggest a derivation, in spite of the difference in prosody, from χρήματα (wealth). If that is intended, it will reinforce the point that Chremes, like Horace, is rich enough already.[135] Here, as elsewhere, Horace pairs the miser with his opposite extreme, the *discinctus...nepos*, the profligate whose dissolute morals are reflected in his dress.[136] Together they represent the vices corresponding to the virtue of *liberalitas/benignitas*. In emphatically rejecting the possiblity that he might act in any way like these embodiments of the vices *auaritia* and *luxuria*, Horace draws attention to the two vices most commonly thought to have contributed to the unending series of civil wars.[137] On this general level, Horace is perhaps simply making the point that excessive desire for riches is not just morally reprehensible but dangerous. The victory at Actium was a first step towards ending civil war. Those who had supported Caesar should not now be endangering those efforts with unseemly demands.

But the closing lines might be yet more pointed. The final quatrain is framed by *benignitas tua* (31) and *discinctus...nepos* (34), Horace's grateful acceptance of the former and his rejection of the latter. This is the first occurrence of *discinctus* in its figurative sense of 'dissolute', 'slovenly': the usage implies a contrast with the traditional dress, and, by implication, the behaviour expected of the soldier (Servius, *Aen.* 8.724 *discinctos dixit inhabiles militiae: omnes enim qui militant cincti sunt*).[138] The use of *nepos* to mean 'wastrel' rather than literally 'grandson', 'descendant' enjoyed something of a vogue in the first century and had apparently been attributed to Etruscan influence by some ancient etymologist, as seems clear from the fragmentary entry in Festus 162.17 (Lindsay): *nepos... Tuscis dicitur...luxuriosae uitae homines appellati*.[139] If this is correct, it would seem likely that the word has some special relevance for Maecenas, who prided himself on his Etruscan ancestors. Similarly, at *Carm.* 4.11.16, in a birthday poem for Maecenas, there is a well-known allusion to the derivation of *Idus* from the Etruscan word *iduare* (meaning 'divide', 'split') in the Latin word *findit* and this is clearly designed to appeal to the addressee.[140]

But there is more to it than that. The word *discinctus* has a particular association with Maecenas. Seneca's famous denunciation of Maecenas for appearing *discinctus* while discharging serious public duties refers to his behaviour at this precise period (*Epistulae* 114.6): *nam etiam cum absentis Caesaris partibus fungeretur, signum a discincto petebatur...tunc maxime ciuilibus bellis strepentibus et sollicita urbe et armata*.[141] It seems likely that he is reflecting contemporary political abuse of Maecenas, since the more positive accounts of his behaviour provided by the Caesarian loyalist Velleius Paterculus (2.88) and by the *Elegiae in Maecenatem* both also refer to the period at the end of the thirties.[142] Dio had explained Caesar's decision first to send Agrippa and then return in person to deal with the troubles of the winter of 31/30 BC by reference to his fear 'that they would despise Maecenas for being an equestrian'.[143] He may have been aware of contemporary criticism aimed at his dress and his *luxuria* as indicative of a man unsuited to his present role and incapable of handling the crisis. Or perhaps they simply complained that while they went unrewarded, Caesar's friends did well for themselves, and cited Maecenas' *luxuria* in evidence. In any event, Horace's emphatic rejection of any desire to play the *discinctus . . . nepos* works in a way similar to his earlier rebuttal of the charge of *mollities*. It carries with it rejection of the criticisms made of Maecenas. The words *haud parauero* (32) recall formally *paratus* (3) and mark closure through ring compostion.[144] But they also serve to recall Maecenas' readiness to undergo the danger that threatens Caesar. By implicitly citing Maecenas' brave decision to accompany Caesar at Actium, Horace implies that both Maecenas and himself are the very opposite of *discinctus*: *omnes enim qui militant cincti sunt*. On this view, Horace offers a defence very similar to that given explicitly by the anonymous encomiast of the *Elegiae in Maecenatem*. Having noted the charge (*quod discinctus erat*, 1.21), he goes on to crown his defence with a catalogue of the occasions on which Maecenas had accompanied Caesar, introducing them with the words (39–40):

> quid faceret? defunctus erat comes integer idem
> miles et Augusti fortiter usque pius.[145]

Although the word *nepos* does not appear among the critical expressions used of Maecenas, he was certainly criticised for his *luxuria* in a wide variety of terms; and given the supposed Etruscan derivation and that *nepos* was a standard term of political abuse, it is quite possible that the word was applied to him.[146] One defence for someone being called *nepos* was evidently to turn the vice to a virtue and dismiss the accusation as a misunderstanding of his open and outgoing nature: so, implicitly, Seneca (*Dialogi* 4.16.3): *simplices uidentur quia expositi sunt. quos quidem non simplices dixerim sed incautos: stultis luxuriosis nepotibusque hoc nomen inponimus et omnibus uitiis parum callidis.*[147] Similarly the author of the *Elegiae in Maecenatem* responds to the charges made against Maecenas in the first instance by attributing them to a misunderstanding of his *simplicitas* (21–2): *quod discinctus eras, animo quoque, carpitur unum: | diluis hoc nimia simplicitate tua.* Horace's strategy is comparable. The final word *nepos*, in combination with *perdam*,[148] is used in the sense *prodigus, luxuriosus*. As such it is in careful antithesis with *benignitas tua* (31), as is clear from Seneca's injunction (*De beneficiis* 1.15.3): *ueto liberalitatem nepotari*. Another word for *liberalitas* is *benignitas*. Having established Maecenas' *benignitas*, Horace is rejecting not only any accusation made against him of being a *discinctus nepos* but also the charges made against Maecenas. His friend has been misunderstood and the implication is that it must be his accusers who are behaving as *auari* or *prodigi* in pressing their incessant demands.

So, in the end, Horace emphatically rejects material recompense for his support in the war at Actium in the confident expectation of the *gratia* of those beneath whose *signa* he would serve *pro milite*, and by so doing sets an example as well as acting as a rebuke to those others who had served similarly but were currently demanding their rewards. They should have acted simply in confident expectation of *gratia*. As Seneca says (*De uita beata* 24.2): *beneficium conlocetur quemadmodum thesaurus alte obrutus, quem non eruas nisi fuerit necesse*. For, as he elsewhere says (*De beneficiis* 3.10.1): *dies praeterea beneficio reddendo non dicitur, sicut pecuniae creditae; itaque potest, qui nondum reddidit, reddere*.[149] There is however an implicit promise, and one that will be lavishly redeemed after the fall of Alexandria. Before the end of 30 BC, 'repayment was made in full to those who had previously advanced loans and to both the senators and equestrians who had taken part in the war with him [sc. Caesar] large sums were given'.[150]

CONCLUSION

Epode 1 has as its dramatic setting the eve of Maecenas' embarkation for the war against Cleopatra in the spring or early summer of 31 BC. At that time the majority of senators and leading equestrians had gathered at Brundisium with their followers to honour the oaths of loyalty and formalised friendship, which they had taken the previous year, as part of the *coniuratio totius Italiae*. But the poem was written to head the collection of *Epodes* which were published at the time of a second mass gathering of the same senators and leading equestrians at Brundisium in January of 30 BC. On this occasion the mood was different. All those who had fought with Caesar at Actium were anxious to receive material recompense for the services they had rendered. The threat of trouble was so severe that he had crossed the Adriatic at the most dangerous time of year, at great personal risk to himself, to deal with the matter personally. The Epode uses Horace's own relationship with Maecenas paradigmatically to explore some of the major contemporary issues relating to the duties and obligations of friends to each other in time of war and the returns they might expect for the services they provide.

The poem takes the form of a propemptikon, a farewell to a departing traveller. This genre is an ideal one in which to explore the theme of friendship, since it focuses on the moment when that relationship is placed under strain by the prospect of separation. But Horace's treatment of the traditional form is highly innovative. His departures from the generic norms serve to throw into relief the particular emphasis of his arguments.

The first section (1–14) sets the scene and establishes a contrast between Maecenas' relationship with Caesar and Horace's relationship with Maecenas. Maecenas has shown his friendship to Caesar by deciding to accompany him to war, in spite of the danger to himself. Contrary to the standard situation in the propemptikon and to normal Roman expectation, Maecenas has shown his friendship for Horace by ordering him to remain behind. Horace responds by showing the same devotion to Maecenas as the latter had shown to Caesar and declares his intention to accompany him in this war and to whatever other dangerous places might require in the future the attention of Caesar and the presence of Maecenas. By overriding the express wishes of Maecenas, Horace establishes the voluntary nature of his action. It is his decision to declare willingness to accompany Maecenas anywhere, just as those who swore their oaths to Caesar in the *coniuratio* did so *sponte sua*.

The next section reiterates the supposed concerns of Maecenas. Horace, cleverly and wittily, presents his request to accompany Maecenas not as an offer to lend military assistance but rather as a request for Maecenas to spare him the fear he would feel in the absence of his friend. Not knowing what was happening, he would fear the worst. This section again underlines the voluntary nature of Horace's action. The value of such support is conveyed by the elaborate simile, unique in the *Epodes*, which brings closure to the first part of the poem. It might also carry the further implication that the senators and the equestrians who, like Maecenas, accompanied Caesar, did so to provide moral support and to honour their oath and show their loyalty rather than to lend significant military assistance.

Breaking with the conventions of the propemptikon, Maecenas changes his mind and grants Horace his request. For all the previous emphasis that Horace has put on this being a favour to him, he now presents his *comitatus* as a service that he is providing to his friend. All he expects in return is *gratia*. Within the framework of the reciprocal exchange of goods and services that defined *amicitia*, there exists an *honestissima contentio beneficiis beneficia uincendi* (Seneca, *De beneficiis* 1.4.4). A *beneficium* may be in part return for benefits received, while simultaneously establishing a claim to *gratia*. Horace immediately and emphatically rejects any implication that he is looking for an immediate material reward in the form of more land. Once it is recalled that at the time of the poem's composition, those who had supported Caesar in the war against Cleopatra were clamouring for their rewards, the pointedness of Horace's example becomes apparent. To quieten their demands Caesar was compelled to offer for auction or exchange the properties belonging to himself and his friends. Horace's elaborate list of possible rewards culminates in a Tusculan villa. It is likely that Maecenas owned such a villa, and, if he did not, then either Caesar or another of his friends will have done. Horace closes instead with recognition of Maecenas' previous generosity, insisting that he already has all he needs. By recalling at the end Maecenas' readiness to undergo the danger facing Caesar, Horace simultaeously recalls and rebuts any charge of unsoldierly dissoluteness that might be aimed at either himself or Maecenas, as he had similarly disposed of the charge of *mollities* at the close of the first section. By the end of the poem the *benignitas* of Maecenas is matched by the *benignitas* of Horace, for, as Cicero observes (*De officiis* 2.54), *non dubium est, quin illa benignitas, quae constet ex opera et industria, ... honestior sit.* Similarly the *gratia* exhibited by Horace, in his affection for Maecenas, his offer of *comitatus*, and his explicit praises of his *benignitas* will be matched in the *gratia* of Maecenas. This exemplary show of *liberalitas*, which encompasses the proper way to receive as well as to give (Aristotle, *Eth. Nic.* 1119b), provides reassurance to those who had rendered support at Actium. The closing rebuttal of the charges of *auaritia* and *nepotatus* implies a stinging rebuke to any who, unlike Horace, insist nevertheless on pressing their incessant demands for immediate material reward.

As has long been recognised, the central theme of Epode 1 is the friendship of Horace for Maecenas. But this is only part of the story. Horace has not chosen to advertise the nature of that friendship just for the sake of it. Given the circumstances in which the poem was composed, his dramatic enactment of the relationship takes on an exemplary quality. The poem was written in difficult and uncertain times: Caesar had stretched his resources to the limit and beyond, and the final outcome of the struggle with Antony and Cleopatra was yet to be determined. He needed the continuing support and loyalty of those who had given it at Actium. Horace provides the example of what friendship means in the circle of Caesar and Maecenas and the proper way to behave in giving and receiving goods and services. As Cicero puts it, quoting with approval the Ennian version of a proverbial saying, at *De amicitia* 64:[151]

quamquam Ennius recte: 'amicus certus in re incerta cernitur', tamen haec duo leuitatis et infirmitatis plerosque conuincunt, aut si in bonis rebus contemnunt, aut in malis deserunt. qui igitur utraque in re grauem, constantem, stabilem se in amicitia praestiterit, hunc ex maxime raro genere hominum iudicare debemus et paene diu-ino.[152]

JAMES E. G. ZETZEL

3 DREAMING ABOUT QUIRINUS
Horace's *Satires* and the development
of Augustan poetry

HORACE'S DREAM

At the opening of the final poem of the first book of his *Sermones*, Horace
responds to (probably imaginary) critics who had objected to his criticism of Lucilius for sloppy writing in the fourth Satire.[1] Lucilius deserves
praise, he repeats from that poem, for his wit and his attacks on vice: *quod
sale multo | urbem defricuit* (10.3–4). At the same time, however, admirable
content does not make a good poem: there is need for constant control
of style and tone, something that Lucilius' model (at least according to
1.4), the comic poets of classical Athens, had attained, and for which they
deserve imitation (16–17):[2]

> illi scripta quibus comoedia prisca uiris est
> hoc stabant, hoc sunt imitandi.

But, he continues, neither Hermogenes nor the *simius* who can only sing
along with Calvus and Catullus has ever bothered to read them (17–19):[3]

> quos neque pulcher
> Hermogenes umquam legit neque simius iste
> nil praeter Caluum et doctus cantare Catullum.

At this point, the imaginary interlocutor – presumably the same imaginary
person as the one who had criticized Horace for criticizing Lucilius –
offers a praise of Lucilius' style (20–1):

> at magnum fecit, quod uerbis Graeca Latinis
> miscuit.

The dialogue continues briefly, Horace pours scorn on the idea of mixing
Greek and Latin, 'in the manner of a two-tongued Canusian' (30), and,
in an apparently autobiographical narrative of his earlier poetic life, he
proceeds to justify his rejection of such blending (31–5):

> atque ego, cum Graecos facerem, natus mare citra,
> uersiculos, uetuit me tali uoce Quirinus

post mediam noctem uisus, cum somnia uera:
'in siluam non ligna feras insanius ac si
magnas Graecorum malis inplere cateruas.'

The young Horace, so his story would have it, had begun by writing
Greek poetry, or at least (to make the story consistent) poetry with a
significant Greek element.[4] But late one night he had a dream in which
Quirinus, the deified Romulus – and thus necessarily the founder of all
things Roman – had told him to stick to Latin: there were far too many
Greek poets already. And he proceeds to tell how it was that he came
to write satire (it was the only form that did not have a major exponent
already among his contemporaries) before returning to the linked issues
of poetic style and the merits of Lucilius.[5]

Autobiographical anecdotes are always suspect, and even more so in the
Satires, in which every statement of almost any kind is suspect, owing to
the constant irony and self-contradictions of the speaker's voice: it is quite
apparent that 'Horace' is not – or at least is not consistently – Horace.
What is more, literary dream-narratives in Latin literature, from at least
the time of Ennius, owe less to the workings of the subconscious than
they do to the traditions of literary polemic, and Horace's dream – as has
long been recognised – is no exception. Like all the other famous literary
Roman dreams, it echoes Callimachus, and in particular his narrative of
a long-ago encounter in his youth with Apollo (fr. 1.21–4 Pf.):[6]

καὶ γὰρ ὅτε πρώτιστον ἐμοῖς ἐπὶ δέλτον ἔθηκα
γούνασιν, Ἀ[πό]λλων εἶπεν ὅ μοι Λύκιος·
... ἀοιδέ, τὸ μὲν θύος ὅττι πάχιστον
θρέψαι, τὴ]ν Μοῦσαν δ' ὠγαθὲ λεπταλέην.

And when first I put my tablet on my knees, Lycian Apollo said to
me '... poet, feed your victim as fat as possible, but, my friend, keep your
Muse thin.'

Equally clearly, Horace's dream was written in full awareness of another,
far closer adaptation of Callimachus' encounter in Virgil's *Eclogues*, a text
made public at most three years before the completion of the *Satires*
(*Ecl.* 6.3–5):[7]

Cum canerem reges et proelia, Cynthius aurem
uellit et admonuit, 'pastorem, Tityre, pinguis
pascere oportet ouis, deductum dicere carmen.'

Seen against this background, Horace's dream-as-justification becomes
considerably more pointed and polemical. In place of the Greek god
Apollo (with his various learned titles), comes the ancestral Roman

divinity Quirinus. Like Apollo in Callimachus, if not in Virgil, Quirinus speaks in homely language, although his second verse, with its combination of alliteration and a ponderous concatenation of long syllables, evokes and parodies the style of earlier Roman poetry.[8] But the changes from the Callimachean–Virgilian epiphany are even more striking: in place of the opposition of long and short poetry is a contrast between Greek (or Hellenizing) verse and home-born Latin; the diminutive *uersiculos* is both a word-formation typical of the neoterics and an element in an attack on neoteric style (the ape who chants Calvus and Catullus). Above all, the very fact and method of parody are highly significant: Callimachus, perhaps the Greek poet most admired in Horace's day, is adapted to attack Hellenism; a foreign source is used to defend native poetry; an elegant poet is used in defence of homely verse. But of course, to give due recognition to Horatian irony, it is not unimportant that Horace is here using a very Callimachean technique, the oblique use of a poetic source to attack itself, to attack the influence of none other than Callimachus.[9] Horace is being both Callimachean and anti-Callimachean, eating his cake and having it too. But what is Callimachus doing in a poetic book which claims to exemplify and describe plain-speaking, moral content, and Roman life?

CALLIMACHEAN SATIRE

'Callimachean' is a term more easily used than defined, for the simple reason that it has more than one meaning. A definition such as 'adherence to the literary principles of Callimachus' is true but both overly vague and tautological, and in fact the most significant aspect of Callimacheanism, at least in Rome, is that writers of more than one sort of poetry could legitimately claim to be followers of Callimachus. Callimacheanism can be many things: in a very broad sense, it is simply an intense concern with detailed aspects of verbal style; a preference for short, elegant, and allusive poetry over long and (from a Callimachean point of view) sloppy writing; or a self-conscious and frequently metapoetic concern with the nature of poetry itself. Beyond that, there are not only particular types of poetic subject (the obscure, the erotic, the personal; poverty and 'simple' life; aetiology) that are found in the writings of professed Callimacheans, but also an interest in previously unknown or uncommon combinations of literary genres and modes ('Kreuzung der Gattungen') and a tendency to elevate to a literary level forms of writing that had not, perhaps, been considered particularly literary before: the epigram, the mime, the curse.[10]

In the broadest sense, Horace can be considered a Callimachean because some or all of these characteristics are virtually universal among Roman poets from the time of Catullus, and possibly from the time of

Ennius and perhaps even earlier; in that respect, to describe a Roman
poet as a Callimachean is redundant, not only because modern criticism
recognizes Roman Callimacheanism, but because the Roman poets themselves drew attention to their Callimachean credentials with considerable
frequency. But while it is perfectly clear that the Horace of the *Odes* and
Epodes was heavily influenced by Callimachean principles, the *Satires* are
a less obvious candidate for such a description.[11] That is not to say that the
Satires are not Callimachean, as will be discussed below. But at the outset
of the book, with its simplistic moralising in the vein of the diatribe, and
through the deliberate roughness of the metre and the apparent avoidance
of the recherché subjects and elegant tone of Callimachus (together with
the presentation of the speaker as a simple and unpoetic poet), the *Satires*
appear, on at least one level, to ignore, and at times to reject, the literary
attitudes and heritage held in common by the other poets of Horace's
generation whose works we possess.

As has long been recognised, however, any attempt to read the *Satires*
as un- or anti-Callimachean falters rapidly. The book displays a thorough
knowledge of Callimachus' works: he not only adapts the dream from the
Aetia prologue, but quotes an epigram, and he seems to make extensive
use of the *Iambs* as well.[12] Among the most interesting of his Callimachean
allusions is his use of the programmatic conclusion of the *Hymn to Apollo*:
in describing Lucilius' poetry as *lutulentus* (4.11; 10.50), he makes it clear
that he subscribes to the Callimachean ideals of brevity and clarity –
something that would in any case be obvious from even a cursory reading
of the *Satires*.

Other aspects of both language and style make it even clearer than specific allusions to Callimachus that in the *Satires* Horace subscribes to the
poetic principles associated with other Roman admirers of Alexandrian
poetry, notably the neoterics. At 4.139 and 10.37 he characterizes his
poetry as *ludus*; at the beginning of his encounter with the *molestus* in *Satire*
9, the poetry that he is mentally composing is described as *nugae* (2).[13]
Consonant with this typically neoteric self-disparagement is Horace's
repeated emphasis (in 4 and 10) on the slow and careful composition
of his poetry, on the need for brevity, and on his choice of audience.
In Satire 4, Horace's foil Crispinus offers a splendid reduction of the
non-Callimachean poetics which Horace rejects (14–16):

> accipe, si uis,
> accipiam tabulas; detur nobis locus, hora,
> custodes; uideamus uter plus scribere possit.

In the tenth Satire, he rejects the public theatre as a suitable place for
the performance of his works, and in listing the critics whose approval

he desires, he urges the would-be poet to ignore the opinions of the mob and to be satisfied instead with the few, qualified readers (10.73–4):[14]

> neque te ut miretur turba labores
> contentus paucis lectoribus.

This exclusivity is clearly an echo of Callimachus, *Epigrams* 28.4, σικχαίνω πάντα τὰ δημόσια, 'I hate everything common.' The theatrical audience, the schools, and the uneducated mob are rejected in favour of those few *docti* whose opinion really matters; this is clearly the same poet as the author of the more emphatic version of the same words of Callimachus at the opening of *Odes* 3: *Odi profanum uulgus et arceo*.[15]

At the same time, however, it is important to recognise that the tenth Satire – from which many of the Callimachean sentiments cited above have been drawn – is not only the clearest expression of Horace's adherence to Alexandrian/neoteric poetic principles, but also the clearest rejection of them. When he refers (18–19) to

> simius iste
> nil praeter Caluum et doctus cantare Catullum,

it is perfectly clear that mindless echoing of the neoterics is not what he considers admirable poetry. In the dream of Quirinus, the contemptuous *uersiculos* (together with the other features of the dream noted above) has a similar effect. The response to his putative critics has two equally important elements: he rejects Lucilius for his style, but he rejects Hermogenes and the *simius* for their content. They have not read the great comic poets; what they admire in Lucilius (clearly his diction and wit, not merely his use of Greek words) is misguided, while they ignore the grand substance of his poetry. Again, the dream of Quirinus makes the important point: Roman substance and elegance of Roman diction are to be sought, and neither the less felicitous aspects of earlier Roman poetry nor the aping of the Greeks is admirable. Horace's imitations of Lucilius' substance are frequent throughout the *Liber Sermonum*; but it is no accident when, in the last verse of Satire 9, Horace's *sic me seruauit Apollo* (78) evokes and implicitly criticizes Lucilius' use of the same Homeric tag in its original Greek.[16]

Horace's poetic style in the *Satires* is immensely varied and brilliantly controlled; he demonstrates constantly his ability (easily a match for Catullus or the *Eclogues*) to manipulate language with wit and precision in just the manner exemplified by Callimachus; that, if nothing else, would show that he, as much as any of his contemporaries, was a master of Alexandrian poetics. This is not the place for a full treatment of Horace's style; but it is worth noticing that in some passages he makes particular use of neoteric stylistic mannerisms in pointed parodies. That is most evident in Satire 5, one of the most carefully polished and poetically polemical poems in the book.[17] The contrast between the occasion (if there was one) for the journey and the pedestrian and vulgar incidents recorded by Horace has been frequently noted; of more importance here are some verbal techniques that have a similar effect. Thus, at 5.4, Horace describes Forum Appi as

> differtum nautis cauponibus atque malignis;

and at 5.86, concerning the trip to the metrically unnameable town, he says

> quattuor hinc rapimur uiginti et milia raedis.

In each of these verses, the language of which is distinctly prosaic, a conjunction is postponed; in the second case, ludicrously so. The postponement of conjunctions is a mannerism with a pedigree, found in its most extreme form at Catullus 66.65 and *Ecl.* 1.14, where a conjunction is postponed by four or five words; and this refinement is clearly associated with Callimachus himself.[18] The combination of Alexandrian word-order with prosaic language can only be seen as a parody of neoteric stylistic affectations.

Less specific, but equally parodic of the same style, are some other passages in *Satire* 5. Thus the evening at Forum Appi, while Horace waits for the canal boat to depart, receives an extremely elevated description (9–10):

> iam nox inducere terris
> umbras et caelo diffundere signa parabat.

It is surely not coincidental that the neoterics seem to have prided themselves (as indeed did the entire Roman hexameter tradition) on elegant descriptions of the time of day, a mannerism brilliantly parodied in the *Apocolocyntosis.*[19] Here too, the elevated time-keeping contrasts beautifully with the shouting barge-keepers who appear in the following verse. Elegant metre and elevated imagery in incongruous surroundings, in fact, are hallmarks of the style of this poem. One example appears at 5.38:

> Murena praebente domum, Capitone culinam.

Again, the fine rhetorical and metrical arrangement jars with the homely subject matter. One final example will suffice, one which seems to have a peculiarly anti-neoteric point. When, at Beneventum, the innkeeper starts a fire that nearly destroys his kitchen, Horace describes it in extraordinarily high style (73–4):[20]

nam uaga per ueterem dilapso flamma culinam
Volcano summum properabat lambere tectum.

The diction of these verses, particularly the metonymy of Vulcan for fire
and the use of the metaphorical *lambere*, has epic overtones; the ornate
word-order, with the first three adjective–noun pairs arranged abc ABC,
clearly shows the influence of neoteric stylistics.[21] The relationship of
language to subject, particularly the juxtaposition of *culinam | Volcano*, is
obviously parodic. In this case, moreover, there is a very specific object of
parody. It was characteristic of Alexandrian poetry to describe the homely
details of everyday life in a heroic context: thus Hecale's entertainment of
Theseus, Heracles in the hut of Molorchus, the aetion of the mousetrap
embedded in the story of Heracles in the Nemean lion, or little Artemis
trying to touch her father's chin, but being unable to reach it. What
Horace does here is to reverse the cliché, by describing a humble event
of everyday life (a chimney fire) in the elevated tones of high poetry.

What programmatic statements and stylistic parodies alike demonstrate
is that Horace both saw his poetry as belonging to the Alexandrian tradition and was willing and able to distance himself from it by parody,
criticism, and revision. The one passage where Horace in fact translates
fairly closely an epigram of Callimachus provides a point and a focus
for Horace's reservations about Callimacheanism. In the second Satire,
where the poet is urging his interlocutor to avoid the dangers of adultery
and to seek the simpler and safer company of freedwomen, the interlocutor compares himself to a hunter who loses interest when the victim is
caught (105–8):[22]

'leporem uenator ut alta
in niue sectetur, positum sic tangere nolit',
cantat et adponit 'meus est amor huic similis; nam
transuolat in medio posita et fugientia captat.'

The source of these lines is Callimachus, *Epigram* 31 Pf.:

Ὡγρευτής, Ἐπίκυδες, ἐν οὔρεσι πάντα λαγωιόν
    διφᾷ καὶ πάσης ἴχνια δορκαλίδος,
στείβῃ καὶ νιφετῷ κεχρήμενος· ἢν δέ τις εἴπῃ·
    'τῇ, τόδε βέβληται θηρίον', οὐκ ἔλαβεν.
χοὐμὸς ἔρως τοιόσδε· τὰ μὲν φεύγοντα διώκειν
    οἶδε, τὰ δ' ἐν μέσσῳ κείμενα παρπέταται.

The hunter, Epikydes, seeks out on the mountains every hare and the
tracks of every doe, enduring frost and snow. If somebody says, 'Look,
that animal was hit', he doesn't take it. My love is of that sort: it

*knows how to pursue what runs away, but passes over what lies in the
open.*

The last two lines of Horace's version are a close translation of the last
two lines of the epigram; and what is most significant about Horace's
attitude is the comment that follows (109–10):[23]

hiscine uersiculis speras tibi posse dolores
atque aestus curasque grauis e pectore pelli?

He continues, in highly Lucretian diction, to advise the interlocutor to
approach the problem of necessary and unnecessary desires more ratio-
nally. In this passage, the Callimachean epigram is placed in the mouth of
the foolish lecher, and the poet's response disparages the ability to quote
Callimachus in no uncertain terms. The epigram itself is described as
uersiculi[24] – the same word used at 10.32 for Horace's putative attempts to
write Greek poetry – and it may well be the case that the lecher's citation of
an epigram (rather than one of the more recondite works of Callimachus)
itself locates him among the Roman amateurs of Greek epigram who had
long been familiar with such relatively easy Alexandrian poetry. Such poetry, both passages make clear, is trivial; and it is not unreasonable to see
the deliberately crude language and morals expounded in Satire 2 as a
whole as a not altogether gentle criticism of Alexandrian erotic posturing,
as exemplified by Epigram 31, by the tales found in Parthenius' *Erotika
pathemata*, and perhaps even by Virgil's second Eclogue.

LIBER SERMONVM, LIBER BVCOLICON

To this point, no mention has been made of what is perhaps the most
obviously Alexandrian feature of Horace's *Satires*, the simple fact that it
is an organised and carefully arranged book of ten poems.[25] The various possibilities of interpreting the shape of the *Liber sermonum* need
no examination here; that it is an extraordinarily complex shape should
be evident. The entire collection shows a concern with the artful disposition of poems characteristic of the most Alexandrian productions of
the Triumviral period, above all the *Eclogues* and the *Monobiblos*; and the
former book not only contains the same number of poems, but is referred
to both explicitly and implicitly in the *Satires*. The most striking of the
implicit references, the dream of Quirinus, has been discussed above; it
is impossible to believe that Horace wrote that passage without the opening of the sixth Eclogue in mind, and it is equally impossible to imagine
that he shaped his book of satires without reference to the *Liber bucolicon*.
As with his attitude to Callimachus, so, it will emerge, with the *Eclogues*:

admiration and homage on the one hand, criticism and revision on the other.

The one explicit reference to the *Eclogues* in the *Satires* is well known; at the very least it establishes absolutely, in a way that nothing else does, the chronological relationship between the two books. In the list of poetic forms that Horace decided not to write, he refers to Virgil in an obviously complimentary context and with equally complimentary language (1.10.44–5):

> molle atque facetum [sc. epos]
> Vergilio adnuerunt gaudentes rure Camenae.

The compliment, however, has a complexity of tone that seems to undercut its praise. The laudatory elements are clear: Horace refers to the Camenae, whom Virgil appears to have resurrected in the *Eclogues*. The description of the *Eclogues* as *facetum*, moreover, is even more complimentary than it might at first appear because of its juxtaposition with *rure*, which seems to correct the traditional opposition between *urbanitas* and *rusticitas*.[26] *molle*, however, is less unequivocally positive: despite all the favourable connotations (as e.g. its contrast with the *duritia* ascribed to Lucilius), it also may have overtones of decadence and effeminacy, and it is so employed, with great pride at times, by Propertius. If the *Eclogues* are a masterpiece of wit and elegance, they may also somehow be decadent and enervated.[27]

The *Liber sermonum* has a far larger range than is entailed by its relationship to the *Liber bucolicon*, but that, as should emerge from this discussion, is precisely the point. Throughout the *Satires*, it is possible to find evidence of a complex mixture of admiration for Virgil's poetic genius with criticism of the way in which he had employed it. While the structure of the *Satires* keeps Virgil's book constantly in the back of the reader's mind, the deliberate plainness of Horace's *sermo*-style of diction and metre makes the reader attentive to the differences between them. Where Virgil's style is mellifluous and constantly recalls his Alexandrian models, Horace's is abrupt, and looks back to Lucilius and Lucretius.[28] Where Virgil has singing shepherds, Horace has moralising street-philosophers; where Virgil's characters inhabit an imaginary countryside, Horace's are to be found in the streets of Rome and the towns of Italy; where Virgil cites Callimachean Apollo and the Heliconian Muses as sources of inspiration, Horace has Quirinus and the practical precepts of his own freedman father. It is not necessary to go as far as Van Rooy in finding precise parallels between each satire and the corresponding eclogue,[29] but it is not unreasonable to see certain poems and scenes in Horace as parody of similar moments in Virgil. As noted above, where the second Eclogue deals with melodramatic erotic passion, the second Satire reduces it to copulation. In the eighth Eclogue, magic is used for an amatory incantation; the eighth Satire has the lurid witches of the Esquiline disturbed by Priapus' fart. The exquisite delicacy of amoebaean song in the pastoral context becomes, in two poems of Horace (5 and 7), mock-epic contests of crude invective, and Putnam has recently argued that the fifth Satire should be seen as a response to the fourth Eclogue, and that the conclusion of the first has links to the last line of Eclogue 10.[30]

But if Horace draws attention to the preciosity of the *Eclogues* and parodies the mannerisms and conventions of the Alexandrian style, his purpose in doing so is not simply to criticise: there is a positive goal as well as a negative one. Once again, the dream of Quirinus is the most explicit demonstration of what Horace finds wanting in Virgil's book: Greek *uersiculi* are to be scorned; the Roman poet is to write in the Roman language and, by implication, about Roman themes in the real world. Similarly, the criticism of the use of Callimachus' *uersiculi* in Satire 2, like Lucretius' attack on the language of Greek erotic epigram in *De rerum natura* Book 4, is meant to draw attention to the artificiality of language and the emotional posturing of that genre. If one looks at the sources of inspiration and ideas named or implicit in the two works, they are radically different. The poetic tradition in which Virgil claims to be writing, the poets whom he cites as models or antecedents, form a familiar group, whose ancestry was convincingly traced by David Ross: from the mythical archetypes of Linus and Orpheus, through Hesiod, to the Alexandrians, to Parthenius, and through him to the Roman Alexandrians – the neoterics and, of course, Cornelius Gallus.[31] But other than Callimachus himself, these are not the writers to whom Horace turns. His overt model is Lucilius, whose pedigree he traces to Aristophanes and the other poets of the Old Comedy. Ennius appears as a figure worthy of admiration. But, aside from Lucilius (whose precise influence is very hard to identify), the single text most frequently alluded to, particularly in the opening poems of the book, is the *De rerum natura* of Lucretius. And what is important about these writers – except for the ubiquitous Callimachus – is not, at least in Horace's explanation, how they wrote, but what they wrote: poetry of substance, social criticism, philosophical speculation, moral commentary. It is the concern for *magnae res* that is most admirable in such poets: *hoc stabant, hoc sunt imitandi* (10.17), and it is no accident that it is unfamiliarity with such authors that Horace most condemns in the poetry of the *cantores Catulli*.

None of this is meant to suggest either that the *Eclogues* are elegant trifles devoid of serious content or that Horace seriously intended to lump Virgil's poetry together with the unknown *simius* who aped the neoterics; but satire (like literary criticism) has a tendency to oversimplify the objects of its attention, and it is worth considering that Horace, in his reading of Virgil, chose to exaggerate certain tendencies in the *Eclogues* that were shared by the work of lesser (and now thankfully unknown) contemporaries. And while recognising that it is an exaggeration, one must consider whether there was something there for the plain-spoken speaker of the *Satires* to exaggerate. It is obvious that the *Eclogues* do not remove themselves from the troubles of contemporary Rome, and that Virgil, however obliquely, does deal with the moral and social issues raised by the civil wars of the 40s and early 30s. It is equally clear, however, that the surface and style of the poems are remarkably precious.[32] The *Eclogues* are a work of poetic genius that manages to transcend its own artificiality, but it surely is artificial: a world of learned shepherds singing mellifluous and recondite poetry in a fictitious never-never land, in a Hellenizing style the peculiarity of which both was and is unmistakable.[33] When the lovesick Corydon in Eclogue 2 praises himself with the lines (23–4)

> canto quae solitus, si quando armenta uocabat,
> Amphion Dircaeus in Actaeo Aracyntho,

the second verse could have been (and perhaps was) written by an Alexandrian poet, and in reading it one feels a certain sympathy with Quirinus' strictures on Greek *uersiculi*. I am fairly certain that Virgil used it in order to mock Corydon's literary pretensions; but it is still Virgil who wrote it.

In the proem to the seventh Eclogue, Meliboeus is invited by Daphnis to leave his sheep in order to witness the poetic contest of Corydon and Thyrsis. He does so, with the following comment (17):

> posthabui tamen illorum mea seria ludo.

A remarkably similar line appears in the first Satire. There, after discussing the choice of careers, commenting on human inconsistency, and introducing the principle of *ridentem dicere uerum*, Horace introduces his interpretation of the opening scene with the line (27)

> sed tamen amoto quaeramus seria ludo.

The last two words (as well as the second, *tamen*) are the same, but the meaning of the two lines is exactly opposite. Meliboeus gives at least temporary preference to *ludus*, but Horace deliberately sets it aside in favour of *seria*. Without pressing too much the significance of a single verse, it remains true that the attitude toward *ludus*, at least Virgilian *ludus*, is emblematic of Horace's attitude to the *Eclogues* as a whole.

WHITHER ALEXANDRIANISM?

A century after Horace wrote the *Liber sermonum*, another satirist launched a far more vitriolic attack on the poetic failings of his contemporaries.
The dyspeptic persona of Persius' first Satire exclaims at one point over
the vileness of literary taste and style (30–5):

> ecce inter pocula quaerunt
> Romulidae saturi quid dia poemata narrent.
> hic aliquis, cui circum umeros hyacinthina laena est,
> rancidulum quiddam balba de nare locutus
> Phyllidas, Hypsipylas, uatum et plorabile siquid,
> eliquat ac tenero subplantat uerba palato.

This passage in particular and the whole poem in general create a picture
of the decay of the poetic tradition by the time of Nero. Tired stories
of Greek erotic legends, precious verses replete with Greek formations,
and refined form without serious content match the hyacinth-coloured
cloak that wraps the portly decadence of the degenerate descendants of
Romulus.

One should obviously not take this to be an accurate portrait of Roman
poetry in the 60s CE, but there are too many similar criticisms to be found
in post-Ovidian literature not to recognize that it contains more than a
germ of truth. The tradition of Callimachean poetry – for that is surely
what is being described in Persius' tirade – had degenerated into a tired
collection of tricks and clichés, an exquisite poetry of no literary merit
whatsoever. And it is worth recognising that, from a very early stage, the
self-conscious style of Alexandrian poetry lent itself to parody and indeed to self-parody. In Rome, it is clear that the poets themselves were
aware that excessive concentration on poetic technique or mere imitation
of some of the subject matter of the Alexandrians could easily overwhelm
any serious thought. Even in the *Monobiblos*, Propertius parodies neoteric
refinement, as in his magnificent description of Cynthia's swimming in
1.11.[34] Ovid in the *Amores* freely resorts to parodying the tradition in
which he wrote, and which he reduced to absurdity.[35] The brilliant parodies of the *Culex* and some of the poems of the *Apocolocyntosis* show
that Persius was not alone in recognising the revolting possibilities of
Alexandrianism.[36] What should surprise us is not that a tradition with
such an instinctive drive for the obscure, the precious, and the melodramatic degenerated as fast as it did, but that poets who were reared at
the feet of Parthenius – himself a good example of technical virtuosity
combined with brainless admiration for Callimachus – ever managed to
do anything else.

All writers who choose to fashion themselves after the manner of another writer run the risk of reducing what was at one time a striking and original style to a collection of tricks and oddities. Seneca demonstrated this in the case of the *Sallustianus* Arruntius, and Quintilian heaped scorn on all those who thought that by producing the clausula *esse uideatur* they had succeeded in writing Ciceronian Latin.[37] With Callimacheanism, the problem was even more acute: to acknowledge one's debt to a style that, for the production of meaning, depends so heavily on allusion, imitation, and variations on earlier texts can easily result in precisely the slavish forms of allusion and imitation that Callimachus himself was so careful to avoid, an aping of the manner devoid of the master's genius. To be a Callimachean involves an inherent impossibility: by imitating Callimachus, one violates Callimachus' own rejection of imitation.

The *Eclogues*, of course, are far from being a servile imitation of anything, but it is not difficult to see that Horace's *molle* has a real point, no matter how much his parody of the Callimachean–Virgilian scene of poetic inspiration oversimplifies the issue. The implicit antitheses that he sets up between his own book and Virgil's are excessively stark: between Greek and Roman, between the country and the city, between imaginary singing shepherds and the plain-spoken moralist, between poetics and ethics. Both poets are Callimacheans; both subscribe to Alexandrian principles of learning, brevity, and careful and elegant composition; and neither one, of course, represents the simple-minded preciosity of the surface Callimacheanism of the unnamed chanters of Calvus and Catullus, of Parthenius, or of the sort of poet derided by Persius. It is not unreasonable, however, to see the *Satires* as a suggestion that the *Eclogues* lean too far in that direction. Virgil does indeed deal with substantial problems and with the realities of Roman and Italian life in the Triumviral age; but, it might be argued (as I think Horace does argue), that to veil the moral and social issues under the mask of pastoral, to emphasize poetics rather than politics, to construct a smooth, elegant, and artificial world and diction is not the best way to write or to live in Rome of the mid-30s. The satirist on the other hand, while maintaining to be sure his own ironic distance, has applied Callimachean principles to his own time and place, and made a close connection between aesthetic and moral principles. Poetry is about something more than itself.

All this seems to go rather far afield, and to stretch perhaps beyond the limit the few lines of the *Satires* that are obviously related to the *Eclogues*. And, if the *Satires* had an influence on the later development of Triumviral and Augustan poetry, it is not altogether easy to see what it is. In particular, is there any evidence that Virgil understood the *Satires* to be saying anything remotely like the interpretation that I have been proposing? There is, in fact, some reason to believe that he did. In the first place, a small philological point. At *Georgics* 3.279, in listing the directions of the compass towards which mares in heat do not go, Virgil uses the phrase *pluuio contristat frigore caelum*; 25 lines later, in discussing the location of sheep-pens, he uses the phrase *extremoque inrorat Aquarius anno*. The content of these lines is not important here, but the diction is. Compare Horace, *Satires* 1.1.36:

> inuersum contristat Aquarius annum.

Virgil has adopted *contristat* in one verse, and *Aquarius annum* in the other, from one and the same line of Horace; and the two allusions to a single verse span the major division of Book 3.[38] A similar homage to the *Satires* occurs at *Aeneid* 2.310–11, where the description of the kitchen fire in Satire 5 discussed above is transformed into the burning of Deiphobus' house.[39]

Echoes of this kind, however, are technical, and serve only to show (what is scarcely surprising) that Virgil knew and respected Horace's book, and gave it an oblique compliment by adapting Horace's words to very different contexts. But the echo in the *Georgics* helps to confirm one of the reasons for the immense change between the *Eclogues* and the *Georgics* in subject matter as well as style. The excessive Hellenism of metre and diction are muted; the artificial shepherds in a fictional landscape are replaced by agriculture and Italy, however poetically transformed. The structural model, and major elements of the style, come from Lucretius, one of the major influences on the style of the *Satires*.[40] And, above all, Virgil deals with philosophical and ethical issues concerning the contemporary world of Augustan Rome, and adumbrates grand themes in a manner which clearly looks forward to the *Aeneid*.[41]

Perhaps such a conclusion is too sweeping: we have lost too much poetry to be able to trace accurately the literary currents of the 30s; and it would be naïve to suggest that one book could change poetic style so dramatically. Not all poets, clearly, were so affected: the *Monobiblos* too looks back to the *Eclogues*, but it shows no sign of Horatian influence. But the *Satires* and their criticism of one type of Alexandrianism offer the opportunity to construct a slightly different background to Augustan poetry than is commonly found. The neoteric version of Callimacheanism is a kind of poetic withdrawal from the public world, the construction of a poetic counter-world with its own values that are aesthetic rather than political, private rather than public; and, in the context of the 50s, it is not difficult to find explanations for that emphasis. But that, of course, not only represents a distortion or narrowing of Callimachus himself, but essentially removed from poetry the possibility of public comment or significance, except through meaningful silences; and, as in fact clearly happened among lesser writers of later generations, it lent itself to triviality and preciosity. But there are (at least) two ways of being a Callimachean in Rome: one is to imitate the style and matter of the Alexandrians, as was largely done by the neoterics; the other is to adapt the poetics of Alexandria to a Roman context – to substitute allusion to earlier Roman poetry for the Alexandrians' adaptations of archaic Greek poetry; to explore aetiology in a Roman, rather than a Greek context; to employ the oblique methods of Callimachus or Theocritus in examining issues of contemporary significance. No serious Roman poet limited himself to one alternative or the other, but it is clear – to consider only the two books that have been discussed above – that the *Eclogues* incline as much in the first direction as the *Satires* do in the other.[42] The *Satires* are not easily to be pinned down to a single theme, and it is not my intention to do so here; but if one seeks a literary explanation for some of the changes in Roman poetry in the process of becoming 'Augustan', then it is clear that the *Liber sermonum* deserves an important place in such an account.

4   *BIFORMIS VATES*
     The *Odes*, Catullus and Greek lyric

I

From the epilogue to the first three books of *Odes* it is clear that Horace saw his principal lyric achievement in terms of *Aeolium carmen* (3.30.13). The commentators on this passage, if they say anything at all, explain that the reference is to Sappho and Alcaeus.[1] Horace uses a similar phrase, *Lesboum ... barbiton*, in the very first ode of the collection (1.1.34), but here the commentators are divided in their explanation. The majority of those writing in the nineteenth and twentieth centuries, including (most recently) Quinn and West, refer likewise to Sappho and Alcaeus;[2] but in the major commentaries of Kiessling–Heinze and Nisbet–Hubbard reference is made only to Alcaeus.[3] This division of opinion is reflected in the statements of distinguished Horatian scholars which are enshrined in successive editions of the *Oxford Classical Dictionary*. Writing in 1970, Williams said that 'Horace claims the early Greek lyric poets, Sappho and Alcaeus, as his model', whereas according to Syndikus, writing in 1996, 'Horace declares that his main literary model in the *Odes* was the early Greek lyric poetry from Lesbos, especially that of Alcaeus.'[4] What seems to be at issue is the degree to which, or even the question whether, Sappho is important for Horace in his *Odes*.

It may be pertinent that the word *barbitos*, used by Horace at the end of his first ode, is not found in the extant remains of Alcaeus and was associated particularly with Sappho.[5] These considerations seem scarcely to support any neglect of Sappho; but, since the former is arguably fortuitous, we should also consider Horace's two following lines, in which he concludes the first ode with an address to his patron, Maecenas (1.1.35–6):

> quodsi me lyricis uatibus inseres,
> sublimi feriam sidera uertice.

There were nine poets in the lyric canon: Horace can be installed in the canon only if he displaces one of its existing members or if the canon is enlarged to ten to include him.[6] Although we cannot tell which of these conceits Horace intended, it is worth noting that an analogous conceit to the latter is that of Sappho as the tenth Muse, which occurs in several epigrams of the *Greek Anthology* (7.14, 407, 9.26, 66, 506, 571) and in Poem 35 of Catullus (15–16). As for the final line of Horace's ode, commentators note that the expression is 'a proverbial phrase';[7] but its first recorded occurrence is in Sappho (52 'I do not expect to touch the sky'),[8] and, in the context of a *barbitos* described explicitly as *Lesbous*, it seems perverse not to believe that Horace is reversing and outdoing a statement of Sappho. It therefore appears that there is more Sappho behind the ending of the first ode than is allowed by the two major commentaries; and this cluster of Sapphic elements provides a neat and natural transition to the next ode, *Iam satis terris*, which is written in the Sapphic metre.[9]

In the overtly programmatic passages of *Odes* 1–3 Horace identifies an Aeolian or Lesbian poet only at 1.32.3–5:

> age dic Latinum,
> barbite, carmen,
>
> Lesbio primum modulate ciui...

Here it is of course clear that the reference is exclusively to Alcaeus: hence it 'may seem strange', as Nisbet–Hubbard remark, that the ode 'should be written in Sapphics'.[10] Moreover, not only does Horace again use the arguably un-Alcaic word *barbitos* but his command to the lyre recalls Sappho 118:[11]

> ἄγι δὴ χέλυ δῖα †μοι λέγε†
> φωνάεσσα †δὲ γίνεο†
>
> Come, divine shell, speak to me
> and find yourself a voice.

Though one might protest that *age dic* is too unmarked an expression to constitute an allusion, it will be noted that the juxtaposed words seem to mimic the sound of Sappho's ἄγι δὴ χ-.[12] And the likelihood of allusion here is strengthened by a later ode (3.11), again written in the Sapphic metre, where χέλυ...φωνάεσσα ('speaking shell') is alluded to by the phrase *testudo...loquax* (3–5).[13]

At 2.13.24–32 Horace depicts Sappho and Alcaeus in the Underworld:

> Aeoliis fidibus querentem
>
> Sappho puellis de popularibus,   25
> et te sonantem plenius aureo,

> Alcaee, plectro dura nauis,
>> dura fugae mala, dura belli.
>
> utrumque sacro digna silentio
> mirantur umbrae dicere, sed magis   30
>> pugnas et exactos tyrannos
>> densum umeris bibit aure uulgus.

No one doubts the significance of this brilliant and evocative passage, some scholars interpreting it as implicitly programmatic. But what is the precise significance? Numerous readers seem to agree with Ferguson that Horace here 'makes clear a preference for Alcaeus to Sappho'.[14] Thus Nisbet–Hubbard say that, 'like the shades in the Underworld', Horace 'rightly found Alcaeus more interesting'.[15] D. A. Campbell refers to 'the unfavourable comparison with Alcaeus'.[16] Yet the matter seems rather more complicated than this. The *umbrae* admire both poets equally (29–30 *utrumque... mirantur*); it is the *uulgus* which is more absorbed by Alcaeus. Now this may be one of those rare occasions on which the *uulgus* 'sees straight' (cf. *Epist.* 2.1.63 *interdum uulgus rectum uidet*);[17] but post-Callimachean poets normally abhor anything to do with the *uulgus*,[18] and in the *Odes* the *uulgus* 'commonly represents the kind of person from whom Horace wishes to distance himself as a select and sublime lyric poet'.[19] That is certainly the case when, a mere three poems later, Horace again mentions the *uulgus* in suggestively Callimachean terms (2.16.37–40):[20]

> mihi...
> spiritum Graiae tenuem Camenae
> Parca non mendax dedit et malignum
>> spernere uulgus.

At the very best it seems that 2.13 cannot be invoked to denigrate Sappho by comparison with Alcaeus.[21]

Thus Sappho refuses to be eclipsed in the very passages which appear, or have been thought, to privilege Alcaeus. On the basis of such evidence it seems that the majority of commentators are right when they say that Horace's references to Aeolian or Lesbian poetry embrace Sappho as well as Alcaeus.

II

The conjunction of Sappho and Alcaeus seems entirely natural. Each poet came from Mytilene on Lesbos, and they were said to be contemporaries and even lovers;[22] Sappho wrote at least one poem which according to

Aristotle was addressed to Alcaeus (137), while Alcaeus allegedly wrote at least one poem in which Sappho is addressed (384); they are frequently mentioned alongside each other by ancient authors,[23] and they are depicted side by side in Greek art.[24] When Horace in 2.13 (above) depicts them as singing together in the Underworld, he is appealing to a familiar tradition.

Yet there are three other respects in which Horace's conjunction of the two poets is not natural at all. Many Latin authors claimed, or were thought by others to have established, a relationship with a single principal model.[25] Ennius was commonly said to be a 'second Homer' (*Epist.* 2.1.50 *alter Homerus*), Sallust was said by Velleius to be the 'rival of Thucydides' (36.2 *aemulumque Thucydidis Sallustium*), Propertius claimed to be the 'Roman Callimachus' (4.1.64 *Romani...Callimachi*).[26] The unfortunate Terence, because he allegedly lacked *uis*, was said by Julius Caesar to be only 'half a Menander' (fr. 1.1 *o dimidiate Menander*).[27] Horace himself is at the opposite extreme from Terence's relationship with Menander: he claimed a generic relationship which, as we have seen, involves *two* poets.

Second, Horace in the epilogue to *Odes* 1–3 claims that he is the first to have imitated Aeolian poetry (3.30.13–14): *princeps Aeolium carmen ad Italos | deduxisse modos*. This claim would be true if it applied only to Alcaeus; but we have seen that it applies also to Sappho, who had already been imitated by Catullus in two famous poems. Horace's claim, at least as it concerns Sappho, is therefore untrue and has placed scholars on the defensive. 'He has to ignore the two Sapphic poems of Catullus', says Williams, 'but this was justified because Catullus did not attempt to represent Sappho's poetry in Latin'; Quinn says that 'Catullus' experiments with the Sapphic stanza, being of limited extent, are ignored.'[28]

Third, unlike Alcaeus and unlike all the other models with whom Latin poets established a relationship, Sappho was a *woman*. This aspect of Horace's imitative claims, like each of the two others, would be unusual in itself;[29] but, when all three are considered together, they seem most extraordinary and in need of an explanation.

III

Some scholars have seen Horace's relationship with Greek lyric poetry exclusively in terms of metre,[30] but Macleod has offered a much more comprehensive interpretation of Horace's relationship with Alcaeus:[31]

> what he imitates is not merely metres or lines or poems of Alcaeus, but a whole poet.... What counts, then, about Alcaeus as portrayed

in Horace's writing is less his techniques or products than the poetic inspiration and the human being that the work contains. He becomes not merely a model, but a matrix, one from which Horace can produce different images of his own work.

Macleod's view of 'poetic inspiration' is illustrated by Longinus' point that 'the genius of the ancients acts as a kind of oracular cavern, and effluences flow from it into the minds of their imitators' (*Subl.* 13.2).[32] Perhaps more difficult is the notion of imitating 'a whole poet'. Yet, if the genre of biography is any guide, it was common for the ancients to see one author in terms of another, transferring to a later author biographical material from an earlier.[33] Such material in its turn might well be derived from an author's own poetry;[34] and, even if such poetry was non-biographical in nature, it would nevertheless allow a reader 'to discern the author's character', as Demetrius put it (*Eloc.* 227). Thus the exiled Ovid maintains that his addressee will derive a *maior imago* of his 'friend Naso' from reading the *Metamorphoses* than from gazing at the poet's portrait (*Tr.* 1.7.9–14). Alcaeus' poetry, on the other hand, gave every appearance of being highly biographical, in the same way as Lucilius was said by Horace to have presented his 'whole life' in his satires (*Sat.* 2.1.32–4 *omnis . . . uita*); and, if Horace in his *Odes* brings to lyric 'something of the self-expression, however stylised, that he borrowed from Lucilius in the *Satires*', as Nisbet–Hubbard have aptly remarked,[35] it is *a fortiori* probable that he also modelled his lyric personality on the figure of Alcaeus which he read in Alcaeus' poetry.[36]

Indeed Macleod's view receives support from Horace's own *Epistles*. In *Epist.* 1.19, published after *Odes* 1–3, Horace claims to have been the first Latin poet to have imitated Alcaeus (32–3):

> hunc ego, non alio dictum prius ore, Latinus
> uulgaui fidicen.

It will be noticed that Horace says 'this man' (*hunc*), not 'this man's poetry'.[37] We might be tempted to dismiss the pronoun as a simple metonymy, but another passage in the *Epistles*, not mentioned by Macleod, makes this dismissal difficult. Imagining himself in a duel with a fellow poet, Horace concludes the episode with these words (*Epist.* 2.2.99):

> discedo Alcaeus puncto illius.

'[I]dentification, not comparison', writes Brink magisterially on this line,[38] referring to the description of Ennius as a 'second Homer' (*Epist.* 2.1.50). Now Ennius did indeed see himself as the reincarnation of Homer, since in the *Annals* he described himself as having received

Homer's own soul by a process of metempsychosis.[39] There seems no reason to doubt that, at least in the *Epistles*, Horace saw himself, and represented himself as being seen, as a second Alcaeus.

IV

If Macleod is right to suggest that in Alcaeus' case Horace was imitating 'a whole poet', and if in the *Odes* Horace's references to Aeolian or Lesbian poetry embrace Sappho as well as Alcaeus, why should Horace's imitation of Sappho not also be that of 'a whole poet'? One response is that there is no mention of Sappho in the very lines of *Epist.* 1.19 which help to support the comprehensive nature of Horace's imitation of Alcaeus:[40] this is a serious objection, to which we shall return later (VIII). Another response is that Sappho's 'fémininité même la rendait, pour un homme, inimitable';[41] yet gender was no barrier to a metaphorical metempsychosis, since Empedocles, for example, alleged that one of his previous incarnations had been as a woman.[42] This notion may be pursued further by reference to Catullus.

Catullus had written two Sapphic poems. Poem 51 has four stanzas, of which the first three are a close translation of Sappho 31 and the fourth has no analogue in Sappho at all.[43] Poem 11 is the converse of this: it has six stanzas, of which the first five have no link with Sappho, except for their metre, but the sixth contains a flower simile which most readers believe to be derived from Sappho 105b. The simile was used by Sappho to describe a young girl, but Catullus has used it to describe his own love (21 *meum ... amorem*). The same transposition occurs in Poem 51. In Sappho's original poem the first-person references are to Sappho herself;[44] in Catullus these same references are to Catullus himself, the change being first indicated by the masculine ending of the adjective *misero* in line 5.

It is as well to be clear what the precise nature of Catullus' imitation is. He has not, as it were, personified a woman: this is not a case like Poem 64, where the male poet puts words into the mouth of Ariadne. Such personification is as old as Greek literature itself and is well exemplified by the *Epistula Sapphus*, where an author has put 220 lines of elegiac verse into Sappho's own mouth.[45] What Catullus has done in Poems 11 and 51 is quite different: he has appropriated, and transposed to a male context, words which were originally uttered by a woman poet about her own or another woman's condition.[46]

It is well known that these are not isolated experiments but part of a much larger complex of transpositions in which Catullus describes his own circumstances in feminine terms.[47] Although most of the numerous examples are too familiar to list, there is an interesting case at 65.13–14, where Catullus likens his own lament for his brother to Procne's lament for her son:

> qualia sub densis ramorum concinit umbris
> Daulias, absumpti fata gemens Ityli.

This comparison is 'female' twice over: not only does Catullus liken himself to Procne but the same comparison had already been used by Penelope of herself in the *Odyssey* (19.518–23). Unlike Homer, however, Catullus refers to the nightingale as 'the Daulian bird', a name which according to Thucydides was used by 'many of the poets' (2.29.3). As it happens, no surviving Greek text exhibits the name, although it recurs in the *Epistula Sapphus* (154 *concinit Ismarium Daulias ales Ityn*). Perhaps the author of the epistle took the epithet directly from Catullus;[48] but where did Catullus get it from? No doubt from one of the now lost Greek poets mentioned by Thucydides; and, given Catullus' evident fondness for Sappho, she must be a strong candidate.[49] Alternatively it might be argued that the poetic epistolographer was constructing a so-called 'window reference' to Sappho via Catullus.[50] Whatever the precise intertextual relationship, it does seem highly probable that behind both Catullus and the epistle there lurks a passage of Sappho, who wrote about, and was herself compared to, the nightingale.[51] At any rate, transpositions of gender, such as this example in Poem 65, are so frequent in Catullus that they may legitimately be called a distinctive feature of his poetic personality.

Now as early as Homer we find a man being compared to a woman by means of a simile (*Od.* 8.523–31),[52] and modern scholarship has investigated the effect of 'playing the other' in Greek tragedy (to use Froma Zeitlin's famous phrase);[53] but Catullus is distinguished by the fact that he has constructed a complex personality of this nature within a single body of poetry and applied it to himself as the author of the text – an author, moreover, who constantly addresses himself and identifies himself by name as 'Catullus'.[54] No scholar seems to have suggested a true precedent for this phenomenon, and we naturally cannot discover what led Catullus to construct such a personality. It may reflect something in his own psychology, which in turn is illustrated by his story of Cybele and Attis in Poem 63;[55] on the other hand, we know from Poem 35 that Catullus was not the only new poet engaged in writing about the cult of Cybele: there may have been a vogue in literary gender-change at the time when Catullus was writing.[56]

It happens that Poem 35 brings together the cult of Cybele and the conceit of Sappho as the tenth Muse (above, p. 54). Is this simply

coincidence? Did the notion of gender-change put Catullus in mind
of Sappho, the most famous woman poet? Of course we cannot know.
Sappho is praised frequently in the epigrams of the *Greek Anthology*, and
some of them are contemporary with Catullus.[57] Alternatively Catullus
may have been introduced to her poetry through the epigram of Valerius
Aedituus (fr. 1), in which Sappho 31 is again rendered into Latin and
applied to the male poet (line 4: *tacitus, subidus*).[58] Indeed Valerius is
the only potential precedent for Catullus' own procedure; but Catullus
is distinguished by the fact that his exploitation of Sappho is more extensive, retains the original metre, and is part of a much larger literary
context of gender-transpositions. Whatever the exact nuances of influence, it seems not unreasonable to say that it was Catullus who was
principally responsible for introducing Sappho's verse in Latin to the
literary élite at Rome. In the words of Richard Jenkyns, 'Catullus took
more interest in Sappho as a source than any Roman poet before
Horace.'[59]

V

I suggest that Horace was decisively influenced by the striking, perva-
sive and seemingly unprecedented dualism of gender which is found in
Catullus' poetry and that, as an admirer and imitator of archaic Greek
lyric, he was particularly interested in the role which Sappho was given
in that dualism. Horace's reading of Catullus made him realise that, by
claiming to imitate Sappho as well as Alcaeus, he might himself repro-
duce – though in a radically different form – the dualism of gender which
is presented by Catullus and to which his own dualism is itself a response.
If (like the majority of scholars) we separate into its two constituent parts
Horace's claim to be the first in imitating Sappho and Alcaeus, the claim
is rendered untrue by the priority of Catullus in imitating Sappho; but, if
both Greek poets *together* are regarded as his *joint* model, Horace's claim
is nothing less than the truth. This conjunction is precisely that which
Williams, whether knowingly or not, expressed in the statement mentioned earlier (p. 53): 'Horace claims the early Greek lyric *poets*, Sappho
and Alcaeus, as his *model*', two poetic personalities forming a single exemplar. Just as joint imitation of both Homeric poems is signalled at the
start of the *Aeneid*, so Horace in his *Odes* claims joint imitation of the two
Lesbian poets in a form of 'personalised *contaminatio*'. The suggestion
of a *biformis uates* will no doubt seem unusual; but it would explain the
three extraordinary elements in the claims which Horace makes in the
Odes (II above).

VI

Catullus' dualism results in his self-portrayal as a man whose emotional responses are describable in womanly terms: in the famous words of Poem 8, he is *Miser Catullus*, and indeed *miser* is a word often used by women in Roman comedy.[60] In another poem Catullus represents his critics as accusing him of effeminacy (16.12–13):

> uos, qui milia multa basiorum
> legistis, male me marem putatis?
>
> uos qui δ: hosque *O*: uosque *G*: uos quod *uulg.*

We do not know what the grounds of the alleged accusation were (even the text of the lines is uncertain),[61] and we have no evidence that it was his Sapphic poems, or the *persona* to which they contribute, that gave rise to the accusation. Nevertheless both the accusation itself and Catullus' reaction to it are a timely reminder that, if a man was seen to be adopting womanly behaviour or characteristics, he was inviting instant attack.

Poem 16 is only one of many cases which bear out M. Gleason's statement that 'Using male effeminacy as a conceptual category... brought primal prejudices into play. In almost every culture known to anthropologists, the proper separation of male and female is felt to be essential to the preservation of the cosmic order.'[62] We may well imagine that in Catullus' opinion his experimental self-portrayal in womanly terms was worth the risk of criticism; but there is nothing in Horace's *Odes* to suggest that he was interested in a similar kind of self-portrait.[63] On the contrary, there is a passage in *Satires* I which, from the presence of the words *uiris* and *pulcher*, seems both to impute a feminine image to Catullus and to reject it in the case of Horace himself (10.16–19):[64]

> illi, scripta quibus comoedia prisca uiris est,
> hoc stabant, hoc sunt imitandi – quos neque pulcher
> Hermogenes umquam legit neque simius iste,
> nil praeter Caluum et doctus cantare Catullum.

If we are to pursue the notion of gender dualism in the case of Horace's claimed imitation of Sappho and Alcaeus, we must look for a different conceptual framework from one which is based on 'the proper separation of male and female'.

VII

'The truth is', noted Coleridge in the year 1820, 'a great mind must be *androgyne*.'[65] The poet was presumably reflecting, or responding to, a general belief of the late eighteenth and earlier nineteenth centuries, when for the Romantics the union or harmonisation of the sexes was a significant intellectual concept.[66] A good example is Wagner, whose prediction in 1849 was that a future great work would issue 'from the fusion of a masculine principle in the form of the poetic intent transmitted by the libretto and a feminine principle in the form of music'.[67] Wagner acknowledged that he was thinking of himself as the artist in whom these male and female elements would be united; is it possible that not dissimilar thoughts had occurred to Horace in the first century BC?

Poets of the period described divinities as uniting the opposites of male and female: thus Jupiter was described as *progenitor genetrixque* by Valerius Soranus (fr. 2.2), and Venus as *femina ... mas*, like the Moon, by Laevius (fr. 26.2–3).[68] Yet such unity was not the exclusive prerogative of gods. The Hellenistic physician Loxus, whose work is known only from later Latin sources, evidently maintained that an *ingenium bonum* requires masculine *uirtus* and feminine *sapientia*;[69] and Philo, a younger contemporary of Horace, saw the male Adam and female Eve as allegories of the two parts of the soul.[70] Such evidence appears to show that there were ways in which male and female could be seen, not just as opposites, but as complementary to each other and that their coming together represented balance, harmony and wholeness.[71] A particularly detailed application of male and female is to be found in Aristides Quintilianus, a musicologist of perhaps the late third century AD.[72] In his work *On music*, which embraces literature and philosophy as well as music, he says that much of the world is to be seen in terms of masculine and feminine. Thus the soul comprises both masculine and feminine, the latter being the seat of 'pain and pleasure', the former that of 'anger and boldness' (2.8). He argues that 'all sensible objects' have powers corresponding to these elements of the soul: those 'which entice us to pleasure and gently relax the mind are to be reckoned as feminine, while anything that excites anxiety or activity belongs to the realm of the male. Those that are neither or both should be assigned to an intermediate category.' One of these 'sensible objects' is poetry, as are the letters, words, expressions and tropes of which poems consist. If we were to apply this theory to the *Odes*, we might say that its incorporation of male and female elements is signalled by Horace's proclaimed imitation of Alcaeus and Sappho and that the collection of poems as a whole falls into Aristides' 'intermediate category'.[73] We know, for example, that Sappho's style was famous for its 'charm' (χάρις) or (in Latin) *gratia*, the very quality which Quintilian attributes to Horatian lyric alongside the masculine 'boldness' (10.1.96 *plenus est iucunditatis et <u>gratiae</u> et . . . uerbis felicissime <u>audax</u>*). It is of course true that Aristides is a much later writer than Horace; but he is recognised to be highly derivative,[74] and his theory is so elaborately worked out that it is unlikely to have originated with himself.

It has often been pointed out that in Horace's poetry generally, and in his *Odes* particularly, there are a number of contrasting features such as public and private, urban and rural, Stoic and Epicurean, grand and plain. Rudd has addressed these antitheses and argued that they are partly artificial, since the strands of each are interwoven with one another.[75] To this list of contrasting features we might now add Alcaeus and Sappho, male and female, whose different qualities have been combined through Horace's imitation to produce the balanced and harmonious whole which we know as the *Odes*. In this very respect the collection represents that *aurea mediocritas* which is so typical of him.

VIII

Although scholars have detected less Sapphic material in *Odes* 1–3 than Horace's claims, thus interpreted, might lead one to expect, it is perhaps worth observing that his patron, Maecenas, deployed allusions to Catullus when addressing Horace in his poetry. In one fragmentary hendecasyllabic poem (fr. 2) he addresses Horace as *mea uita*, as Catullus had addressed Lesbia (109.1),[76] and uses the rare adjective *Thynicus* as Catullus had used the noun *Thynia* (31.5). In another such poem (fr. 3) he expresses his affection for Horace in the terms of Catullus 14.1–2 and ends a line with *tuum sodalem* in the same way as Catullus had ended lines with variations on *meus sodalis* (10.29, 12.13, 35.1, 47.6). Courtney wonders 'how Horace felt at being addressed in Catullan terms',[77] but perhaps Maecenas recognised the importance of Catullus for Horace. If that is so, one may speculate that Horace was not so much interested in a direct and detailed engagement with Sappho as in how he might present his own 'answer' to the dualism of gender which she epitomised in Catullus. As often in the *Odes*, the distinction may be seen in terms of 'classicism' rather than 'romanticism' – which is in no way to depreciate Horace's extraordinary originality.

Yet, when Horace within three or four years of the publication of *Odes* 1–3 turned to discuss the originality of his collection, his claim embraced Alcaeus but excluded Sappho, who is mentioned merely to provide a transition to Alcaeus from Archilochus (*Epist.* 1.19.23–33):[78]

Parios ego primus iambos
ostendi Latio, numeros animosque secutus
Archilochi, non res et agentia uerba Lycamben.   25
ac, ne me foliis ideo breuioribus ornes
quod timui mutare modos et carminis artem,
temperat Archilochi musam pede mascula Sappho,
temperat Alcaeus, sed rebus et ordine dispar:
nec socerum quaerit quem uersibus oblinat atris,   30
nec sponsae laqueum famoso carmine nectit.
hunc ego, non alio dictum prius ore, Latinus
uulgaui fidicen.

Horace nevertheless goes out of his way to describe as *mascula* the poet
whom his contemporary, Antipater of Thessalonica, described as 'the
female Homer' (*Anth. Pal.* 9.26).[79] The famous epithet *mascula* seems to
confirm that Horace was engaged in seeing poetry in gendered terms;[80]
but it also serves as an oblique defence against any misconceived criticism
to which he was liable as a result of claiming in the *Odes* to have imitated
Sappho. Fraenkel saw *Epist.* 1.19 as expressing Horace's disappointment
at the reception of the *Odes*;[81] perhaps one aspect of that reception had
been the imitation of Sappho which his reading of Catullus had led him
to claim.

When Horace published *Odes* 4 some years later still, he described
Sappho 'in such a way and with such affection', says Fraenkel, 'that
the reader is given at least some idea of the true nature of her poetry'
(9.10–12):[82]

spirat adhuc amor
uiuuntque commissi calores
Aeoliae fidibus puellae.

Is *spirat* here used simply as a convenient synonym for *uiuit*? Or is Horace,
by now the author of the Sapphic *Carmen saeculare* of 17 BC, defiantly
referring to the 'effluences' which are given off by her poetry and which
he had claimed to transmute in his earlier lyric collection?

5 THE *ODES*
Just where do you draw the line?

How did ancient readers of poetry books, working their way through Callimachus or Cercidas or Catullus, know when they had reached the end of a poem? Scribal conventions offered some visual aid: the conclusion of a long lyric poem might be marked by a big wiggly *koronis* in the left margin, while shorter epigrams were separated by the more economical *paragraphos*, the same 'dash-mark' which was used to indicate change of speaker in dramatic texts. If the book were an anthology like the *Garland* of Meleager, a new name would mark both change of authorship and change of poem. Yet such *external* graphic signals were subject to the hazards of careless transcription, and might be omitted or misplaced; errors would propagate themselves throughout subsequent copies.[1]

Internal evidence offered surer clues to the reader. Just as play-scripts, lacking stage-directions, were designed to be self-sufficient ('But who is this I see approaching? – surely not Tiresias again?'), so poets deployed a regular set of termination-routines, of which ring-composition is perhaps the most familiar.[2] Writers drew on a common stock of cues, and could rely on their readers to pick them up.[3] A fan of Pindar or Propertius would soon develop an instinct for their favoured pointers. And even if the reader of a text unequipped with *sigla* failed to spot an ending as it passed, an immediately following strongly marked *opening*-formula, combined with a sharp change of subject, ought to have corrected the error in most cases. But here too verbal cues were ambiguous. Catullus uses *quare* with an imperative to mark closure in poems 1, 6, 21 and 69 (and it signals stanza-end at 62.17); not so at 12.10 or 39.9.[4]

A reader capable of crashing heedlessly through both external and internal signals would at least, surely, be brought up short by a change of *metre*. Even in a series of dactylo-epitrite poems, in which the conclusion of a triad constitutes a necessary but not sufficient condition for poem-end, the appearance of a new rhythmic combination of the double-short and single-short elements signals the start of a different poem. And when scazons turn into hendecasyllables, it is clearly time to stop and make a new beginning. If, that is, we are lucky enough to be dealing with a book of mixed metres. If not, one need only look at the state of the text of Theognis or Propertius to see how editors confronted with an unreliably partitioned stream of elegiacs have agonised over the problem of poem-division.[5]

Horace's *Odes* provide the perfect laboratory in which to carry out an investigation of these issues. The text is in pretty good shape. There is a strong tradition of commentary going back to antiquity (and we shall see that the third-century scholar Porphyrio's views are of particular interest). Finally, Horace's desire to seek *variatio* of all kinds means that there is a regular change of metre between poems; so the area of uncertainty is strictly limited. Only in a few cases do blocks occur where editors traditionally recognise *different poems* although the metre continues unchanged. These are: 1.16 and 17; 1.26 and 27; 1.34 and 35 (all contiguous alcaics); 2.13–15 and 19–20 (again, alcaics); 3.1–6 (the great series of 'Roman Odes', alcaics); 3.24 and 25 (asclepiads); and 4.14 and 15 (alcaics). What I shall be doing here is to examine the three alcaic pairs in Book 1, and the Roman Odes, to see whether there is a case to be made for altering the conventional presentation; and I shall conclude that we should renumber the first book, and seriously rethink the internal divisions of the Roman Ode cycle.[6]

BOOK I

Each of the first three books, which were published as a trinity, adopts a different metrical strategy for its opening. The third starts with *minimum* variation – 84 stanzas of alcaics. The second alternates Horace's favourite workhorses, alcaics and sapphics, up to and including the eleventh poem.[7] The first presents *maximum* variation: the famous 'parade odes', nine in a row before repetition occurs. The poet is demonstrating the range of his technique, showcasing his talent. And the variation on display here is surely the principle employed throughout the book. There are no other examples of contiguous poems in the same metre, except the three alcaic pairs already mentioned. What if these pairs were in fact intended to stand as single poems? Would that not make the principle of variety stand out out even more impressively?

Before we examine these alcaic siblings, let us cautiously test the possible relevance of another consideration: what we may dub the 'five and dime' principle of book construction during the early Augustan period, within which Horace's first books of *Odes* fall. Just as Proteus, when he took a roll-call of his seals in Book 4 of the *Odyssey*, 'fived' them (πεμπάσσεται, 412), so Horace's contemporaries seem to have followed the same practice, making up their books in multiples of fives and tens.[8] Here are the figures: Virgil, ten *Eclogues*; Tibullus, ten elegies in Book 1;

Ovid, *Amores* (2nd edition)[9] Book 1, 15; Book 2, 20; Book 3, 15.[10] The
intentions of Propertius are by now almost impossible to excavate, poem-
boundaries having been first ignored by the MS tradition, and subsequently obscured, often hopelessly, by omissions, transpositions, and
corruptions. But Skutsch argued plausibly for 25 poems in Book 3 and
20 (after a fashion) in Book 1.[11]

When we turn to Horace, we find ten poems in *Satires* 1, and twenty
poems in *Epistles* 1.[12] The odes present us with the following break-
down: fifteen in Book 4, thirty in Book 3, twenty in Book 2 ... and 'die
merkwürdige Zahl'[13] thirty-eight in Book 1.

Eduard Fraenkel declared, *more suo*, 'Book 2 twenty [poems], Book 3
thirty; in the case of Book 1 there was an overflow.'[14] I am not disposed
to accept 'overflow' as a legitimate critical term. There must be at least a
prima facie case that this first book, too, conformed to the contemporary
fashion for fiving. Being of a cautious disposition, I discount the possibility that it might once have consisted of (say) 45 or 50 poems, with seven
or twelve poems lost, or 30 or 25 poems, with eight or thirteen suppositi-
tious interlopers by unknown hands. I will even concede that 40 is a total
which we can rule out, for the transmission of Horace (unlike that of
Catullus) is excellent, and there is no reason to suspect even lost lines or
stanzas, let alone entire poems swallowed up without trace.[15] That leaves
as a provisional working target the number 35; and to achieve it we would
need, somehow, to reduce the book's total by three.

Robert Graves' headmaster rapped him over the knuckles in his school
report for 'preferring some authors to others'; and I too am fonder of
some of Horace's lyrics than others. However lukewarm my admiration
for his less successful efforts, though, there can be no question but that
everything in the book bears the stamp of the master. If we are to bring the
total down to 35, it must be by combining poems, running them together,
not deleting them. And the most obvious way to combine six poems into
three is to amalgamate the adjacent alcaics, 16 and 17, 26 and 27, 34
and 35. Which is where we came in. If we could find it in our conscience
to regard these neighbours as constituting a unity, and knock down their
party wall, we should confer (it seems to me) a double benefit on Horace,
restoring both perfect metrical *variatio* to the book and slimming it down
to a desirable figure, the vital statistic of 35. Will it work?

POEMS 16 AND 17

Horace announces in 1.16 that he has previously abused this anonymous
'lovely mother's still more lovely daughter', has suffered for it by losing
her love and friendship, and now pleads for forgiveness. He promises
that he will now write *mitia* instead of *tristia*, nice poems to efface the

memory of the nasty ones. In itself it seems a perfectly satisfactory, self-sufficient poem, mention of the satiric iambics marking beginning and end by ring-composition. So why should 17 have anything to do with it?

This girl-friend addressed in 1.17, unlike her immediate predecessor, has a name: Tyndaris, daughter of Tyndareus, *Helen*; and that Horace is indeed hinting at Helen is perhaps suggested by the songs that the girl will sing under the midsummer shade – *dices laborantis in uno* | *Penelopen uitreamque Circen*. When the disguised Iris went to deliver a message to Helen in the third book of the *Iliad*,

> she came on Helen in the chamber; she was weaving a great web,
> a red folding robe, and working into it the numerous struggles
> of Trojans, breakers of horses, and bronze-armoured Achaians,
> struggles that they endured for her sake at the hands of the war god.
>
> (3.125–8, tr. R. Lattimore)

Homer's Helen is peculiarly self-aware of her tragic place in history, and it is wholly appropriate that Horace, following this lead, should represent her in another act of artistic contemplation, this time conjuring up not the Iliadic theme of Paris and Menelaus competing for her own body, but the complementary Homeric tug-of-war between Circe and Penelope for the love of Odysseus.

Helen is definitely in Horace's mind, then, and meant to be recalled to ours, even if the poet later elusively (and typically) blurs the image by shifting at the end to a different picture, that of the unwanted attentions of the Hellenistic gigolo Cyrus. And Helen is the key to the link between the two poems. The name Helen is quite compatible, to put it no more strongly, with the periphrastic description of 16's dedicatee: the still more lovely daughter's lovely mother will be Leda, who was after all beautiful enough to catch Zeus's eye.[16] So both of Helen's human parents have been alluded to, Leda as well as Tyndareus. But there is more. Poem 16 is a palinode, and is so described in the MSS. The archetypal palinode of antiquity was that of Stesichorus, who, tradition had it, insulted the reputation of Helen in his poetry, was blinded, and only recovered his sight when he produced his recantation:

> οὐκ ἔστ' ἔτυμος λόγος οὗτος,
> οὐδ' ἔβας ἐν νηυσὶν εὐσέλμοις
> οὐδ ἵκεο πέργαμα Τροίας

> It is not true, that tale;
> you never went upon the well-benched ships,
> nor came to Troy's walled town.
>
> (*PMG* fr. 192)

Now we can see the picture. The last stanza of 16 promises praise poetry, ἔπαινος, to compensate for the earlier iambic slander (ψόγος) and it promises it *nunc* (25). Poem 17 is the immediate fulfilment of that promise, simultaneously and ambiguously a hymn which summons Helen-as-goddess, in Sapphic vein, to the place of worship, and an erotic invitation which lures Tyndaris-as-contemporary-lover to the *locus amoenus*. Horace is making amends as he said he would.

I am not the first person to make this connection. Scholars had already grasped the point in antiquity, and Richard Heinze finally accepted it in his third revision (1930) of Kiessling's commentary: 'Porphyrio hat die Ode als Ankündigung der folgenden ... gefaßt. ... Diese Kombination wird alt sein und richtig.'[17] This change of mind drove Fraenkel, who describes it as an 'astounding volte-face',[18] to a fit of temper. Pages 207–9 of his Horace book are devoted to a lengthy diatribe against the position espoused by Porphyrio and Heinze, on the grounds that it is held to violate Buttmann's principle that data drawn from outside the poem in question must be deemed irrelevant to its interpretation. Since 1.16 and 1.17 are different poems, says Fraenkel, they cannot be used to throw light on each other. This is a magnificently brazen circular argument, since the point at issue here is precisely where the boundaries of these adjacent alcaics are to be drawn. Such is the vehemence of Fraenkel's tirade that it drives him to say, of the dedicatee of 1.16, 'Horace appears to be very anxious not to lift the veil of anonymity that shrouds the lady in question'; a statement which itself surely violates Buttmann's rule, implying an independent and autonomous biographical reality behind the poetry.

I add one further point: poem 15 immediately preceding is a poem about Paris eloping with Helen, in which Nereus is made to utter a grim prophecy of the fate which the Trojan prince is drawing down on himself. Rather than acquiesce in a sequence which moves from Paris (15) to an echo of a palinode to Helen (16) and on to a love-poem whose addressee just happens to be called 'daughter of Tyndaris' (17), it is surely neater to think of a responding pair of poems, a nasty one about Paris followed and balanced by a nice one to a Helen-persona; just as Propertius included a matching pair of Homeric poems in his fourth book.[19] Propertius 4.7 sees Cynthia returning to haunt the poet in his sleep, echoing the accusations that Patroclus made to Achilles in Book 23 of the *Iliad*; 4.8 is the comic Odyssean pendant, with a Propertius–Penelope found dallying at home with rival lovers by a Cynthia–Odysseus who returns unexpectedly to reclaim her matriarchal rights.[20]

To sum up, 16 is the overture to the performance of 17; and while they represent distinct parts, they jointly constitute a unity and should be thought of as together forming a single poem. Since this is the pattern which I shall argue applies also in the other two cases we shall be examining, it would be as well to pause for a while to establish whether such a bipartite structure – 'preface + performance' – is attested elsewhere in ancient poetry.

The answer seems to be a qualified 'yes'. I do not know of any examples in the area where I should most like to find it, in the lyrics of Alcaeus or Anacreon, on whose poetic strategies Horace is building; but there are plenty of general models. The shorter Homeric Hymns are, explicitly, προοίμια composed to introduce epic recitations. The four dactylic hexameters of Alcman's fr. 26 have been mooted as a 'solo hexameter prelude to a choral song'.[21] Pindar speaks at *Nem.* 4.9–11 as if the preceding eight lines of the ode have constituted a ὕμνου προκώμιον, a 'prelude to the hymn'. From the Hellenistic period onwards the conceit of the 'covering letter' becomes a regular form. Thus Theocritus 11.1–18 comprise an introduction addressed to Nicias (cf. too 13); and Catullus 65 is a preface to Hortalus, enclosing 66. More generally, one may think of the five-line preamble by the goatherd of Theocritus 3, which acts as introduction to the Amaryllis song itself. Still later, Mesomedes' *Hymn to the Sun* (Heitsch no. 2) has a six-line prologue invoking a holy silence before the hymn itself, equipped in two of the MSS with musical notation, gets under way.[22]

In Horace's own *œuvre*, 3.11 conforms to this general scheme. An initial hymnic invocation to Mercury and the lyre requests them to tell a cautionary tale to his recalcitrant girlfriend (25–6 *audiat Lyde scelus atque notas | uirginum poenas*), which then accordingly follows. Admittedly there is not in that poem a clear stanza boundary between packaging and contents, as I shall argue for the three poems in Book 1; nor is the poet himself speaking in two successive, and distinct, registers. But the *aporia* presented in the first three stanzas of 1.12, *Quem uirum*, etc., 'What man, what hero, what god?' is clearly *preliminary* to its own resolution, and the poem's consequent picking up of a clear direction. And if we look at 1.24 – the memorial poem for his friend Quintilius – we not only find the kind of tonal shift I have in mind, but can also perhaps dissolve an apparent problem on the way.

> Quis desiderio sit pudor aut modus
> tam cari capitis? praecipe lugubris
> cantus, Melpomene, cui liquidam pater
>   uocem cum cithara dedit.
>
> ergo Quintilium perpetuus sopor
> urget; cui Pudor, et Iustitiae soror
> incorrupta Fides, nudaque Veritas
>   quando ullum inueniet parem?

multis ille bonis flebilis occidit,
nulli flebilior quam tibi, Vergili;
tu frustra pius, heu, non ita creditum
   poscis Quintilium deos.

quid si Threicio blandius Orpheo
auditam moderere arboribus fidem?
num uanae redeat sanguis imagini
   quam uirga semel horrida,

non lenis precibus fata recludere,
nigro compulerit Mercurius gregi?
durum! – sed leuius fit patientia
   quidquid corrigere est nefas.

1–8 tetrasticha inter se mutat Campbell, coll. Serm. 2.5.101 sq.

Shackleton Bailey (1985a), whose apparatus I reproduce, thought Campbell's citation of the parallel in the *Satires* worthy of mention because that poem too refers, in its first line, to the news of a friend's death: *ergo nunc Dama sodalis | nusquam est? unde mihi tam fortem tamque fidelem?* If the other passage is a valid model, it looks as though *Ergo* ought to stand at the very beginning of the poem. And it is true that many other Latin poems, especially poems on death, do lead off with just that word: for example, Propertius 3.7 and 3.23; Ovid, *Amores* 2.7 and *Tristia* 3.2.[23]

Campbell was right – but also wrong. *Ergo* is indeed the first word of Horace's poem; but no transposition is required. The first stanza is *prefatory*. It represents Horace casting around for inspiration, appealing to the Muse for the right words in which to express his grief in the poem proper, which then follows. He does this again in the first stanza of *Carm.* 3.4,[24] where it is Calliope's turn to be asked for help; also, if I am right, in the next two cases I want to consider in Book I.

POEMS 26 AND 27

The short, very short, 1.26 is the excited (note the emphatic anaphora) announcement of an intention to write poetry in a new strain – 'an ode | in the Alcaic mode', as Michie (1964) correctly interprets *Lesbio | plectro*. Commager, after Wilkinson, notes that the appeal to the Muse to 'weave a garland for my friend Lamia', properly decoded, means 'inspire a poem for Lamia'.[25] Where then is the poem? Apparently, say the commentators, '26' itself. The medium is the message. It is a 'performative utterance', the very thing which it promises: a perfect example of ὁμοουσία, being of one substance with itself.

Poems of this 'recursive' nature do of course exist, and in the *Odes*.[26] But three measly stanzas hardly justify all this trumpeting. If I were Lamia, I should have responded: 'The wrapping-paper's pretty. The book jacket is indeed delightful. I like the blurb, too. But (to change the metaphor) – where's the beef?'[27]

The beef is the following poem: '27' is the poem which '26' heralds.

What links can we see between that and the prospectus that Horace sent to Lamia in 26?[28] First, to start as we did in the previous case simply at the level of compatibility, note that 27 depicts Horace at a drinking party; that chimes very well with the straightforward meaning of *necte meo Lamiae coronam* at 26.8, for the provision of garlands for the guests at the symposium was one of the necessary preparations. Horace invites his friend to a party in 26, and sings a song for him at the party in 27.

Secondly, 27 is a version of a poem by Anacreon, as Porphyrio tells us[29] and as we know from fragments of the original (fr. 356 *PMG*). If Horace is here presenting Lamia with his newly turned version of a Greek poem, this matches Catullus' present of 66, his translation of Callimachus' *Lock of Berenice*, to Hortalus, the addressee (as we saw) of 65, the covering note. Now we come to the interesting point. Anacreon's poem was composed, not surprisingly, in anacreontics. Horace has transposed it into his favourite alcaic stanza. And that is exactly what the 'please find enclosed' note to Lamia told him to expect. *hunc fidibus nouis,* | *hunc Lesbio sacrare plectro*: 'Muse, produce something for Lamia in a new, Lesbian, metre, the metre of Alcaeus' – not the 'Tean' metre in which Anacreon originally composed it.

Finally, what of Lamia himself? He reappears as a *bon vivant* and party-goer in 1.36. We may assume that he was a friend who shared Horace's sophisticated sense of humour. His *nomen* must inevitably have led to a certain amount of banter among his friends, for it is identical with that of the voracious Greek bogey-woman Λάμια.[30] Now Nisbet–Hubbard observe, rightly, that in 1.27 'Chimaera' not only refers to a man-eating myth-monstress but is also attested as a Greek hetaera-name; when we note that exactly the same is true of Λάμια – Demetrius Poliorcetes had a mistress of that name[31] – it should be clear that it is Aelius Lamia's own name which at least facilitates, and may indeed have suggested, the reference to Charybdis and Chimaera as predatory females in '27'. Yet another reason to draw the two poems together as a complementary pair or (as I am arguing here) two parts of the same poem.

This is the point at which I must declare that, just as I found myself to have been at least partly anticipated on the question of 16 and 17 by Porphyrio and Richard Heinze, so too Ross Kilpatrick came to some of the same conclusions that I have reached about this poem, by a rather different route, twenty-five years ago.[32] I quote: '*Carm.* 1.26 and 27 are in essence two components of one metrical recapitulation. The former's function in the collection is to introduce the spectacular 1.27, and dedicate it ... to Aelius Lamia.' What makes the case worth restating here, nevertheless, is that Kilpatrick offered only a weak version of the thesis which I am here presenting in its strong form: he still talked about separate poems, the first serving as an introduction to the second.[33] My aim is more strictly focused: to assert that, at least in Book 1, there is no such animal as adjacent poems in the same metre.

POEMS 34 AND 35

Here, at least, there is no dispute that we are dealing with a symbiotic pair.[34] Fraenkel handles these two together, but in topsy-turvy fashion, just as he had done in the case of 16 and 17: the latter first (251–3), then the former (253–7). I am not going to dispute his assertion that 34 'serves as a preparation for the prayer to Fortuna that follows it' (253). This is true as far as it goes, which is not far enough. From my perspective, '34' is the preface to '35', and what the MSS offer as two poems in the same metre is in fact a single poem, a meditation on the unpredictability and mutability of life which leads into a direct address to the responsible goddess. I will draw attention only to what seems to me the inelegant repetition of *ima summis | mutare* (34.12–13) in the first stanza of 35. But that is a problem, if it is a problem, whether you take the poems as separate but successive, as 'prayer prepared for' (Fraenkel's formulation), or as two parts of the same piece.[35]

I hope this survey of the three pairs of alcaic odes in Book 1 may have established that in each case there are intimate links between the two members. The individual analyses would not, perhaps, quite constitute absolute proof that the pairs should be designated single poems. It is the overall picture, together with the considerations of metrical variety and book total, that prove decisive. I recommend that future editors of Horace should renumber the book, holding firm against the feeble cries of those who may protest at the ensuing confusion.[36]

BOOK 3

When we turn to the third book, we find that it opens with a block of 84 stanzas, 336 verses, all in the same metre.[37] The third-century scholar Porphyrio regarded this long stream of alcaics as constituting a single poem;[38] so, even if he had in front of him a text equipped with *paragraphoi* or other markers of sub-division, he did not think them worth noting. The possibility thus exists that here too the boundaries between the poems we know as 3.1–6, now so familiar, may have been illegitimately introduced at some early stage in the transmissional process, perhaps in order to make the sprawling mass more digestible. At the very least, we are entitled to enquire whether the divisions offered by the MSS[39] look convincing.

There seem to me to only two points between 3.1.1 and 3.6.48 at which one can state with confidence that the flow of Horace's expression stops and makes a fresh start: 3.5.56 | 3.6.1 and 3.3.68 | 3.4.5.

First, 3.5.56 | 3.6.1. The marvellous picture of Regulus striding off to face torture and death in Carthage, as stoically calm as if he were departing for his country cottage after a hard week in the city, falls into the closural category of 'quasi-photographic images' which I mentioned (see n. 3). When we move on to the stanza beginning *Delicta maiorum inmeritus lues,* | *Romane,* . . . , it is surely clear that we have crossed a strong boundary – whatever we call it. 3.6 *is* a separable unit, a coda to the long sequence which began at the start of the book.

Secondly, 3.3.68 | 3.4.5. Juno's long speech ends; and 'hanging speeches' are another favourite terminating device (see n. 3). There then follow two stanzas, in the first of which the poet remonstrates with himself for engaging in out-of-area activities, only to renew an appeal for inspiration in the one which follows:

> non hoc iocosae conueniet lyrae:
> quo, Musa, tendis? desine peruicax
>   referre sermones deorum et
>   magna modis tenuare paruis.
>
> descende caelo et dic age tibia
> regina longum Calliope melos,
>   seu uoce nunc mauis acuta,
>   seu fidibus citharaue Phoebi.

Then the inspiration arrives:

> auditis, an me ludit amabilis
> insania? audire et uideor pios
>   errare per lucos, amoenae
>   quos et aquae subeunt et aurae.

and Horace begins the personal reminiscences which lead him on to the subject of Augustus as an earthly Jupiter, and back once more into a high, Pindaric style.

Here then, if anywhere in 3.1–3.5, the great cycle comes to a halt, then rolls forward again. But it is not at all obvious that there is anything which could be called a clear poem-boundary. Editors divide '3.3' from '3.4'; and, since we are committed to the conventions of modern typography, we must do *something*. Come back, *paragraphos*, all is forgiven. We should put one at the end of Juno's speech; and two more to mark off the strong pauses after the two stanzas to the unnamed Muse, and Calliope, respectively.[40] In the same way, the very first stanza of the whole cycle should be separated from what follows. It is a 'striking up', a priestly introit, a prelude to all that follows.

What of the other traditional divisions? That the opening sequence of the cycle should be brought to an end with

> cur ualle permutem Sabina
> diuitias operosiores?

may seem unsurprising. At *Carm.* 2.12 we find not only another question-ending[41] but a question-ending which asks, as here, 'would you prefer to *permutare x* for *y*?' It will no doubt have been this strong parallel that caused the ancient editors of our text to mark a poem-division here. But the Epicurean message, though we have heard it many times before, seems in this context to strike a false note. This is not just another of Horace's personal musings but the opening salvo of the 'Roman Odes'. It is surely odd that the first poem in a cycle whose avowed aim is to proclaim a moral crusade to the Roman public should end on such a meanly selfish note.

While the first poem appears to end by recommending *pauperies* as the solution to Horace's own life-style problems, the second appears to open by prescribing the same medicine to the budding young soldier. This could be no more than an example of what we may call the 'leapfrogging' device used elsewhere in the cycle, by which a thematic idea emerging towards the end of one poem (or 'section') is used as the springboard for the next.[42] On the other hand, it could be an indication that Horace's personal frugality is not a concluding motif but a merely transitional one; in which case the objections outlined above melt away.[43] The poet's personal concerns are seen in this perspective as a preparatory idea leading up to a much more important, public issue: for the *puer*-destined-to-be-soldier in 3.2.2 can be recognised as one of the *pueri* who Horace declared in 3.1.4 were targeted as his audience.

I do not, therefore, think that a strong break should be marked after 3.1.48. Indeed, if we were to seek a point at which we could say that the opening themes of the cycle seemed to have reached a natural conclusion, it would be rather at the end of the second poem, whose last stanzas recapitulate material from the exordium in the familiar ring-compositional pattern. Jupiter opened the poem proper (3.1, second stanza), and recurs at the end (3.2, last stanza). The priestly persona in which Horace robed himself at the outset comes once more to the fore in 3.2.26ff. (*uetabo, qui Cereris sacrum | uulgarit arcanae*, etc.);[44] and the silence which the priest enjoined in 3.1.2 is picked up at 3.2.25–6 in the Simonidean *est et fideli tuta silentio | merces*. The vote-seeking politician of 3.1.10ff. is alluded to at 3.2.17–18 (*Virtus repulsae nescia sordidae*, etc.), and the *profanum uulgus* of 3.1.1 rears its head again at 3.2.23. All these features tie the end of '2' back to the beginning of '1' and make it a more plausible candidate than 3.1.48 for a first resting-point on the long journey through the cycle. And it is also appropriate, to continue the metaphor, that we should have covered a fair amount of ground before our first pause; better a determined hike of twenty stanzas than two short strolls of twelve and eight.

Not a 'poem-end', perhaps, at 3.2.32, but a place for a *paragraphos* or for extra space; a minor way-station *en route* to the end of Juno's great speech in heaven.

If, as I have tried to show and as Collinge observed,[45] there is no strong break between the image of the omnipotent Jupiter at the outset and the point at which Juno reaches her peroration,[46] then we may expect '3.4' and '3.5' to form a balancing counterweight between the two central stanzas directed at the Muse and the coda, '3.6'.[47] How convincing is the firm boundary offered by editions at 3.4.80?

Once more I take as my starting-point what seems to me to be a peculiar and unsatisfying ending. The final stanzas of 3.4 describe the eternal punishment suffered by rebels against Jupiter's authority: the Giants are crushed under mountains, the vulture rips at Tityus' liver, and finally

> amatorem trecentae
> Pirithoum cohibent catenae.

It is easy enough to see why a late Roman editor casting around for a way to articulate the alcaics into more manageable units should decide to snip the sequence at this point, for *Carm.* 4.7 also concludes with the punishment of Pirithous.[48] There the conclusion seems to me natural and moving; here, the impression left is one of unfinished business. Certainly the *oddity* of the Pirithous ending was recognised by Fraenkel, for in the very act of lauding 'this concluding diminuendo' he used the phrase (the tell-tale phrase) 'by the happiest inspiration' – acknowledging that this was by no means an off-the-peg ending, nor (we may reasonably add) one which the reader could be relied upon to pick up.[49]

Caelo tonantem (which follows on the heels of Pirithous) is such a famous 'opening' that I realise the difficulty of re-visualising it as a mere transitional stanza. Yet the hurried progress from Jupiter, via Augustus, to the remnants of Crassus' army all in the space of five lines is so precipitate, and so unlike the normally grandiose and expansive openings of Horace's big Pindaric efforts, that it hardly assures us that we have just crossed a watershed between discrete poems. If I were asked to mark a pause-point in this second block, it would not be here but earlier. At line 42 of '3.4' Horace introduces the theme of Jupiter's crushing of cosmic rebellion: the fate of the Titans, the Aloadae and (in greater detail) the Giants is adduced to show the hopelessness of resisting Olympian rule. The stanza 65–8 seems to offer a *gnōmē*, a point-to-ponder, to conclude this idea:

> uis consili expers mole ruit sua;
> uim temperatam di quoque prouehunt
>   in maius; idem odere uiris
>   omne nefas animo mouentis.

We now expect a new development of thought. But instead we find a further exemplification of the *gnōmē*:

> testis mearum centimanus Gyas
> sententiarum, notus et integrae
>   temptator Orion Dianae
>   uirginea domitus sagitta, etc.

... as if we had not already heard enough about the dangers of challenging the powers-that-be. It is as if one were to say: 'Standing up against Stalin was a dangerous business. Look what happened to Bukharin. That proves how risky the attempt was. After all, look what happened to Trotsky.' True, in moralising on the fate of monsters Horace is here following Pindar's sequence of thought at *Pythians* 8.12–18, which moves from *exemplum* to *gnōmē* and then again from *gnōmē* to *exemplum*; but that does not necessarily mean that he must be tied to Pindar's 'archaic' articulation. In fact, if we are to mark a pause anywhere in this 'second block' (and perhaps we shouldn't be doing any such thing), 3.4.64 | 65 seems a much better place to rest and restart than the 3.4 | 3.5 boundary.

Consider first the putative resumption at 3.4.65, *uis consili expers mole ruit sua*. The powerful Pindaric *gnōmē* is now backed up by evidence to launch it on its way – like 3.3 *Iustum et tenacem*, or 1.22 *Integer uitae*.[50] The hundred-handed Gyas, the rapist Orion and the other criminals now form a legitimate set of *exempla*, no longer the tedious reprise of a point already made; though the start of this section, with its emphasis on the need for *consilium*, does pick up the theme of its predecessor, 'leapfrogging' onwards in a way which is characteristic of the Roman Odes throughout.[51] And the idea behind the transition to '3.5' is: 'Jupiter's punishment of rebels against his own command explains our respect for his rule in heaven. Augustus' forthcoming treatment of the surly Britons and Persians will justify his earthly dominion in the same way.'

If 3.4.65 is a candidate for a new beginning, we now need to look backwards and ask whether 3.4.64 displays any of the hallowed stigmata of closure. The preceding stanza celebrates Apollo as victor in the Gigantomachy, the god

> qui rore puro Castaliae lauit
> crinis solutos, qui Lyciae tenet
> dumeta natalemque siluam,
> Delius et Patareus Apollo.

Like the following Regulus poem, it ends its section on a note of glorious tranquillity, the commanding but relaxed image of Apollo effortlessly quelling the unruly opponents of the heavenly family. Pindar's First Nemean provides a model: there too Herakles' life of struggle, wrapped up as here with the Gigantomachy, concludes with a picture of the hero enjoying eternal bliss.[52] The final words, a recital of the god's name and cult-titles, possess a semi-magical incantatory power all of their own: compare the last line of Catullus 4: *gemelle Castor et gemelle Castoris*. More significantly, the domination of the section's conclusion by Apollo the warrior links back to the theme of poetry which has been the central concern of the ode since its restart at 3.4.1ff.: Calliope had been invited to appear with Phoebus' *cithara*, if she so wished, at the end of the introductory stanza. As often, Apollo is seen by the Augustans as simultaneously the victor of Actium and the poetic *Mousagetes, Citharoedus*.[53] Similarly, the *dumeta natalisque silua* at the close recalls the *pii luci* through which Horace wandered at the beginning. Like the first section of the first block ('3.1' + '3.2'), then, this part also seems to be structured by ring-composition.[54]

To sum up, and come clean: as in Book 1, where I tried to make the case that new poems should only be recognised where we encounter a change of metre, so here I follow Porphyrio in seeing the 'Roman Odes' as a single great canto.[55] The book is thus reduced from 30 to 25 poems, but still fits the 'five and dime' criterion laid down in the discussion of Book 1. This monster mega-poem – *carmina non prius | audita* indeed – does however contain, inevitably, a certain amount of internal articulation. I have talked of two great blocks of poetry. They are preceded by the invocatory stanza; separated by the two stanzas to his muse which first express doubt in his project and then celebrate its renewal; and concluded by the 'coda', conventionally known as 3.6. It is the architecture of the main blocks which is so difficult to analyse. I am unhappy with the traditional break-points (those between '3.1' and '3.2'; and '3.4' and '3.5'), and have proposed alternatives for consideration. But Horace really is attempting to build some quite new kind of structure here, in which themes spring up and fade away only to vault back into the foreground; there are several other points at which one has the sense of a re-launch, a fresh impulse, like the anaphoric stanzas on *uirtus* at 3.2.17ff. All the same, one can perhaps discern the outlines of the big pattern Horace was after:

- introit (3.1.1–4)
- *first block*, in two movements: the first dominated by Jupiter, and structured by ring-composition (3.1.5 – end of 3.2); the second dominated by Juno, launched by a *gnōmē* and culminating in a speech on Rome and Troy (3.3.1–68);
- two stanzas on doubt and renewed confidence (3.3.69–3.4.4);
- *second block*, also in two movements: the first dominated by Apollo, and structured by ring-composition (3.4.5–64); the second dominated by a human hero, Regulus, launched by a *gnōmē* and culminating in a speech on Rome and Carthage (3.4.65 – end of 3.5);
- pessimistic *envoi* (3.6).

The general picture that emerges is one of a complex poetic structure which, once brought to a conclusion, is then repeated after a pause, with a shift down towards more recent historical events; the coda considers prospects for the future. And if this sounds like a pseudo-triadic structure, what could be more appropriate for Horace's Pindaric ambitions?

6   A WINE-JAR FOR MESSALLA
Carmina 3.21

O nata mecum consule Manlio,
seu tu querelas siue geris iocos,
   seu rixam et insanos amores,
     seu facilem, pia testa, somnum,

quocumque laetum[1] nomine Massicum   5
seruas, moueri digna bono die,
   descende, Coruino iubente
     promere languidiora uina.

non ille, quamquam Socraticis madet
sermonibus, te negleget horridus: 10
   narratur et prisci Catonis
     saepe mero caluisse uirtus.

tu lene tormentum ingenio admoues
plerumque duro; tu sapientium
   curas et arcanum iocoso   15
     consilium retegis Lyaeo;

tu spem reducis mentibus anxiis,
uirisque et addis cornua pauperi,
   post te neque iratos trementi
     regum apices neque militum arma;   20

te Liber et si laeta aderit Venus,
segnesque nodum soluere Gratiae,
   uiuaeque producent lucernae,
     dum rediens fugat astra Phoebus.

(1) *O born with me in Manlius' consulship, whether thou bearest wrangles or merriment, or brawls and insane love-making, or easy sleep, kindly[2] jar, (5) in whatever description the Massic rejoices that thou preservest – inasmuch as thou art worthy to be brought out on an auspicious day,*

descend, for Corvinus bids produce a languorous wine. (9) He, though steeped in Socratic dialogues, will not uncouthly despise thee: they say that even old Cato's virtue often grew hot with unmixed wine. (13) Thou dost apply gentle torture to a talent that is generally stiff; thou dost reveal wise men's preoccupations and confidential plans by the aid of the merry Liberator; (17) thou restorest hope to troubled minds and bestowest strength and horns on the poor man, who after thee quakes neither at the raging diadems of kings nor soldiers' weapons. (21) Bacchus and Venus, if she is glad to come, and Graces that are slow to loose their belts, and undimmed lamps will progress with thee, till returning Phoebus routs the stars.

Horace did not usually write for *nobiles*,[3] but the Hymn to the Wine-Jar is a conspicuous exception. M. Valerius Messalla Corvinus was the most accomplished aristocrat in Augustan Rome, and the subject of this chapter will be the relation of the poem to its recipient. His very name commemorated the history, real or invented, of the Republic. The patrician Valerii claimed descent from P. Valerius Poplicola, who was supposed to have been one of the first consuls in 509 BC. The cognomen 'Messalla' was acquired by an ancestor (*cos.* 263) who rescued Messana from the Carthaginians at the beginning of the First Punic War. The agnomen 'Corvinus', the name that Horace uses here, went back to M. Valerius Maximus Corvus (sometimes himself called 'Corvinus'), six times consul, and a dominating figure in the Samnite Wars in the second half of the fourth century. We shall meet him again later in this chapter.

Messalla Corvinus was himself an experienced soldier.[4] In 42 BC he served under Cassius at Philippi (cf. Tac. *Ann.* 4.34.4), but transferred to Brutus on the right wing (Plut. *Brut.* 40.6), who needed his help more: he must have recalled the deeds of his legendary ancestor who joined a Brutus at the expulsion of the kings (cf. Livy 1.59.2). After the suicide of his leaders he declined the command of the Republican remnants, but with an aristocrat's realism negotiated the surrender to Antony on Thasos (App. *B Civ.* 4.17.136); as a member of Brutus' staff (cf. *Sat.* 1.7) Horace may have been near him in these events, as previously in 45 as a student at Athens (cf. Cic. *Att.* 12.32.3). With characteristic flexibility Messalla joined Octavian at some stage, and fought for him against Sextus Pompeius and in the Bellum Illyricum; in 31, the year of his consulship, he held a command at Actium (App. *B Civ.* 4.6.38). He then served in Syria and Gaul, and in 27 BC celebrated a triumph for the conquest of Aquitania: Tibullus might well call him *magna intonsis gloria uictor auis* (2.1.34, a contrast with Messalla's own sophistication), and Virgil must have had him in mind when he wrote of an Italian warrior *haud expers Valerus uirtutis auitae* (*Aen.* 10.752). He was appointed Prefect of the City in 26 BC, perhaps about the time of Horace's ode, but with a show of independence resigned after a few days.[5] When somebody is as grand as Messalla, the trappings of office add nothing to happiness.

Messalla was an important person in Latin literature as well as in war and politics. As a young man in 43 BC he was already commended by Cicero for his eloquence (*Ad Brut.* 23 [= 1.15].1); and he became one of the most eminent orators of the day, distinguished for suavity and charm, though compared with Pollio lacking in force. He translated Greek speeches into Latin, and competed even with the *Phryne* of Hyperides (Quint. *Inst.* 10.5.2 *difficillima Romanis subtilitate*). He wrote an invective against Valerius Laevinus (Plin. *HN* 35.8), whose *imagines* he would not admit among his own.[6] As a grandee of literature he showed the same hauteur towards minor versifiers like Furius Bibaculus and Valerius Cato, whom he called a *litterator* or school-teacher (Suet. *Gram.* 4.2).

On the other hand Messalla gave encouragement to favoured poets, including Horace himself: see *Sat.* 1.10.84–6 *ambitione relegata,*[7] *te dicere possum,* | *Pollio, te, Messalla, tuo cum fratre,*[8] *simulque* | *uos, Bibule et Serui.* It is significant that in this group of important *amici* Servius Sulpicius and Bibulus seem to have been related to our Messalla: the former (the son of the great jurist) married his sister Valeria,[9] and Bibulus was perhaps brother of his wife (below, p. 86). Messalla encouraged other poets who will all appear later in this chapter: there was the mild and elegant Tibullus (qualities that must have appealed), who wrote a famous poem in honour of Messalla's birthday and his Aquitanian triumph (1.7); Sulpicia, Rome's only woman poet worthy of the name, daughter of the Servius mentioned above, and so Messalla's niece; Cornutus, who under the pseudonym of Cerinthus may have been Sulpicia's lover (she was probably also his anonymous bride at Tibullus 2.2); C. Valgius Rufus (*cos.* 12 BC), who is teased by Horace for his sentimental elegies (*Carm.* 2.9). There were also three anonymous poems addressed to Messalla, the tedious *Panegyricus Messallae* (= Tib. 4.1), the more interesting *Catalepton* 9 in the *Appendix Vergiliana*, and the *Ciris*, that post-neoteric 'epyllion', where the addressee is surely our Messalla. As well as encouraging others, Messalla wrote poetry himself; what sort of poetry will emerge at the end of this chapter.

Messalla does not himself appear till line 7 of the ode. In the meantime Horace teases the reader with frivolous misdirections: first he seems to be addressing an old love, born like himself in 65 BC (1 *O nata mecum consule Manlio*); then it appears that the addressee is really a wine-jar (4 *pia testa*); as another element he uses liturgical language,[10] as if the wine-jar were a deity. But once it transpires that Messalla is the true recipient, the date of Horace's wine may seem particularly appropriate. According to Jerome's *Chronicle* (154 Helm) Messalla was born in 59 BC by our reckoning; but in that case he would have been only seventeen when he rallied the Republicans after Philippi, which was too precocious even for this *fulgentissimus iuuenis* (as Velleius 2.71.1 calls him). He became consul in 31 BC, which somebody of his ancestry is likely to have done at the earliest permitted age, when he was about thirty-two or thirty-three; so it is now generally assumed that he was born in 64[11] (*Caesare et Figulo coss.*), which was confused with 59 (*Caesare et Bibulo coss.*). I suggest that even at the cost of losing this explanation we might push his birth back to 65, the consulship of Manlius; in that case the wine-jar is an exact contemporary not just of Horace but of Messalla himself. Coevals might feel a particular bond of sympathy, and *mecum*[12] could evoke memories of shared experiences at Athens and Philippi; but Horace is too tactful to boast directly of an association with the great man.

A date like *consule Manlio* exemplifies the Roman organisation of chronology (Greek poetry had nothing similar), but it also has resonances that are not easy to recover fully:[13] Manlius Torquatus was presumably the grandfather of Horace's friend in *Epistles* 1.5 (a poem with affinities to our own), and the Valerii had an old association with the Manlii (as will emerge below). An interest in birth-dates and birthdays was also typically Roman, and is particularly noticeable in the circle of Messalla: Tibullus 1.7 is a genethliacon for Messalla, 2.2 for Cornutus, 3.11 (anonymous) for Cerinthus, 3.12 for Sulpicia, while in 3.14 and 3.15 Sulpicia writes about Messalla's invitation for her own birthday. Indeed the 'auspicious day' of line 6 of the ode might be the birthday of Messalla himself (as Denis Feeney suggests). In the case of Maecenas such concern for the calendar suggests astrological interests (Hor. *Carm.* 1.20, 2.17, 3.8); with Messalla one thinks rather of an old-fashioned ritualist who took the Genius Natalis seriously.

The imitations of hymnal style in the first two stanzas are also appropriate to Messalla; he seems to have had a precise understanding of the flavour of words, and the elder Seneca describes him as *Latini ... sermonis obseruator diligentissimus* (*Controv.* 2.4.8). But beyond that the sacral language suits a family at the heart of the religious establishment; for the Romans had no professional priests, but trusted *res diuinae* to public men of suitable antecedents and temperament. Corvinus himself was made an augur, though there was no vacancy, when still under thirty (Dio 49.16.1), and later was admitted as one of the Arval Brethren,[14] which is why Tibullus wrote on the Ambarvalia in his honour (2.1). His son Messalinus was installed when very young as one of the *quindecimuiri sacris faciundis*;[15] Cornutus, who may have married his niece, was also an Arval Brother;[16] Messalla 'Niger' (*cos.* 61), who was probably Corvinus' father,[17] was a pontifex;[18] Messalla Rufus (*cos.* 53), who was probably his father's cousin, wrote an authoritative book on the auspices, which he was well qualified to do as an augur for fifty-five years (Macrob. *Sat.* 1.9.14).

Potitus Valerius Messalla, who was perhaps Corvinus' brother rather than his second cousin (n. 8), was another *quindecimuir sacris faciundis*;[19] when suffect consul in 29 he performed the sacrifices on Octavian's return from the East,[20] which is reflected by Virgil at *Aeneid* 8.281 *iamque sacerdotes primusque Potitius ibant*. The original Valerius Corvus, from whom the name 'Corvinus' was derived, was said to have been so called because a raven settled on his helmet during a battle (Livy 7.26.2–5; *RE* 7A.2414–15); he was portrayed thus in the statue that Augustus was to erect in his forum (Gell. 9.11.10). The story surely originated because the raven was a bird of augury;[21] Corvus seems to have been an expert augur.

We may now ask if there is a particular reason why Messalla should be offered Massic wine (5), bearing in mind how often Horace's wines have a power of association. The Mons Massicus runs inland from Sinuessa at the north-western edge of the *ager Falernus*, the important wine-growing district of Campania to the north of the Volturnus; the area was taken over by Rome in 340 BC[22] at the end of the Latin War that came between the First and Second Samnite Wars. Accounts of the campaign are inconsistent and unreliable: Diodorus records a Roman victory at Suessa (16.90.2), which controlled the gap between the Mons Massicus and the dominating Monte Roccamonfina to the north; other sources mention a stream called the Veseris,[23] which is unlikely to have been far away. The battle was familiar to everybody because of two exemplary stories: T. Manlius Torquatus, the Roman general, executed his son for disobeying orders, and the elder P. Decius Mus 'devoted' himself to save the army. In the same year Livy describes another victory of Torquatus (unless it is a duplication) at Trifanum, which was situated 'between Sinuessa and Minturnae' (8.11.11); so when Horace offers a Torquatus wine from precisely the same area (*Epist.* 1.5.5 *inter Minturnas Sinuessanumque Petrinum*), he is certainly alluding to this battle.[24] As Sinuessan wine was a kind of Massic,[25] it seems that a similar point is being made in our passage. Corvus was regarded by Livy as the greatest general of the period (8.16.4 *maximum ea tempestate imperatorem*), he was perhaps present at the battle of the Veseris (below, p. 91), and he may have been given credit for Rome's conquests by the historian Valerius Antias, who notoriously exaggerated the achievements of the Valerii.[26]

Other points may be considered summarily. Perhaps Horace calls the great man 'Corvinus' (a name not normally used in Augustan poetry) not just to distinguish him from other Messallae, but to recall the deeds of his famous ancestor; similarly in the *Satires* 'Corvinus' is used to emphasise the glories of Roman history and the Latin language.[27] When the Massic wine-jar is called *pia* (line 4), even if the epithet in its context primarily means 'kindly' (n. 2), it might in retrospect hint that the jar honours the family[28] that fought for its own countryside. And if we are right that

Corvinus was born in 65 BC, the consulship of Manlius Torquatus, the
first line would recall the fruitful association of the first Corvus and the
first Torquatus, who derived their names from parallel legends,[29] and
between them annexed the Mons Massicus.

When Horace says *Coruino iubente* (7), commentators disagree about
whether Messalla is the host or the guest. It has been argued that in real life
somebody as important as Messalla would not readily visit Horace; but
social distinctions were played down to some extent even in the Roman
symposium,[30] and the Valerii seem to have prided themselves on *ciuilitas*
(up to a point).[31] Horace was more active in the world of affairs than
he pretends, and his talent for eulogy made his friendship worth having: Messalla was not his *patronus* in the Roman sense of the term, and
he wished to distinguish himself from the clients who as Cicero puts
it 'cannot invite us to their houses'.[32] At least for the purposes of the
ode Horace is directing the arrangements and specifying the wine, just
as in the parallel poem to Torquatus (*Epist.* 1.5); he could not do this in
Messalla's house. When he says *Coruino iubente*, the verb is less imperious
than 'orders', and should be translated 'bids' or 'asks'.

In line 8 the wine is described as *languidiora*, 'on the languid side'.[33] The
vocabulary of taste is imprecise and the metaphors of connoisseurs are
opaque, but the adjective seems to imply that the wine has become bland
and mellow from its repose of forty years (cf. 3.16.34–5 *nec Laestrygonia
Bacchus in amphora | languescit*). That suits the easy charm of Messalla
himself, whom Quintilian describes as 'underplaying his strength' (*Inst.*
10.1.118 *uiribus minor*); Horace would not have represented the vigorous
and austere Pollio as asking for such a drink. Some moderns might wish to
suggest that *languidiora uina* is a metaphor for the poem (as at 1.26.8 *necte
meo Lamiae coronam* there is no garland other than the ode). That would
go too far (for the wine has a significance in its own right); but it is true
that Horace is adopting a relaxed style to suit the manner of the recipient.

In 9–10 *ille* and *te* (isolated before the break in the line) are both emphatic; if an allusion to the fourth-century campaign is accepted, Horace
is saying 'a *Corvinus* at any rate will not despise *Massic* wine'. *Socratici
sermones* are the Socratic dialogues of Xenophon and Plato, whose style
and content must both have appealed to the Ciceronian Messalla. *madet*,
'is steeped', suits Attic charm[34] as well as drink, but here there is an
element of paradox: a philosophical treatise was expected to be dry.
horridus by contrast suggests dryness; it suits the unkemptness of Socrates
but not Messalla, who was famous for the *nitor*[35] of his personal and
literary style.

In line 11 with mock-seriousness Horace produces an *exemplum* from
Roman history: *narratur* appeals to tradition without implying that the
story is false. 'Old Cato' whose *uirtus* grew hot with wine points at first

sight to the censor of 184 BC: he is described as *priscus* by Horace himself (*Epist.* 2.2.117 *priscis memorata Catonibus*), and Plutarch tells us that his original cognomen was 'Priscus' rather than 'Cato' (*Cat. Mai.* 1.2). Though he drank water when on campaign (ibid. 1.7), Cicero pictures him enjoying convivial occasions in the country.[36] In view of his exaggerated reputation for ruggedness, there is humour in choosing him as a model for the urbane Messalla.

Proper names in Latin *exempla* are sometimes ambiguous,[37] though caution is needed in assessing the expectations of the original readership. Here there seems to be a hint of the younger Cato; though he had died only twenty years before, *priscus* could be used in its sense of 'old-fashioned', and *narratur* might imply that he was already a legendary figure (as at 1.12.35–6). His heavy drinking is attested much more explicitly than the Censor's, and seems to have figured in Julius Caesar's *Anticato*;[38] Plutarch tells us that 'as time went on, he grew particularly fond of drinking, so that he often continued over his cups till dawn'[39] (just as Messalla is invited to do at the end of Horace's ode). See also Seneca, *Dial.* 9.17.4 *et Cato uino laxabat animum curis publicis fatigatum*; some think that he is talking about the Censor, but there are repeated references to the younger Cato in this essay, notably just below at 9.17.9 *Catoni ebrietas obiecta est*. On this interpretation *uirtus* would have a philosophical implication, which suits *Socraticis sermonibus*; for the younger Cato had Stoic ideals,[40] whereas the Censor professed to think Socrates a babbler.[41]

There might be a further reason for connecting our passage with the Younger Cato. Without using Horace's ode Syme suggested that Messalla's wife, apparently a Calpurnia, might be the daughter[42] of M. Calpurnius Bibulus (*cos.* 59) and the sister of L. Bibulus, Messalla's close associate;[43] when acquaintanceship with suitable women is restricted, men have often married the sisters of their friends. So when M. Bibulus remarried Cato's daughter Porcia about 58 BC, the young Calpurnia could have looked on her stepmother's father[44] as a *domesticus auctor* (to use a Ciceronian phrase). In that case Horace is gently hinting to Messalla that there was authority for drinking among his own connections.

In the last three stanzas Horace lists the virtues and capacities of the wine-jar, and his 'aretalogy' continues the language of liturgy to suit the religiosity of Messalla. Here there is probably a reference to a lost dialogue by Maecenas called the *Symposium*, which included among its characters Virgil, Horace, and a Messalla. A fragment shows Messalla discoursing on the virtues of wine (*Serv. Dan. Aen.* 8.310): *idem umor ministrat faciles oculos, pulchriora reddit omnia, et dulcis iuuentae reducit bona* ('the same liquid provides indulgent eyes, makes everything lovelier, and brings back the blessings of sweet youth'). The natural assumption is that this is Messalla Corvinus, and that he was celebrated in both the dialogue and the ode as a connoisseur of wine: for the same reason Tibullus commemorates Messalla's birthday by introducing Osiris in the unfamiliar guise of a wine-god (1.7.35–45). By alluding to this *Symposium* Horace is able to flatter Messalla without making Maecenas think that he has transferred his allegiance.

However Cichorius followed by Syme thought that the character in the *Symposium* was not Corvinus at all, but his red-haired relative, the elderly Messalla 'Rufus' (*cos.* 53).[45] He argued that the same man was given the title-role in Varro's *logistoricus* 'Messalla de ualetudine', where he might have praised wine as conducive to health. It might be relevant that Potitus Messalla, who is often regarded as the son of Rufus (n. 8), owed his recovery from illness to a Lucanian wine called 'Lagarinum' (Plin. *HN* 14.69): could this information have come from a remark attributed to his father in Maecenas' *Symposium*? Yet Potitus may in fact have been the brother of Corvinus (n. 8); in any case the detail about the Lagarinum could derive from Potitus himself (Plin. *HN* 1.19 cites his treatise on horticulture). Potitus was perhaps a connoisseur like Corvinus, as he seems to have given his name to one of the fine Mamertine wines of Messana: see Plin. *HN* 14.66 (close to the passage about Lagarinum) *ex iis* [sc. *Mamertinis*] †*Potulana* [*Potitiana* Detlefsen], *ab auctore dicta illo cognomine, proxima Italiae laudantur praecipue*. As has been mentioned above, the first Messalla (*cos.* 263) derived his cognomen from Messana; perhaps Mamertine wine had a sentimental attraction for the family, like the Massic in Horace's ode.

Cichorius argued that Messalla's phrase about the blessings of youth shows that the speaker is an old man, which suits Rufus but not Corvinus. But even the middle-aged may envy the young, and Horace himself, the coeval of Corvinus, mentions 'sweet youth' as something now past (1.16.23). Cichorius also maintained that Corvinus had no connection with Maecenas,[46] but a poem by Sulpicia points the other way (Tib. 3.14 = 4.8):

> Inuisus natalis adest, qui rure molesto
> et sine Cerintho tristis agendus erit.
> dulcius Vrbe quid est? an uilla sit apta puellae
> atque Arretino frigidus amnis agro?
> iam, nimium Messalla mei studiose, quiescas;
> non tempestiuae saepe, propinque, uiae...

Sulpicia is being invited by her kind uncle Messalla to spend her birthday at his country-house, when she would much rather be with Cerinthus in Rome. The interesting thing for our purpose is that Messalla's estate is at Arezzo in Etruria, the ancestral home of Maecenas; so Maecenas had every excuse for bringing him into his *Symposium*. Cichorius added that there was no reason to associate Virgil with Corvinus, but a link will be suggested at the end of this paper.

To turn to details, when Horace talks of wine's 'bland torture' (13 *lene tormentum*), commentators compare Bacchylides' oxymoron about its 'sweet compulsion' (fr. 20 B 6 γλυκεῖ' ἀνάγκα), but the Latin is more specific: just as torture was used in legal proceedings to make witnesses talk, so wine makes inhibited talents fluent and men of affairs indiscreet. This formulation springs less from lyric poetry than from prose writings about the symposium (as notably in the first two books of Plato's *Laws*); thus Plutarch says 'some people have an inventive nature that as long as they are sober remains unadventurous and stiff, but when they start drinking they let off exhalations like incense from the heat'.[47] Bentley thought that Horace might be hinting at his own purported lack of fluency (cf. *Sat.* 1.4.17–18), but 'wise men's preoccupations and confidential plans' are much more applicable to Messalla; Horace claimed to know no state secrets (*Sat.* 2.6.50–8), and he would not make jokes about his own lack of discretion (cf. *Epist.* 1.18.38 *commissumque teges et uino tortus et ira*). *duro . . . ingenio* may seem tactless when applied to the great orator, but for similar teasing by Horace see the eulogy of wine addressed to the eloquent Torquatus: *fecundi calices quem non fecere disertum?* (*Epist.* 1.5.19). Messalla affected an agreeable diffidence about his own abilities;[48] so perhaps we have a paraphrase here of something that he is represented as saying in Maecenas' *Symposium*. On the other hand the commonplaces in the fifth stanza seem humorously inappropriate to the character of Messalla, who was not afraid of Eastern kings.

In the last stanza Horace describes the thiasos or escort of the divine wine-jar, a feature common in kletic hymns (cf. 1.30.5–8). First comes Bacchus under his old Latin name of 'Liber', which like the Greek 'Lyaeus' above (16) suggests the liberating power of wine; his presence is particularly appropriate in view of Messalla's standing as a connoisseur (cf. Tib. 1.7.39–42). Venus is mentioned next, not Cupido, for the homosexuality of the Greek symposium would not have suited the impeccable Messalla (contrast *Carm.* 1.4.19 to Sestius). The drinking goes on till dawn as in the *Symposium* of Plato, perhaps also of Maecenas; Phoebus as the morning sun balances the lamps and the stars, but he is also a god to balance Bacchus and Venus, and perhaps one with a particular relevance to Messalla (see below).

Something more must be said about the Graces (22) and their relation to Messalla. When Horace says that they are *segnes nodum soluere*, 'slow to loose the knot', most commentators think that *nodus* refers to the characteristic circle of three, familiar from Botticelli's *Primavera* and Canova's less beautiful sculpture, a grouping that has been traced back to the art and literature of the ancient world.[49] Seneca explained that the Graces held hands because good deeds are indissolubly linked (*Ben.* 1.3.4), and Servius in repeating this explanation actually cites our passage (on *Aen.* 1.720); but such allegorical interpretations are too far-fetched. *nodus* here naturally refers to a belt, as at Martial 9.101.5 *peltatam Scythico discinxit Amazona nodo*. The Graces, when they wore clothes at all, did not normally tie their belts, and Horace invites them to come to Glycera's house *solutis zonis* (1.30.5–6). But in our passage they are un-typically strait-laced: at a symposium for Messalla *insani amores* would be inappropriate.

The Graces particularly suit Messalla because of the charm of his writings, not only in prose (as is well attested) but also in verse. The author of *Catalepton* 9 mentions one of them among the deities who have helped Messalla with his poetry: *ea quae tecum finxerunt carmina diui | Cynthius et Musae, Bacchus et Aglaie* (59–60). The nature of this poetry is clarified earlier in the same poem (13–20):

> pauca tua in nostras uenerunt carmina chartas,
>   carmina cum lingua tum sale Cecropio,
> carmina quae Phrygium, saeclis accepta futuris,
>   carmina quae Pylium uincere digna senem.
> molliter hic uiridi patulae sub tegmine quercus
>   Moeris pastores et Meliboeus erant,
> dulcia iactantes alterno carmina uersu
>   qualia Trinacriae doctus amat iuuenis.

> *Few are your songs that have found a place in my pages, Cecropian* [i.e. Attic] *both in language and in savour, songs that finding acceptance with future generations, deserve to outdo the old man from Phrygia* [i.e. Priam] *and from Pylos* [i.e. Nestor]. *Here at their ease under the green shelter of a spreading oak were the shepherds Moeris and Meliboeus, bandying sweet songs in alternating verses, such as the accomplished young man of Sicily loves.*

In other words Messalla wrote elegant pastoral poetry in the manner of Theocritus, all about shepherds under a tree, just like Tityrus in Virgil's first eclogue. But unlike Virgil, Messalla wrote his verses in Greek, and apparently Attic (14 *Cecropio*) rather than Doric, which made them an oddity for pastoral poems.

Nestor is mentioned at *Catalepton* 9.16 primarily because of his longevity:[50] he was said by Homer to have seen three generations of men

(*Iliad* 1.250–2), which is expanded by Roman writers to three centuries. But Homer also says in the same context that Nestor was 'the clear-toned orator of the Pylians, from whose tongue flowed a voice sweeter than honey'.[51] The mellifluousness of Nestor is mentioned repeatedly in Latin: that is why the *Panegyricus Messallae* (45–51) uses him as an analogy for the speeches of its hero. A fragment of Valgius uses the same analogy for a poet called 'Codrus' (fr. 2.1–4 Courtney):

> Codrusque ille canit quali tu uoce canebas
>   atque solet numeros dicere, Cinna, tuos,
> dulcior ut numquam Pylio profluxerit ore
>   Nestoris aut docto pectore Demodoci.

So when the author of the *Catalepton* piece associates Messalla's poetry with Nestor, he is surely thinking of their mellifluousness as well as their long life.

The Codrus of Valgius must be a real person as he is compared with the real and influential Cinna. He also appears in Virgil's seventh eclogue (21–6):

CORYDON   Nymphae noster amor Libethrides, aut mihi carmen
           quale meo Codro concedite (proxima Phoebi
           uersibus ille facit) . . .
THYRSIS   Pastores, hedera crescentem ornate poetam,
           Arcades, inuidia rumpantur ut ilia Codro . . .

It is sometimes said that Codrus in the *Eclogues* is fictitious and that Valgius has wrongly assumed that he was real. But Valgius could not have made such a mistake, for he was a contemporary of Virgil and Horace: Horace's ode to him (2.9) must have been written before 23, and the *Panegyricus Messallae* suggests him as an alternative panegyrist (177–80):

> non ego sum satis ad tantae praeconia laudis,
> ipse mihi non si praescribat carmina Phoebus.
> est tibi qui possit magnis se accingere rebus
> Valgius: aeterno propior non alter Homero.

Clearly Valgius belonged to Messalla's own circle.

All this goes to show that the Codrus so admired by Valgius is none other than Messalla himself, as suggested by Rostagni in a neglected article.[52] When Virgil's Corydon hopes to compose songs like those of Codrus, that suits Messalla's Greek pastoral poems mentioned at *Catalepton* 9.17–20 (above, p. 89). When Valgius compares Codrus with Nestor, that suits the comparison of Messalla with Nestor at *Panegyricus*

45–51 and *Catalepton* 9.16; when he compares Codrus with Cinna, it should be noted that the *Ciris*, a poem dedicated to Messalla, shows clear signs of Cinna's influence.[53] Valgius regards the voice of Codrus as sweet, and the same adjective is applied at *Catalepton* 9.19 to the poems of Messalla; similarly the Delia of Tibullus is to pick for Messalla 'sweet apples from choice trees' (1.5.31–2 *cui dulcia poma | Delia selectis detrahat arboribus*), and Tacitus says of his prose style *Cicerone mitior Coruinus et dulcior* (*Dial.* 18.2). We may also note repeated references to Phoebus, which suggests that Messalla claimed a relationship with the god:[54] Virgil's Corydon says that Codrus makes songs next to those of Phoebus (*Ecl.* 7.22–3); the *Catalepton* poem says that the Cynthian god (i.e. Apollo) helped Messalla with his poetry (9.60); the panegyrist says that he could not sing adequately of Messalla even if Phoebus told him what to say (178, cited p. 90); and as for Horace's ode, the emphatic last word is *Phoebus*.

Codrus was the name of a legendary king of Athens, who is associated in Greek proverbs with antiquity, noble birth, and simple-mindedness.[55] It seems a suitable pseudonym for the patrician Messalla with his old-fashioned tastes and his curious penchant for writing bucolic poetry in Attic Greek; his translation of the *Phryne* of Hyperides shows his fondness for Attic purism. Messalla is associated elsewhere with legendary kings of Athens: the poem in the *Catalepton* talks of his 'Cecropian savour' (9.14 *sale Cecropio*); the invocation to him in the *Ciris* mentions the 'Cecropian' garden of Epicurus (3); and when Tibullus celebrates his birthday he says *liba et Mopsopio dulcia melle feram* (1.7.54), an allusion to Mopsopus, another king of old Athens, as well as to the mellifluousness appropriate to Messalla. Rostagni missed the parallel in Tibullus, but included a more speculative point: Codrus sacrificed himself for his city,[56] and when Messalla joined Brutus and Cassius, his friends may have seen a resemblance to the legendary king. However that may be, there is surely significance in *Catalepton* 9.49 where Messalla is said *saepe etiam densos immittere corpus in hostes*; even if he was called 'Codrus' in the first instance because of his poetry, the line could allude to the king's act of self-sacrifice. Messalla had a special interest in such ritual acts: when the elder Decius Mus immolated himself at the battle of the Veseris, an exemplary instance of *deuotio*, the pontifex who was said to have pronounced the sacred formula was a M. Valerius, very possibly Corvus himself.[57]

It may be argued against Rostagni's identification that Codrus in the *Eclogues* was a bad poet; but when Thyrsis hopes that Codrus may burst with envy (7.25–6, cited p. 90), the remark diminishes not Codrus but Thyrsis, who loses the singing-match. In the fifth eclogue a shepherd invites Mopsus to sing if he has any praises of Alcon or abuse of Codrus

(5.11 *iurgia Codri*); but at the most that shows that some poets of the period made fun of Messalla's old-fashioned Greek bucolics. It is true that 'Codrus' has become a type-name for a bad poet at Juvenal 1.2 *uexatus totiens rauci Theseide Codri;*[58] but by that time the man's identity could have been forgotten. Virgil's own more favourable view of Codrus emerges from the eulogy by the victorious Corydon (*Ecl.* 7.21-3); indeed if Messalla wrote his bucolics when a student at Athens in 45, Virgil is likely to have imitated his charm as well as his subject-matter. All this goes to confirm against Cichorius that the Messalla who discourses on wine with Virgil and Horace in the *Symposium* of Maecenas is none other than the recipient of Horace's 'Ode to the wine-jar'.

Messalla attained great eminence in war and politics, but Horace's poem says nothing about his achievements, not even his recent conquest of Aquitania. The reason may partly be political discretion: Horace was closer to the centre than Tibullus, and might be wary of building up a man who was never in the inner imperial circle. But it was a matter also of literary tact: a sensible poet might be deterred by the blatant flattery of the *Panegyricus Messallae*, a recent and exemplary demonstration of how not to praise famous men. An interesting analogy to Horace's approach may be found in the last of his major poems: when Piso the Pontifex returned from Thrace about 10 BC, having reduced the Bessi and won *ornamenta triumphalia*, Horace said not a word about his victories but greeted him with a distinguished and inconsequential literary essay, the so-called *Ars poetica.*[59] Similarly in the 'Ode to the wine-jar' nothing is said about Messalla's deeds in peace and war: instead we get a parody of liturgical language to suit the religious proclivities of the family, humorous references to wine to suit the connoisseur, a mention of Massic to suit the conquests of his ancestor, a joke about Socratic dialogues to suit the Attic purist with philosophical tastes, discreet banter about Cato to suit a family relationship, reminiscences of the *Symposium* of Maecenas to flatter two important *amici* simultaneously, references to the Graces to suggest the great man's charm and propriety, and to Phoebus to suggest his interest in poetry and augury, above all an urbane and agreeable manner that evokes the aristocratic distinction and languid elegance of Messalla himself (contrast *Carm.* 2.1, the energetic and realistic ode to Pollio). In Horace's poems the style reflects not just the author but sometimes also the recipient.

7   FEMININE ENDINGS, LYRIC
     SEDUCTIONS

GARLANDS AND KNOTS

This essay explores some of the aesthetic and erotic effects produced by hair as a closural motif in Horace's poetry. In taking up this some-what recherché topic, I take encouragement from the fact that Horace chose to make 'hair' the last word of his collected *Odes* 1–3 (*comam*, 3.30.16, revising the 'crown' of Horace's head, *uertice*, from the end of 1.1). The closural appeal of hair is no doubt connected with the ultimacy of its position at the body's edge and top. And yet there is also some-thing inconclusive or even anticlosural about this substance. In the *Ars poetica*, Horace faults the maker of bronzes who knows how to represent 'fingernails' (*unguis*, 32) and 'soft hair' (*mollis . . . capillos*, 33)[1] but not how to fashion a whole (*ponere totum*, 34). Though the main antithesis here is between part and whole, decorative detail and encompassing design, Horace's pairing of hair with fingernails is instructive. Like the nails, hair is a peculiar thing: not exactly part of the body, but a detachable extension of it; essentially lifeless, nerveless and insentient, but also curiously alive in its ability to continue growing after the body's death.[2] At the mar-gins of the body, hair blurs the difference between subject and object, life and death. It may have a similar effect in the final line of Horace's collected *Odes*, in a poem so much taken up with the question of the poet's afterlife.

On the other hand, it is important to note that this hair, however fore-grounded by its final position, is caught up in a sentence that decrees its garlanding: 'with Delphic laurel graciously bind, Melpomene, my hair' (*mihi Delphica | lauro cinge uolens, Melpomene, comam*, 3.30.15–16). Hair makes less strange an ending when it is thus bound within the honorific wreath of Apollo's laurel. Certainly the garland, invoked by Meleager in the title of his lyric anthology the *Stephanos*, furnishes an apposite closural emblem for a collection of poetry. This may be one reason that Horace chose to end *Odes* 1 with a poem (*Persicos odi*) that is so much preoccupied by the proper composition of a garland.[3] But the garland, circular and circumscribed, is also a good emblem for the individual poem. Thus in the final line of *Carm.* 3.25 Horace contains Bacchus' dangerously centrifugal energies within an ivy garland ('it is a sweet danger to follow the god, binding brows with green ivy', *cingentem uiridi tempora pampino*, 20), and at the first, false conclusion of 4.1 he imagines himself (while disclaiming any interest in) 'binding [his] brow with fresh flowers' (*uincire nouis tempora floribus*, 32). A figurative counterpart to the garland is provided by the closural *nodus*, the 'knot' or 'coil' of hair. In the final line of Epode 11, Horace dreams of 'a shapely boy tying back' – or perhaps 'undoing' (I will return to this ambiguity later) – 'his long hair' (*teretis pueri longam renodantis comam*, 28); at the close of *Carm.* 2.11, he summons Lyde to join his party, 'hasten[ing] here with her ivory lyre, having bound up her hair, Spartan style, in a neat coil' (*eburna dic age cum lyra | maturet, in comptum Lacaenae | more comam religata nodum*, 22–4).[4] The same image helps produce a simulacrum of closure in *Carm.* 3.14, where Horace orders a slave to tell 'clear-voiced Neaera to hurry and tie up her perfumed hair in a coil' (*dic et argutae properet Neaerae | murreum nodo cohibere crinem*, 21–2).[5]

The garland and the knot picture closure by gathering up something multiple and linear into a circular unity. This is a unity of time as well as space. When Horace writes *uincire nouis tempora floribus*, he is punning on *tempora* and perhaps on *uincire/uincere* as well: the lyric 'flowers' of the ageing poet ('nearing fifty', as he tells Venus, *circa lustra decem*, 4.1.6) are his way of binding and thus (figuratively) conquering the flow of time. This 'fixing' of time is also expressed by Horace's focus on the music of Neaera and Lyde (Neaera is 'clear-voiced', Lyde carries a lyre) alongside their hair. Their music and their hair are alike self-reflexive figures of poetry, or rather the one is the textualisation of the other: a fugitive lyric performance is rewritten and objectified in the form of the *nodus*.

Such closural gestures of containment tend also to carry a moral message, especially when they are directed at women. As Kenneth Reckford has pointed out, Lyde's *nodus* suits Horace's party, which is to be not a wild carousal but a decorous relaxation, as befits its white-haired participants (cf. *canos... capillos*, 2.11.15).[6] In Horace's poetry, women with loose hair are less seductive than threatening. In *Satires* 1.8, Canidia's feet are unshod and her hair dishevelled (*pedibus nudis passoque capillo*, 24) as she sets about her witchcraft. In *Epodes* 5, about to launch upon a still more ghastly ritual in the hopes of winning back a straying lover, Canidia has braided snakes into her hair – a hairdo that results in a head that is precisely *unkempt* (*Canidia breuibus inplicata uiperis | crinis et incomptum caput*, 15–16; contrast Lyde's *comptum... nodum, Carm.* 2.11.23–4); these *vipers*, parodic *uittae*, embody the wildness of the hair they are purportedly called upon to tame.[7] Likewise Sagana, Canidia's partner in crime here, has spiky hair which bristles like a sea urchin or a boar (*horret capillis ut marinus asperis | echinus aut currens aper*, 27–8).

Whereas loose hair signals a woman's freedom – which to Horace regularly means her resistance to (formal, emotional, sexual, societal) control[8] – bound hair figures her compliance. Lyde may be an 'elusive whore' (*deuium scortum, Carm.* 2.11.21), paradoxically at once difficult of access and universally available, but, if she attends Horace's party, she will curb, for the occasion at least, not just her hair but herself. When Horace asks Pyrrha 'For whom are you tying up your blond hair?' (*cui flauam religas comam, Carm.* 1.5.4),[9] he is in effect restating the poem's famously iconic opening, which catches Pyrrha within her lover's embrace (*gracilis te puer*, 1), with the difference that it is now Pyrrha who willingly binds herself over to her new relationship. This opening scenario will of course be devastatingly reversed in subsequent stanzas, where Pyrrha will elude that embrace and, instead of 'mooring' her hair to her new lover (*religas*, 5; the nautical connotation comes into focus only retrospectively), will herself provide the emphatically untamed waves upon which his minute and helpless bark will be tempest-tossed.[10] Compare the complex ending of *Carm.* 1.17, where the carefully crafted enclosure into which Horace invites Tyndaris is disrupted, Tyndaris herself disfigured, by a lover who is imagined as ripping 'the garland clinging to your hair, and your undeserving dress' (*scindat haerentem coronam | crinibus inmeritamque uestem*, 27–8). Tearing off the garland and the dress may be not (only) an expression of rage but the prelude to sexual intercourse, which can itself be represented as the untying of the girdle's 'knot'.[11] Near the end of *Carm.* 3.21 Horace describes the Graces, those epitomes of feminine charm, as 'slow to untie the knot' (*segnesque nodum soluere Gratiae*, 22; the expression renders a Greek phrase such as ζώνην λύεσθαι) – a seductive postponement that mirrors the prolongation of Horace's proposed party until daybreak.

FUGITIVE TRESSES

As this last example implies, while the *nodus* suggests the tight coil of the finished poem, it can also point to its unfinished business. Consummation, both erotic and readerly, waits on the untying of the *nodus*; sexual satisfaction figures the textual denouement. But Horatian lyric is wont to frustrate the reader along with the lover, or rather (since 'frustrate' discounts lyric's particular pleasures in favour of more typically narrative satisfactions), to shield both alike from the threat of a premature conclusion.[12] This tendency is dramatised by *Carm.* 2.5, a poem that

begins by addressing an urgent heterosexual desire for immediate grat-
ification but ends quite otherwise, with a lingering description of a boy
graced with long loose hair (*solutis | crinibus*, 23–4). At the start, Horace
advises an unnamed 'you' of the sexual immaturity of 'your heifer', who
is 'not yet' ready to be yoked or mounted (1–12):[13]

> Nondum subacta ferre iugum ualet
> ceruice, nondum munia conparis
>   aequare nec tauri ruentis
>   in uenerem tolerare pondus.
>
> circa uirentis est animus tuae
> campos iuuencae, nunc fluuiis grauem
>   solantis aestum, nunc in udo
>   ludere cum uitulis salicto
>
> praegestientis. tolle cupidinem
> inmitis uuae: iam tibi liuidos
>   distinguet autumnus racemos
>   purpureo uarius colore.

> *Not yet is she strong enough to bear the yoke on tamed neck, not yet
> [strong enough] to meet a partner's duties or to endure the weight of the
> bull rushing in for love. Your heifer's thoughts are on green fields, as she
> now dips in the stream to ease the oppressive heat, now longs passionately
> to play with the calves amid the moist willows. Give up your desire for
> the unripe grape: soon parti-coloured autumn will pick out for you with
> purple the dull blue clusters.*

With the *iam* ('soon') of line 10, Horace initiates a movement that will be
completed in the next stanza (13–16):

> iam te sequetur: currit enim ferox
> aetas et illi quos tibi dempserit
>   adponet annos; iam proterua
>   fronte petet Lalage maritum.

> *Soon she will follow you; for savage time races on and will add to her the
> years it has deducted from you; soon Lalage will level her wanton forehead
> at a husband.*[14]

At this point, the poem has travelled from its opening 'not yet' to a
thrice reiterated 'soon', a movement that mirrors Lalage's transformation from elusive maiden to mature sexual partner. Had Horace stopped
here, the poem would not have seemed incomplete; readers might indeed
have processed *maritum* ('husband' or 'lover') as the climactic realisation

of the first line's 'yoke' (*iugum*, 1; cf. *con-iugium*, 'marriage' or 'sexual union').[15] Lalage's yoking, like the binding of Lyde's hair in *Carm.* 2.11, would then function as a model of the poem's own achievement of closure.

On the other hand, the mature Lalage is not envisioned as docilely submitting to her mate. Instead of offering herself up to him as an erotic object, she will begin actively to direct her own desire toward him. In retrospect, it becomes clear that the beloved 'heifer' is characterised not by the absence of desire but by its misdirection (from 'your' point of view);[16] note especially the enjambed (hence not only semantically but formally 'excessive') *praegestientis* ('longing passionately', 9), which instantly evokes, as if in defensive response, the speaker's further reduction of the heifer to a cluster of grapes (an 'objectification' which turns 'her' into a passionless 'it'). Thus when we read *iam te sequetur; currit enim ferox | aetas* ('Soon *she* will follow *you*; for savage runs | time') we might mistake the maturing heifer for the subject of *currit* – a misconception which will be corrected as soon as we read across the line break to the next line, which provides the proper subject.[17] Still, it is no longer the man who plays the part of the aggressive bull. There are two zero-sum games being played out here simultaneously; what time transfers from the man to the woman is not only years but desire. Lalage's warmth, far from heating her lover, makes him grow cool. Her pursuit makes him flee.[18]

This flight carries the poem past the narratively and rhetorically overdetermined marital conclusion of stanza four[19] and into images of obscurity and imprecision (17–24):

> dilecta, quantum non Pholoe fugax,
> non Chloris albo sic umero nitens
>   ut pura nocturno renidet
>   luna mari Cnidiusue Gyges,
>
> quem si puellarum insereres choro,
> mire sagacis falleret hospites
>   discrimen obscurum solutis
>   crinibus ambiguoque uoltu.

> *more beloved than fugitive Pholoe, or white-shouldered Chloris gleaming like the cloudless moon shining in the night sea, or Cnidian Gyges, who, if you set him in a dancing circle of girls, would miraculously escape detection by his clever visitors, hard to tell apart with his loosened hair and confounding face.*[20]

These stanzas return us to the sphere of the 'not yet': Lalage will 'seek out a mate', but Pholoe is 'fugitive'; Lalage will become distinct as she ripens, but Chloris shimmers like the moon reflected in water; Lalage will leave her playmates behind, crossing over into marital heterosexuality, but Gyges obscures the very division between the sexes. The 'not yet' is transformed here, moreover, into something more than a preliminary; the threshold becomes a terrace. The georgic, sunlit, workaday world of the opening stanzas, in which heifers are destined to prepare the earth to produce fruit and to produce young themselves, and grapes are worth nothing until they are ready to eat, is displaced by a set of figures who embody a value we might call aesthetic, a value here associated with non-consummation, night, moonlight, reflection, and finally with homo-erotic ('fruitless', from a georgic perspective) desire. There is a narrative 'not yet' at issue here too, since the situation Horace hypothesises for Gyges – blending in with a circle of girls to deceive his suspicious visitors – is blatantly patterned on Achilles' transvestism on Scyros (a story which also decorates the end of *Carm.* 1.8).[21] For Homeric epic, this episode can be but a prelude to Achilles' heroic entrance into war. But for lyric, this moment on the threshold of manhood is something to be prolonged and celebrated. It is in this kind of interlude or interval that lyric best knows how to linger.

Pholoe, Chloris, and Gyges are all ostensibly invoked to serve as foils to Lalage, *dilecta* (*dis-lecta*, suggesting 'chosen out', 'singled out' as well as the dictionary meaning 'beloved') beyond all others. But poetic negations are never final, and the *non* preceding this list of slighted lovers does not cancel out Horace's loving description of their charms. The paradoxical effect of these final comparisons is to obscure and finally displace Lalage as an object of desire. Gyges' loose hair has its part to play in this affair. The phrase *discrimen obscurum solutis crinibus* might be translated (until we reach the conclusion of the sentence, which forces a less concrete rendering of *discrimen*) 'the part [in his hair] rendered hard to see by his loosened tresses'.[22] What seems to be undone in these lines is the coiffure of the Roman bride, whose hair was traditionally first parted by her husband-to-be (with a spear-head!) and then arranged in a style known as *sex crines*, 'six tresses'.[23] The detail about Gyges' hair thus recapitulates the movement of the poem as a whole, from marital binding to erotic loosening.[24] Moreover, whereas women's loose hair implies the unleashing of potentially threatening forces, Gyges' tresses pose no such threat, perhaps because the beloved boy is consistently envisioned as the passive object of masculine admiration, never as a voracious subject of desire. The dangerous economy of heterosexual desire does not apply to the homoerotic liaison. Once he crosses the line into sexual maturity, Gyges, unlike Lalage, will not turn his desire toward his lover but will instead become an image of him, directing his desire in turn toward indifferent boys and fugitive girls.

The wilfully supplementary character of this ending is underscored by Horace's syntax. It is a free apposition, *dilecta*, that gets the ode under way again after the apparently terminal completion of *petet Lalage maritum*; here, as elsewhere,[25] Horace generates a closural extension by appending a descriptive clause to a proper name. In this instance, the strategy is duplicated – first *Lalage* and then *Gyges* closes one stanza and generates another. The resulting syntax might be identified, in Roman terms, as 'errant' or 'loose' or even 'effeminate'. Especially relevant to my purposes here is the style decried by the author of the treatise *Ad Herennium* as 'lax' (*dissolutum*), 'sinewless' (*sine neruis*), 'wavering' (*fluctuans*), and unmanly in its inability to arrive at a goal (*nec potest confirmate neque uiriliter sese expedire*, 4.16). As the sentence quoted to exemplify this style suggests,[26] what the author has in mind is a syntax that tends toward paratactic addition and that progresses (or slides away) from main to subordinate clauses – as if the speaker had set forth without knowing where his sentence was heading. Compare Seneca's famous critique of Horace's patron Maecenas, a man notorious for his literary and personal 'laxity' (*Ep.* 114.4):[27]

> non oratio eius aeque soluta quam ipse discinctus? ... magni vir ingenii fuerat si illud egisset uia rectiore, si non uitasset intellegi, si non etiam in oratione diffflueret. uidebis itaque eloquentiam ebrii hominis inuolutam et errantem et licentiae plenam.

> *Wasn't his literary style as loose as he himself was loose in dress [unbelted]? ... He would have been a man of great talent if he had guided it more firmly, if he hadn't avoided being understood, if he hadn't rambled even in his literary style. And so what you'll see in him is the obscure, wandering, licentious eloquence of the drunkard.*

Within the *Ad Herennium*, as elsewhere, the antithesis of this effeminate errancy is the manly embrace of the circular period (*perfectis uerbis amplectitur*, 4.16) within which the orator locks his subject (and thereby simultaneously captures his audience).[28]

As has often been remarked, Horace tends, even in his most sober and serious odes, to avoid this kind of strongly figured closure.[29] What interests me here, however, is Horace's recurrent conjunction of this errant syntax with the figure of a long-haired boy. In the final stanzas of *Carm.* 2.5, Horace proceeds by addition (Pholoe, Chloris, Gyges) and by branching elaborations (*dilecta quantum*, 17; *quem si*, 21) that carry us, syntactically and imagistically, a great distance from their source. Compare the end of *Epodes* 11 (23–8):

> nunc gloriantis quamlibet mulierculam
>   uincere mollitia amor Lycisci me tenet;
> unde expedire non amicorum queant
>   libera consilia nec contumeliae graues,
> sed alius ardor aut puellae candidae
>   aut teretis pueri longam renodantis comam.

> *Now love for Lyciscus, who prides himself on outdoing any woman in softness, holds me tight; from whom I can't be extricated by the outspoken [and 'liberating'] advice of my friends, nor by their stern rebukes, but only by another passion for a fair girl or a shapely boy, tying back [or: undoing] his long hair.*

As far as syntax and metrics go, the poem might have ended with the closural embrace of line 24 (*amor Lycisci me tenet*). By continuing on, Horace broadens his horizon; unlike the infatuated lover, trapped within his current *amour*, the relatively disengaged self-observing poet is in a position to appreciate the grand ongoing comedy of desire in which he himself plays so signal a role.[30] The large-scale ring composition that characterises this poem – these final lines restate Horace's opening claim that love aggressively seeks him out to make him 'burn for soft boys or girls' (*mollibus in pueris aut in puellis urere*, 4; cf. *graui*, 2, matched by *graues*, 26) – suggests that the poet is trapped not by any one love but by the very condition of desire. On the other hand, the shift from the plural 'boys and girls' of line 4 to the singular 'girl or boy' of lines 27–8 reminds us that the entrapped lover and the analytic poet cannot be so readily disentangled. With his final, just slightly prolonged glance at the 'shapely boy' who lies somewhere in his erotic future, Horace both loosens the grip of Lyciscus and readies himself to enter another erotic nexus – a double movement well captured by the ambiguity of *renodantis* (knotting back/unknotting). Thus against the poem's overarching structure – a structure corresponding to the poet's (self-)knowledge – there plays the local disorder effected by the fugitive syntax of these closing lines, with their freely appended elaborations (*unde*; *nec* (preceded not by *nec* but by *non*, as if Horace had not foreseen the second member of this pair); *sed*; *renodantis*).[31] These centrifugal clauses are in effect the linguistic counterpart of the tresses which supply the poem's final image.

Another long-haired boy is featured in *Carm.* 3.20, a brief poem which takes indecision as its very theme. The poem begins in the excitement of an imminent conflict (1–8):[32]

Non uides, quanto moueas periclo,
Pyrrhe, Gaetulae catulos leaenae?
dura post paulo fugies inaudax
    proelia raptor,

cum per obstantis iuuenum cateruas
ibit insignem repetens Nearchum,
grande certamen, tibi praeda cedat
    maior an illa.

Don't you see, Pyrrhus, at what peril you steal the cubs of a Gaetulian lioness? Soon you will flee the hard battle, a cowardly ravisher, when she comes through the crowds of young men to reclaim amazing Nearchus – a great contest [to decide] whether the prize shall fall to you, or she prevail.

But the contest thus envisioned is at once postponed and, once postponed, never resumed. The epic pretensions of Pyrrhus, who views himself through the magnifying glass of Homeric simile, are deflated not only by Horace's predictions of his future cowardice but also by the subsequent description of Nearchus (9–16):

interim, dum tu celeris sagittas
promis, haec dentis acuit timendos,
arbiter pugnae posuisse nudo
    sub pede palmam

fertur et leni recreare uento
sparsum odoratis umerum capillis,
qualis aut Nireus fuit aut aquosa
    raptus ab Ida.

Meanwhile, while you're getting out your swift arrows and she's sharpening her terrible teeth, the umpire of the fight is said to have put the palm under his bare foot, and to be cooling his shoulders, overspread with perfumed tresses, in the gentle breeze – such a beauty as Nireus was, or the boy snatched from watery Ida.

With a sudden shift of perspective, Horace relegates the industrious rivals to the background and focuses all his attention on the contested beloved. The metaphorical language of this second pair of stanzas implicitly corrects the simile of the first pair by casting Nearchus not as prey or prize but as the awarder of prizes, the Jupiter-like *arbiter* of battle. In this light, the rivals' fierce preparations are revealed to be mere bravado; it is Nearchus who will decide the outcome.[33] And yet the judge is supremely indifferent to the contest he is called upon to decide. The object of desire is himself untouched by desire.

As in *Carm.* 2.5, so again here the progress toward a narrative *telos*, a decisive outcome, is interrupted in favour of a lyric in-between. The multiple dimensions of this in-between are suggested by the various mediations performed by *interim* (temporal), *arbiter* (intellectual), and *fertur* (discursive; contrast the immediacy of *Non uides*...?).[34] The suspension is also figured at the levels of gender and syntax. Note that neither of Nearchus' lovers acts in accordance with the norms of his/her gender: Pyrrhus, like the effeminate Paris of the *Iliad* (and unlike his namesake, the son of Achilles), is but a 'timid rapist' (*raptor inaudax*, 4), while his female rival plays the aggressive warrior, lion-like in 'his' rage.[35] Nearchus too, with his long, loose, perfumed hair, crosses gender categories; the poem arrests him, as Jupiter captures Ganymede, in a condition of sexual ambiguity – a condition which is, however, not comically indecorous but proper to his age, and beautiful. Nearchus' floating hair is syntactically figured by the poem's final divergence into a simile (as in *Carm.* 2.5, Horace closes not with the tenor but with the subordinate vehicle), a simile that is further divided into two alternatives, the second more elliptical than the first (15–16).[36] The poem thus ends in a condition not of narrative suspense but of lyric suspension.

Here as elsewhere, the narrative that is thus suspended can be identified as the grand, perhaps the ultimately authoritative narrative of Homer's *Iliad*, which is the source of the mythical beauties to whom Horace compares Nearchus in his ode's final lines. Nireus makes a single brief appearance in the 'Catalogue of Ships' (*Il.* 2.671–5), where he is described as the most beautiful of the Achaeans after Achilles, though no great warrior; Ganymede is the Trojan boy snatched up to serve as Jupiter's Olympian cupbearer (*Il.* 20.232–5) and (in post-Homeric tradition) 'catamite'. Michael Putnam has written eloquently of the power of the triple anaphora that Homer lavished upon Nireus, an anaphora that Ovid read as the symptom of a lover's passion for his beloved (cf. *antiquo Nireus adamatus Homero, Ars am.* 2.109).[37] Horace's conjunction of Nireus with Ganymede suggests not only that he read the Homeric passage similarly but also that he was interested in discovering, within Homeric epic, moments and models that could be recuperated for lyric.[38] Ganymede (raped long before Helen) and Nireus (whose subsequent fortunes at Troy pass unrelated) appear within the *Iliad* but elude its epic action; they are glimpsed but remain unknown. So too Horace's Nearchus partially disappears behind the screen of simile, while Ganymede hides behind the participle that holds the place of his name – *raptus*, 'carried off', ironically countering *raptor*, 'rapist', at the end of the first stanza (the beloved boy is to be carried off by no mortal lover).[39] Nearchus thus remains permanently available to, and seductively out of reach of, the wider audience of potential lovers composed of Horace's readers.

Two other odes belong in the company of *Carm.* 3.20. In *Carm.* 1.4, thoughts of springtime 'loosening' (*Soluitur*, the poem's first word, sets its key) unleash the spectre of 'pale death'. Once the comfortably rigid categories of winter have yielded to the mobile transgressions of spring, time proceeds on its rapid course toward a second, figurative winter (13–17):

> pallida Mors aequo pulsat pede pauperum tabernas
>   regumque turris. o beate Sesti,
> uitae summa breuis spem nos uetat incohare longam:
>   iam te premet nox fabulaeque Manes
> et domus exilis Plutonia.

> *Pale Death pounds with impartial foot at the inns of poor men and the towers of kings. Blessed Sestius, life's brief total forbids us to set in train a long hope: soon you'll be constrained by night and the fabled Manes and the meagre home of Pluto.*

Death, which brackets this passage (*pallida Mors . . . domus exilis Plutonia*) and provides an ominous frame for the name of Sestius, is of course a most conclusive end. But Horace evades this stifling conclusion by appending two relative clauses, the second of which, as in *Carm.* 2.5 and 3.20, evolves out of the proper name of a beautiful boy (17–20):

> quo simul mearis
>   nec regna uini sortiere talis
> nec tenerum Lycidan mirabere, quo calet iuuentus
>   nunc omnis et mox uirgines tepebunt.

> *where, once arrived, you won't throw dice for the kingship of the wine or admire tender Lycidas, whom all the young men are hot for now and the girls will warm to soon.*

Like Gyges, Lycidas is at the threshold between boyhood and manhood. But here the *telos* that is displaced is not marital consummation but its narrative equivalent, death. The translation of Sestius' imminent passage into the Underworld (*iam*, 16) into Lycidas' imminent passage into manhood (*mox*, 20) – a translation marked by the fading echo of Death's explosive kick in the girls' sexual warming (*omnis et mox tepebunt*, 20; cf. especially *tabernas*, 13) – arrests the headlong momentum of the ode by scaling down its temporality to one indeterminate interval within the life course.

Something similar happens at the end of *Carm.* 4.1, though here it is Horace himself who takes on the role of Sestius. The ageing poet begins by banishing Venus, claiming to be too old for her service. But this attempt at an ending is disrupted by the intrusion of Ligurinus, who compels the poet to return to love and lyric. The ode ends not in waking reality but in the twilight of dreams (37–40):

> nocturnis ego somniis
>   iam captum teneo, iam uolucrem sequor
> te per gramina Martii
>   campi, te per aquas, dure, uolubilis.

> *In dreams at night now I catch and hold you, and now follow you flying across the grassy Campus Martius, follow you, hard boy, through the chattering waves.*

This ending discards the garland of line 32 for the flowing waves of the Tiber, the resignation of old age for a perpetually renewed erotic pursuit. Though Horace does not mention the hair of either Lycidas or Ligurinus, it is virtually present in the discursive context of these poems (boys who are the object of masculine desire are regularly characterised by long hair). Hair could also stand as an emblem for the centrifugal arguments of these elusive endings.

FEMININE ENDINGS

The term 'feminine ending', once widely used to describe a verse ending with an unstressed syllable, has fallen out of favour, and for good reasons; few critics are comfortable with the synonymy (feminine = weak, trailing, disposable) which this term implies.[40] If I revive the term here, it is to draw attention to the way this synonymy is activated and underscored by Horace's conjunction of 'weak' form and effeminate content.[41] Such endings effect a displacement of marriage by seduction, (self-)possession by erotic pursuit, inevitable death by ineluctable desire, thereby rediscovering, somewhere within the middle of the ongoing narrative, a space of lyric delay or dallying. This effect is replicated, moreover, in the relation of reader to poem. The absence of a clean break makes it harder for the reader to separate from the poem. Gyges' loose hair entangles not only Horace's imagination but the reader's; the poem that represents Gyges also itself partakes of his seductive appeal.

Poems such as *Carm.* 2.5 could be said to put into practice the erotics of reading that underlies Horace's recurring comparisons of his poetry and/or his poetry-writing self to a desirable *puer*. The most clear-cut cases are *Epistles* 1.20, where Horace personifies his poetry-book as a beautiful boy bent on self-prostitution (i.e., publication), and *Epistles* 2.2, where he compares his failure to provide poetry to the truancy of a very attractive slave.[42] A similarly eroticised identification of artist with artwork closes the passage of the *Ars poetica* on the maker of bronzes who fashions realistic hair but incoherent wholes: 'If I took it upon myself to compose something,' Horace proclaims, 'I wouldn't want to be him any more than to live with a crooked nose, though admired for my black eyes and black hair' (*hunc ego me, si quid componere curem,* | *non magis esse uelim, quam naso uiuere prauo,* | *spectandum nigris oculis nigroque capillo,* 35–7; cf. Horace's description of Alcaeus' *eromenos* Lycus, *nigris oculis nigroque* | *crine decorum,* *Carm.* 1.32.11–12). The slippage from 'it' to 'I' here is really remarkable. Horace focuses not, as expected, on the defective artwork (i.e., 'I wouldn't want to make a work that was beautiful only in parts') but on the imperfect attractions of its maker – as if it were not a statue but the body of the maker that was for sale. Also relevant here is the way *Carm.* 4.1 rewrites the reader's (and perhaps Augustus') demand for more Horatian lyrics as the speaker's unseasonable longing for Ligurinus – a chain of desires that links the poet (and/or his poems) with the desirable boy. Horace's most exalted figure for the conjunction of lyric poetry and long-haired effeminacy is the perpetually adolescent Apollo; a more problematic model is supplied by Apollo's protégé Paris, the effeminate seducer who prides himself on his beautiful hair and who wields, like Apollo and like Horace himself, the 'unwarlike lyre'.[43]

As I have already suggested, this erotics may also be activated by the figure of a woman. In fact one of the best embodiments of Horatian poetry, with its paradoxical blend of recherché deviancy and wide availability, is the *deuium scortum* whom Horace invites to the party of *Carm.* 2.11.[44] The ode anticipates pleasures that it does not represent itself as providing: it ends with Lyde's *carmen* still to be peformed, her sexual 'knot' still to be untied. Compare *Carm.* 3.28, where Horace invites Lyde to join him in antiphonal song, a performance that will culminate in a (seemingly jointly performed) celebration of Venus and Night. *dicetur merita Nox quoque nenia,* 'Night too will be hymned in the song it deserves' (16) – thus Horace glosses, in the ode's last line, the passage from song to sex. And despite the exemplary finality of the reference to night, the line, like the poem as a whole, defers its consummations, opening up a vista which is at once and indistinguishably erotic and poetic. The poem seduces by luring the reader into a circle which leads from the poem to its represented future and then back to the self-cancelling presence of the poem – which is the only object that the reader has within her grasp. The same confusion of desires marks the end of *Carm.* 4.11, where Horace asks Phyllis, 'last of my loves' (*meorum* | *finis amorum,* 31–2), to learn his poetry so she can sing it back to him *amanda* | *uoce,* 'with a voice deserving to be loved'

(34–5).⁴⁵ Across the line break, desire flows from Phyllis to her voice, and thence, for the reader, to Horace's.

HAIRLINES

In *Epistles* 1.7, Horace laments his own receding hairline, nostalgically recalling the days when he sported 'a brow narrowed by black curls' (*nigros angusta fronte capillos*, 26). In *Carm.* 4.3, he attributes his poetic character to the shaping powers of 'fertile Tibur's waters, and the dense foliage of its groves' (*quae Tibur aquae fertile praefluunt | et spissae nemorum comae*, 10–11). The fertility and luxuriance of this landscape mirror the vitality of the poet who claims elsewhere that he will 'grow forever fresh in posterity's praise' (*usque ego postera | crescam laude recens*, *Carm.* 3.30.7–8). Near the end of *Carm.* 3.19, Horace praises a desirable youth for his 'thick hair' agleam with perfume (*spissa te nitidum coma*, 25). The phrase is the same as the one I rendered above as 'dense foliage', and it carries similar implications of virile prolificacy.⁴⁶ It is as if the trees of Tibur supplemented Horace's diminishing supply by garlanding him with their own superabundant *comae*, thereby restoring to him a simulacrum of his lost youth. In fact this supplementation is already under way in Horace's previous lyric collections, each of which ends with an enhancement or transformation of Horace's plumage. *Carm.* 1.38 not only provides the recipe for a garland but produces its own immediate effect of garlanding by placing the poet under a 'dense vine' (*sub arta | uite*, 7–8); *Carm.* 2.20 decks the poet in the feathers of a swan; *Carm.* 3.30 crowns his hair with laurel.⁴⁷ The bodies of Horace's poems, which live on in simultaneous relation to and detachment from their author, not only sport their own version of hair but in effect compose Horace's hair, holding his readers fast in their elusive implications.

ALESSANDRO BARCHIESI

8   THE UNIQUENESS OF THE *CARMEN
    SAECVLARE* AND ITS TRADITION

QUALITY

The *Carmen saeculare* occupies an average of four pages in the printed
editions of Horace, and leads a quiet life in an *angulus* at the margins
of his lyric corpus. It was transmitted by our medieval manuscripts and
is occasionally quoted by late antique grammatici, just like the rest of
what Horace published. Yet there is some uneasiness in the background
of modern and contemporary interpretation. The 76-line poem has never
been the subject of specific commentaries, nor is it normally included in
twentieth-century annotated editions of the *Odes*, or given a fair amount
of space in book-length essays and *explications de texte*. The only clear
exception flags itself as an exception, because Eduard Fraenkel's extended
treatment in his *Horace* (1957) is a tense and vibrant apology, not a normal
example of academic discussion. Had the author written in the same vein
about, say, *Carm.* 1.10, he would be considered an eccentric instead of a
master of Latin studies.

Two reasons for this special status deserve mention here. One is that
the poem was performed in a context that for a long time, and for some
time to come, can be perceived as pre-Fascist, and was mostly admired
in the moral climate of European twentieth-century nationalism. I do
not wish to contest this association on grounds of common-sense historicism: people make of ancient texts what they can, and as a viewer of
Ettore Scola's important movie *Una giornata particolare* and as an Italian
of my generation I can easily collapse the ideology of the *Carmen* with
old people's memories of Saturday exercises in nationalism and imperial
rhetoric, and feel the peculiar mix of a dull sense of being protected and
a hidden but perceivable threat against human rights. This association
is hardly useful for a specific interpretation, but it was clearly part of
the atmosphere of lost innocence against which Fraenkel, for example,
reacted, and the main problem remains that nobody seems able to say
anything about Augustan ideology unless some kind of modern analogy
is invoked, or invoked to be contested. For lack of a solution, I turn to

the second difficulty, the one that will be addressed in this chapter, but I promise not to forget the issue of politics when reading this text.

The second problem is that the poem was *performed*, full stop. This is the only surviving poem in Latin of which we know time and place of a choral performance, and independent evidence[1] confirms that this definitely happened. This detail affects the interpretation of the *Carmen* enormously, and is enough to explain many anomalies in the history of modern reception. As a once-performed text the *Carmen* has entered a life of resurrected performance in contemporary culture, has been put to music, broadcast, aired, chorally sung in schools. As a performance poem originating in a post-oral culture and resurrected in a bookish ambience, the *Carmen* has been invested by a powerful dichotomy between oral and written, and between (secondarily but not marginally) Greek and Roman.

As a result of this dynamics, scholars turn out mostly not to like the poem as a text, and this has affected interpretation, teaching, practices of close reading. The *Carmen* has not been subjected to the same strategies of reading that are accepted as regular for mainstream Augustan poetry. Let me briefly focus on some details of the literary texture that are not normally considered worthy of mention because, I surmise, the unique nature of the *Carmen* makes critics uneasy about its poetic value and so, implicitly, about the value of passing detailed comments to make the text enjoyable and interesting: a situation that would not be acceptable if the *Carmen* was read as, say, poem 3.31 or 4.0 in the Complete Works of a master. (With this last sentence I am briefly admitting that the present chapter too is part of this standard rhetoric of literary studies, that we all write to discover hidden preciosity in the works we study.)

> iam mari terraque manus potentis
> Medus Albanasque timet securis
>
> (53–4)

This is the first extant occurrence where *Albanus* links an explicit reference to Rome and an implicit reference to the Julian family, descended from Alba Longa. The geography of the context is important: Horace's point is that people at the edges of the earth are learning to respect Roman power. A witty *double entendre* helps the point: if you are a Medus you would normally react with apprehension at the very name Albani – those axe-wielding barbarians at your northern frontier. Horace exploits the coincidence between the Latin ethnic and the name of a Caspian nation, first attested in Rome in Pompey's triumphal formula (Plin. *HN* 7.98), then in Augustus' *Res gestae* as a symptom of Rome's successful expansionism under his command (31.2),[2] and the ambiguity between the axe as a symbol of legitimate Roman power or as a weapon of barbarian guerrillas in the mountains (cf. the Amazonian *secures* of the Alpine tribesmen in *Carm.* 4.4.20), and shows the surprise of people who are discovering a new far-off power raising dust at their own border. In the next two lines

> iam Scythae responsa petunt, superbi
> nuper et Indi   (55–6)

Horace extorts a similar surprise effect from Virgil: according to the *Aeneid*, more than eleven centuries (ten *saecula*, we might say) before the *Carmen*, Eastern people were already (*iam nunc*) scared by the divine *responsa* about the coming of Augustus:

> huius in aduentum iam nunc et Caspia regna
> responsis horrent diuum et Maeotia tellus
>   (6.798–9)

but now, in real time (*iam*), they ask not for some more oracles, but for *responsa* from the emperor himself, both as their new god,[3] and (in a more Roman vein and a different turn of the word *responsa*) as a civilising power able to dictate principles of administration and justice.

The legal language of the most infamous stanza in classical poetry

> diua, producas subolem patrumque
> prosperes decreta super iugandis
> feminis prolisque nouae feraci
>   lege marita   (17–20)

has been defended by Fraenkel (1957) 374 with an invocation of Aeschylus' legalistic formulas, but even if one accepts the tone as intentionally formal and unpoetic, one could well admire the force of *patrumque*: placed between *matres* (14) and *feminis* (19), the word expresses the vigilant foresight of the Senate but also connotes the identity between being a 'father' and a father in Roman culture. In taking care of demography and family, the senators have proved that their right name is 'Fathers'.[4] In the meantime *iugandis* performs the important function of bridging the gap between legal language and the latent force of *Iuno*, the indispensable goddess of the marriage yoke, absent from the text of the song yet present in the celebrations, and presumably envious of the nominal epiphanies of Venus (only at 50: see next paragraph) and Jupiter (only at 32 and 73).

The power of contextual and referential implications is even stronger in the only stanza where Augustus is visible:

quaeque uos bobus <u>uene</u>ratur albis
clarus Anchisae <u>Vene</u>risque sanguis,
impetret, bellante prior, iacentem
    lenis in hostem   (49–52)

The *princeps* is overdetermined by genealogy (Anchises plus Venus via
Virgil) and performance context – participants at the *Ludi* knew that
only he (with Agrippa) had been sacrificing white bullocks and cows.
Genealogy and sacrifice are merged through etymology when the only
mention of Venus in the poem follows after the co-radical verb *ueneratur*.
Moreover, the colour of the sacrificed animals,[5] *albis*, not only recalls the
importance of ritual prescriptions and joins a rich isotopy of shine and
gleam in the entire poem, but also polarises itself, across *clarus*, with the
implied redness of *sanguis*. It takes a moment for the reader to realise that
this is not the blood of slaughtered bulls, nor that of the conquered enemy[6]
of the following line: one might say that the suppression of visual details
of sacrifice leads to the substitution of Augustus' divine lineage for the expected colour contrast.[7] The original audience is invited to supply some
visual impression of the sacrifice, and the readers to use the idea of an original audience as a medium to intensify their perception of the proceedings.

alme Sol, curru nitido diem qui
promis et celas aliusque et idem
nasceris, possis nihil urbe Roma
    uisere maius.   (9–13)

The movement from Phoebus (1) to the sun-god has caused problems
for modern scholars. The bottom line is that Apollo as a radiant god
(Phoebus) is almost never completely identical with Sol, and almost never
clearly dissociated from Sol, so critics seem to dislike the halo of indeterminacy that irradiates from this choice. But this semi-merger, as we
shall see, has Greek forerunners, and moreover the text wittily plays with
its Apollo/Sun dynamics. In this context, after a whole tradition of same-
ness and alterity between Apollo and Sun, to say that the sun is Other and
Same is pointed;[8] being itself, the sun is nothing but the day, since *idem*
and *diem* are anagrams;[9] being another, *alius*, the sun is the same again,
but in Greek, the Pindaric *aelios*, and so again related to the Greek god
Apollo, the one who is 'also' called *Eélios* (*Sibylline oracle*, p. 57.17 Pighi).

tempore sacro

quo Sibyllini monuere uersus
uirgines lectas puerosque castos
dis, quibus septem placuere colles,
    dicere carmen   (4–8)

By the final day of the proceedings, when the *Carmen* was performed, the participants had had occasion to hear at least six times the introductory formula *uti uobis/tibi in illeis libreis scriptum est*, reported in the official inscription[10] as an address to the Moerae, Jupiter, Ilithyia, Juno, Terra, and Apollo. The formula had the important function of grounding the exceptional celebrations in the prescriptions of the Sibylline Books. Being used to the repetition, the audience will have appreciated the change from *libri* to *uersus*, now that the focus is on song for the gods, *Carmen*, as part of the ordained ritual of sacrifices for the individual gods: the simple change shows that this event in the history of Roman poetry, a live performance[11] of Latin sapphics, is sparked by a book-roll of Greek hexameters.

> certus undenus deciens per annos
> orbis ut cantus referatque ludos
>
> (21–2)

Condescension for Horace's sad duty of saying '110' in poetry may have obscured two good moments in these lines. The *certus orbis* that brings back the *Ludi* and the *saeculum* must be a cycle, the kyklos of hundred and ten years that is forecast at the beginning of the Sibylline oracle – 'But when the longest span of a human life shall have elapsed, across a cycle of 110 years, do not forget, O Roman...' – but after all this solar activity in the previous lines (9–12 *promis ... celas ... nasceris ... possis ... uisere*) the *orbis* must be also the solar disk,[12] since the sun is the one divine power that guarantees continuity. Secondly, it should not escape attention that the poet, in anticipating the next celebration, has put 'song' first and 'games' second.[13] This choice suggests that next time, in another 110 years, there will emphatically be Latin song again: a promise of national stability, but also a hint that Roman poetry will survive and that the *Carmen*, for all its uniqueness, will be no mean factor in this development. If reperformed at the next *Ludi*, the poem will prove its own vitality: because the reperformance will allow the ambitious Horatian text to play precisely the same matrix role that the Sibylline books had played *vis-à-vis* the Augustan celebrations – a poetic text that anticipates a festival set in the distant future. The next *Ludi* will be able to look back to the *Carmen* just as the Augustan *Ludi* look back to a hoary[14] Greek prophecy.

I introduced these sophistications at the outset not because they are all equally believable, but to raise the problem of why certain hermeneutic strategies (I included double-takes, etymology, bilingual wordplay, allusion, and a model reader who is a bit more similar to the one servicing the *Odes* nowadays than the usual stodgy epigraphist supposed to be interested in the *Carmen*) are normally accepted by the reading community when the text is a 'regular' ode, while the *Carmen* has long been suspected of being incapable of niceties and poetic riches. I fear that the uniqueness of having been composed for performance is a reason why: the situation is not very different if we turn to another typical interpretive strategy, the quest for a genre and a Greek background.

GENERIC IDENTITY

It is equally anomalous that, against the traditions of classical scholarship, students of the *Carmen* have for a long time dodged discussions of the generic aspect. After some initial hints in the early twentieth century,[15] the question of the generic background, which also means the Greek background, for this choral poem seems to recede from sight. Yet, as we shall soon remark, the poem has a much clearer generic definition than many other Augustan poems. Perhaps the presence of so many pointers to a societal setting – the city of Rome, the festival, the ritual, politics, imperial *committenza*, performance – has made the category of literary genre superfluous to many readers: genre is often used in literary criticism as a substitute for lost or weak links to society, occasion, and historical context. Why bother with genre if we have, for once in Roman literature, the real thing?

However, the very ease with which the *Carmen* can be generically understood in Greek terms of reference should attract attention, and some scholars have remarked on it very recently: 'More generally, if I may be slightly dogmatic, the *Carmen* is a Paian'; 'The *Carmen* was identified in antiquity as a paean. This is affirmed in two related Greek sources, including the Sibylline text which provided the festival with its sacral basis and legitimacy'; 'Horace's *Carmen*, which is mostly devoted to the praise of Apollo and Diana, could be considered an example of a "Latin paian".'[16] Those formulations are parallel, independent and motivated by slightly different concerns. I happen to agree with the first quotation (unsurprisingly, since it is from a paper of mine), and with the third, but I have problems with the implications of the second. In his paper, Alex Hardie argues that (i) the link between *Carm.* 4.6 and the *Carmen*, and the link between 4.6 and Pindar's *Pae.* 6, taken together, indicate that Horace wanted to advertise the paeanic nature of the *Carmen*, (ii) the request of the Sibyl that 'Latin paeans' should be sung at the *Ludi* 'identifies' the *Carmen* as a poem of the genre paean, (iii) and this analogy in turn proves that 4.6 is a performance poem, linked to the performance of the *Carmen*. I cannot agree on (ii) and (iii),[17] and (ii) is what concerns us most here. The Sibyl's definition of 'Latin paeans' must be evaluated within the text of the Sibylline oracle, which is in Greek and purports to be very old. There is a possibility that the entire text has been invented from scratch to suit the programme of the new *Ludi* or that, more likely, traditional material has been refashioned to fit the project of the celebrations, including that of a song by Horace. But the fact remains that the reference to the Sibyl has the effect of distracting our attention from the challenge met by Horace: if we take for granted that the *Carmen* is a 'Latin paean' we lose the tension between Greek tradition and the specific occasion. Commissioning 'a Latin paean' is not as simple and easy as consecrating some more cakes. The Sibyl refers to a long continuous Greek tradition of religious song, and 'paeans' is often used without a specific reference to a generic label, especially when Apollo is involved in the context. We cannot cut the knot of the genre of this poem simply by recourse to an oracle, if we want to understand the peculiar situation faced by Horace. Worse still, the generic definition has the effect of obscuring the dynamics of the text, the effort and the negotiation involved in the invocation of such a distant background: effort and negotiation are part of the literary meaning, not of its compositional pre-history. Graeco-Roman intertextuality is a process, not a state, and is predicated on the mismatch and slippages between the two cultural systems.

Let me briefly rehearse what we happen to know about the paean tradition in Greek culture.[18] This is an area, more than a clean and clear-cut department, within the production of religious songs. Perceptions and definitions of what counts as paean vary, but most observers in various moments of Greek culture agree on some crucial points. It is a genre of song to be performed by a chorus, with choreography, and has to do mostly with Apollo, and subordinately with his sister Artemis. An appropriate song for certain religious festivals and gatherings, the paean often includes praise and invocation of Apollo, and sometimes themes of civic and collective importance. The typical performers are a group of young male citizens, the metre tends to be complex and organised in triadic stanzas. The fragments show recurring interest in prophecy, divine justice and foresight, ritual and sacrifice, and justify the assumption that the function of the genre is that of mediating at the level of verbal communication between the occasion – ritual, sacrifice, procession – and the gods.

Those generalisations are of interest for students of Horace, but it is also important to remember how we happen to have evidence on paeans. The tradition climaxes with the success of some masters of sixth- and fifth-century choral lyric, Pindar in particular, and steeply declines from the fourth century onwards. By 'decline' I am referring (but not without bias) to a combination of various evidence: no other author of paeanic poetry becomes a classic and exerts a wide influence; later paeans, most of them preserved in inscriptions, are composed, and the older ones are reperformed, but the metre and scope of the new texts becomes much more simple and formulaic, the song-and-dance tradition loses momentum, the reduced importance of *poleis* and festivals weakens the visibility of this kind of poetry. Paeanic traditions contribute to songs in honour of individuals, not communal gods, but this way the genre loses autonomy and is submerged within a wider area of praise poetry. In parallel, an intense scholarly work begins: the Pindaric paeans are collected in a book of the Alexandrian edition, critics discuss criteria of generic identification of this and adjacent genres of poetry, ways of presenting metre in a textual format become a focus of research.

Horace and his contemporaries respond to the tradition and to its crisis, to the reception of Pindar and to the reception of his critics and commentators. Horace had certainly access to live (re)performances of Greek song, and to many more texts than we have, but like us he is separated from the *floruit* of religious lyric and has to read his way backwards. This is not to say that people became indifferent to the social setting and original context of this kind of poetry: but the approach to those distant origins is now mediated through books. If Horace, as I would assume, was reading learned editions of Pindar and other Greek masters,[19] he would be in a position similar to our own, that of trying to imagine a distant universe through written *testimonia*. This does not mean that he would make no distinction between, say, Pindar's paeans and a collection of Hellenistic epigrams. True, both would be available to him in Greek books, but the epigrams book would bear eloquent witness of its 'written' origins while the paeans book had been revised, selected and assembled and edited by Greek people who had an interest in religious traditions and communal performances: there is still a long way to go before those songs/texts become purely aesthetic objects or archaeological data. For example, paeans in Alexandrian editions are normally prefaced by a heading where the group of first-time performers is named and the location is indicated – e.g. 'for the Thebans at Delphi'. A poet writing for a festival taking place on a June day in Rome would have been immediately aware that the Pindaric text was able to produce multiple experiences – first-time performance, reperformance, readerly reception; and the last-named could become a complex experience, including the memory of the original occasion and its progressive fading away. He could certainly be invited to fantasise about the past performances of those texts but, just like us, he could not make a clear-cut separation between the poetics of Pindar and the Alexandrian edition that has redefined paeanic performance by making a canonic textual choice of its documents.

So there is no wholesale opposition between 'live' songs and books of poetry: reading a Pindaric book could not, of course, be a surrogate for the experience of live performance, but the book would be a trace and a memory of occasions and performances. As a result, the poet responds to a tradition and co-operates in continuing it, but does not attempt a systematic re-enactment. Some of the typical markers and functions of classical paeans are in place in the *Carmen*, some are transformed.

The poem is definitely a song for Apollo and Artemis to be performed by a group of young singers and dancers – more exactly, it points out that it is being performed this way. The choral self-definition in the very last two lines (75–6)

> doctus et Phoebi chorus et Dianae
> dicere laudes

matches – and indeed surpasses in precision – some of the typical learned definitions of paeans in antiquity: 'the paean is typically a praise of Apollo, but it is also used imprecisely of praise of others, hence Pindar called *paeans* his work in praise of men and gods' (Serv. on *Aen.* 10.738); 'the paean is a kind of song that can be written for all the gods nowadays, but in antiquity it was specifically destined for Apollo and Artemis, and performed to celebrate the end of plagues and diseases' (Procl. *Chrest.* 320a 21ff.) 'and to deprecate political discord (*stasis*)' (Schol. Dion. Thr. p. 451.12 Hilgard), and finally, fundamental among extant testimonia, the Pindaric fr. 128c, from the *Threnoi*: 'On the one hand there are the seasonal (/periodical/springtime)[20] paeanic songs for the children of Latona of the golden distaff, on the other hand songs from crowns of blossoming ivy, belonging to Dionysos ... '

If one decides to accept this generic link, further similarities emerge. Important themes of the *Carmen*, prophecy, collective welfare, youth, protection, the future of the community, are also prominent in the Pindaric fragments. There are also individual clues and shared stylemes. The initial Apollo/Diana invocation (1 *Phoebe ... Diana*) is not exclusive to paeans, but is featured in a number of poems that were included in the Alexandrian volume, and it is a reasonable inference that the editor considered them a significant clue, e.g. *Pae.* 4.1 Apollo (conjectural) + Artemis; *Pae.* 5.1 'Ieie, Delian Apollo!'; *Pae.* 7b.1 'Apollo ... you and ... mother'.[21] The important time marker *tempore sacro* (4) establishes the occasion for the song in parallel to what seems to be a convention of the genre, cf. *Pae.* 1.5–6 'Ieie, on this occasion the complete Year and the Seasons have come to Thebes'; *Pae.* 3.14 ὥριον ποτὶ χρόνον 'in appropriate/seasonal time'; *Pae.* 4.11 'time' (of performance in festival?[22]) and especially *Pae.* 6.5–6 'welcome me, the interpreter of the Pierides, famed in song, at this sacred time' (ἐν ζαθέῳ ... χρόνῳ).

The extant remains also show 'clusters' of topics, divine addressees, and visual elements that reappear in various combinations in the *Carmen*. Without entering the many problems of reconstruction, I quote the evidence in its fragmentary state. *Pae.* 12 combines: nine Muses, prophecy, Fates and Eileithuia, light and solar imagery. In particular 14–17 'When the twins shone like the sun, moving towards the bright light, Eileithuia and Lachesis emitted a great noise from their mouths' highlights the birth of Apollo and Artemis as gods but also as quasi-heavenly bodies: instead of being born to see the light, like any other, they were born to shine. Horace has linked Apollo, the nine Muses (62 *acceptusque nouem Camenis*), Ilithyia and child-birth (14), Parcae (25) and the same fade-to-brightness effect (2 *lucidum caeli decus*).

Other promising scraps in *Pae.* 3[23] ('fragrant ... altar ... appropriate time ... Apollo ... moon and its path ... shining aether ... sacred voice of *auloi* ... sacrificing') suggest a mix of self-reference, cultic action, representation of time, Apolline cult and 'big sky' atmosphere. It should now be clear that the play of identifications at the beginning of the *Carmen*, where Diana is also the Moon but Apollo 'is and is not' Sol, must have had ample precedent in Pindaric strategies. A famous text, *Pae.* 9, begins by offering the same cultural syllepsis: the bold start is an address to the sunbeam, the foil to the poem being the crisis brought by an eclipse, and only later does the poem move on to ritual invocation of Phoibos, so that identity and difference between the god and the sun are a main subtext for the entire song.

Another general point that can be suggested, although I have no space to offer a stylistic analysis, is that both the paeans and the *Carmen* are peculiar in the lyric work of their own composers for a relative simplicity and restrained attitude, to be read both as a generic marker of difference from other registers of lyric style, and as a careful response to the problems of performance, instruction, and decorum that were raised by the ritual occasions. Both Pindar and Horace are conditioned in their choices by similar factors, including the peculiarity of the theme – Apollo, not (for instance) Dionysos – and the social and moral personality of the performers – groups of young people saying things and using words that are perceived as appropriate to their age.[24]

The problem with this kind of identification of genre is that it tends to privilege similarities over difference. And yet one of the effects of this link with a distant Greek genre is to enhance difference. For example, one of the striking things about the *Carmen* is that an apotropaic function is not central:[25] Apollo the Healer is briefly hailed at 63–4, dangers and crises are only implicitly present. So the new poem distances itself from a typical perception of paeans, as attested by textbook definitions and poetic fragments, in terms of a defensive song, performing/celebrating liberation from political crisis, disease, danger. This is what Horace himself seems to imply as an expectation, when he defines this communal function of poetry in the epistle to Augustus:

> auertit morbos, metuenda pericula pellit   (*Epist.* 2.1.136)

in terms reminiscent of the *Carmen* and of the ancient etymology of paean from *pauo* and *katapausis*,[26] except that his own paeanic poem is less simple than that.

The privileging of Apollo and Diana is neatly mirrored by the gender division of the chorus, but it would be wrong to maintain that this kind of double chorus was characteristic of paeans. Indeed, a singing chorus of boys and girls is extremely rare in Greek culture, participation of female voices in paeanic performance is anomalous,[27] and Alexandrian editors would have been embarrassed by a text for Apollo and Diana that suggests both an all-female partheneion and an all-male paean. All the testimonies confirm that young men or boys were the expected performers of paeans, while extant partheneia are very different in tone from the Horatian poem. It is best to develop a point made by Peter White,[28] that this innovative poem is heir to a shadowy tradition of Roman festivals, apparently dominated by chthonic cult, apotropaic purification, and regularly featuring choruses of virgins. The double chorus could be a compromise and a short cut for the merger between tradition and innovation. So one sensible way to describe Horace's innovation would be that a tradition of 'Latin partheneia' has been modified by the insertion of a new model, the 'Latin paean', with the new Augustan *Ludi* strongly supporting the new centrality of Apollo, daytime rituals, and non-chthonic elements. This compromise could also have had a deft metaliterary function for those who brought an experience in Latin poetry to the Augustan *Ludi*: because the only places where double choruses of boys and girls had been performing in this style were poems in books, the Diana songs at Catullus 34 and Horace, *Carm.* 1.21.

Being exceptional in Roman culture as a performed song for Apollo and Diana, and also a successor to an infinite series of Greek songs for the same gods, the poem is being quietly daring and witty in its address to Apollo and Diana as (2–3) *colendi semper et culti: semper … culti* is the avowal of a Greek tradition which has never become Roman before, and it is up to this new song to make the tradition happen. To say that Apollo

is and has always been by tradition a theme of songs is indeed very Greek
(*Hymn. Hom. Ap.* 19–21), but the *topos* becomes a programme when
transcribed in a different language and culture.

HELLENISATION

'The poem is too Hellenized to be representative' (Nisbet–Hubbard
(1970) 253)

The reason why I insisted on the dialectics between Greek genre and
Horatian text is that this dynamic negotiation involves more than just
poetics and literary choices. Viewed thus, the poem is a meditation on the
unique status of Rome *vis-à-vis* Greek culture, as well as a self-reflexive
utterance about the position of poetry in Roman society.

The stunning variety of Greek performances for the gods is evoked
within the poem through similarity and difference. Modes of Greek communal song include local pride, verbal links between ritual and divine
power, negotiation of transitional moments in life, apotropaic prayer,
politics, and military history, self-assertion and self-definition, education and celebration, as well as attempts at pan-Hellenic synthesis. Now
those modes of public communication are rehearsed, selected and re-
formulated within a poetic act that comments on the peculiar status
of Rome. If they agree to view Rome through the traditions of Greek
communal performance, the Romans end up with some kind of double
perspective. On the one hand, Rome is a *polis* writ large, on the other
it is a puzzling and threatening exception. The *Carmen* comments on
this ambiguity by eliding mediations: the link with the Sibylline oracle
perpetuates an antique image of a city-state ruling over ancient Latium,
and the *Carmen* is completely silent about one of the main themes of
Augustan literature, Italy.[29] The ripples of Roman horizons in this poem
seem to end at Mt Algidus, the battlefield where the Early Republic had
struggled with an alien Latium, a spatial as well as historical benchmark.
The vertical landscape[30] of the poem connects the seven hills, the privi-
leged Palatine and Aventine, Jupiter's seat on the Capitoline, Alba Longa,
and the Algidus, but ignores the lowlands of Italy and mentions the *litus
Etruscum* only as a beach-head to be conquered (38): nor is there any personal glance towards Daunia or Apulia. In this perspective, the *Carmen* is
just another Greek-style song for a nuclear *polis*, celebrating its privileges,
charter myths, traditions, and divine protectors. At the opposite extreme,
the mention of Medi and Indi brings in a sense of expansionism that
pointedly contradicts the defensive Hellenism of the city-song. A Greek
Apolline song mentioning the god's protection against the Medes makes

an interesting comparison: 'Lord Phoibos, you yourself once fortified the high city . . . now likewise keep the hybristic army of the Medes away from this city, so that to you the people may convey memorable hecatombs in joy when the spring comes, delighting in the lyre and heartwarming feast and the choruses of paeans and shouts around your altars' (Theognis 773–9 about a *polis* in the early fifth century). The Palatine altars of Roman Apollo have proved much more powerful, and require a different song for a unique community, a contradictory entity in Greek terms, as unitary as a *polis*, as panoramic and totalising as the pan-Hellenic centres of Delphi, Olympia and Delos where Greek religious song had reached its zenith.

The unique nature of Rome is also demonstrated by the ongoing discourse of Hellenisation, and here again the invocation and transformation of paeans is a move within a broader strategy, cultural and political. It is important to remember, with Feeney (1998) 28, that the *Ludi* – even without the song – are already a major step in the competitive and contested history of Roman Hellenism. All the sacrifices were performed *Achiuo ritu*, the traditional signifier of the empowerment of Roman religion:[31] the Romans recognise their cults as made in two ways, their own way and the Greek way, and they keep those two traditions, the Roman and the other, separated and co-existent. This 'Greek' enclosure within traditional religion is in fact very Republican, but by re-enacting it the Augustan cult revels in ambiguity: the Greek element is both revival and revolution. No Roman magistrate had ever performed 'Greek style' quite the same way. The *Ludi* co-operate with this duplicity by alternating old-style shows and 'modern' theatre, both appropriations of Greek culture, but linked to different periods. The *Carmen* contributes to this dynamics and marks advances in the web of Graeco-Roman connections. The Parcae of 25–8, singers, spinners, goddesses of Fate, are a transcription of Greek Moirai that is different from the Moerae of the night-time *Ludi*, and their name brings out a competence over childbirth that is emplotted in a different way in the Greek Moirai, and not explicitly recalled in the ritual, while their power of singing the truth offers a Latin transference of the Sibylline Greek textuality. The other divine power related to childbirth, Eileithuia, is also present in the night-time proceedings, but the song adds a significant multiplication of names

> lenis, Ilithyia, tuere matres,
> siue tu Lucina probas uocari
>   seu Genitalis;   (13–16)

a stimulating choice, because the Latin version of Eileithuia has to decide whether she is closer to Diana or to Juno (both regular bearers of the name

Lucina in Rome), and if she opts for Romanisations such as Lucina and Genitalis, instead of being the Ilithyia of the night-time ritual, she will also become a much more benevolent (*lenis*) goddess: Eileithuia is basically a goddess of birthpangs and *mogos* (labour), while Lucina is perceived in Latin as a luminous goddess of deliverance[32] and bringing to the world.

The choice of restarting the long-lost and perhaps never Romanised tradition of paeans is important in this context. Like Augustus, Horace is an antiquarian and an innovator. He recuperates Pindar, a difficult challenge *vis-à-vis* the more obvious attractions of Hellenistic praise poetry, but the paeanic echoes highlight precisely the boldest innovations in the ritual, Apollo, the solar imagery, the Palatine complex, the sacrificing emperor. Fraenkel qualifies the *Carmen* as 'revolutionary',[33] to emphasise its original synthesis of old and new, and independence from the political context, and he was certainly conscious that the same strong language had been used by Mommsen[34] to define the aggressive and subversive political strategy that finds expression in the *Ludi saeculares*. It is not very useful to try to dissociate those two semiotic projects. In this light, the recall of Pindar is not merely a sophisticated ornament of literary allusion or the result of an independent artistic research. The *Carmen* goes beyond the Republican tradition of linking political achievement and competitive appropriations of Greek art and culture. The analogy between poet and *princeps* is closer than in Republican tradition: Horace is inventing a tradition and his poetry cannot use a ready-made cultural code or advertise a new import, but has to re-create its own Greekness; the Augustan programme is a bricolage of antiquarianism and Hellenism oriented on the invention of an *una tantum* event of sacrifice and palingenesis.[35]

GENRE, TEXT AND IDEOLOGY

Discussions of the ideology of this text face well-known dilemmas. The poem can be read within the context of the *Ludi*, at the risk of becoming a passive and marginal contribution to the overall message of the Games. It can be recuperated *qua* vintage Horatian poetry, as by Fraenkel, but at the risk of losing significant connections. The wisest operative solution is the model of interpretation tried out by Feeney:[36] the *Carmen* and the *Ludi* are both semiotic, communicative protocols of the highest complexity. The *Carmen* does not simply mirror the festival – indeed, it stands at a very oblique angle to the celebrations and would severely distort our vision of what really happened, unless we had other independent evidence – but it is also true that it interacts with the proceedings. Neither the *Ludi* nor the *Carmen* are copies of a master-discourse, a pre-existent ideological model, but both are involved in the production and the workings of ideology.

White (1993) 124–7 has warned us that the *Carmen* does not fit the model of a court poem written under programmatic pressure from Augustus. It is easy to check the explicit presence of the *princeps* in the text, and the result is that Augustus is central only to a short vignette, as a sacrificer and a conqueror, but most of the poem is given over to communal prayer and traditional institutions – senate, *XVuiri*, cults. But of course it would be easy to retort that this subtle approach to politics is precisely what has always been characterised as Augustanism: *res publica restituta*, a voluntary containment of the imperial power, mediation, coalescence and integration of republican traditions and new authority. The real dilemma then is whether we recognise the *Carmen* as an active player in this area, or as a reflex of a stereotyped ideological construct. But his reception of Greek communal lyric should have warned Horace that this kind of communication is always complex and cannot escape a considerable responsibility: the song is both about the audience and to the audience; the message reflects shared ideology and affects shared ideology.

The issue of genre and poetic choices is again relevant here. By turning the clock back to Pindar and classical Greece, Horace eschews precisely the kind of celebratory poetics that White considers as a road significantly not taken in spite of the Augustan occasion. Perhaps the poem comments on this bifurcation when the address to the sun refracts a communal prayer by Pindar (above, p. 116), because the obvious alternative, should the poem belong to the Hellenistic tradition of paeans as celebrations of rulers, would be to read the *alme Sol . . .* stanza as a straightforward celebration of the emperor. By hymning Demetrios the Besieger as a Sun-god and a saviour god,[37] the fourth-century Athenians had substituted a new ideology for the communal tradition of civic paeans. Horace alludes to precisely the same approach in a curious intratext of *Carm.* 4.2.46–7: the trochaic slogan *o sol pulcher, o laudande* is a collective utterance and is quoted within the poem as an example of the unsophisticated celebrations that are called for in real life, outside the space of monodic lyric. So the poetics of the *Carmen* is a return to classical Greece, and confirms the autonomy from celebration that White finds so characteristic – save of course that this choice too can still be read as a quintessentially 'Augustan' choice. It will always be possible for the address to the sun to be linked to the solar imagery of imperial rule,[38] but the poem offers only a potential, paratactic link, not a direct syncretism, and relies on a co-operative audience. The discarded possibility, celebrative poetry that crudely mixes hymnic forms and ruler cult, enhances the bold poetics of the *Carmen*, and its ambitious imagining of a communal function for a new Roman *uates*. The ironical undertone is that this important communicative act depends on the slender thread of one individual poet's negotiation with the most difficult of Greek traditions, without any support in the traditional positioning of poets in Roman society.

All the other main aspects of the poetics of the *Carmen* have inescapable Augustan implications. The revolutionary emergence of Apollo with Diana in the traditional pantheon of the *Ludi* has been regularly viewed as the cypher of the Augustan intervention, but now we can also notice that the generic choice of the 'neo-Pindaric paean' is a deft commentary on this cultic politics. The spectator who is conversant with the Hellenic tradition of cult poetry will quickly realise that precisely *qua* paean the *Carmen* will be entitled to go much further than the Augustan intervention in the programme of the *Ludi* has dared to go. In the proceedings, people had seen Apollo becoming a central god of Rome, precisely when the archaising poetics of the *Ludi* would have allowed only a different space for him, a Greek god traditionally set ouside the pomerium. The inclusion of the Palatine, the offer of one of the sacrificial days to Apollo and Diana, were clear indications, but there was still so much that sounded as recuperation of the antique: Eileithuia and the Moerae, the chthonic offerings, Juno and Jupiter, the Capitoline cult. And here, at the end of the proceedings, Horace shows that poetry can go even further, and be both more backward-looking and more innovative than the festival. With striking economy, the author of the *Carmen* recuperates a neglected Greek genre that is recognised as specifically Apollo's genre. The generic choice opens up a sequence of hesitations and witty negotiations with divine powers, with some traditional gods exploiting crevices and blanks to make their presence perceived – Juno, for example, in the reference to marriage (*iugandis*) and in the diffraction of Lucina between herself and Diana – in the paeanic dominance and radiance of Apollo and Diana. The more delicate positioning of Jupiter is facilitated again by the Greek model, since Zeus had always been lateral but powerful in the classical paeans. The rhetorical strategy exploits indeterminacy and even referential ambiguity: the impressive strophic beginning

Roma si uestrum est opus ...   (37)

does not allow an easy decision between the couple Apollo–Diana (the last-named gods who were invoked in the context at lines 33–6) and the general likelihood that some of the main state gods are also, or even mainly, being implied, and this alternative is enhanced by the repeated invocation *di* that follows, unspecific, at a certain distance (45–6).

So when the poet addresses the gods to remind them of the offers

Quaeque uos bobus ueneratur albis   (49)

it was only through the discovery of the epigraphical *Acta*[39] that modern scholars have come to realise that those are not, after all, Apollo and Diana again, because it was for the Capitoline gods that cattle were sacrificed, as the original spectators would have known. In other words, the first-time audience was in a position to realise how partial the poem was to the children of Leto, while the readers, doubtless equipped with Greek learning, were bound to bring to the text a generic competence, in order to make sense of the poetic recreation of the secular programme. The spectacular asymmetry of the poem in the context of the *Ludi* has a Hellenising meaning in this perspective: the omission of the night-time rituals,[40] the ones that were looking back to the 'chthonic' tradition of Republican *Ludi* in the Campus,[41] fits the generic mould perfectly. Paeans had always been the opposite pole of chthonic cults, darkness, and death ritual. Conversely, the isotopy that aligns Apollo, the sun, the Palatine, Augustus, Alba, and whiteness, is the Roman version of a paeanic idiom.

Readers conversant with Pindaric poems 'for the gods' would also have easily realised that there is no mutual exclusion between strategies of representation and self-representation.[42] The paradox of the *Carmen* is that the Greek tradition that it invokes requires regular repetition and a rich calendar of performances (paeans are 'seasonal' or 'periodical' unlike, for example, dirges[43] or marriage songs) and so is at home in a communal song-and-dance culture; but the setting of the *Ludi* guarantees that for Horace, as a Latin poet of communal lyric, the sun will shine only once.[44] Common sense has it that you cannot have a genre *just once*: one individual text can hardly be recognised in generic terms; only serial repetition and variation can constitute a generic matrix. But here again, it is wrong to separate the *Carmen* from its social setting. As a Latin paean, the poem was one of a kind, and must have been more challenging and innovative than we usually assume: the choice of a unique revival of a long-lost Greek genre mirrors the idea of the Augustan *Ludi*, because *Ludi saeculares* means once in a lifetime.[45]

9   *SOLVS SAPIENS LIBER EST*
     Recommissioning lyric in *Epistles* I

Horace begins his first book of *Epistles* by answering the question that many in his audience were asking. It has been put to him by Maecenas concerning the long dry spell that has passed since the publication of *Odes* Books 1–3. 'Will there be a curtain call?' Maecenas has asked. 'When can we expect the sequel to those spectacular *carmina* of three years past?' To which Horace replies: 'I am retired now, like old Veianius who dedicated his arms to Hercules after so many battles in the arena' (*Epist.* 1.1.4–6). Hidden away in his country estate, he says, he is glad to be rid of the ring, the notoriety, and the noise. His answer is the standard 'no' or 'not now' of an Augustan poet backing away from a big, laborious project. But here the refusal has a not-so-standard edge, aggressive and cynical, that derives from an uncharacteristic deployment of two ancient metaphors for the poet's high epic pursuits. The chariot race had been used as a symbol of martial epic and epinician since the days of Choerilus and Pindar, and the metaphor figuring such high-flying projects as a kind of warfare and/or Olympic *agon* was equally ancient and well worn.[1] But here the figures have passed from their original Greek setting into a Roman one, and with that transfer they have picked up an alien and indelible tarnish. For the chariot-driver of Hor. *Epist.* 1.1.7–9 is no Olympian aristocrat, well born and godlike in his moment of victory. He is a slave or, at best, a freed slave. No *eques*, but equine in being owned and driven. Likewise the gladiator whose feats of strength, in marked contrast to those of an Olympic champion, actively degrade rather than ennoble.[2] Moreover, these images put Maecenas in an unflattering role as well. He, it seems, is the *lanista*, a ludic entrepreneur, or at least an adoring fan, determined to wrench one last fight from a favourite retired gladiator, one last chariot race from a former champion driver.

Thus, with the oddly Romanised figures that open this poem we have a picture of the poet's lyric enterprise that the *Odes* themselves never paint – never even hint at. Namely, lyric song as ludic spectacle (*lyrica = ludicra*). And with that odd figuring comes a radical shift in the way we are made to view the poet's world, his work, his relationship to Maecenas, and to his once proud public achievements in lyric. The warrior and *triumphator* of *Carm.* 3.30 has been remade here, and cheapened. The priest of the Muses (*Odi profanum uulgus, et arceo, Carm.* 3.1), regrettably, has gone Hollywood. The story this one-time *uates* now tells is of a jaded popular performer, done with playing to Rome's grimy crowds and risking his life as a star in their tasteless *ludi.* All tongue-in-cheek perhaps, and it would be easy to exaggerate the picture's potential to shock. Still, the image has a rough edge to it that readers must work to ignore. But ignoring it may be the wrong tack to take. For in this opening *recusatio* we have what turns out to be only the first of many suggestions of the poet's ultimate disgust, and of his having lost that old sense of self that he so proudly proclaimed in his *Odes.* Disillusionment, exhaustion, and the loss of his old, noble self are themes touched on not just here but in many, if not all, of the poems that follow. And that gives me reason to suspect that this opening *recusatio* is not simply a handy 'way into' the *Epistles,* that is, a way of initiating one generic enterprise by signalling the end of another. Rather, it is a key to how we figure the poet's purposes in taking up this work, and how we handle his disillusionment in the poems that follow, that famous malaise that gets wrestled against and purged in the course of the book. For his jadedness is obvious already in his initial 'ludic' perspective on his past achievements. It is not simply ironically toyed with there, tongue-in-cheek, then set aside as he gets on to the 'real business' of the *Epistles.* It *is* the real business of the *Epistles,* set up as such in the first lines of the book's first poem. The search for spiritual and physical health, his desire to locate a new direction for his talents, and recover a lost freedom, themes underscored in *Epist.* 1.1 as central aims of the book, do not simply follow upon his opening refusal, they derive from it and persist in reflecting back upon it in significant ways.

Recently A. Traina has argued that the whole of Book 1 can be read as 'the longest and most involved [*recusatio*] that the poet ever addressed to Maecenas'.[3] I take up that suggestion here, but with a different emphasis, arguing that perhaps the book is less about refusing (or *just* refusing), as Traina expertly maintains, than it is about finding a way to accept. That is, the performed agonies of this book have to do with coming to terms with Maecenas' offer, chafing at its too narrow limits, and redefining it to suit the poet's own terms. Thus, I maintain, inside the search for strength and spiritual health is a second search for the resources needed to produce the lyric poems that Maecenas, and his adoring public, now expect from him, a retired lyric champion. But how can he do this without, in turn, becoming the servile ludic performer that he imagines himself becoming in the opening lines of *Epist.* 1.1? That is the Catch 22 of his patron's 'generous' offer, the place he is stuck as the book begins. The poems that follow are a means to his breaking free. Saying 'no' to Maecenas, in the end, involves telling him the 'when' and 'how' of his return as *uates*, so a necessary part of the project involves taking a stand and speaking to Maecenas in uncharacteristically aggressive ways, something we see already in the first lines of *Epist.* 1.1. For by speaking that way, the poet actively demonstrates the αὐτάρκεια ('self-reliance') that he so desperately seeks through these poems, the true freedom that these *Epistles* take as one of their central themes. In speaking that way, the poet shows that his epistolary regime is working. For every letter in the book, regardless of content, persists in saying 'no' to Maecenas, and thus contributing to that desired αὐτάρκεια. For every letter prolongs his absence from the lyric fray, by offering to Maecenas yet more of what he so obviously has not asked for.

But what, precisely, does Maecenas want this time? How can he think that *Odes* Books 1–3 were not enough, and that Horace has somehow left something undone? Too often commentators on the *Epistles* assume that the offer refused in the opening lines of Book 1 is simply an invitation to write more of the same. But here again Traina, following Cima and Gigon, has made an excellent case for limiting the scope of the poet's refusal.[4] He draws on the claim of *Epist.* 1.1.10 *uersus et cetera ludicra pono* to show that 'Horace's renunciation is not so much of lyric in general as it is of erotic lyric.' And thus, he says, 'by saying nothing of civil lyric, which is not *ludere* but *canere*, and constituted no small part of his Aeolic program, Horace has left the door open for his return as *uates*'.[5] It is an excellent suggestion, and I am altogether convinced that the poet's refusal in the poem's opening lines is not as far-reaching as it is commonly assumed to be. But I think that Traina may have reversed the poles of 'civil' and 'erotic' in his treatment of *Epist.* 1.1.1–10. For while I agree that the issue in these lines has something to do with the poet's return as *uates*, I am not convinced that the claim of line 10 shuts the door on erotic poetry and leaves it open for the civil/Aeolic. In fact, it may do just the opposite. For the poet has just cast his return to lyric as a return to the city, to the crowds, and to the two principal venues of the *ludi circenses*. Maecenas, he says, wants to shut him up in his old training-school (*includere ludo*). So what can he be thought to have sworn off with *uersus et cetera ludicra pono* in line 10? Is he saying goodbye to his 'youthful trifles' (*OLD* s.v. *ludicrum* 1), or to the horse-driven strains of grand, public lyric, cast here as a kind of 'public entertainment' (*OLD* s.v. *ludicrum* 2)?

But perhaps the more important question here concerns not what the refusal says about what is being sworn off, but the way it affects our figuring of Maecenas' offer; that is, what it says about what he wants *this time*. For perhaps that is the reason that the poet's lyric work is given such an uncharacteristically debased look in the opening figures of *Epist.* 1.1. Maecenas is not asking for a return to lyric *per se*, but to the grand and engaged songs of the public fighter and benefactor; to epinician and to songs of war, as the figures suggest. The more relaxed, private sides of the poet's lyric self (playboy, subumbral lounger, etc.) are absent from the poem's opening figures, perhaps because Maecenas has not asked the poet to bring them back. We recall from the first poem of *Odes* Book 4 that Horace begins his return to song by paring away his old lyric self, telling us not to expect Cinara's old lover this time. In lines that deliberately recall the opening figures of *Epist.* 1.1, he says that Venus has attempted to stir in him old 'wars' and to 'steer' him, horse-like, into his accustomed erotic haunts. But he objects that he is now too 'stiff with age' to obey her soft commands, so he hands over erotic themes to the young and noble Paullus Maximus.[6] The songs of Book 4, we are led to believe, will be of a different, and more mature sort. Building temples to Venus, he says, belongs to the young. This book is concerned with monuments of a different kind.

So, in retrospect, we know that Horace does return to lyric in his *Carmen saeculare* and fourth book of *Odes*, but that the lyric he returns to there is the most openly political and least nugatory of all the poems he ever wrote.[7] In case we failed to notice, the martial and equine allusions opening *Carm.* 4.1 remind us that the 'refusal' of *Epist.* 1.1 was short-lived, so with Traina I prefer to see that *recusatio* less as a refusal *per se*, than as a way of hinting at the poet's eventual return to lyric, and of his chafing at certain restrictions being put upon that return, making it seem both common and servile. He objects in line 4 of *Epist.* 1.1 that he is now too old for the fray: *non eadem est aetas*. But that may touch on not only his ageing, but on changes in 'the age' in which he now finds himself living. New pressures have been brought to bear, not because of any imagined failure on his part – so often assumed to trouble the writer of these letters – but because of his magnificent, even 'spectacular' success. With that success, given the times and the (un)usual workings of Roman power-relations, come new expectations of what he should now write, and how he should write it. What does it mean to be a high-profile friend of Maecenas now, not in 23 BCE, but in the early days of 19 BCE, as a re-tired champion of the lyric fray?[8] What expectations does success bring? How can he, a man of obscure, if not servile, origins, now handsomely rewarded for his talents and deeply involved in high-profile friendships, including even a friendship with Augustus himself, find anything like the true freedom of, say, an Aristippus whose *cultura potentis amici* was so famously flexible and insouciant?[9] More importantly, how can that kind of freedom actually express itself in poems that are at once reciprocal, and thus engaged with the social and political concerns of his well-placed friends, and yet true to the poet's own likes and beliefs?

Such are central questions of *Epistles* Book 1, at the core of the poet's performed discontent. The lessons taught here, to others, are lessons that the poet needs to hear first for himself, not in dialogue with himself, but as lessons directed *from him to them*. He needs the letter form. For by telling friends what they need to hear, in letters that speak to them openly (with one stunning exception[10]) and, at times, aggressively ('you're money-obsessed, Quinctius', 'watch your tongue, Lollius', etc.), he gets to see and hear himself in the role of a well-intentioned friend, confident in himself, and unmuzzled in his relationships with Rome's current and up-and-coming élite. Thus, in these letters he experiments with what he wants to become, sampling the freedom he wants to achieve. And that is the healing property of the epistolary form. The letters are not just about finding a stronger self, they are the regimen that makes such healing and reintegration happen.

Epistles 1.7, the second letter of the collection addressed to Maecenas, begins with yet another refusal. Not a different refusal this time, but the same refusal differently figured. The poet has been away from Rome, just as he was in *Epist.* 1.1, and Maecenas has wanted him back for some time. Convalescing at his villa, he is determined to stay away for at least one month more. But if winter sets in, he says in lines 11–13, he may be away a bit longer:

> ad mare descendet *uates tuus* et sibi parcet
> contractusque leget: *te, dulcis amice*, reuiset
> cum Zephyris, si concedes, et hirundine prima.

> *your* uates *will go down to the sea and take it easy on himself, huddled up with his books. If you allow it, sweet friend, he will come to see you again (in spring), with the coming of warm Zephyrs and the first swallow.*

Maecenas is 'sweet friend' to Horace, Horace is *uates* to Maecenas. His own *uates*. The terminology matters, for again it lets us think that conditions have been put upon the poet's return. Maecenas wants the prompt return of his beloved *uates*, a term that Horace uses consistently in his works to designate not his lyric self in its full, varied character, but his higher 'public' lyric voice.[11] That, it seems, is the role Maecenas is anxious to have him revive: 'I'll be your (extra-generous) friend. You be my own *uates*.'

Then follows the story of the Calabrian host who urges his well-fed guest to eat more of his pears in order to obligate the man to himself all the more.[12] 'You are not like that', Horace says to Maecenas in lines

14–15. That is to say, 'you have given me gifts precious to both you and me alike, not mere hog-fodder. And I am terribly grateful for them.' And yet, despite the disclaimer, it is clear that Maecenas resembles the pushy Calabrian in one important sense: he is pushing! He wants *his* poet to take more of the fine feast he has set before him, and to linger a while longer even though he has by now fed himself quite full. Horace says in lines 24–8:

> dignum praestabo me etiam pro laude merentis.
> quodsi me noles usquam discedere, reddes
> forte latus, nigros angusta fronte capillos,
> reddes dulce loqui, reddes ridere decorum et
> inter uina fugam Cinarae maerere proteruae.

> *I will show myself worthy, even considering my benefactor's renown. But if you don't want me to go away anywhere, then give me back my strong flank, my dark, thick hair, give me back my sweet talk, an attractive laugh, and, over the wine, let me grieve over losing come-hither Cinara.*

The dinner-party metaphor is still active here. Maecenas, taking the host's part, insists that his favourite guest stay, have a drink, and enjoy the party. But the poet has had enough. He wants to leave (*discedere*) because his playboy days, he claims, are done, his sexual stamina spent. Clearly the lines can be taken as a lament for lost youth, and there is no reason to think they are not that. But perhaps they hint at something else as well.[13] For we have just been told that Maecenas wants the prompt return of his *uates*, a word that shuts out so much of what Horace was in so many of his more nugatory modes in *Odes* Books 1–3. Perhaps there really is a sense in which Maecenas can give all of these lost components of late-night partying back to the poet and make him young again. The lover-boy of these lines can come back easily enough in song, but is that what Maecenas wants? Perhaps this time he wants song of a different, more restricted, sort.

And so, at this point in the poem, the tone becomes edgy and unusually aggressive. Two quick exemplary tales are told, then a long one, each inviting a different view of the tension introduced between generous (but pushy) host and put-upon guest. In the first of these stories, the little vixen resembles the dinner guest of lines 14–19 in being fed full and unable to leave. 'If I am squeezed in by the image', the poet says in line 34, that is, if I am like that fox stuck in the bin, 'then I sign everything back.' 'And watch me do it with a smile', he adds in line 39.[14] In the second tale he recalls the events of Homer, *Od.* 4.601–8, where Telemachus politely refuses the horses offered to him by his host, Menelaus, on the grounds that Ithaca, his homeland, is unsuited for horses, with no open plains for racing.[15] *paruum parua decent* Horace says in conclusion, in words that strongly recall his many refusals to write poetry of a certain grand and martial type.[16] He prefers 'unwarlike' Tarentum, he says, and 'empty' Tibur to 'kingly' Rome.[17] And so the language of horses and racing plains, of small things preferred to large, of leisure to war, and so on, just as the language of 'thin' (*tenuis*) versus 'corpulent' (*pleno . . . corpore*) in the story of the over-fed fox above, all conspire in this story to suggest that the 'gift' being refused here, and so aggressively agonised over, is not a basket of pears, nor even a simple invitation to return home.[18]

In the final long tale of Philippus and Volteius Mena we have yet another story of a 'horse-loving' (= *phil* + *hippus*) gift-giver who pushes too hard, and of a receiver not well suited to the gift he has been given. Philippus first spies Mena 'delicately cleaning his nails' in the empty shade of the barbershop in lines 50–1, and this clearly does not bode well for what follows. For just how likely is it that a man who likes to lounge about in the shade and keep his nails clean will do well as a dirt-farmer? To his credit, Mena first says 'no' to the rich man's overtures. But, with time, after his best excuses have been spent, and Philippus has refused to take the hint, he finally gives in and becomes a regular guest at the rich man's feasts. A bad choice. His old lounge-about freedom quickly disappears, and like a fish on a hook (*piscis ad hamum*, 74), he becomes a steady client at the morning roll-call, a dinner guest at the evening *cena*. But even more oppressive is the gift of the farm that follows. This is no pleasurable retreat set high in the Sabine hills, but a place of wearisome toil, with vines to be tended, fields to be ploughed, sheep and goats to be fed (and not an inspirational spring in sight!). The city-boy tries his best, but the work gets the better of him. Quickly that ill-fitting gift turns sour, and he returns to Philippus late one night, filthy and unshorn, having not seen a barber in months, and he begs that he give him back his old life: *uitae me redde priori*, 95. His last words deliberately recall Horace's own plea to Maecenas in line 27: *reddes dulce loqui, reddes ridere decorum*.

The story does not fit with what we 'know' of the relationship of Horace to Maecenas from earlier versions of the same tale. Most obviously, it has Philippus finding Mena, then pursuing him relentlessly, quite unlike the way Maecenas kept Horace wondering and waiting in *Sat.* 1.6. The sweet little villa of *Sat.* 2.6 here becomes a sweatshop and a money pit, with the terms of Maecenas's outright 'gift' now rewritten as a comparably small 'loan' to be paid back. Thus, some have seen this story as evidence of a rift between Horace and Maecenas, and the poem itself as an outright conclusion of their friendship.[19] I prefer to see it not referring to any dire crisis in the poet's relationship with Maecenas, or to any frustration with his work-a-day life on the farm. Rather it helps us imagine what that relationship has the potential to become in 19 BCE, describing what that once famous friendship will look like if Maecenas persists in pushing Horace too hard to accept a gift that is much too big for his talents, and too grimy for his well-trimmed nails. The gift will be ruined through the shade-lover's ineptitude, and there will be hard feelings on both sides. Certainly we are meant to compare this story with earlier ones and to feel the mismatch that exists between them.[20] And just in case we are too literal-minded in matching this exemplary tale to its frame, Horace is quick to remind us in the poem which directly follows that his farm is thriving. There he tells Albinovanus Celsus that no hail has crushed the vines, no heat has sapped the olive trees. His malaise, he says, is a physical and spiritual one. And no amount of doctoring has managed to make it any better.

The companion piece to *Epist.* 1.7, where Horace warns Maecenas that he plans to 'go down to the seaside' (*ad mare descendet*, 11) when the first snow flies, is *Epist.* 1.15, where he asks his friend Vala about the winter weather in the region of Veglia and Salerno, then wonders whether he might borrow his villa there by the sea (*ad mare*, 18). The winter convalescence projected in 1.7 is being mapped out in 1.15. The Muse has prescribed it, he says. Antonius *Musa*, the physician who in 23 BCE brought Augustus from the brink of death with a unique cold-water regime, cold driving out cold, has refused to let Horace visit the warm springs at Baiae.[21] In his *Life of Horace*, Suetonius records that it was precisely when Augustus was ailing and unable to meet the demands of his daily routine (presumably in 23 BCE) that he approached Maecenas in a letter and asked him to urge Horace to step away from his leisure-loving table and to take on the bigger responsibilities of an official letter-writer in his court. A subsequent letter from Augustus to Horace indicates that the poet declined the emperor's offer *by citing his own ill health*.[22] Yet he takes up letter-writing all the same, as his next poetic work, and this project he describes not as a detriment to his health, but as a means to his healing. Thus we have put before us in these lines one of the great ironies of the poet's epistolary convalescence. Augustus cannot write letters when sick. Horace, precisely because he is sick, must write them. Not for Augustus, as requested, but for himself.

Horace wants to winter at Baiae, and to steep his ailing frame in its warm sulphur springs. But his doctor-Muse has forbidden it, insisting instead on the cold-water regime that was his signature therapy, so Horace looks for other options. Thanks to Musa, he worries openly about what waters he will find there, at his borrowed villa by the sea. He asks Vala in lines 14–16:

> maior utrum populum frumenti copia pascat,
> collectosne bibant imbres puteosne perennes
> iugis aquae – nam uina nihil moror illius orae.

> *(I wonder) whether the grain supply feeding the populace is bigger there,*
> *whether they drink rainwater gathered in tanks, or from springs that never*
> *go dry – for I don't like the wine of that region.*

The poet's worries bear an uncanny resemblance to the inspirational language of poets since Pindar, for whom the rain-trough figured as a symbol of counterfeit inspiration, common and secondhand, against the true and natural genius of the clear-flowing spring.[23] Pindar claims (on numerous occasions) to have drawn his inspiration from the waters of Dirce, his home-town spring, and thereby to have become himself a gushing fountain of song.[24] So the poet's concern for waters, here, under strict orders of Musa, has the distinct packaging of a quest for poetic inspiration and purpose. By casting those concerns in the pre-loaded, symbolic terms of Pindar (besides Callimachus, and many others), he triggers for us a second quest inside the first. We hear him ask, 'What inspiration will I find there, in the healing waters of that place?' A way of asking 'What kind of poet will I become?' And we are left to wonder about the spring that flows in his own backyard, the one that was supposed never to run dry. What has become of its inspiration and restorative powers? Why are his old haunts at Tibur, Baiae, and Tarentum no longer enough?

The ague of *Epist.* 1.1 persists, prominent again in 1.15, where the poet casts about for a borrowed villa and cure.[25] The water-trough and spring of lines 15–16 remind us of Pindar, thus touching one of the more obvious sides of Horace's lost lyric self. But the draughts of the lines that directly follow work to quite another effect, even though they must be imagined as part of the same seaside regime. The poet tells Vala in lines 17–21:

> rure meo possum quiduis perferre patique:
> ad mare cum ueni, generosum et lene requiro,
> quod curas abigat, quod cum spe diuite manet
> in uenas animumque meum, quod uerba ministret,
> quod me Lucanae iuuenem commendet amicae.

> *At my own country place I can tolerate and survive any (wine) you please.*
> *But when I come to the sea, I require one pedigreed and smooth, one to*
> *drive away my cares and, with its rich hope, to seep into my veins and*
> *mind. Wine that will serve me with words, make me young again, and*
> *attractive to my Lucanian girl.*

Here, the second side of the poet's cure, recalling the second pole of his lost lyric self. No water, this time, but wine, and of an amazingly restorative sort. He imagines himself remade by it, getting back his old sensualist ways by easing it down in long, lingering draughts (*manet*). Significantly, he imagines that wine 'serving' him with words, giving him a voice, and powers of charm and seduction long forgotten.[26] With the right amount of pampering, he says in line 24, he will return to the city (*inde domum*) a well-fed Phaeacian.

The emphasis here is no longer on staying away, but on finding a way to return, a long-lost Odysseus, restored by the waters and wine of a borrowed, Phaeacian villa. The poems that follow are framed by book-end scenes of the poet's water therapy (1.16.12–14, 1.18.104–12), but their central concern is with issues of freedom and self-reliance in one's dealings with men in power; that is, as *Epist.* 1.1.17 has it, with *regibus uti* ('using kings/patrons', repeated in lines 13 and 14) without stepping into the standard, unsavoury roles of a flatterer or an angry cynic. The lessons taught in these poems, offered to younger friends by a man who over the years has risen far, and played many of the roles his lessons teach and/or warn against along the way, lead into *Epist.* 1.19 in a special way.[27] For this is Horace's last letter to Maecenas, the man *he* has called 'king' (*rexque paterque | audisti coram*, 1.7.37–8), so we hear its teachings not simply as a continuation of the lessons taught from expert to ephebe, but as a case-study in those lessons, a performance of Horace's own *cultura potentis amici* in a pressure-filled interaction between a handsomely rewarded poet and his powerful, demanding friend. The poem opens by drawing together the principal themes of the poems that immediately precede, making water-drinking/wine-drinking, and the poet's search for health and independence, all part of the same question (*Epist.* 1.19.1–5):

> Prisco si credis, Maecenas docte, Cratino,
> nulla placere diu nec uiuere carmina possunt,
> quae scribuntur aquae potoribus. ut male sanos
> adscripsit Liber Satyris Faunisque poetas,
> uina fere dulces oluerunt mane Camenae.

> *If you believe old Cratinus, learned Maecenas, no songs written by water-drinkers can last for long and continue to gratify. Ever since Liber enrolled the sick/unsteady among his satyrs and fauns as poets, the sweet Muses have pretty well stunk of wine at daybreak.*[28]

We should assume an earlier letter here, a worried letter, from Maecenas to Horace. Later in the poem (lines 35–6), Horace has us imagine Maecenas pressing for answers about the mixed reception of his *Odes*.

And that, I believe, is the background we are to posit for these lines as well. Maecenas, we are to imagine, has been wringing his hands over the success of the published *carmina*. He has worried openly to the poet about their longevity, and their ability to 'gratify' (*placere*) for long. That word was given a special, Pindaric turn at *Epist.* 1.17.35, where *principibus placuisse uiris* ('gratifying [Rome's] leading men') recalls the parting wish of Pi. *Pyth.* 2.96 ἀδόντα δ' εἴη με τοῖς ἀγαθοῖς ὁμιλεῖν ('and may I gratify noble men, and keep company with them'). Horace will later recast Pindar's wish as a boast at *Epist.* 1.20.23 *me primis urbis belli placuisse domique* ('I have gratified the city's leaders at home and at war'). But here the issue is treated as unsolved, and we are left to worry with Maecenas and wonder whether the *Odes* have what it takes to both 'gratify' men in power, and 'last'. Has Horace failed at what Pindar, so famously, achieved? Has he been, for Maecenas, Pindaric enough?

If you believe Cratinus, Horace begins, maybe what your poet needs, is a good, stiff drink. Just consider the magnificent successes of heavy-drinking Homer (*uinosus*), and Ennius, who never took up the fight of panegyric epic unless reeling drunk (*nisi potus*). 'I will issue a decree assigning the sober to the forum and Libo's well. Serious sorts I will deprive of their right to sing.' Make that decree, he adds in lines 10–11, and there will be no limit to the number of poets stinking at daybreak.

The options considered are inelegant and extreme, with no suggestions of a happy middle-ground between Liber and Libo; between martial/panegyric epic and the gnarly oratory of the Elder Cato; nothing between fist-fighting delirium and dreary sobriety. And thus we are left with no sense that, like the mending poet of 1.15, one might drink just so much water and just so much wine as part of a mixed therapy, and that the inebriation achieved might be of a milder, more controlled sort, rendering one attractive rather than belligerent. Instead we are left without a middle; given, as it were, the flatterer and grumpy cynic of 1.18, with no Aristippus to negotiate between them. And what ultimately gets under the poet's skin about being left to deal with such ungainly theories of inspiration is that, in the deliberate contrast between *Liber* and *Libo*, we hear them being pawned off as rival expressions of 'freedom'. Thus, the famous apostrophe of lines 19–20, *o imitatores, seruum pecus*. For his part, Horace sees only slavishness here, not freedom. And in the lines that follow he paints a different picture of the freedom that he himself has achieved in song:

libera per uacuum posui uestigia princeps,
non aliena meo pressi pede. qui sibi fidet,
dux reget examen. Parios ego primus iambos
ostendi Latio, numeros animosque secutus

Archilochi, non res et agentia uerba Lycamben.
ac ne me foliis ideo breuioribus ornes,
quod timui mutare modos et carminis artem:
temperat Archilochi musam pede mascula Sappho,
temperat Alcaeus, sed rebus et ordine dispar.

(21–9)

*Free are the tracks that I have put down while leading the way across
an empty frontier. No one else's have I impressed with my foot. He who
is confident in himself directs the throng as their leader. I was the first to
show Parian iambs to Latium by following the rhythms and violent moods
of Archilochus, not his themes and the words that harried Lycambes. And
if, for this reason, you should decorate me with a scantier crown of leaves,
because I feared changing the measures and art of his song, it was with
her foot that manly Sappho tempered Archilochus' muse, and Alcaeus,
too, though in a different arrangement and with different themes.*

No 'gratifying the great' here, but a poet who is himself both *princeps* and
rex (*dux reget examen*). But some leaves have fallen from the laurel-crown
of *Carm.* 3.30. By now some have pegged him as a follower, rather than as
a truly original leader, for having kept with the basic metrical schemata of
his Greek models. Others, it seems, have thought him too free in his adaptations, wondering why he left Lycambes behind, and those kinky, lesbian
affairs of Sappho. But Horace re-states his case for the triumph he claimed
in *Carm.* 3.30 by arguing that following established metrical forms does
not necessarily make one a slavish imitator, nor does tossing aside the
themes that went with those metres make one irresponsible and licentious.
Line 24 makes the point with a neat antithesis: *ostendi Latio, numeros animosque secutus*. In claiming to have 'shown' foreign iambs to Latium, the
poet puts himself back in his old role of *triumphator* displaying conquered
troops and goods to the crowds at Rome. But that puts quite a different
spin on his 'following' Archilochus at the line's end – how, we may ask,
can there be anything free and ennobling in that!? But the image reminds
us that following is precisely what conquering generals do: they come last
in the procession, driving the conquered ahead of them, with never a hint
of their becoming anything less than godlike in their following.[29] Thus,
the poet makes a (hard to make) case for *leading by following*, to suggest that middle way his critics could not abide. And he makes a similar point in the case of the 'tempering'/'softening' (*temperat. . .temperat*,
28–9) of Archilochus' aggressive song by Sappho and Alcaeus. Here a
wine metaphor, matching the 'tempering' of bold Archilochus to the
'softening' of strong wine by the infusion of just the right amount of

water.[30] And thus, in a poem obsessed with the rival inspirational merits of water and wine, he opens a middle way between the ungainly extremes considered in the poem's opening lines.

But the lines not only teach these lessons about adapting and tempering, they exemplify them by stirring memories of earlier poems of Lucretius, Virgil, Propertius, and even Horace himself. Thus we hear them not simply as this poet's final say on what trailblazing poets do, and the ways of their tempering, but as his sample lesson in the ways of 'free' adaptation. Most obviously, the lines cue us to a number of similar scenes of trailblazing and triumph in Lucretius' *De rerum natura*, especially to Lucr. 3.3–4: *te sequor, o Graiae gentis decus, inque tuis nunc | ficta pedum pono pressis uestigia signis*.[31] Oddly, the message in these lines is not about leading, but about following, and that is the great irony of their being remembered in Horace's claim to have stepped in no one else's tracks. For by seeing this passage inside the claim, we spy Horace stepping in Lucretius' tracks, and right at the point where Lucretius pushed Callimachus aside to claim that he was not leading, but following straight in the tracks of his conquering hero, Epicurus.[32] Thus, the freedom vaunted comes packaged with suggestions of following, and of Horace's being led along in a rather long train. Still freedom, he insists, but not absolute. Perfect self-reliance, it seems, is the stuff of philosophical speculation, a pipe-dream kept alive by those who have never penned a line of poetry in tradition-obsessed Latin, or spent a single day in Rome as the poet-son of a freed slave. The freedom he knows from his dealings with patrons and his precursors in Greek and Latin poetry is of a much more limited, Aristippean kind. It is the freedom to shuttle between pre-set and tightly binding options.

Horace stood out as *triumphator* in *Carm.* 3.30, bringing a conquered, foreign song to Rome. We remember that image here (itself a remake of the proem to *Georgics* Book 3), but not without some colourful and, in the end, 'liberating' interference from the immediate context in which it is set. It is this interference, in the end, that renders the motif unspoiled, and the poet's tracks 'free'. For when he makes his claim to have stamped out 'free tracks' for himself, he has us imagine his champion, this time, not leading a procession up the Capitoline hill (though we remember him doing exactly that), but off in some remote, unspoiled place, wearing a leafy crown (*me foliis … ornes*, 26), at the head of a devoted 'throng' (*examen* = Gk θίασος) as their leader. Dionysian imagery has been filtered into the picture. Like the handsome stranger despised by Pentheus, the poet brings foreign customs in his wake, songs to be embraced by the common crowd. He has made Alcaeus a household name (*hunc … uulgaui*, 32–4), and taken great delight in 'bringing things un-remembered' (*immemorata ferentem*, 33) to Rome. This, on the heels of Liber's conscription of heavy-drinking poets in his ranks in lines 3–5, has us think of Horace not as a follower in a sacred band of poets, but as its leader. His steps are truly *libera* 'free' because they are those of an inspired θιασάρχης, or of Liber himself.

Thus, the image is doubly suggestive, poised between the rival iconographies of Bacchus on a distant hillside, and the *triumphator* in downtown Rome.[33] So, we ask, which is he really? The engaged military champion we remember (and are meant to remember) from *Carm.* 3.30, or the inspired θιασάρχης revelling among his maenads in a pristine, shady landscape?[34] Answer the question and you have ruined the picture, for it is there to be pondered and wondered about as a double-exposure, rather than decisively set straight. For inside the double-exposure we spy the poet doing his acrobatic, Aristippean dance, shuttling between the extremes of engagement and disengagement, triumph and revelry, sanity and sobriety, water and wine. What we are left with is a blended, 'tempered' image, defined by the rival extremes of the poet's own lyric self. Thus, in it, the suggestion of freedom achieved, and an epistolary mission accomplished: *solus sapiens liber est = solus sapiens Liber est.* In the next poem, the book itself (*liber*) is set free, released to experience firsthand the kind of second-rate *libertas* available to a poor but handsome *libertus* in Rome.[35] A brand of freedom that Horace apparently understands all too well: *me libertino natum patre* (1.20.20).[36]

But the success described has failed to impress many in his audience. The poet tells Maecenas in the last lines of *Epist.* 1.19 that, although the private reception of his *Odes* has been quite favourable (*laudet ametque domi*), his reader has proved *ingratus* ('thankless') and unfair towards his poems in public. The language is that of Roman social relations and political canvassing, with the reader here compared to a faithless friend, or to one among Rome's fickle mob of voters who feels stinted by the *opuscula* ('puny little works') that have been tossed his way. That word denigrates, shifting us abruptly into the mindset of the stinted voter, letting us hear, as it were, the word on the street: 'Horace's *carmina*, though clever and delightful, are lean on martial and panegyrical muscle. Sure, men of noble rank are addressed by them – many are even flattered by them! But they are mere trifles compared to those wine-inspired praise-poems of Ennius. He doesn't get my vote, because he doesn't drink deeply enough.[37] He lacks what it takes to "last" and "continue to gratify".' But Horace adds that, if he has no large and devoted clientele in Rome, it is because he has not spent lavishly on dinners and threadbare gifts. He has not 'canvassed the tribes' of grammarians, nor has he made his mark in the court-room of Rome's recitation-halls as a 'hearer and avenger of writers of noble

rank' (39–40). In other words, he has not used his poems to get ahead
with the right people and in the right venues. He has not done enough
name-dropping, pandering, outright defending and praising. His well-
tempered *Carmina* have not marked him as someone politically engaged
and determined to get ahead.

But the tables quickly turn on this argument in lines 41–4:

> 'spissis indigna theatris
> scripta pudet recitare et nugis addere pondus'
> si dixi, 'rides' ait 'et Iouis auribus ista
> seruas.'

*If I say that it embarrasses me to recite in public writings that fall below the
'dignity' of packed theatres, and to add weight to fluff, someone chimes
in with 'You're joking.' And 'You're saving those writings for Jupiter's
ears.'*

Horace has just claimed that his poems are not of a canvassing sort (*ambire
tribus*, 40), offering none of what sells in Rome, and puts one in the good
graces of Rome's powerful élite. But his interlocutor, a clever sort, buys
none of it.[38] 'Well of course you don't need a packed recitation hall', he
counters. 'You've got the ear of Augustus himself! So, remind me again
of how your poems have no political ambitions about them. Tell me – I'm
terribly curious – exactly how does that work? Go ahead and try!'

He makes a good point, unflattering to the poet, but rock-solid. Horace
may claim, as much as he wants, that he is singing unassuming 'trifles',
weightless and ambition-free, but uncooperative readers, such as this one,
do not have to see it that way. They are free to emplot the known details
differently; to imagine a strong causal connection between poems for
Maecenas (and for those two dozen or so other noble addressees) and
that sweet little villa of his in the Sabine hills, and to see similar finan-
cial and social 'ambitions' not-well-hidden inside his most recent collection of songs, some of which have caught the ear of Augustus himself
because they blend so beautifully with the political and social tunes playing under his direction, in *his* harmonic, cosmogonic sphere, *his* Rome.
'Songs for Jove's ears', the crass interlocutor calls them in line 43, re-
minding us just how outlandish the emperor-god's praise could get. The
phrase takes us back to *Epist.* 1.13.17–18, where the problem-package,
whatever it is (*uolumina, libelli, sarcina chartae, clitellae, onus, fasciculus*), is
said 'to have the power to detain the eyes and ears of Caesar'. As that letter
opens, the chosen terminology invites us to think that Horace is send-
ing off a bundle of 'signed'/'sealed' letters (*signata uolumina*) that he returns to Augustus (*Augusto reddes*) at his request.[39] In other words, inside

the poem Horace has us imagine him about the business of Augustus' letter-writing rather than his own. That is, he is acting in the role that Augustus had in mind for him as a writer in charge of his official correspondence, the very role the poet had recently declined. And he lets us see just what *that* letter-writing work does to him as a writer of letters, the sickening down-side of such an assignment, within the context of his own healing, epistolary regime. The confidence exuded from the surrounding poems is conspicuously absent here, giving way momentarily to the nervous bustling of a minor administrator on Augustus' payroll. Augustus himself is not directly addressed by the poem, and the problem of there being no address to this particular 'friend', in a book of letters addressed to friends, both noble and ignoble, is a huge one.[40] Moreover, the precise nature of the friendship imagined, if friendship can be imagined between *princeps* and *this* letter-writer, is quite out of keeping with the direct and egalitarian relationships imagined elsewhere in the book. Instead of the self-assured, balanced tone we have come to expect from these letters, here we are treated to 'don't screw up, Vinnius! For god's sake, whatever you do, make sure Augustus is in a good mood! And be sure to stand up straight and hold the package just so!' (*sic positum*, 12).

So we ask, who is the *sedulus minister* here? Vinnius, or the man who shares with him an asinine cognomen (*Flaccus*), the one barking orders to his dullard assistant like any good social climber bustling about Augustus' business, agonising over whether his work will be well received? And what exactly does this 'burden' of his contain, the one that is so heavy (*grauis . . . sarcina . . . onus*) and causes the carrier so much sweat (*sudauisse ferendo*)? In line 17 we are shocked to hear that the mystery load contains *carmina*. But can he really mean that? *Carmina*, as in his *Odes*? Why so heavy here when elsewhere, as in 1.19, they are virtually weight-free? Surely he means other poems, or imaginary poems; or, if his *Odes*, he intends us to see the whole thing as a joke and nothing more. Or can he really intend for us to think that his *Carmina* are *mandata* ('things commissioned/ordered', line 19), or anything even remotely so mercenary and mundane, a mere job to be done for the emperor to keep his machine running and the officious worker employed?

If this is a joke, it is a joke that unsettles and leaves the listener stung by a hidden barb. There is real agony in it. For that ugly perspective, the one we are invited to take here, is precisely the view that any less than co-operative reader, like the cynical interlocutor of 1.19, might take of Horace's *Odes*: mere pandering, work done, cash-in-hand. But worse, this may well represent the view that Augustus himself took of Horace's 'liberating', 'triumphal' achievement. For, although we are never told how he received these poems, we know that in 23 BC, the year of his desperate illness and the same year that Horace published *Odes* Books 1–3, Augustus asked Maecenas to send Horace away from his 'parasitic table' to his 'kingly' one so that the poet might help him with his letter-writing chores. How might that look to the clever cynic of 1.19? How might he emplot these scattered bits into a story? Quite easily this way: Augustus reads these *Carmina*, songs that ostensibly put the poet on a par with him as *princeps* and *triumphator*, and he says, 'Damn fine poems, friend! Really nice. Look, you're a good writer, I've got a job for you up on the Palatine. After all, that's what this was all about, wasn't it – you writing those poems to enmesh yourself with me? Well, you've done it. You've hit the jackpot! Come, sit at my table, and have a drink.'

The cynic of 1.19 takes exactly this view of Horace's relationship to Augustus – perhaps Augustus' own view! And who is to say that he cannot read this way? Not Horace. It is a good story, and all the parts fit, so the poet cannot wiggle his way out of the hold it puts him in. Instead of fighting, he cuts away from the argument, from the poem, from Maecenas, and from us in the last lines of *Epist.* 1.19, by comparing himself to a wrestler forced to call for a *diludia* ('break in the *ludi*') because the terms of the match are not to his liking.[41] This, it seems, is a match he cannot win, putting him in a hold he cannot escape, and against an opponent with very sharp, incisive nails. And so, with that slippery sidestep, we are left holding the bag, still pondering the question his interlocutor has posed. Thus it becomes our problem to solve; or better, to leave dangling. We ask, are his *Carmina* really as disengaged and ambition-free as the poet claims they are? If so, how? Can poems penned for Augustus' hearing ever really be just that? But answering the question too decisively will only put Horace in a hold that he will refuse to be held by. Like the mysterious stranger (Liber) held tight in Pentheus' chains at the end of 1.16, he can slip away from us, and from any too-controlling Pentheus/Maecenas whenever he chooses. And he does exactly that at the end of 1.19, slipping away from us, and from Maecenas, like the wiliest of wrestlers, leaving us to wonder just how long his 'break from the *ludi*' will be, and what terms he will finally settle upon for his return to the fray.

10 POETRY, PHILOSOPHY, POLITICS AND PLAY

Epistles 1

Scholars disagree over the philosophical and political aspects of *Epistles* 1. While earlier generations (represented by Heinze, Courbaud and Fraenkel) talked freely of 'philosophical conversion' and Macleod, Kilpatrick, Ferri and Harrison still see the book as philosophical, Williams, Mayer and Rudd deny it even formal philosophical status, although both Rudd and Mayer project Horace as a moralist.[1] Similarly, where Williams and Mayer see unequivocal praise of Augustus and Maecenas, Seager, Lyne and Oliensis detect disengagement, even disaffection.[2] These questions entail general questions about Roman poetry: the relationships between literature and life, between *persona* and person, between literature and politics and between poet, patron and addressee.

This chapter[3] argues that the *Epistles* are both formally and profoundly philosophical; that the philosophical and political interrelate; and that the poems express some tensions, ambiguities and reservations in Horace's attitudes both to public life and to Maecenas and Augustus, tensions which inform a wide-ranging and radical debate about the pros and cons of engagement in, or withdrawal from, that public life.

PHILOSOPHICAL POETRY

Prima dicte mihi, summa dicende Camena,
spectatum satis et donatum iam rude quaeris,
Maecenas, iterum antiquo me includere ludo?
non eadem est aetas, non mens. Veianius armis
Herculis ad postem fixis latet abditus agro,   5
ne populum extrema totiens exoret harena.
est mihi purgatam crebro qui personet aurem:
'solue senescentem mature sanus equum, ne
peccet ad extremum ridendus et ilia ducat.'
nunc itaque et uersus et cetera ludicra pono: 10
quid uerum atque decens, curo et rogo et omnis in hoc sum:
condo et compono quae mox depromere possim.

ac ne forte roges, quo me duce, quo lare tuter:
nullius addictus iurare in uerba magistri,
quo me cumque rapit tempestas, deferor hospes.   15
nunc agilis fio et mersor ciuilibus undis
uirtutis uerae custos rigidusque satelles,
nunc in Aristippi furtim praecepta relabor
et mihi res, non me rebus, subiungere conor.   (1.1–19)

When Maecenas requests more of the same (3), Horace likens his previous poetical activity to a gladiatorial *ludus*: that was his old school, he
has retired and put all that aside (10 *ludicra* ~ 3 *antiquo... ludo*). His
new activity (11),[4] necessarily also a *ludus*, seems to be philosophy, an
activity appropriate for those of mature age (4). *rogo* evokes philosophical
'enquiry' (what more philosophical question than 'What is truth?').
decens has a triple philosophical aspect: firstly, 'the neuter sing. of adjectives ... is turned into a noun to provide philosophical technical terms';[5]
secondly, *qua* participle, *decens* is an even closer calque upon the Greek
prepon than the customary *decorum*; thirdly, as we shall see, at least retrospectively, *decens* glosses the specifically Panaetian understanding of
prepon. And *omnis in hoc sum* suggests the absoluteness of philosophical
conversion.

Since the metaphorical gladiatorial *ludus* subdivides into individual *ludi*
(14), the same applies to philosophy. Thus far *ludus* and cognates have
four applications: (a) the *ludus* of gladiatorial combat; (b) the rejected
ludus/ludicra of Horace's previous poetry; (c) the *ludus* of philosophy;
(d) individual philosophical *ludi*. To these we may add a paradoxical
(e). Inasmuch as Horace's philosophical *ludus* is still expressed in poetry, some association between *ludus* and poetry remains (I shall return
to this). Horace's polysemous exploration of 'play' will be a key element
in the structure, imagery and argument of 1.1 and of the whole book.

The treatment of individual philosophies acquires definition in 13–19.
The philosopher Aristippus is explicitly named in 18. His polar opposite
(16–17) is also a philosopher: the orthodox Stoic, 'active' in political
life (*agilis* ~ *praktikos*), emblematic of virtue in a strong sense (*uirtutis
uerae* ~ 11 *uerum*), and imaged in terms of warfare (*custos*) and 'hardness'
(*rigidus*).[6] A good reason for (sometimes) attaching philosophical labels to
poetry is that they are one of Horace's own thematic categories, whether
explicit (18–19) or implicit (16–17).[7]

Numerous allusions underpin the philosophical texture. Line 5 *latet
abditus* glosses the Epicurean tag 'live unnoticed' (λάθε βιώσας). Line 7
evokes Socrates' *daimonion*, appropriately 'deterring' Horace from poetry.
Maecenas' anticipated question in 13 assumes Horace's adhesion to some

philosophical master. The sectarian religious imagery of 13 *quo lare tuter* suggests philosophical exclusiveness. Line 14 echoes the Academic non-commitment of Cicero, *Tusculans* 4.7 (*sed defendat quod quisque sentit: sunt enim iudicia libera, nos institutum tenebimus nullisque unius legibus disciplinae adstricti*), and contrasts with the Epicureans' oath to their master's doctrines. Line 15 echoes *Academica* 2.8 (*ad quamcumque sunt disciplinam quasi tempestate delati*). Line 15 *hospes* glosses Aristippus' claim to be a *xenos* everywhere (Xen. *Mem.* 2.2.13). Line 17 *custos* and *satelles* image virtue as a king, glossing Stoic 'kingship'. Line 18 adapts *Academica* 2.139 (*uideo quam suauiter sensibus nostris blandiatur: labor eo ut adsentiar Epicuro aut Aristippo*); 18 *furtim*, echoing 5, nicely characterises Epicureanism. Line 19 glosses, via the yoking metaphor, Aristippus' boast 'I have, but I am not had' (Diog. Laert. 2.75).[8] The combination of that yoking metaphor, of the horse metaphor for Horace's rejected earlier poetry (8–9) and of the name 'Aristippus' (= 'best at horses' or 'best horse') recalls the contrasting horses of *Phaedrus* 246bff. And beneath the polarity of 16–19 lies Hercules' choice between Virtue and Vice/Pleasure and their corresponding roads, a choice put to Aristippus (*Mem.* 2.1.21–34) and alluded to in *Academica* 2.139. Although the primary contrast in 17–19 is between an unchanging conception of virtue and a flexible ideal, virtue–vice, hard–soft and virile–effeminate contrasts are also latent. Given this Aristippean colouring, 3 *includere* must be read (restrospectively) as including a (prospective) gloss on Aristippus' refusal to 'shut himself into' (*Mem.* 2.1.13) any *politeia*.

Horace's deployment of his immense philosophical erudition[9] accommodates different levels of readership: philosophically erudite readers can enjoy the depth and ingenuity of allusion, but the main philosophical divisions are spelled out, and all readers can understand both the need for some form of philosophy and the difficulties of putting it into practice.

The conclusion that the *Epistles'* subject matter is philosophy might be supported by certain (admittedly controversial) generic considerations.[10] But the general conclusion is sure. Yet the standard objections to it[11] require consideration, since they illuminate the complexity of Horace's engagement with philosophy and indeed of the very activity of philosophising.

OBJECTIONS TO A PHILOSOPHICAL READING

(a) The first objection is the alleged *naïveté* of supposing that Horace had had a philosophical conversion, especially given his earlier philosophical poems. But the latter factor does not preclude a broad distinction between non-philosophical and philosophical matter, no doubt exaggerated to suit the rhetoric of conversion, and the main point foists upon philosophical interpreters a crude biographical model to which they are not committed.

But this objection does point an important question: the relationship between literature and life. No one still believes that the *Epistles* are 'real letters'[12] and many stress the presence of motifs from the *Satires*, a linkage strengthened by their common status as *sermones*.[13] Yet Maecenas, like all the addressees, is a real person, and the subtlety of Horace's allusions to addressees' characteristics and interests is well recognised.[14] Whatever the truth of Horace's self-description in 94–7, Maecenas' fussy reactions suit a notorious fop; Maecenas *was* Horace's patron; he *did* request poems; Horace *was* pressured into producing *Odes* 4.[15] In short, if, on the question of the relationship between the *Epistles* and real life, the theoretical possibilities are: (i) elaborate, self-conscious, fictionality; (ii) literal truth; and (iii) poetic truth à la *Poetics* 9 (allowing a degree of historicity – real people, broadly historical circumstances and events), then the world of the *Epistles* includes all three and rather more of (ii) than many moderns concede. If we do not attribute some substantive truth to that world, Horace's proffering of his own life-experience and his fitful moral progress through the text will fall flat. For the poems to engage the reader emotionally, socially and morally, there must be some recognisable relationship between 'Horace' (the literary construct) and Horace (the 'real person').

This point is reinforced by the *sphragis* of the last poem, Horace's farewell to his book (20.19–28):

> cum tibi sol tepidus plures admouerit aures,
> me libertino natum patre et in tenui re   20
> maiores pennas nido extendisse loqueris,
> ut, quantum generi demas, uirtutibus addas;
> me primis urbis belli placuisse domique,
> corporis exigui, praecanum, solibus aptum,
> irasci celerem, tamen ut placabilis essem.   25
> forte meum siquis te percontabitur aeuum,
> me quater undenos sciat impleuisse Decembres,
> collegam Lepidum quo dixit Lollius anno.

Line 23 echoes 17.35 *principibus placuisse uiris*, of Aristippus, who, as we shall see, there represents one side of Horace. Epistles 1, 7 and 19 (to Maecenas), 9 (to Tiberius) and 13 (on Augustus' receiving the *Odes*)[16] attest that worldly success. And 26–8 ring with 1.4: Horace has indeed changed; he is ageing. His allegedly new interest in philosophy is psychologically and chronologically plausible. An inevitable gap remains between writer and text (a gap upon which 1.20 itself elegantly plays), but the two connect.

(b) The second objection claims that Horace cannot be maintaining a distinction between poetry and philosophy: his words scan; he *is* writing poetry. There are self-conscious thematic overlaps with the *Satires*. Any poetry–philosophy distinction in favour of the latter is challenged by the opening of Epistle 2: Homer tells us what is fine, what is base, what is useful, what is not, more clearly and better than Chrysippus and Crantor (1–5). Epistle 4's and Epistle 13's allusions to *Satires* and *Odes* respectively bring those poetic types closer to the *Epistles*. Epistle 12 (to Iccius) intertexts with *Odes* 1.29.[17] And Horace's defence of his poetry in Epistle 19 centres on *Odes* and *Epodes*.

Now it is clearly true that Horace presents the *Epistles* as both different from some or all of his previous poetry and as part of his whole poetic corpus, the latter emphasis predominating in the second half of the book. Yet the paradox of the *Epistles'* being *both* poetry *and* not-poetry but philosophy is created and emphasised in 1.10–11:

> nunc itaque et uersus et cetera ludicra pono:
> quid uerum atque decens, curo et rogo et omnis in hoc sum.

These lines of verse make a polar opposition between verse and all other play-things *and* philosophy; *uersus* cannot be restricted to lyric, since this excludes the *Satires* and the term can include poetic *sermo*: hence 10–11 do not appeal to the prosaic status of *sermo* (as many argue), but to the simple idea that philosophy is something distinct from poetry – cf. Socrates and Plato[18] (simple, though of course highly paradoxical when the text propounding it is itself poetry).

Now if the *Epistles'* subject matter is philosophy, they themselves must constitute a philosophical text. Horace says so: 12 *condo* and *compono* ('put together') are literary terms. The *Epistles* are Horace's own 'store-house' now that he has 'put aside' *uersus et cetera ludicra* (12 *compono* ∼ 10 *pono*). And when in 23–5 Horace envisages the eventual possibility of *total* commitment to philosophising (25 *agendi* ∼ 16 *agilis* and 25 *nauiter* ∼ 15),[19] rather than the make-shifts of 14–19, and when he says *restat ut his ego me ipse regam solerque elementis* (27), *his . . . elementis* must gloss the *Epistles*. This reading receives confirmation from 20.17–18 *hoc quoque te manet, ut pueros elementa docentem | occupet extremis in uicis balba senectus*. There the book will be reduced to teaching *elementa* of an even more 'elementary' kind. Similarly, while within the sickness metaphor the *ter pure lecto . . . libello* of 37 is the booklet of spells used in propitiatory rites, outside the metaphor it is the *liber* which will make Horace's readers 'pure', i.e. the *Epistles*. Furthermore, Epistle 1 rings with Epistle 20: Horace's own *liber* frames and instantiates the teachings of the collection. It is not true that Horace never recommends philosophical texts;[20] he does: his own.

Beneath the irony, wit, self-depreciation etc., the implicit claims for the philosophical potential of the *Epistles* are huge, although to derive maximum benefit both Horace and his readers will have to re-read the poems repeatedly (*ter lecto* ...).

The paradox of the *Epistles'* being *both* poetry *and* not-poetry but philosophy still requires explanation. Of course, once Horace the poet decides to write philosophy, he is committed to that paradox. But this does not *explain* it. One factor is that the *Epistles'* place in his whole poetic corpus helps to make Epistles 19 and 20 into a general *apologia pro vita sua*, and some aspects of that *vita* (e.g. Horace's ability *primis urbis ... placuisse*, 20.23) antedated the alleged conversion of 1.10–11, yet show one possible philosophical road. Another factor is that both the writing and reception of poetry function as a sort of metaphor for a range of moral behaviour in life. We shall see something of this in Epistles 3 and 4, and it is an important aspect of Epistle 19.[21] Nor is it just a matter of metaphor: Horace moves progressively through the book towards a more philosophical conception of poetry. More radically still, some such paradox is inherent in the best philosophical writing itself. On the one hand, such writing is superior to other types of writing such as poetry, because of its philosophical commitment and rigour; on the other, it has an inevitable relationship with such writings; again, even to write about philosophy is a poor substitute for the real thing. The ambiguity of Horace's presentation of the *Epistles* – poetry-not-poetry, of enormous value, merely an elementary propaedeutic – is paralleled in writings that are indubitably philosophical, such as Plato's.

The same applies to Horace's fizzing wit and irony; many of the greatest ancient philosophers are witty and ironic (most relevantly, Socrates, Aristippus, Plato and Diogenes). It was the Socratic *daimonion* that caused Horace's conversion (7) and Socrates is important to Horace's self-presentation[22] – or *persona*. For although 7 *personet* means 'sounds through', Horace here acknowledges the decisive influence of an identifiable philosopher; there is (as we shall see) a general Panaetian influence upon the epistle; Panaetius made much of *persona*-theory; and later in the collection Horace himself exploits Panaetian *persona* theory.[23] *personet*, therefore, introduces, precisely, Horace's Socratic *persona*. Then, Horace's irresolute changes of philosophical position (15–19) humorously recall Socrates' wanderings in search of knowledge (Pl. *Ap.* 22a) and his encounters with the Roman people in the colonnades (7off.) suggest Socrates' debates in the *agora*. The epistle even sketches a certain rudimentary Socratic *elenchos*: Horace 'asks' what is true (11), Maecenas may 'ask' who Horace's philosophical master is (13), the Roman people may 'ask' Horace why he does not share their judgements and tastes (70), it is one of the aims of philosophy to teach one to 'respond' to Fortune (68): a 'response' underpinned by Socratic *elenchos*.

Socrates, too, was the paradigm of 'the laughing philosopher'. The epistle is full of allusions to laughing (*rideo*), whether justified (9, 10, 91) or misplaced (95, 97, cf. 101). Moreover, in 59–60 Horace cites the children's game of 'kings' as pointing the right moral lesson: *at pueri ludentes* '*rex eris*' *aiunt* | '*si recte facies*'. On a banal level, this gives the term *ludus* a sixth application, that of literal children's 'play' or 'games'. But the appeal to the *ludus* of *pueri* as a moral standard is polysemous. The implicit etymological connection (more prominently trailed in 2.67–8) between *puer* and *purus*[24] underpins a central paradox, which, *mutatis mutandis*, unites the thoughts 'now I am become a man, I have put away childish things' (10 *ludicra*, cf. 3) and 'except you become as little children you cannot enter the kingdom of God' (59). To begin the quest for virtue, at whatever age (26), one must become as *purus* as a *puer*. Thus the children's *ludus* is at least potentially philosophical, so that *ludentes* suggests not just philosophy as a *ludus* but *ludus* as a way of doing philosophy. Thus *ludentes* glosses Socratic 'play' (*paizein*)[25] (the seventh application of *ludus*). And since the concept of *ludus* here appears in juxtaposition with *pueri*, the collocation *pueri ludentes* glosses the Socratic/Platonic pun *paideia/paidia*: 'play' is a thing for children (*paides*) but children point towards right moral behaviour – true 'education' is a form of 'play'.[26] *Ludus* thus acquires an eighth application: 'education'. Even a ninth: Horace also suggests a punning allusion to the moral/philosophical idea of 'serious play' (*spoudaiogeloion*), the vehicle used by Socrates, and after him, the Cynics, and the satirical Horace himself, for philosophical teaching.[27] Thus the phrase *pueri ludentes* is itself complexly and brilliantly philosophical. And 59 intimates a potential clarification of the paradox of 10–11: poetic 'play' will yield to philosophical 'play', or, rather, to 'philosophical play' expressed in poetic form.

The tenth application of *ludus* is to the 'school' that children attend, imaged in 53–69. Horace imagines Janus teaching both young and old the supreme value of wealth. Then he himself appeals to the children's jingle (59–62) to suggest a better lesson. This further application of *ludus* explains the challenge of Epistle 2: the poem is a protreptic to philosophy, and in a protreptic one returns to school, to the beginnings of moral wisdom, the teaching of Homer. This stance, which philosophers themselves could take (Antisthenes, Plutarch etc.), is not Horace's final word but the first step in one's philosophical career. A poem which comes after Epistle 1 sequentially is anterior to it logically (because Epistle 1 sketches the whole philosophical process), a point made by the interaction between 2.1–2 *Troiani belli scriptorem . . . relegi* and 1.37 *ter pure lecto ... libello. relegi* is 'pre-cut' by <u>ter</u> *lecto*. The *Epistles'* philosophical potential *exceeds* Homer's.

The complex and intricate 'play' element does not erase the *Epistles'* philosophical seriousness, but there is an implicit challenge to readers to penetrate the 'play' to that underlying seriousness. They may fail. The rich philosophical potential of pure *pueritia* at school may degenerate into a dismal and familiar reality: 20.17–18 *hoc quoque te manet, ut pueros elementa docentem | occupet extremis in uicis balba senectus.* The hopes of 1.27 may never be fulfilled. Reading/interpreting/implementing philosophy requires unremitting commitment and effort by both poet and readers.

There is the possibility even of an eleventh application of *ludus*: 'playing a part';[28] lines 2–3 are not far from this and the idea of the Socratic *persona* (7) helps.

This analysis may seem to give insufficient value to the self-depreciation which overlays Horace's philosophical self-assertion. There are indeed several aspects to that self-depreciation (including the needs to respond tactfully to Maecenas and to explore the inevitable shortfalls from philosophical precepts), but self-depreciation, whether real or assumed, is an essential part of the Socratic tradition. Socrates, notoriously, knew nothing. The Socratic philosopher teaches and learns in a reciprocal relationship with his pupils: hence the interaction between Socrates, his *daimonion* and Horace (7), between 7 *purgatam* and 37 *pure*, between Horace's ear (7) and his readers' ears (40).[29] Horace's self-depreciation simultaneously ingratiates, challenges and teaches.

(c) The third objection is that 14–19 are philosophically unorthodox in the refusal to enlist under one master and in the appeal to Aristippus, who had no contemporary followers. Yet on *one* level Horace's eclecticism (problematic but useful term) must be taken seriously, because it parallels his refusal to be 'included within any (poetical) *ludus*' (3). Such admitted eclecticism is rare in ancient philosophy but not unknown,[30] and there is a carry-over from 7: no ancient philosopher more truly exemplified the principle *nullius addictus iurare in uerba magistri* than Socrates. Similarly, as we have seen, 15–19 playfully echo Socrates' famous wanderings in search of knowledge at the start of *his* philosophical career. Moreover, as already noted, the wording of 14 extends to philosophy at large the eclecticism that is found *within* Academicism. As for Aristippus, contemporary philosophy could still allude to him and discuss his ethics (as did Panaetius and Cicero).[31] Finally, to be philosophically unorthodox is, logically, to be philosophical (no mere sophistry, as will become clear).

On another level, however, Horace's eclecticism is vulnerable: he is making a complete hash of his philosophical options. When he tries Stoicism, <u>mersor ciuilibus undis</u> (16);[32] then *furtim ... relabor* (18):

compared with the Stoic ideal, however ironised, 'Aristippeanism' is a 'furtive' second best, not the *'best* philosophical horse'. Some scholars[33] have seen Aristippus as Horace's ideal: he is not, he is simply one possibility. Here his attractions are recognised but formally decried; conversely, in 1.17 he wins the debate against Diogenes over whether or not to associate with 'kings', in which respect he does reflect Horace's own view and practice, but then in 1.18 Aristippus' own claims are implicitly criticised (he is too much the *scurra*: 2–4). Nor does the irony of 1.1.16–17 and 108[34] entail Horace's dismissal of orthodox Stoicism: on the contrary, he has the highest respect for it (1.16), although it is not, ultimately, for him personally.[35] Thus the eclecticism of 14–19 can be read alternatively as a serious eclecticism, to be justified as the book progresses, or as an eclecticism destined for refutation: one particular philosophy may after all hold the key to right living. But, however read, Horace's assumed eclecticism has obvious structural advantages, allowing the relatively unprejudiced exploration of a range of philosophical alternatives.

(d) The fourth objection is that the *Epistles* are about life, not philosophy. But the dichotomy is false. The *Epistles* are about *recte uiuere* (60) as interpreted by different philosophies. The fact that a few Epistles resist philosophical categorisation does not undermine the book's philosophical classification. General, non-doctrinaire, moralising is found extensively in philosophers such as Cicero, Seneca, Musonius and Plutarch and in the popular philosophical writings of the Cynic tradition, of which Horace was in some respects heir.[36]

In sum, the *Epistles'* subject matter is philosophy; they themselves constitute a philosophical text; and they register – indeed enact – many of the problematics of writing philosophy.

PHILOSOPHICAL ARGUMENTS AND STRUCTURE

The next question to consider is the philosophical argument of 1.1, beginning with its ambiguous Stoic *color*. Lines 16–17 imply that orthodox Stoicism is 'best' and the flavour of 68–9 *an qui Fortunae te responsare superbae | liberum et erectum praesens hortatur et aptat?*, on the gains available from philosophy, is heroically Stoic.[37] The poem ends (106–8) by endorsing the Stoic *rex*, the 'answer' to the question of *recte uiuere*, though that endorsement is finally ironised.

But there are counter-elements. There is much that is objectively consistent with the moderated Stoicism of Panaetius: *decens* (11), which *could* gloss Panaetian *prepon*; the eclecticism of 14–19; the appeal to Aristippus; the idea that some progress is better than none – 32 *could* gloss the Panaetian concepts of *profectus* and *proficiens*; the modest definition of *uirtus* in 41–2; the awareness of individual difference as frustrating universal norms (80–93); the ironisation of the sage. Should we, then, add a Panaetian label to our existing collection of orthodox Stoic, Aristippean and Epicurean? McGann, in his seminal philosophical investigation, claims: '*decens* . . . can in Rome at this time, less than a quarter of a century after the publication of *De officiis*, point in one direction only, to the ethics of Panaetius'. This is perhaps exaggerated, but Panaetius certainly comes into the frame with the parallel definition of philosophy in 2.3 (*quid sit pulchrum, quid turpe, quid utile, quid non*), so only a little retrospective reading (which 1.37 entails) activates his presence in 1.11. There is, then, a tension in the poem's Stoic *color*. While formally the Stoic elements push towards an orthodox Stoic solution, sub-elements advocate more modest, and pluralist, Panaetian goals.[38]

And there are other elements. Partly in their own right (5), partly through Aristippus, the Epicureans 'lurk' (appropriately) in the background. Aristippus himself represents both a certain conception of pleasure and philosophical flexibility. The Socratic element promotes the claims both of non-doctrinaire pluralism and of dialectical pursuit of truth. Orthodox Stoicism re-emerges really only in Epistle 16, but it provides a convenient, indeed the obvious, initial standard of virtue with (as it were) a capital 'v'. All other elements conduce better to the exploration in subsequent poems of a range of philosophical alternatives, to Horace's own developing pluralist philosophical *persona* and to ever more direct engagement between philosophy and life.

Hence the final philosophical aspect of Epistle 1: its architectural role. While there are many organising principles in this most intricate of poetry-books,[39] the philosophical one is primary. Horace's basic procedure is to provide preliminary sketches of the main figures of the philosophical landscape, which he then tries out on the real people of the *Epistles*, himself included, matching temperament to philosophical choice, in a series of dramatic situations, whose individual rationales and interlocking permutations are characteristically explored through recognisable philosophical positions. The concepts of *ludus* and *persona* help to articulate this shifting scenario.

Lines 16–19 institute a complex polarity between orthodox Stoicism/virtue/consistency and Aristippus/adaptability/pleasure, a polarity resolved and not resolved by the description of the *sapiens* at the poem's end: *qua* ironic, this description suggests the Panaetian perspective otherwise implicit in the poem; the Epicureans are also in play, partly through their implicit association with Aristippus. Epistle 2 deploys a similar polarity, between Virtue/Wisdom/Odysseus (17–22), implicitly linked with the addressee Lollius, and Pleasure/Folly/Companions/Phaeacians (23–31), and it ends by compromising between the two (70–1). This compromise looks like Panaetian *profectus*, and the initial philosophical formulation (3) is definitely Panaetian. By analogy with Epistle 1 Odysseus' virtue must be broadly Stoic (or Cynic), as confirmed by the link between 2.22 *immersabilis* and 1.16 *mersor* (Odysseus and Horace are 'swimming' in the same philosophical 'sea'). One naturally reads the opposing Pleasure as vulgar Epicurean, as confirmed by the link between 2.26 *sus* and 4.16 *Epicuri de grege porcum*. The lurking Epicureans of Epistle 1 replace Aristippus as the polar opposite of Virtue, though their portrayal, unlike Aristippus', is now straightforwardly negative.[40] And the foppish Maecenas of Epistle 1 now looks rather Epicurean (2.29 ~ 1.94 ff.).[41]

Epistle 3 is difficult, but 3.5 asks if Florus (the addressee) and his friends are behaving like Phaeacians / vulgar Epicureans, and the poem's unifying thought is that true wisdom involves concord/friendship with oneself, one's fellows, one's *patria* and the *cosmos* (28–9). This is Stoic and indeed directly Panaetian (*De off.* 1.50–8).[42] The argument works with the same essential polarity as Epistles 1 and 2, though Panaetian Stoicism now appears in a loftier light. Epistle 4 recycles that polarity yet again but this time favours Epicureanism (notwithstanding Horace's ironic self-description) over Albius' austere Stoicism.[43] Favourable redefinition of Epicureanism continues in Epistle 5 addressed to the Epicurean Torquatus: Augustus' birthday allows a busy man to implement Epicurus' advice of 4.13.[44]

So much, for now, for the *Epistles*' philosophical architecture. To change the figure, in this poetic corpus the dramatic situations are the skin and tissue, the philosophies the bones and sinews.

PHILOSOPHY AND POLITICS

Epistle 1 foregrounds programmatically the questions of political participation, linked to choice of philosophy, and of the moral well-being of the *patria*. But the central social/political question of the poem itself is Horace's relationship with Maecenas.

Maecenas is Horace's alpha and omega, a compliment reflected in the structure of both poem (1, 105) and book (Epistle 1 ~ 19), though in both cases the ring that is Maecenas is outflanked by other, and larger, concerns.[45] Maecenas tries to restrict Horace to his old poetic *ludus*; Horace responds with the *Epistles*, which are something new. Reproof jostles with compliment. It is paradoxical that the *Epistles* can give Maecenas freedom (69) when he seeks to restrict Horace's (3); that he laughs at Horace's unkempt habits (95, 97), not the things that are truly *ludicra* (10); that he remains Horace's *tutela* (103), when Horace seeks a *tutela* elsewhere (13). Can it really be true that Horace still 'looks to' Maecenas (105), when he himself no longer wants to be 'looked at' (2)? Is he really still 'dependent' on Maecenas (105), when he himself wants freedom from his old poetry to concentrate on philosophy and freedom even within philosophy? Horace tries to bring Maecenas within the philosophical process by extensive second-person-singular addresses, some of which must at least include Maecenas.

The compliments remain, including the compliment of being able to take public reproof, yet with all the urbanity and joking Maecenas' attitudes are objectively criticised, and he is implicitly on probation.[46] Maecenas the *laudandus* is an addressee in a philosophical book most of whose addressees are criticised or admonished. And 'figured-speech' theory[47] admits criticism through compliment.

Epistle 3 warns against strife among young careerists in a military camp, who risk the *stultorum regum ... aestus* of *Iliad* and *Odyssey* (2.8); broaches the possibility of poetic commemoration of Augustus' *res gestae* (7); and elevates devotion to the *patria* (29). The apparently slight and urbane epistle to Tibullus contains one jarring allusion: 4.3 *scribere quod Cassi Parmensis opuscula uincat*. As in Epistle 3, poetic rivalry functions partly as a metaphor for civic strife. The Epicurean Epistle 5 celebrates the birthday not of Epicurus but of Augustus: implicitly the good king, who in Epicurean political thought can be the guarantor of Epicurean quietism.[48] No tension here between Epicureanism and Augustanism or between country and city. Epistle 7 reintroduces Maecenas, complaining that Horace has stayed away for a month rather than the promised five days; compliments and endearments abound but Horace maintains his position (metaphorically and literally). Panaetian relativism allows individuals to choose what is right for them (44, 98; cf. Cic. *Off.* 1.110), here, for Horace, a form of rural Epicureanism.[49] In Epistle 10 Horace's happiness at the crumbling shrine of Vacuna, Sabine goddess of victory whose name suggests *uacare*, pointedly subverts worldly values, and in Epistle 11, with the right attitude of mind, happiness is available at Ulubrae for Bullatius (29).[50] By contrast, in Epistle 12 imperial successes and bumper crops in Italy point the unreasonableness of Iccius' discontent with his managership of Agrippa's estates (25ff.). Epistle 13 commemorates Augustus' receiving the *Odes* a few years before: like Epistle 9 and others it advertises Horace's connections with the court. Still, Augustus is nowhere addressed, as he himself was to complain (Suet. *Vita Hor.*, Loeb ed. 2.486), and, unlike Maecenas (1.1), he is not formally 'first and last': even in his own poem he comes in the second and penultimate lines.[51]

In the majestic and philosophically rigorous Epistle 16[52] Horace is on his farm (1–16), master (2, 10) of his simple natural bounty and 'safe' in his Epicurean retreat: 15 *hae latebrae dulces* ~ 1.5 *latet abditus; dulces* glosses Epicureanism,[53] 16 *incolumem* that 'security' (*asphaleia*) obtained by Epicurean 'withdrawal' (Epic. *KD* 14). The addressee, Quinctius, is politically active in Rome (17–79). The poem operates with a *rus*/Epicurean–Rome/Stoic contrast, hence the latter's appeal to Stoic doctrines: only the wise man is happy (20), virtue and vice are absolutes and vice is rejected through love of virtue, not fear of punishment (52–4), and all sins are equal (56).

What, within this Roman context, does *recte uiuere* mean? Who is *beatus*, or *sapiens* and *bonus*? Worldly honours are no criterion: they can exaggerate a man's worth (if he is flattered as if he were Augustus) or be removed at the donor's whim (34). (Who he? one wonders, and, at least retrospectively, the answer must be: 'Augustus'.)[54] Loss of worldly honours does not degrade a virtuous man. Is the *bonus*, then, the man who does good public service (40)? Not necessarily, for his household and neighbourhood may know that he is base within (a common philosophical contrast between outer and inner). The absolute materialist (67) has deserted the post of Virtue (contrast the Stoic ideal of 1.17). The captured deserter should not be killed but sold as a slave, when he can usefully become a shepherd, ploughman, or whatever: although the complete materialist is a moral slave his immoral activity has some commercial benefit for society.[55] This section highlights the qualities of the polar opposite of the moral slave, the truly free man, who, as the last lines of the poem emphasise, may face loss of all his possessions, imprisonment or even death.

> uir bonus et sapiens audebit dicere 'Pentheu,
> rector Thebarum, quid me perferre patique
> indignum coges?' 'adimam bona.' 'nempe pecus, rem,   75
> lectos, argentum: tollas licet.' 'in manicis et
> compedibus saeuo te sub custode tenebo.'
> 'ipse deus, simulatque uolam, me soluet.' opinor,
> hoc sentit 'moriar'. mors ultima linea rerum est.

These lines adapt the scene between Pentheus and Dionysus from Euripides, *Bacchae* 492–8. Philosophical exegesis of literary passages is commonplace; that Epictetus also uses this scene[56] suggests a common Stoic source. The move from 'real life' to 'myth' imitates a concluding philosophical *muthos*. The scene also provides a concrete dramatic representation of 1.68–9 *qui Fortunae te responsare superbae | liberum et erectum praesens hortatur et aptat*. It also crowns the philosophical argument. The *uir bonus et sapiens* is finally revealed (outer and inner united), the criterion being his unflinching response to tyranny. Whereas Epicurean retreat gives 'safety' and autonomous self-'mastery', Stoic engagement risks collision with a tyrannical 'external' *dominus*. But it is impossible for the

tyrannical *rector* to degrade the man of virtue, whose virtue and freedom
are underwritten by the freedom of suicide. Horace transmutes Euripides into pure Stoic doctrine, reinforced by the notion of 'the god within'
(78–9): in Euripides Dionysus simply says: 'the god will free me from
imprisonment', whereas Horace's exegesis makes Dionysus mean: 'I can
release myself by suicide.'

The closing *sententia* – 'Death is the last line of things' (like the line at
the end of a race) – is no mere banality. For the man of virtue, it is conso-
latory: untimely death as a necessary response to tyranny is no evil since
we all die sometime; for the tyrant, it is admonitory: you can compass
the death of the man of virtue, but you gain nothing, since you yourself
have to die. For such Stoic insouciance there are (again) good parallels in
Epictetus, e.g. when (1.25.22) the philosopher Demetrius says to Nero:
'you threaten me with death but nature threatens you'. Further, as applied to a pursuer of the philosophical *rectum*, the image of the *line* fittingly
adorns a *noble* death. There is still another implication, again applicable
both to man of virtue and tyrant, though again in different ways: 'you
can't take it with you': *rerum* also interacts with 75 *rem* and 68 *re* (both
of property). Lastly, the image of the line achieves a final modification
of the poem's architecture: if the poem works, as it were, horizontally,
with a polar opposition between Epicureanism and Stoicism, then, as it
were, vertically, all polar oppositions are resolved in death, though the
Epicurean and Stoic attitudes to death are of course different, and this
also is part of the densely condensed meaning.

What are the consequences for political interpretation? Formally set in
legendary Thebes, the heroic final scene must also play in contemporary
Rome, the setting of the whole Stoic section. Not only is the scene the
culmination of the argument, but Thebes itself can function as a metaphor
for civil-war Rome. It is so used by Virgil and Ovid, and, as we shall see,
by Horace himself in 18.41ff. Also relevant is the Pindaric/Theban *color*
of Epistle 3, with its warnings against intestinal and fraternal strife.[57]
Further, the word *rector* (74) recalls Cicero's conception of the *rector*,
which envisaged Pompey and was in some sense fulfilled by Augustus,[58]
who is within the frame of the poem. This *rector*, however, is the antithesis
of *recte uiuere*. Thus the concluding *muthos* implies an analogy between
the political status of Pentheus and that of Augustus, 'monarch'[59] and in
certain contexts, from certain focalisations, also 'tyrant'. Ancient theories
of 'figured speech' easily accommodate such radical implications. No
concidence, then, that Epictetus (also) applies the Euripidean scene to
tyrannical emperors.

Does the man of *uirtus* suggest any specific allusions? Certainly not
to the materialistic[60] Quinctius, for whom the point of the scene is the

extremely high stakes risked by his Stoic political engagement under the new monarchy. But Cato Uticensis and Brutus must qualify:[61] Cato who committed suicide rather than endure the clemency of Augustus' father and whom Horace introduces as a paragon of Stoic virtue in a thematically related later poem (19.12–14); Brutus, Horace's erstwhile *imperator*, who had recognised Stoic affiliations, whose last words before his suicide denounced Octavian,[62] and who cannot be excluded from the *primi* of 20.23 (*me primis urbis belli placuisse domique*). But also Horace himself, for, while, dramatically speaking, Horace here plays the Epicurean role, it is Horace the poet who voices this existential struggle between Stoic virtue and Caesarian tyranny. Despite all the material benefits showered on him by Augustus and Maecenas, in an ultimate sense the poet-philosopher remains morally and politically free, inspired by the examples of Cato and Brutus and by Stoic ethics at their most magnificently uncompromising. Nor does its tremendous moral power exhaust the poem's political quality. Du Quesnay has persuasively argued that some of Horace's poetry shows detailed inner knowledge of the political thinking of Augustus and his *consilium*;[63] by contrast, this poem contemplates unflinchingly one of the new dispensation's supreme costs: the death of men of true *uirtus*. Had it been written under Tiberius or any of the later 'tyrant'-emperors, the poem would not, perhaps, have been in this respect very remarkable; that it was written early in Augustus' reign and by a poet so closely involved with the imperial court is eloquent testimony to Horace's political acumen.

The worldly and practical Epistle 17 reshuffles the cards. The players are Panaetians, Epicureans, Aristippeans and Cynics. The aim is *maioribus*, even *regibus*, *uti* (2, 13, 14), clearly recalling Epistle 16, though *reges* now include patrons as well as kings. As in 16 Epicurean withdrawal is a legitimate and virtuous option (9 ~ 36). Cynicism's claim to a virtuous but independent life within the city is refuted by the flexible and Panaetian Aristippus. It is virtuous and onerous *principibus placuisse uiris* (35), and honour and reward rightly attend such success. There are strong shades of one side of Horace here: perhaps, after all, orthodox Stoic heroics are avoidable, even without Epicurean withdrawal. So Epistle 18 explores the problem of successful social engagement with the great. Cynic behaviour *within* society is merely boorish and does not confer *uirtus*, but you must not be an unprincipled parasite. You can be a true *amicus* of the great, thereby attaining *uirtus . . . medium uitiorum* (9).[64] How? On Bowditch's[65] attractive 'figured-speech' reading, Horace's mature poetic *ludus* plays dangerously with the covert realities of Augustan Rome – Augustus' supremacy as *dux* and *patronus*, loss of *libertas*, the intestinal nature of Actium – as a way of warning the young and excessively *liber*

Lollius. But on any reading the tone is grim enough: 86–7 *dulcis inexpertis cultura potentis amici:* | *expertus metuet*, a sentiment, incidentally, applied by Pindar fr. 110 to war.

But *inter cuncta leges et percontabere doctos* (96). Although simultaneous with cultivation of powerful *amici*, this activity is preferable: to be a friend to yourself, to be Horace's friend, matters more.[66] That the *docti* are at least primarily philosophers is confirmed by many things:[67] 96's echo of *Academica* 2.1.2 (*partim in percontando a peritis, partim in rebus gestis legendis* (of military matters) and 4 (same process in philosophical matters); the Socratic *percontabere* (contrasting with the nosy 'enquirer' of the body of the poem and ringing with Horace's Socratic *elenchos* of Epistle 1); the contrast with Iccius' high-flown philosophical interests; the thematic echoes in 98–9 of Epistles 14, 6 and 16 (all strongly philosophical); the Stoic *mediocriter utilium*; the question of 100; the Aristippean 102; and the Epicurean 103. And the *docti* must include Horace, Lollius' present counsellor, the ironic *docendus* of Epistle 17, then pointedly revealed as *doctus* (17.16), the poet of the *liber* with such vast philosophical potential (1.36–7). And seventeen lines after 18.96 Epistle 19 begins: *Prisco si credis, Maecenas docte, Cratino*. As at the book's beginning, Maecenas is *doctus* in poetry, not in the *doctrina* of 18.96–103, or, if the latter, only because he has *learned* (become *doctus*) from Epistles 1–18. Poets, then, are included only to the extent that Horace himself is a philosophical poet, promoting a philosophical conception of poetry.

Lollius must choose which philosophy suits him best. Then he must keep at it: philosophising never stops. Back once more to Epistle 1: the cure is philosophy. But from Socratic non-commitment and the relativism which exists within Academicism, Panaetianism and Aristippeanism, Horace has fashioned a relativism which allows individual choice between philosophies: an original and creative philosophical move, and one based on a simple but profound psychological truth: individual personality greatly influences – and should influence – philosophical, political and intellectual choices. For Horace himself, now, the Epicurean way is most suited, it cannot be for ever (104 *quotiens*), because we are none of us completely free – only the *liber* is *liber* (Epistle 20),[68] but may it last at least a year (109). Maecenas will have an even longer wait than Epistle 7 requested. Indeed, Horace's final praise of Maecenas is conditional upon Maecenas' approving of Horace's philosophical talk, upon his allowing Horace greater freedom, and upon his trying himself to become a better person.

Is, then, *Epistles* 1 'anti-Augustan' (robustly useful term)? Are the praises of Maecenas in Epistles 1, 7 and 19 (praises themselves not unequivocal), of Augustus in Epistles 5 and 13, and of patriotism in 3 sapped by the

Epicurean 7, by the Stoic heroics of 16 and by the grimness of 18? Augustus did not find the *Epistles* sufficiently complimentary.[69] But, logically, deconstruction must work both ways: such is the interactive economy of the circular book. And the pleas of 3 for concord seem real enough, while 5 floats the possibility of reconciliation between praise of Augustus and Epicureanism within Rome. Augustus could not get angry. Nevertheless, along with Horace's pride in 'pleasing the *principes*' and his insistence that each must choose his own philosophical road goes recognition of the increasing dangers of cultivation of the mightiest *amicus* (Epistle 18), of the fact that under him the truly virtuous may have to die to preserve their virtue (Epistle 16), and of the ever-greater attractions of Epicurean withdrawal (Epistles 7, 16, 18). The social and political backdrop to the *Epistles'* exploration of the range of philosophical choices is not inert: Horace registers the ever-sharper challenges of the new monarchy. Ultimately, Epicurean withdrawal is where Horace's own heart lies. But this is a conditional Epicureanism, non-doctrinaire, and untainted by the smugness which disfigures orthodox Epicureanism and enfeebles its intellectual processes. In important respects, Horace's Epicureanism is better than the real thing. Here, too, so far from rejecting philosophy or even just moving outside it, Horace shows himself to be a philosopher and a thoroughly useful one.

But individuals must make their own philosophical choices. They must balance one philosophical position against another. They must read and re-read the text, much of whose complexity derives from the poems' kaleidoscopic shifts of viewpoint, which create an interactive dynamic which itself constitutes a kind of Socratic dialectic. And they must constantly interface this complex text with the complexities of life. The *Epistles*, then, are what they claim to be: both formally and profoundly philosophical, although to gauge their full philosophical profundity readers are required to penetrate the poems' polysemous 'play' in an act of interpretation which itself unites the aesthetic, the moral and the philosophical and itself promotes their philosophical growth, if, that is, they are prepared to do so (20.17–18).

MICHÈLE LOWRIE

11   HORACE, CICERO AND AUGUSTUS,
     OR THE POET STATESMAN AT
     EPISTLES 2.1.256

Horace and Cicero: poets with a philosophic bent, Republicans who
came down on the losing side of civil war in the wake of Caesar's as-
sassination but nevertheless admired the man who became Augustus,
authors preoccupied with their own immortality and who thought hard
about art's commemorative task. Augustus and Cicero: statesmen with
a literary bent, whose prose was more successful than their poetry, who
wrote accounts of their own accomplishments, and took especial pride
in saving the state from civil disturbance, who were hailed as *pater patriae*
and thought of themselves as new founders, but whose role in bringing peace came with the terrible price of putting Roman citizens to
death without trial.[1] My tendentious descriptions emphasise the many
similarities linking Horace, Cicero, and Augustus despite all the differences: Cicero's poetry was an afterthought to his political career; the
death of the Catilinarians could be defended in legal terms while the
triumviral proscriptions could not; Augustus succeeded where Cicero
failed.

I will argue that Cicero triangulates the relation of Horace to Augustus
in *Epist.* 2.1. Horace cites Cicero's poetry in declining to write the *princeps'*
res gestae:[2]

> o fortunatam natam me consule Romam   (fr. 8[3])

> et formidatam Parthis te principe Romam   (*Epist.* 2.1.256)

Horace's line also shares a verbal similarity with Augustus' own *Res gestae*.
Augustus says *me principe* (13) in talking about the closing of the gates
of Janus, mentioned in the previous line of Horace's epistle – the pronoun is Cicero's, the noun Horace's.[4] Cicero shares the role of poet and
laudator with Horace, of statesman and *laudandus* with Augustus.[5] Why
Cicero?[6] And why here, when Horace stakes out a claim to an important
social function for literature, only to disavow the greatest story of the age,
Augustus' *res gestae*, and in the next poem to disavow poetry altogether for
philosophy? Extensive allusion to Cicero in the epistles to Augustus and

to Florus tells a story about the relation of poetry to politics, of republic to principate, of philosophy's role in removing us from such concerns.[7] This story corroborates the surface level of Horace's combined panegyric of Caesar and refusal to write such panegyric, but also says much that his decorum leaves unsaid.

Cicero is cited frequently in Horatian contexts for parallels in ancient literary theory and for general cultural or philosophical background.[8] Fraenkel, for instance, peppers his reading of *Epist.* 2.1 with comments that make Cicero exemplary of real life.[9] These are parallels that never meet, not passionate allusions.[10] The assumption is that these similarities derive independently from the *tertium quid* of Roman life, which supplies sufficient meaning in itself. Horatians tend to look through Cicero: he transmits citations of the poets Horace 'really' alludes to.[11] In a literary context, we separate poetry from prose (disregarding Cicero's poetry), and poets from men of action (disregarding Horace's military career).[12] In arguing for allusion, I do not, however, mean to argue for a literary relation as a thing apart. Horace evokes Cicero to underscore a difference between cultural realities then and now. The change in literary taste he argues for – against a view best represented for us by Cicero – goes hand in hand with a change in politics. Our separation of literature from politics and both from philosophy is nonsensical for Cicero, though Horace's division of himself from the *princeps* in *Epist.* 2.1 seems perfectly natural. The Horatian perspective blinds us to the possibilities of the prior generation.[13] The necessary division between writer and addressee in the epistolary format corresponds to a division between functions: Augustus the statesman stands as second person against the poet's first. The division between poetic and philosophical pursuits in *Epist.* 2.2 posits a further split between aspects of Horace's self. By contrast, Cicero's favourite pronoun *ego* encompasses political, philosophical, and literary capacities alike. This is not egotism: Cicero's utilitarian conception of intellectual pursuits as handmaidens of the statesman grants literature a social function Horace could well envy.

The *Pro Archia*'s explanation of poetry's worth reveals the assumptions Horace inherited and altered. We start with *topoi*. Cicero attributes complementary functions to the Muses: to offer respite for the tired man of the world and to commemorate his actions so another generation may aspire to his example. Horace would doubtless agree with the former:[14]

> quaeres a nobis, Gratti, cur tanto opere hoc homine [Archia] delecte-
> mur. quia suppeditat nobis ubi et animus ex hoc forensi strepitu
> *reficiatur* et aures conuicio *defessae* conquiescant. (Cicero, *Arch.* 12)

> uos [Camenae] Caesarem altum, militia simul
> *fessas* cohortis abdidit oppidis,
>   finire quaerentem labores
>   Pierio *recreatis* antro.
>   (Horace, *Carm.* 3.4.37–40)

Commemoration is more tricky. Horace certainly believes in offering *exempla* to the next generation. His addressing the children at the beginning of the Roman Odes (*Carm.* 3.1.4) accords with the picture of literature's pedagogical function he presents in the epistle to Augustus:

> mox etiam pectus *praeceptis* format amicis,
> asperitatis et inuidiae corrector et irae;
> recte facta refert, orientia tempora notis
> instruit *exemplis*, inopem solatur et aegrum.
>   (*Epist.* 2.1.128–31)

Horace redirects toward ethics an education that inspired Cicero to glory:

> nam nisi multorum *praeceptis* multisque litteris mihi ab adulescentia suasissem nihil esse in uita magno opere expetendum nisi laudem atque honestatem, ... sed pleni omnes sunt libri, plenae sapientium uoces, plena *exemplorum* uetustas. (*Arch.* 14)

Augustus also was interested in models for ethics or glory and would make excerpts of *praecepta et exempla publice uel priuatim salubria* (Suet. *Aug.* 89.2). Where Horace offers *exempla* for others to follow, and Cicero here presents himself as following others' *exempla*, Augustus positions himself as both follower and originator:

> legibus nouis me auctore latis multa *exempla* maiorum exolescentia iam ex nostro saeculo reduxi et ipse multarum rerum *exempla* imitanda posteris tradidi. (*Res gestae* 8.5[15])

Horace does recognise that *exempla* derive from *recte facta*, but, when it comes to praising them himself, he demurs. Whereas Cicero defends Archias for writing up the achievements of the Roman people (*eum qui uos, qui uestros imperatores, qui populi Romani res gestas semper ornauit*, *Arch.* 31), Horace hesitates when it comes to Augustus': *nec sermones ego mallem | repentis per humum quam res componere gestas, | ... si quantum cuperem possem quoque*, *Epist.* 2.1.250–7. The grounds are aesthetic: *nec praue factis decorari uersibus opto*, *Epist.* 2.1.266. He does not object on principle, given his admiration of Virgil and Varius (*Epist.* 2.1.247), but, were he to try, it would result in bad art.

Bad art, however, cannot be defined merely on aesthetic grounds independent of praise and blame. The bad poetry Horace would rather not be subject to in the passage cited above (*praue factis uersibus*, 2.1.266) recurs not only in the context of aesthetics (*incultis uersibus*, 2.1.233; *carmine foedo*, 2.1.236; *chartis . . . ineptis*, 2.1.270), but in that of defamation (*malo . . . carmine*, 2.1.153). The two axes – praise/blame, good/bad – cross:[16]

> *sedulitas* autem stulte quem diligit urget,
> praecipue cum se numeris commendat et arte:
> discit enim citius meminitque libentius illud
> quod quis deridet, quam quod probat et ueneratur.
> (*Epist.* 2.1.260–4)

The first two lines about artistic ineptitude segue neatly into two comparing the relative ease of remembering mockery over praise. The points of contact between the epistle and the *Pro Archia* here become more specific. Horace implies he could not end up on the positive side of both axes, as a good praise poet, but, should he try, would produce something along the lines of the *malus poeta* whose *sedulitas* Sulla rewarded on the condition he write no more (*Arch.* 25). Cicero argues Archias should be valued as a good poet since even bad poetry wins some reward (25) and since poetry is so inherently valuable that Q. Metellus Pius lent his ears even to Spanish poets with thick and foreign accents (*etiam Cordubae natis poetis pingue quiddam sonantibus atque peregrinum, Arch.* 26). Horace takes a dim view of *Alexander*'s reward of Choerilus' bad verse (*Epist.* 2.1.233) and would himself blush to be given a 'rich' gift (*ne rubeam pingui donatus munere, Epist.* 2.1.267).[17] In the same passage, Cicero tells a rather different story of *Alexander*, that, despite the numbers of poets he kept in his entourage to write up his deeds (*scriptores rerum suarum, Arch.* 24), he envied Achilles' having Homer as his publicity agent.

To these thematic and verbal parallels, we can add others.[18] But such correspondences mark a greater and more delicate problematic. Horace in this poem rejects the role of commemorative poet as defined by Cicero. His citation of the *Pro Archia* highlights the difference. Where Cicero tolerates bad praise poetry – with a certain amount of irony, of course – Horace draws the line. Unlike Archias, he does not tell of the Augustan equivalent of Lucullus' Mithridatic war. If Archias is Cicero's ideal, he represents a model Horace cannot embrace, at least not directly or extensively.

For a negative foil, Horace shares more with Archias than we might expect. Horace actually does tell of Lucullus' Mithridatic war in the following epistle (*Epist.* 2.2.25–40).[19] It is not a war story, but rather an *exemplum* explaining why he has not sent poetry to his friend Florus. Like Horace, the argument goes, a brave soldier made efforts solely to avert penury. Once the soldier wins his reward by a heroic exploit, and Horace saves himself from poverty by writing verse (51–2), each becomes unwilling to take further pains. In short, Horace's *Mithridatic War* justifies another poetic refusal, an inversion of Archias' poem. Florus rather resembles Archias as the general's literary companion in Asia, with Lucullus and Tiberius both conducting business in Armenia.[20] Cicero, in his version of Archias' poem, says the Romans opened Pontus, which was fortified by royal wealth as well as nature: *populus enim Romanus aperuit Lucullo imperante Pontum et regiis quondam opibus et ipsa natura et regione uallatum* (*Arch.* 21). Horace likewise stresses royalty, wealth, and fortification, along with a marker of citation: *praesidium regale loco deiecit, ut aiunt, | summe munito et multarum diuite rerum* (*Epist.* 2.2.30–1). Does 'they say' refer to Cicero's Archias?[21]

Archias, however, also offers Horace a positive example for withholding commemorative verse. Cicero mentions Archias' having begun a poem on the events of his consulship (*Arch.* 28), but is later disappointed in his failure to progess (*Ad Atticum,* 1.16.15, 1.20.6). If Horace makes Archias into an *exemplum* for himself, does that in turn imply Cicero as an *exemplum* for Augustus?[22] Cicero kept trying to induce others to write up his accomplishments, but, because no one did, ended up writing them himself.[23] The comparison appears absurd: true, the Augustan poets kept declining to write the *res gestae* Augustus himself composed,[24] but Cicero's position seems ridiculous while Augustus' was, well, august. The differences have to do with power – social, political, and rhetorical. Cicero was a *nouus homo,* Augustus *diui filius*; Cicero lost, Augustus won; authors of various stripes actually refused Cicero's requests, while the Augustan poets praised Augustus indirectly with elaborate *recusationes*.

Another text of Cicero's takes us to the next stage in Horace's articulation of the relation between poet and statesman. In his letter to Lucceius requesting a historical account of the deeds surrounding his consulship and exile, Cicero returns to similar concerns Horace finds of interest in the *Pro Archia*.[25] Alexander serves as an *exemplum* again, this time one more similar to the Horatian passage: he shows good artistic taste in wanting to be painted only by Apelles and sculpted by Lysippus.[26] Close on the heels of each passage comes another comparing literature favourably to the figurative arts (*Epist.* 2.1.248–50, *Fam.* 5.12.7). A further similarity is that Cicero wants recognition *within his lifetime*:

> illa nos cupiditas incendit de qua initio scripsi, festinationis, quod alacres animo sumus ut et ceteri uiuentibus nobis ex libris tuis nos cognoscant et nosmet ipsi uiui gloriola nostra perfruamur. (*Fam.* 5.12.9)

Horace distinguishes Augustus from a series of culture heroes exactly in this regard. Romulus, Liber, Castor and Pollux, who were transferred to heaven after death, complained of a lack of recognition (*Epist.* 2.1.9–10); Hercules found that envy was overcome only by death (12). By contrast, Augustus is honoured as a god on earth (15). Horace has, of course, changed the equation by putting Augustus into more heroic company: divine honours are not on the cards for Cicero. Praise within one's lifetime also underlies the transition to the next section, a transition ostentatiously frivolous, though something serious is at issue.[27]

The opening of the epistle to Augustus takes for granted the commemorative task of a poem addressed to a statesman. The first four lines outline Augustus' job in war and peace; next comes a flattering comparison to divinised culture heroes where the very subject is commemoration; the climax presents Augustus as a god on earth. When Horace complains (20) that, unlike the good judgement they show regarding their supreme statesman, the people appreciate nothing else, and especially literature, unless it is dead, our poet turns the tables on Augustus. The poem ceases glorifying the *princeps*; instead he will have the privilege of having an essay on poetics directed his way. The unexpressed link turns on commemorative literature. How can a poet who receives no recognition in his lifetime write something worthy of a *princeps* who does? It is a structural problem: you cannot be praised by a dead poet (*quod Libitina sacrauit, Epist.* 2.1.49)[28] and contemporary poets receive no praise: therefore, Horace implies, Augustus cannot receive his due. Cicero regards it the utmost glory to be praised by a man deserving of praise:

> placet enim Hector ille mihi Naeuianus, qui non tantum 'laudari' se laetatur sed addit etiam 'a laudato uiro'. (*Fam.* 5.12.7[29])

By receiving recognition on his own without poetry, Augustus sets a conundrum for Horace.[30] *Carm.* 4.8 shares two similarities with *Epist.* 2.1: a passage juxtaposing literature with the visual arts (*Carm.* 4.8.5–12, *Epist.* 2.1.248–50) and an almost identical list of immortalised culture heroes (Hercules, Liber, Castor and Pollux at *Carm.* 4.8.29–34, Romulus in addition at *Epist.* 2.1.5–12).[31] The burden of Horace's message in *Carm.* 4.8 is *caelo Musa beat* (29). In achieving divinity on his own, Augustus sets in question one half of the purpose of poetry as understood by Cicero. If its commemorative function has become obsolete, does that leave mere delectation? The epistle's defence of aesthetics and definition of a social role for poetry answer this question,[32] but, if Horace does not write commemorative poetry in any straightforward way, he still cannot for that reason stop talking about it – and his talk about Augustus' not needing commemoration and his own inability to provide it commemorates Augustus willy-nilly.[33]

In asking Lucceius for a historical account, Cicero envisions a relationship between author and statesman that excludes the likes of Horace. Cicero wants to be praised by another *statesman*, not as Timoleon was by Timaeus or Themistocles by Herodotus; he wants not merely genius or the Homeric *praeconium* Alexander envied Achilles, but the *auctoritas clarissimi et spectatissimi uiri et in rei publicae maximis grauissimisque causis cogniti atque in primis probati* (*Fam.* 5.12.7). The statesman and the man of letters coincide. They do not necessarily, as the terms of his distinction between Marius and Catulus show (*Arch.* 5). But the combination of *uirtus* and *doctrina* results in *illud nescio quid praeclarum ac singulare*. The examples he lists are a group of Ciceronian heroes, Africanus, Laelius, Furius, Cato (*Arch.* 15–16), who follow on the heels of his own confession to a devotion to literature (12). We have now reached an issue with no obvious correspondence in Horace, who defines Augustus as a statesman and himself as a poet without overlap between their roles.

Or is there? Cicero's understanding of literary commemoration helps Horace define exactly what he disavows, but with the relation of poet to statesman Horace becomes less explicit. The epistle to Augustus opens with a sharp division between the important work of the statesman and the trivial distraction of *sermo* (*Epist.* 2.1.1–4).[34] This clear distinction between first and second person, poet and statesman respectively, becomes clouded at the poem's conclusion. Horace puts himself as first person in the position of the *laudandus*. The *scriptor* who would write his praises, as poorly as Horace would Augustus', is a third person:

> nil moror officium quod me grauat, ac neque ficto
> in peius uultu proponi cereus usquam,
> nec praue factis decorari uersibus opto,
> ne rubeam pingui donatus munere, et una
> cum scriptore meo, capsa porrectus operta,
> deferar in uicum uendentem tus et odores
> et piper et quidquid chartis amicitur ineptis.
>
> (*Epist.* 2.1.264–70)

Putting oneself in the place of the addressee is not adverse to the rhetoric of praise; indeed, Pindar does so in moments of tact.[35] Tact is at issue here, since the poet takes on himself the descent into the ridiculous.[36] But by putting himself – up to now the *laudator* – in the position of the *laudandus*, Horace suggests the same person can occupy both positions. This move stands out, given Horace's transformation of Cicero's line just above. When Archias failed to write a poem on Cicero's *res gestae* in the year of his consulship, Cicero did it himself, collapsing the roles of *laudator* and *laudandus*, poet and statesman.

Horace's version of Cicero's line is the climax of his sample of the poetry he here declines:

> o fortunatam natam me consule Romam					(Cicero, fr. 8)
>
> et formidatam Parthis te principe Romam					(*Epist.* 2.1.256)

He makes a number of changes relevant to the issues, spoken and unspoken, of the epistle. One is aesthetic: he erases the jingle -*natam natam,* thereby implying that Cicero's poetry did not meet Horace's standards.[37] Another political: the statesman no longer holds an office, but has become a first citizen. Barchiesi understands these corrections as a statement that a new good taste inheres in panegyric that accords with a new discourse of power: Augustus demonstrates good taste by declining monarchy just as the poet declines poetry that would compromise his demanding aesthetics.[38] But arguments from tact are notoriously slippery, and there is more. The change of just three letters – *tun* to *mid,* with a chiastic exchange of dentals for nasals – marks a vast difference: from the fortune of renewal (*fortunatam*) to a mature and feared empire (*formidatam*). Horace divides the self-reference in Cicero's *me* into a poet's *ego* speaking of a statesman's *te,* and further replaces reference to a civil disturbance, Catiline's conspiracy, with a respectable foreign opponent in the Parthians (a standard Horatian move since *Odes* 1–3).[39]

Civil war has more to do with Horace's division between poet and statesman than first appears. It is essential to the autobiography Horace presents in the epistle to Florus, since it disrupts his studies, first literary at Rome, then philosophical at Athens, and throws him into the world of war and politics:

> Romae nutriri mihi contigit, atque doceri
> iratus Grais quantum nocuisset Achilles.
> adiecere bonae paulo plus artis Athenae,
> scilicet ut uellem curuo dinoscere rectum,
> atque inter siluas *Academi* quaerere uerum.
> dura sed emouere loco me tempora grato,
> *ciuilis*que rudem belli tulit *aestus in arma*
> Caesaris Augusti non responsura lacertis.
> unde simul primum me dimisere Philippi,
> decisis humilem pennis inopemque paterni
> et laris et fundi, paupertas impulit audax
> ut uersus facerem.					(*Epist.* 2.2.41–52)

Horace's foray into the world failed and he turned to poetry to make a living. The distortion of Horace's account is often noted, since he supported himself by purchasing a post (*scriba quaestorius*, Suet. *Vita Hor.*) before poetry won him Maecenas' patronage. This distortion allows for the development of an argument. Since his only (alleged) reason to write was to avert poverty, and he now has what he needs, writing poetry has become superfluous (52–4). This argument in turn informs the discussion of avarice in the second half of the poem, a moral consideration he had presumably pondered at the Academy when learning right from wrong, true from false (44–5). Horace's claim to renounce poetry to devote himself to philosophy distracts from an earlier renunciation. He had already left an unsuccessful political and military career for poetry[40] – precisely because of civil war, the kind of internal conflict he learned about when studying how much Achilles harmed the Greeks. Hindsight and Horace's ironic treatment of his past make the very idea of our genial poet engaging in war or politics laughable,[41] but things may have looked different at the time.

Urania, in Cicero's poem on his consulship, tells a similar story of his being snatched from study at the Academy by public affairs:

> inque *Academia* umbrifera nitidoque Lyceo
> fuderunt claras fecundi pectoris artis.
> e quibus ereptum primo iam a flore iuuentae
> te patria in media uirtutum mole locauit.
> tu tamen anxiferas curas requiete relaxans,
> quod patria uacat, id studiis nobisque sacrasti.
>
> (fr. 10.73–8[42])

The result, however, is antithetical to Horace's story. Not only does Cicero become an important statesman, but he devotes his spare time to philosophical studies and the Muses. He can juggle politics, philosophy, and poetry – if not quite all at once, at least all within the same person. Horace did not have this option and sees these as mutually exclusive pursuits.

Before rushing to the conclusion that Horace saw in Cicero the ideal of the Renaissance man, an ideal he perhaps aspired to when as a student at Athens he imagined emulating the renowned *nouus homo* in his defence of the Republic, an ideal that died in the disturbance of civil war, let us remember that Urania presents a rosy picture Cicero elsewhere contradicts. Even in this passage, philosophy and the Muses, as leisure activities, yield to public affairs. Elsewhere philosophy affords Cicero consolation when out of power and substitutes for politics (*philosophiam nobis pro rei publicae procuratione substitutam*, *Div.* 2.7). As soon as he can return to government, he does. Literature is for leisure (*quantum uacabit a publico officio*, 2.7). Civil disturbance (*armis ciuilibus*, 2.6) drove him, like Horace, out of the public arena into writing.

If Cicero offers Horace an *exemplum*, it is one of a failed ideal for politics and poetry alike.[43] Both men ran aground in civil war, but, in addition to political failure, Horace's transformation of Cicero's line on his consulship reveals aesthetic objections as well. The erasure of the jingle is a correction according to principles advanced earlier: *emendata ... | pulchraque et exactis minimum distantia (Epist.* 2.1.71–2).[44] Furthermore, the citation of Cicero's line occurs in Horace's sample of the praise poetry he disavows (*Epist.* 2.1.252–6). He implies that, were he to write such poetry, it would sound like Cicero – a reason not to.[45] As in *Carm.* 1.6, a sense of decorum (*pudor* 9) keeps him from singing the *laudes egregii Caesaris* (11): *nec meus audet | rem temptare pudor quam uires ferre recusent (Epist.* 2.1.258–9). A sense of violated decorum would also attend his hypothetical receipt of bad art: *ne rubeam pingui donatus munere (Epist.* 2.1.267). But the ridicule attaching to Cicero's line concerns more than the parallel with Volusius' turgid poetry Horace makes at the poem's end, where he cites Catullus' conceit of bad poetry's fate as wrapping-paper (Poem 95). The line is ridiculous because it praises its own author – a violation of decorum – something that happens only when poet and statesman are one.[46]

The ridicule Juvenal heaps on the line comes paired with admiration for Cicero's eloquence and courage:[47]

> ingenio manus est et ceruix caesa, nec umquam
> sanguine causidici maduerunt rostra pusilli.
> 'o fortunatam natam me consule Romam':
> Antoni gladios potuit contemnere si sic
> omnia dixisset. ridenda poemata malo
> quam te, conspicuae diuina Philippica famae,
> uolueris a prima quae proxima.
>
> (Juvenal 10.120–6)

Bad poetry is not dangerous like good oratory. Juvenal conjoins the two to highlight their incongruity. In his argument, the former is preferable to the latter with regard to personal well-being, but Horace falls between the cracks. His aesthetics cannot tolerate bad poetry, and history precluded a public career. Besides, his list of admitted vices includes fear of death (*Epist.* 2.2.207). Whereas Juvenal splits the laudable from the ridiculous, poetry from prose, true courage from silly self-involution, poet from statesman, in Horace the allusions to Cicero lie without comment under the text's surface: positive, negative, merely analogous all together.

Well, not entirely without comment. Barchiesi sees the relevance of the ridicule in lines 262–3 to the citation of Cicero's line: *discit enim citius meminitque libentius illud | quod quis deridet, quam quod probat et ueneratur.*[48]

But the comment again leaves us wondering – if Cicero's verse is laughable, is there a part Horace would 'approve and respect'? Can we, like Juvenal, separate bravery from the ridiculous, the poet from the statesman? So far, we have been considering Cicero as a (failed) *exemplum* for Horace. He also pertains to Horace's addressee. Can the context of citation recover another side to Cicero?[49]

> terrarumque situs et flumina dicere, et arces
> montibus impositas et barbara regna, tuisque
> auspiciis totum confecta duella per orbem,
> claustraque custodem pacis cohibentia Ianum,
> et formidatam Parthis te principe Romam
> *(Epist.* 2.1.252–6)

The *res gestae* of Augustus which Horace declines to tell include two historical realities, the closing of the gates of Janus, and the recovery from the Parthians of the lost standards.[50] If we recall that Augustus first closed the gates in 29 BCE, the year of his triple triumph, when civil war's end was officially celebrated,[51] we do find a parallel to Cicero: instead of ending a civil war, he prevented one from starting. If we also recall that the standards were recovered from the Parthians in 20 BCE by diplomacy rather than war, we at least find Cicero being honest about the preferability of civil resolution to force: *cedant arma togae, concedat laurea laudi (De cons. suo,* fr. 12).[52] Augustus was no better a general than Cicero, and the cross-reference to *arces | Alpibus impositas (Carm.* 4.14.11–12) reminds us Augustus largely prevailed militarily through delegates, whether Drusus and Tiberius or Agrippa.[53]

Here I go too far. Comparison of Augustus to Cicero is categorically unacceptable.[54] Horace makes sure to couch the return of the standards in complimentary military terms: *formidatam (Epist.* 2.1.256). To suggest otherwise reads against the grain. My suggestion that Augustus did things comparable to the accomplishments Cicero immortalised in his silliest verses undoes the tact scholars attribute to Horace throughout this epistle, and good manners, as Mayer emphasises, are crucial to the *Epistles.*[55] Tact has two sides, one a 'keen sense for what is appropriate, tasteful, or aesthetically pleasing', the other a 'keen sense of what to say or do to avoid giving offense'.[56] Does the emphasis on aesthetic pleasure here accompany an avoidance of offence? Is there so much to avoid? Horace can remake Cicero's poetry according to his own standards, but he cannot remake Augustus' treatment of Cicero. Horace has aesthetic, but not political control. Rudd lists among things one could say about Augustus – but Horace did not – his 'complicity in the murder of Cicero'.[57] Rudd brings up what cannot be suppressed.

To be fair, the evidence for Augustus' dealings with Horace points to similar tact and aesthetic judgement to that which the poet exercises with him. As Horace suggests, Augustus was concerned that celebration of him be outstanding:

> componi tamen aliquid de se nisi et serio et a praestantissimis offendebatur, admonebatque praetores ne paterentur nomen suum commissionibus obsolefieri. (Suetonius, *Aug.* 89.3)

In Horace's epistle, the *exemplum* about Alexander answers to Augustus' concern about *praestantissimis*, and the allusion to Cicero's poetry to *serio*. Unlike Cicero's letter to Lucceius where he hankers for praise in his lifetime, Augustus turns his request around:

> post sermones uero quosdam lectos nullam sui mentionem habitam ita sit questus: 'irasci me tibi scito, quod non in plerisque eius modi scriptis mecum potissimum loquaris; an uereris ne apud posteros infame tibi sit quod uidearis familiaris nobis esse?' (Suetonius, *Vita Hor.*)

Augustus expresses no desire for praise, he rather wants address; the poet's reputation among posterity replaces praise of himself during his lifetime; he displaces a request into a question. Certainly, the question is ironic because it occludes a demand, but such is tact: good taste in the avoidance of giving offence. It goes both ways.

It would be easier to understand what Horace tells Augustus if he made as sharp a distinction between literature and politics as between good and bad art. The moral would be one of decorum, where each person fulfils his function in an ordered and tactful universe: you stick to public affairs (*Epist.* 2.1.1–4), and leave literature to me; do not write up your deeds in verse, or you risk the ridicule of a Cicero. Instead, Horace sees no harm, however misguided, in everyone's writing verse (*Epist.* 2.1.109–10, 117–19), though there is no reverse possibility for everyone to engage in politics. Moreover, Horace slips out from the position of the commemorative poet that such a partition would lead us to expect. It would also be easier to understand his refusing this role if he categorically stated *res gestae* make for bad poetry. Cicero's example points that way, but Virgil and Varius support the proposition that one can write good praise.[58]

On second glance, however, Horace says nothing about Virgil or Varius offering praise, however clear the implication. Rather, what Horace says reverses the entire direction of praise, and disrupts the panegyrical contract. In commemorative poetry, the poet praises the statesman. Here the statesman earns praise by his choice of poets to honour:

> at neque dedecorant tua de se iudicia atque
> munera, quae multa dantis cum laude tulerunt,
> dilecti tibi Vergilius Variusque poetae.
>
> (*Epist.* 2.1.245–7)

The competition has moved from *uirtus* to taste: the statesman who rewards the best poet wins. The price is a treatise on poetics instead of one's deeds.[59]

It would be nice if the story ended here. In the next poem, however, Horace plans to abandon poetry altogether to work on his character. The desire to return to philosophy essentially puts him back at the Academy of his youth. Is this a desire to erase subsequent history, the civil war that disrupted his studies, and his ensuing poetic career?[60] But Horace himself refuses to allow a neat demarcation between 'now' and 'then'. If the *sorites* paradox removes any dividing line that would allow us to determine poetry's worth according to age (*Epist.* 2.1.39–49), the same can apply to the political situation. There were no 'good old days' for poetry or anything else. Before civil war disrupted Horace's studies, it intervened in Cicero's life, and that was hardly the beginning. Besides, Cicero does not provide an example he, or Augustus, would (entirely) emulate.

So where are we? The allusions to Cicero invite us to compare him as a poet to Horace, and as a statesman to Augustus – and vice versa. He further opens the door to philosophical concerns that question poetry's value as well as politics'. While he appears to function mostly as a negative *exemplum* for a bad poet and a failed politician, our inability to control allusion's power conjures up a (rejected) positive *exemplum* – a philosopher poet king? Whichever way we turn, our thoughts pursue a line that undoes the poet's tact. The ridicule Horace insists on discussing with the aim to divert makes us wonder what could be so ridiculous. I do not mean Horace's panegyric of Augustus fails. As Barchiesi points out, Horace's line *nil oriturum alias, nil ortum tale fatentes* (*Epist.* 2.1.17) surpasses Cicero's fondest hopes.[61] Far from providing the last word, however, this line falls close to the poem's beginning, and the rest of the poem takes us elsewhere, to poetry.

The epistle's panegyrical beginning does not actually mention poetry. The culture heroes complain about not receiving *fauor*, Hercules' death brings *inuidia* to an end, the one who blasted lesser merits finds love (*amabitur*) upon death (9–14). These words have to do with popularity independent of artistic praise. Art comes up as poetry's distraction of Augustus from business (*sermone*, *Epist.* 2.1.4), and as the generalised 'arts' Brink translates as 'skills, practices, merits', not as commemoration.[62]

Horace's poetry *does* commemoration without talking about it. What keeps this section, then, from falling to the strictures of the poem's final section where he rejects commemoration?[63] Precisely that they both occur in the same poem, that the poem concerns something else, namely literature and its history. The humorous twist into the poet's complaint that, like Hercules, he does not get his due while alive, the inclusion of a sample panegyric Horace disavows writing, both avoid the ridiculous through wit. Talk of killing verse at the end enables the poem's opening to do what it says, namely give a living hero his due.

Tact, wit, allusion all keep something simmering under the surface, contain that something and show that it could burst into the open, but does not. A less decorous poet would remind us that Cicero's bad poetry did not bury him in the oblivion of the spice district. Rather, *inuidia* during his lifetime and his second Philippic nailed the *disiecti membra oratoris* to the Rostra. But let us not whitewash Cicero. If the thought Horace cannot keep us from thinking is Augustus' complicity in Cicero's death, we will also remember that the suppression of the Catilinarian conspiracy for which Cicero composed his infamous lines also entailed the execution of citizens without trial.[64] Does the parallel between Augustus and Cicero justify empire, or drag the republic down? Augustus heeded Horace's warning and wrote his own *Res gestae* in such a style that people could not make literary hay of political resentment.[65]

12 *VNA CVM SCRIPTORE MEO*
Poetry, Principate and the traditions of literary
history in the Epistle to Augustus

On the first day of fighting at Philippi, the watchword and battlecry for the
tryannicides' army was the inspiring 'Libertas'.[1] It is probable, however,
that the 22-year-old Horace did not hear it – as if in anticipation of the
confused failure to come, the tickets with the watchword were still being
passed along to the officers when Brutus' legions spontaneously hurled
themselves against the forces of Caesar opposite.[2] Returning to Rome
after the eventual catastrophe of the Republican cause, Horace carried
on his fumbled engagement with *libertas* as he tackled the two genres,
one archaic and Greek, one only a century old and Latin, whose entire
raison d'être consisted in the exercise of unrestrained outspokenness; as
has often been remarked, his *Epodes* and *Satires* make a major theme out
of why and how they do not live up to their generic trademarks in the
unparalleled political environment of triumviral Rome.[3]

The transformations of the conditions for speech in the ever-changing
Principate continued to engage the poet throughout his career, as he and
his near coeval, Caesar Augustus, remade their respective traditions. In
what is very probably his penultimate work, possibly his last, the Epistle
to Augustus, Horace addresses the man against whom he fought thirty
years before, each of them now supreme in his own field. They have both
reached their position of classic status in a surprisingly short time and
from beginnings which had promised any outcome but this. Revolution-
aries in their twenties, now, in the summer of 12 BCE, at the age of 50
for Augustus and 52 for Horace – suddenly, as it must often have seemed
to them both – they were the established order.[4] Horace's Epistle to the
Princeps simultaneously analyses and enacts the interplay between the
new poetry and the new Principate, and my main purpose in this chapter
is to chart the strong 'gravitational pull' exerted by this pair's bonding.[5]

In tackling 'the place of the poet ... in contemporary society',[6] 'il rap-
porto fra poetica e potere',[7] Horace is certainly continuing his career-long
interest in the possibilities of speech in the given political and social environment, but in this Epistle there is a new dimension, for now he is
attempting to contextualise this long-standing interest within the field

of literary history. This represents a challenge, for us as well as for him. For us, the limits of literary history, and especially of the claims to explanatory power of its various contextualisations, are a topical problem; and Horace's experiment may provide us with a salutary test-case. For Horace, the experiment is even more difficult, since his inherited traditions of literary history and criticism do not afford him any models for such a politically informed investigation of the social status of poetry.[8] The poem treats us, then, to the spectacle of Horace struggling with a recalcitrant literary-critical tradition that barely gives him the purchase he needs. Yet he persists in the struggle, for, as we shall see, Horace needs to construct for himself some kind of critically informed sense of the social conditions for poetry at Rome before he can engage with a situation without precedent in Rome – a quite novel political and poetical power and pre-eminence, implicated in and defining each other, and joined together in the immortality of posterity as they both knew they would be.[9] The momentum of this Epistle shows how Augustus and Horace depend upon each other for the immortality they both covet so much. It is Horace and his poetic peers 'who will eventually be in control of the *Princeps*' posthumous fate', as the *aeditui* of the temple of Virtus.[10] Conversely, it is now Augustus who is in charge of access to the libraries, housed in his temple of Apollo (214–18). They each control the temple that will guarantee the other's immortality.

The two men's shared and mutually implicated hopes of immortality are only one example of numerous points of identity between them, tokens of the inextricability of their spheres of eminence. At the end of the poem, famously, addresser and addressee are collapsed together in the phrase which provides my title, when Horace puts himself into Augustus' shoes as the object of panegyric and fantasises about being consigned to oblivion by and together with the inept person writing about him (264–70). This culminating identification is hinted at already in the first sentence of the poem, which offers the obverse, with its glimpse of the *Princeps* as a super-artist or super-critic, 'adorning' and 'emending' the state (*res Italas . . . moribus ornes,* | *legibus emendes,* 2–3).[11]

The poem's very first line signals the most obvious point of identity, with the emphatically placed *solus*, 'alone', at the end, describing Augustus. Undecidable as the issue of the Epistle's dating must ultimately remain, there is much in favour of the often canvassed date of 12 BCE, not least the consideration that this was the year when Augustus did indeed find himself definitively alone at the summit of affairs.[12] On 6 March of that year Augustus claimed the one prize left and was elected by 'a multitude from the whole of Italy' to the office of *pontifex maximus* which had finally been vacated by Lepidus' recent death.[13] Two weeks later he heard that M. Agrippa, just arrived in Campania from Pannonia, was seriously ill; rushing to see him, he found already dead the man who had been his right hand for thirty years, his son-in-law, father of his adopted sons, colleague as consul (twice) and as quindecimuir (and doubtless other, undocumented, priesthoods), joint holder of supreme *imperium* and *tribunicia potestas*.[14]

In his own sphere, the poet was just as isolated, the sole survivor of his generation. For him the crucial year will have been 19 BCE, when he had lost Virgil, Tibullus and (probably) Varius.[15] Some two decades before writing to Augustus, at the beginning of his career, when closing the first book of *Satires*, Horace had presented a battery of names, fellow-composers and readers, a crowd of individuals representing the new wave which Horace was hoping to catch. As Horace's fellow-composers we are shown Fundanius, Pollio, Varius, Virgil (*Sat.* 1.10.40–5), and thirty-five lines later as his ideal audience we meet Plotius, Varius and Virgil again, together with Maecenas this time, then Valgius, Octavius, Fuscus, both Visci, Pollio again, Messalla and his brother, Bibulus and Servius, Furnius, and 'a good number of others, learned men and friends of mine too, whom I discreetly skip' (*compluris alios, doctos ego quos et amicos | prudens praetereo*, 87–8). There is a striking contrast with the later Epistle, from which the Satire's throng of sympathetic and cooperative peers has vanished. Of all those names from the Satire only two return in the Epistle, Virgil and Varius (*Epist.* 2.1.247) – and they are dead.[16] The poet is left alone with the *Princeps*, who had been 'discreetly skipped' in the Satire, or masked by the nearly homonymous Octavius (*Sat.* 1.10.82). Before, there had been many estimable poets. Now, there is only one.[17] Before, there had been many people whose judgement counted. Now, there is only one.[18] Horace's like-minded contemporaries are gone, and, as we shall see below, the judgement of those who are supposedly professionally qualified to judge, the *critici*, is exposed as valueless by Horace, their criteria systematically lampooned; now, the important *iudicia*, no longer 'merely' literary-critical, are those of Augustus (*tua ... iudicia*, 245), and it is inclusion in his library on the Palatine that determines survival.[19]

Horace's contrasts between these two literary *sermones* highlight the novel isolation he occupies in 12 BCE – an isolation which mirrors that of the *Princeps*.[20] In the Epistle he further highlights his exposed position by the affinities he constructs with literary-historical traditions, for the Epistle presents wide views over literary and social history of a kind that are absent from the Satire. We shall be examining his engagement with his literary-historical traditions in more detail shortly; at this stage, we need only remark how this literary-historical context puts a great deal of pressure on Horace's exposed isolation, calling attention to the fact that he alone is being mentioned and discussed. The point is that the histories and canons of his tradition regularly restricted their attention only to authors who were already dead. The presence of Virgil and Varius in the Epistle is acceptable on these terms, but that of Horace is anomalous. It is well known that Quintilian, a century later, did not discuss living authors in his survey of the canons, and in this restriction he is openly following the Hellenistic scholars Aristarchus and Aristophanes.[21] In the generation before Horace, Cicero says quite explicitly that in his survey of Latin oratory down to his own time he will not discuss living authors (*Brut.* 231): the evaluation of living orators is skilfully entrusted to the other speakers, Atticus (Caesar, 252–3) and Brutus (Cato, 118, Metellus Scipio, 212, Marcellus, 249–50).[22] When Pollio opened his new library in the Atrium Libertatis in the 30s, Varro – appropriately enough for the author of a book called *Imagines* – was the only living writer who had a bust there (Plin. *HN* 7.115). This was because he was 'too old to envy',[23] for envy was the enemy of the living author, as Horace makes very clear in the opening section of the Epistle (especially 86–9).[24]

Alive, and hence out of the reckoning according to the traditional critical procedures of the kind he engages with in the Epistle, Horace yet finds himself at a fascinating juncture in the history of literary history, for he is in the unprecedented position of belonging to the first generation of authors to be school-texts in Rome while they were still alive.[25] In the middle 30s BCE, in *Satires* 1.10, he can ask an adversary with scorn if he 'wants his poetry to be dictated in the cheap schools' (74–5), although this anticipates by a few years our first secure independent evidence for the teaching of contemporary poets in Roman schools.[26] Certainly by 20 BCE, when he releases the first book of the *Epistles* to its public, the two-edged fate of being in the curriculum stares him in the face (1.20.17–18).[27] A classic in his own lifetime, his reception out of his control, he is imitated by others, pawed over by the uncomprehending, the object of envy, plagiarism, and inevitable misreading. Isolated as he now is when he writes to Augustus, he can observe the distortion of his and his peers' accomplishments, mordantly contemplating, for example, the collapse into pat neoteric cliché of the hard-won aesthetic victories of his generation, in which they had reworked and upgraded the Callimacheanism of the neoterics, making it a suitable engine for their grander ambitions.[28] Now, with a heavily ironic first person plural he pictures the poets of the day recycling the hackneyed jargon as they lament that people don't notice 'our "toils", and our poems "spun with fine thread"' (*cum lamentamur non*

apparere labores | nostros et tenui deducta poemata filo, 224–5; Pope catches
the mood brilliantly in his *Imitation*: 'we ... lament, the Wit's too fine | For
vulgar eyes, and point out ev'ry line', 366–7).

Already in *Epist.* 1.19 Horace had openly shown his anger and hi-
larity at the antics of those who misunderstood the multi-layered nature of his art in their attempts at imitation (esp. 19–20). The third
poem in that collection is a much more indirect piece of advice and exemplification, offered to the young Florus as a model of how to deal
with the neoteric inheritance as one element in a manifold tradition.
The worthy Florus is a member of the *cohors* of Tiberius, travelling
somewhere in the East (*Epist.* 1.3.1–5). Perhaps he is covering the same
ground as Catullus had covered some thirty-five years earlier, in the
last years of corrupt Republican provincial government, when he had
gone to Bithynia in a very different kind of *cohors*, with a very different kind of governor, Memmius.[29] Florus may be at the Hellespont (4),
like Catullus visiting his brother's tomb;[30] perhaps he is in Asia (5).[31]
The deft allusions to the earlier poetic *cohors* signal the enormous social
and governmental gulf that had opened up in the intervening generation, an object lesson in how to work dynamically with neotericism.[32]
As Horace moves on to discuss the poetic projects of Florus and his
friends, he illustrates the perils of imitating the classics of ancient Greece
and contemporary Rome, likewise giving lessons in how to do it properly as he goes. His own dextrous reworking of Pindar in the course
of this poem, illustrated by Hubbard, casts a pall over the Pindaric attempts of Titius (10–11).[33] Further, as Hubbard points out, 'Horace
very well knew what could be done in Latin with Pindar, and he had
done it himself in the sapphics of *Odes* 1.12 and the alcaics of *Odes*
3.4';[34] this perspective suddenly gives Horace's politeness at line 12 a
distinctly feline tone, as he enquires 'How is Titius getting on? *Is he
keeping me in mind?*' (*ut ualet? ut meminit nostri?*). The dangers of plagiarism are the explicit subject of the next lines, where Celsus is warned
to look to his own stocks and keep his hands off the writings in the
temple of Apollo Palatinus (15–17). Finally, in addressing Florus himself, Horace treats us to a delightful reworking of a living Roman classic
from Apollo's temple, transforming his addressee into one of the bees
from Virgil's fourth *Georgic* (21–7).[35] The Epistle as a whole is a show-
piece for the confident artist's creative engagement with poetry from
classical Greece and from neoteric and contemporary Rome – including
his own.

If we return to 12 BCE, eight years later, Virgil is now dead, and Horace
is now even more exposed in his novel status as the only living classic,
who cannot be accommodated by the received wisdom of the critical

tradition. How does he position himself and his achievement when writing to Augustus, his counterpart as a living classic, prematurely divine, who cannot be accommodated by the received wisdom of the political tradition?[36]

His fundamental tool for the analysis of the unique position he now occupies in the Rome of Augustus is literary history, a literary history which he contextualises within historical and social frameworks to a surprising degree. I say 'surprising' because, as I remarked at the beginning of this essay, Horace's critical traditions offered him very little to go on by way of such frameworks. As Brink astutely observes, when remarking on the two motifs of Horace's theorising in this poem (the 'technical', on the one hand, and the 'human, social, political, religious and moral', on the other): 'Clearly the models of Horace's literary theories did not provide him with a notion that unified these two large groups of subjects.'[37]

What, then, did he have at his disposal? It is well known that 'the historical study of literature in antiquity was very rudimentary by modern standards'.[38] There was rather more of it than one might think: the Peripatetics in particular wrote voluminously on the histories of various forms, especially drama, compiling lists of victors, chronologies, and lives of authors;[39] and the Romans carried on the tradition, with Accius' prose *Didascalica* and the verse works of Porcius Licinus and Volcacius Sedigitus taking up questions of authenticity and chronology, before we reach the crowning researches of Varro.[40] Still, we lack systematic attempts at historically informed literary history, of the kind that aims at what Williams calls an 'understanding of the relationship of author and genre to the historical environment'.[41] As Williams goes on to point out, their oratorically based theory had no more to offer than '"canons" or lists of the great' and 'survey in an antiquarian fashion'.[42]

The history of Roman literary history shows three exceptions standing out clearly against this broad background: Cicero, pre-eminently in the *Brutus*; Tacitus, in Cicero's footsteps, in the *Dialogus*;[43] and Horace in our Epistle, likewise, as far as I can see, profoundly influenced by Cicero. Horace responds to the gaps in his tradition's capacities in two ways. First, he lampoons the conventional procedures of canons and lists and antiquarian survey, exposing their inadequacy as a tool of thought, often precisely on the grounds of their lack of historical sense; second, he attempts to chart ways of thinking about the place of poetry in Roman cultural history which will help him plot the new conditions of writing in the new regime. I shall deal first with the more straightforward, negative, side of his strategy, before turning to the much more problematic question of what his constructions of literary history can and cannot achieve.

First, then, his attacks on the conventional unhistorical critical procedures. After his introduction, Horace opens his attack on the archaists, who revere only the antique, with 18–27, 'one long and flexible sentence';[44] the long and flexible period is itself a demonstration of his superiority, for this periodic technique is not to be found in the pages of the *ueteres*.[45] In 28–33 he keeps up the attack on those who think the old is good, but brings in a vital extra point when he claims that his adversaries praise the old by analogy with Greek literary history: in Greek literature the oldest is the best, so it must be true of Roman literature too. His hostility to this unthinking and unhistorical use of cross-cultural analogy is extremely deep. He sees it as purely mechanical, and in 28–9 he ridicules it by going back to one of the first images used to lampoon mindless comparison-making, the weighing scale of Aristophanes' *Frogs* (1365–410).

At 5off., and especially 55ff., he explodes the whole revered procedure of the κρίσις ποιημάτων ('judgement/criticism of poems') as carried on by the κριτικοί ('critics') – the transliteration *critici* which he uses in 51, instead of the native Latin calque, *iudex*, has a derisorily hypertechnical, jargony tone.[46] He is attacking many targets at once in these lines: first, the whole enterprise of the comparison of Greek and Roman authors; second, the ranking of authors in a canon; third, the summary encapsulation of an author with a telling word or phrase. He is, in other words, attacking the entire underpinning of what we later see as Quintilian's procedure in *Inst.* 10.1.46–131, a procedure which in Roman literary history goes back at least to Volcacius Sedigitus, whose scholarly poem *De poetis* included a ranking of the Roman comic poets, from Caecilius Statius as Number One to Ennius as Number Ten.[47] In line 3 of that fragment Volcacius uses the Latin word for κρίσις, *iudicium*, to justify his canon, just as Quintilian later uses *iudicium* of the process of making a canon selection (1.4.3; 10.1.54, 60). To Horace this kind of procedure is not a proper use of the judging faculty: proper *iudicium* is what the *uulgus* are delivering if they agree with Horace about the *ueteres* (68); the poem will at the end, as I have already noted, return to the *iudicia* that now really count, those of Augustus (245).

Horace derides the thumbnail one-word summing up of an author's essential characteristics: Pacuvius is *doctus*, Accius is *altus*, Caecilius has got *grauitas*, and Terence has got *ars* (56–9). It is sobering to remind ourselves how many people still think they are doing criticism when they come up with this sort of thing.[48] Most importantly, Horace derides the comparison of Roman authors with Greek: Ennius is *alter Homerus,|ut critici dicunt* (50–1);[49] Afranius is Menander, Plautus is Epicharmus (57–8). In order to appreciate Horace's originality here, we have to remind ourselves of how fundamental a tool the σύγκρισις ('comparison') was for literary critics, within the Greek tradition or across the two traditions.[50] Horace will have none of it. In this Epistle such συγκρίσεις ('comparisons') are made in order to be ridiculed, as here, or else the συγκρίσεις are negative: Virgil and Varius are *not* Choerilus, at the end of the poem, as Augustus is *not* Alexander (229–47).[51] At the root of his objection to the comparison-mentality is his conviction, ultimately inherited from Cicero, that the historical patterns of Rome and Greece are distinct and cannot be compared to each other without absurd distortion.[52]

At the end of the section about the fans of the *ueteres*, Horace narrows down, finally, to himself (*nostra . . . nos nostraque*, 89). But then he veers away, and moves into his panorama of first Greek and then Roman cultural history, which will eventually take us all the way down to the present day and the resumption of his direct address to Augustus (214–18). Here we may take up the second, constructive, side of his reaction to his literary-critical tradition, for it is here that he embarks on his elusive literary history, which circles around and around the issues of the status of poetry in Rome since its inception, in order to create a background that will put his own contemporary status in perspective.

It is important to be clear about what Horace is and is not doing as a literary historian, for if we do not place his attempts properly we run the risk of claiming too much or too little for him. It is plain that Horace is not writing cultural and literary history for its own sake (whatever that means). What interests him is poetry now, his poetry, in Augustus' Rome;[53] whatever he writes about the Greek and Roman cultural past arises from his apprehension of his own position in contemporary Rome, which colours his whole retrospective view, and inevitably focuses teleologically on the present. In many important respects, therefore, Horace's literary history resembles what Perkins, following Nietzsche's essay *On the advantage and disadvantage of history for life*, calls 'critical' literary history, which 'does not perceive the literature of the past in relation to the time and place that produced it, but selects, interprets and evaluates this literature only from the standpoint of the present and its needs'.[54] In other words, like all literary history, it is very bad history.[55]

For all that, Brink goes too far when he claims that 'the relativities of modern historical thought are wholly alien to these absolute judgements . . . [T]his kind of "history" is literary judgement or theorizing applied to the past'.[56] On the contrary, Horace is perfectly capable of seeing the historically relativistic point that what is now archaic was modern in its day (*Epist.* 2.1.90–1),[57] and it may be that he applies this insight to his judgement of Ennius' attempt to supplant Naevius (50–4);[58] he is perfectly capable of saying that if Lucilius were alive now he would not be the same author (*Sat.* 1.10.67–71).[59] Fundamentally, he has learnt well the Ciceronian lesson that the relative conditions of Roman literary history are very different from those of Greek – this is, as we have seen, the basis of his objection to a great deal of his literary-critical tradition, with its unthinkingly unhistorical apparatus of cross-cultural analogy, and we shall see shortly how profound are the differences Horace constructs between Greek and Roman culture.

There is, then, a more historically informed sense at work here than is often allowed, even if modern scholars are quite right to remark that the result does not look very much like what most modern practitioners of literary history produce. I take this lack of overlap with modern practice, however, to be a merit of Horace, principally because I agree with Perkins (1992) in regarding as illusory the causal or explanatory value of the Zeitgeist contextualisations offered by conventional literary history (whether of the Old or New Historical variety). We cannot explain (in any rigorous sense of the word) the way any given literary text is shaped by its contexts, because it is impossible to know what kind of causal relationship we might be talking about: the nexus of cause and effect is irrecoverable,[60] and the number of contextualisations to be taken into account is insuperably large.[61] And Horace is not given to such explanatory or causal contextualisations – indeed, as we shall see, at a certain level the production of poetry at Rome is to him an anomalous, even unaccountable phenomenon, and a great deal of his literary history is devoted precisely to highlighting how out of place poetry is at Rome, rather than to explaining the circumstances of its production.

What historical contextualisation *can* do, however imperfectly, is alert us to a set of possibilities (if always at the expense of closing off others) by organising and creating patterns out of the data-bank of the past: as Paul Veyne puts it, 'Historians of literature and historians per se, including sociologists, do not explain events ... They explicate them, interpret them.'[62] Horace needs to have *this* set rather than another, and I am trying to explicate the motivations he constructs in this poem, without implying that the set Horace identifies for his purposes is historically the 'right' or only possible one. My own historical situating in this essay, in other words, tracks and responds to Horace's (more 'gravitational pull'), and does not purport to explain why Horace's text is the way it is rather than some other way. From this perspective, it becomes more clear why Horace's own position in Augustus' Rome is what lies behind his entire project of literary history; in following what he says about the position of poetry in the life of Rome, we will need to keep that teleological aim as clearly in view as Horace did. Underlying everything is his apprehension of the possibilities and constraints that go to shape what he can say in poetry, an apprehension which he expresses, in different ways throughout his work, from the *Epodes* on, and which culminates here, in his address to the *Princeps*.

We see this apprehension powerfully at work throughout the Epistle, most openly in his account of the origins of Roman literary history. The entire section begins with Greece's cultural acme after the Persian wars, and is rather flippant and tongue-in-cheek in its characterisation of Greek nature (93–102); the beginning of the Roman section after that is similarly flippant and tongue-in-cheek, drifting from a general picture of how different pre-literate Rome was from Greece down to the current mania for poetry (103–17). For our purposes, looking ahead to the conclusion, the key Horatian antithesis to perceive in this juxtaposition is that between, on the one hand, the 'naturalness' of poetry in Greece, part of a whole range of artistic activities that the Greeks take to with the natural spontaneity of a child, even an *infans* (99), and, on the other, the isolation of poetry in Rome as the only cultural pursuit, undertaken by the fickle people on a whim (103–10): in the early part of the Epistle Horace had used the idea of Romans excelling at other Greek arts (painting, playing the cithara, wrestling) as a self-evident absurdity to cap an *argumentum per impossibile* (32–3). Tragedy in Greece is presented as the offshoot of a natural predisposition which manifests itself in other, related, ways (athletics, sculpture, painting, music); in Rome, poetry is an unmotivated and unique cultural phenomenon, represented as being at odds with what Brink calls the 'national psychology, attuned in Rome to enduring institutions of commerce and law'.[63] For all that, Horace can eventually claim a place – however ironically at first – for the value of the poet to the educational and religious life of the city (118–38). This section climaxes in the central panel of the poem, with 131 lines on either side, an idealised and free-floating image of the social function of choral lyric, which clearly, yet entirely indirectly, looks to Horace's own *Carmen saeculare*, performed five years before at the Ludi Saeculares (132–8).[64]

At 139 Horace resumes, backtracking to the origins of Roman literature, moving into an historical register which is rather different from what preceded – the very fact that he offers us *two*, rather different, Roman literary histories is itself a sign of his nuanced historicism, for this tactic acknowledges that there is not one single story to be told about this question, any more than about any other.[65] Again, we must recognise that Horace's historical register does not overlap with that of many modern literary historians: commentators quite rightly stress that Horace in this second historical section does not supply definite dates, when he might easily have done so, but instead uses apparently specific but actually recalcitrant phrases such as *Graecia capta* (156) and *post*

Punica bella (162).[66] Horace is interested in very broad and tenacious cultural movements, which do not fit into neat demarcations of time; his refusal to pin down one particular moment as the decisive impact of Greece on Rome brings him close to a view canvassed by Hinds (in 'deliberately overstated terms'), casting Rome's 'Hellenizing revolutions' 'as recurrent but essentially static renegotiations of the same cultural move'.[67]

The start of this section concerns the beginnings of Roman literature. Even before the impact of Greece in line 156 Horace shows some kind of compositions taking place in Rome, and it is notorious that the very start of this enterprise is enmeshed in state regulation according to his presentation: at 145-55 we are told that *licentia* and *libertas* got out of hand and had to be curbed by law. The history of Roman literature, then, is for all intents and purposes co-extensive with the history of the state's regulation of it. This stance is especially striking in someone who, as I stressed at the start, had begun his career in the two genres, Greek and Latin, which had the exercise of *licentia* and *libertas* as their *raison d'être*. The regulation of expression that Horace is talking about in the Epistle to Augustus is not just the origin of Roman literature, but the origin of Horace's career – a very deep aetion, then.

We may of course accuse him of bad faith in deliberately creating a Roman literary history without a golden age, with no predecessors who were not hampered by legislation and constraints upon their speech. It is important, however, to go on from there to see how the Epistle develops this long-standing preoccupation of his. In the *Epodes* and *Satires* he had been obsessed with the strange figure he cut as an impotent follower of outrageously frank predecessors, becoming a pioneer in a new mode of unavoidably polite and (self-)restrained expression;[68] in the first book of *Epistles* he had shifted tack, taking up more explicitly the philosophical interest in παρρησία, freedom of speech, turning his book into a test case in the post-classical shift in register of παρρησία, as public outspokenness has become domesticated into the urbane frankness of private individuals.[69] In the Epistle to Augustus he is writing 'directly' to the figure who embodies the public transformations against which he has played out this long dialectic, and he is confronting, not exactly head-on, the problem of how the two of them can negotiate with each other.[70] The major theme of the close of the poem will be the difficulties Augustus faces in getting the poetry he deserves and the difficulties Horace faces in providing it,[71] and Horace takes the debate into Augustus' realm of public display in order to begin closing in on that theme. For it is commonly remarked upon that when Horace talks about Roman literary history after the Greek invasion he focuses on the drama, and quickly focuses even more specifically on the aspect of spectacle and display – signalled in advance by the mimetic *aspice*, 'look', with which he introduces Plautus (170) – from where he leads up to the eventual antithesis between spectacle and private reading that begins the poem's finale (*uere age et his, qui se lectori credere malunt | quam spectatoris fastidia ferre superbi, | curam redde breuem*, 214–16).

It is the compulsion to engage with Augustus' world, and the resulting momentary assimilation of Augustus' world of display to Horace's world of poetry and criticism, that helps explain the interest – so often seen as puzzling – in Roman dramatic performance in this penultimate section of the poem (177–213). Certainly, there are other important factors at work, well enumerated by Williams.[72] But I wish to concentrate on the dialectic Horace constructs between his world of art and Augustus' world of public display; and here, to set up our conclusion, we return to the themes of the beginning of the chapter, for to Horace his and Augustus' worlds define each other, by repulsion as much as by attraction.

Habinek likewise locates Horace's interest in spectacle within a promisingly political framework, but, following his book's procrustean programmatic obsession with the binary antithesis between élite and mass, he systematically misreads Horace's argument on this score: 'What troubles Horace about spectacle is that it . . . appeals to the least common denominator within the population . . . [T]he *Letter to Augustus* articulates a new set of oppositions, pitting elite against masses . . .'[73] This is precisely incorrect. Horace criticises the appeal of spectacular drama not just to the *plebecula* in 186 but also (*quoque*) to the *eques* in 187. Pope, in the 'Advertisement' to his *Imitation*, puts his finger, as usual, on the right point: '*Horace* here pleads the Cause of his Cotemporaries, first against the Taste of the *Town* . . .; secondly against the *Court* and *Nobility* . . .'[74]

Crucially, of course, Pope goes on to say – 'and lastly against the *Emperor* himself'.[75] As Barchiesi puts it, Augustus is at once student and teacher in this poem,[76] and Horace's didacticism is close to the surface as he develops the momentum that will lead to his explicit contrast between public display and literature for reading (214–18). In Horace's poem the world of the popular theatre overlaps with the world of public display and pageantry, as he gives us a glimpse of what recent scholars have called the 'political theatre' of the Principate.[77] Already in the *Satires* Horace had merged the two worlds in his description of Scipio and Laelius withdrawing from the mob and the stage (*a uulgo et scaena*, *Sat.* 2.1.71).[78] In this section of the Epistle, his presentation of the theatre is dotted with vocabulary and imagery appropriate to politics: the playwright who competes on the public stage is like a politician competing for votes, dependent on the whim of the onlooker (177–80); the audience is split like an historian's public assembly, with the ignorant many outnumbering the virtuous and high-born few (183–4); Roman spectacles are like triumphs, with which the *ferus uictor* (156) is still obsessed (189–93: note especially 193, *captiuum portatur ebur, captiua Corinthus*[79]). This is a world of public judgement and competition from which Horace always removes himself;[80] but it is one that means a great deal to Augustus, not merely because he has a well-known taste for the old Roman comedy, but because in his new Rome the theatre has 'an outstanding importance ... as a substitute for public life'.[81] It is an arena in which he takes an active interest, recovering the discriminations between the orders, stamping out the mixed seating of the slack last days of the Republic, with all its overtones of *libertas*, so as to make the theatre a template for his 'whole hierarchic vision of the society of the Roman Empire'.[82]

Horace appears to have his doubts about the desirability and feasibility of this enterprise.[83] Indeed, one of the reasons, perhaps, that Horace objects to this world of pageantry and display is that, as an *eques* who is *caelebs*, he may have been legally barred by his addressee's marriage and theatre legislation from attending the theatre at all. The evidence is indirect, but suggestive, that senatorial and equestrian bachelors were barred from the *ludi* for a period of some years, from perhaps as early as 22 BCE.[84] Before this period, it appears that Horace had been entitled to sit in the equestrian order's Fourteen Rows along with Maecenas (*ludos spectauerat una*, Sat. 2.6.48);[85] writing in 12, he may be commenting on the spectacular dimension of a great theatrical world which he cannot actually see.

Whether or not this is the case, he certainly does not regard the public as educable, and, as he shows when he begins the concluding section at 214ff., he wants to retreat even from this more regulated public world into a world of readership, instructing the *Princeps* to accompany him if he wishes his regime to leave an enduring literary legacy: *uerum age et his, qui se lectori credere malunt | quam spectatoris fastidia ferre superbi,|curam redde breuem, si munus Apolline dignum | uis complere libris*, 214–17.

Augustus should be more Horatian, it seems. At this most didactic moment in the Epistle, with its *age* plus imperative leading into the culminating instructions for the *Princeps*, we see more clearly than anywhere else in the poem that Horace's discourse is not simply mimicking or tracking that of Augustus.[86] Certainly, he is compelled by the 'gravitational pull' of his addressee into a particular kind of dialectic, and comparison with his other literary-critical epistles throws this power-relationship into relief:[87] if, for example, you are talking drama to the Pisos, as Horace is in the *Ars*, you might not find yourself pulled into a political and spectacular realm of imagery and thought, but if you are talking drama to Augustus, it appears, you will. Brink, consequently, regularly calls attention to the differences in this respect between our Epistle and the *Ars*, remarking that the *Ars* 'does not explicitly dilate on the historical situation of poetry in its own time', and 'avoids the political entanglements that cause strains and stresses in the letter to Augustus';[88] we may acknowledge the justice of his point, even if we do not follow him in marking the *Ars* up and the Epistle to Augustus down accordingly. Nonetheless, what we are watching in the Epistle to Augustus is part of a dialogue, with the poet both reacting to and applying pressure; as Oliensis puts it, 'Horace's poems are not detached representations of society but consequential acts within society.'[89] Brink's 'strains and stresses' are the result of the friction generated as Horace and Augustus interchange the roles of teacher and student: at this point, Horace's reservations about the value of spectacle are not just those of a literary critic, and when he moves into instructions on how rulers and poets should conduct relations, he is at once responding to and moulding one of the ruler's most dear concerns, his current and posthumous image.

Santirocco well remarks that 'Augustus has been co-opted to the poet's own agenda', with the first of his Horatian roles being to stand in, 'as the object of the people's admiration', for 'the contemporary poet who deserves to be judged by the same critical standard'.[90] The interplay between the roles of addressee and addresser becomes a strange identity by the end of the poem, as Horace finally puts himself in Augustus' shoes and becomes the one who has a writer attached to him, running the risk of being commemorated in ignominy *una|cum scriptore meo*, 267–8. The main lever he uses to get into this position is the long-lived conundrum of what Hunter, in an outstanding discussion of Theocritus 16, calls 'the doubleness of the patronage relationship', an issue that goes back to Simonides and Pindar, for whom 'poet and patron need each other, and are in much the same boat'.[91] The boat will carry poet and patron down the river of time together, as objects of reverence, envy, or ridicule.[92] A failure of Augustus' taste in fostering poets will make him a laughing-stock, as happened to Alexander, whose taste in painting, sculpture and classical poetry was not matched by his taste in contemporary poetry (232–44).[93] If the poet fails, the risk for both is colossal, as the closing allusion to Catullus 95 makes clear:[94] poet and *laudandus* alike will be ranked with the infamous sheets of Volusius, wrapping-paper, consigned to death.

The concluding section, in which Horace skirmishes with these huge topics, is an advertisement for his classic status, as a master who dominates every aspect of his tradition. He begins with a ringing allusion to Ennius in line 229, showing that – whatever he may have said about the *ueteres* earlier in the poem – he knows that a Roman poet writing about praise and poetic apotheosis cannot avoid engaging with the poet of the *Annales* and the *Scipio*.[95] From this point on, the close of the poem outdoes even *Epist.* 1.3 in being an object lesson in how to use allusion to all the important layers of tradition simultaneously: classical Greek (Simonides and Pindar), Hellenistic Greek (Theocritus), archaic Roman (Ennius), classics of the previous Roman generation (Cicero and Catullus) and the current one (Virgil and, no doubt, if we had more of him, Varius).[96]

This parade of credentials is impressive, clinching the author's right to rank with Virgil and Varius. Still, once we have admired the credentials Horace parades here, we need to stand back and ask what it is that he actually delivers with them. The poem is full of things Horace cannot or will not do (tragedy, comedy, and especially panegyrical epic), although its principal argument is that he is the last member of a literary movement that has carried Roman poetry to a peak that matches the eminence of the restorer of the state. The poem ends with a strange, yet typically Horatian, mixture of confidence and incapacity, and we may conclude our analysis by using Horace's literary histories as a way of bringing this simultaneous sense of power and helplessness into focus.

First of all, the power and importance of poetry receive strong attention. The *Princeps*, for his part, wants to foster poetry, even if he needs instruction in how to do it consistently, and the poem closes by being acutely self-conscious that poet and *Princeps* will live together in this medium. The apprehension of poetry's power is highlighted, as regularly in Horace's late poetry, by its superiority to the visual arts, of painting, or sculpture.[97] Poetry is more expressive of character than these other arts (248–50); above all, throughout the closing section the immortalising power of poetry is the focus, and here Horace continues to assert, as he had in his *Odes*, that words on papyrus are a more potent form of commemoration than the apparently more durable and impressive medium of statuary.

If we bring to bear the perspective provided by Horace's literary histories, however, another dimension comes into play, which is now not necessarily an enabling one for the poet. Behind the antithesis between poetry and sculpture or painting there regularly lies another antithesis, that between Roman and Greek.[98] The Greek Alexander is perfectly at home as a connoisseur of the painter Apelles and the sculptor Lysippus (239–41): 'in this field, Greeks are still unchallenged'.[99] The radical Roman ambivalence to the Greek visual arts, and to the general culture they typify, is plain over the Epistle as a whole. Earlier in the poem painting was one of the Greek arts singled out for traditional ridicule (32–3); we have already noted Horace's scorn for the parade of Corinthian sculpture (193);[100] and the whole range of Greek culture is presented as the product of decadence and fickleness (93–8); yet the cultural energy that produced these arts is admired – the Greeks do it because they *enjoy* it (*gauisa*, 98) – and the arts are part of a coherent cultural drive, whereas in Rome they are not.[101] We remember that Horace's literary history showed poetry in Greece as one manifestation of a general tendency; at Rome, by contrast, poetry is always being, as it were, written against the grain, at odds with the national character,[102] legislated against, misunderstood by the public, the only one of the *artes* to be cultivated.[103] Against the background of Horace's literary histories, the isolation of poetry as the only part of Greek μουσική to find anything like a secure home in Rome is all the more accentuated – a paradox about Roman Hellenisation with which most modern literary historians would agree.

This uniqueness makes the poet powerful, because he is the sole figure in his domain, and weak, because he is isolated. One may see why Horace's last three projects are concerned with the writing of poetry. He is gradually writing himself, or being written, into a corner. On the conventional dating, after this Epistle, only the *Ars poetica* remains.[104]

EPILOGUE

After two dozen pages of dense discussion, in which the conventional evidence for Virgil's life is subjected to close analysis, an expert recently concluded: 'It may now be apparent that very little external information indeed may legitimately be used in the understanding of Virgil and his work.'[1] In fact the reader of that discussion may be forgiven for thinking that the only items which survive detailed scrutiny are the dates of Virgil's birth (15 October 70 BC) and death (21 September 19 BC). Virgil's friend Horace, by contrast, seems to have been so profligate with the personal information inserted into his poetry that we appear scarcely to need external evidence at all. Horace himself mentions the year of his birth three times (*Epod.* 13.6, *Carm.* 3.21.1, *Epist.* 1.20.26–8), and this, together with other passages, presents us with – or allows us to construct – the figure of the poet with which we are all familiar.

Yet this very familiarity is deceptive and elusive. In the first place, all readers have their own 'Horace'. As L. P. Wilkinson wrote (evidently during his time as a code-breaker at Bletchley Park during the Second World War), 'We English think of him as one of us; but it appears that no less to the French he is one of them, and even to the Germans one of them.'[2] Secondly, there is the ever-present problem of the relationship between 'literature' and 'life'. Just how much of Horace's apparent self-portrayal over roughly a quarter of a century and several different poetic genres can we really take to be a portrayal of self? Moles in this volume thinks that the 'real Horace' must be felt at least in *Epistles* 1, if the moral issues raised there are to come alive; yet this sensation of real contact need not correspond to biographical actuality for its effect to work. Thirdly, familiarity becomes self-fulfilling: if one of our duties as scholarly readers is to test evidence and treat it sceptically, it is the most familiar passages and poems which are the most difficult to dislodge.

Fraenkel in his book on Horace was concerned to interpret the words of the poet rather than to repeat the interpretations with which the poetry had become encrusted,[3] yet the sum effect of his book is to demonstrate just how elusive that goal really is. Because of their familiarity there is perhaps an in-built resistance to G. Williams' radical re-interpretation of the passages where Horace describes himself as a freedman's son.[4] Although Horace often tells us the year of his birth, as has been noted, we need Suetonius' *Life* of Horace to provide us with the extra item of information that his date of birth in 65 BC was 8 December; now Bradshaw has argued that *Carm.* 3.28 is not the summer poem that we had always imagined but is a winter poem whose setting is Horace's birthday. The argument depends upon the cross-cultural fact that Neptune, celebrated in the ode, is the Roman equivalent of Poseidon, whose month is December, as would be known to many cultured Romans, especially if, like Horace himself, they had sojourned in Athens at some time. There is nothing exceptionable about Bradshaw's argumentation, since time and again the contributors to this volume have explained Horace's poetry in terms of things Greek and/or the experiences of Horace's own life, while Nisbet remarks on the popularity of birthday poems amongst the Augustan poets; but how many readers will welcome the re-orientation of the horizon?

Perhaps the most testing case is that of Griffiths, who challenges the canonical totals of *Odes* 1 and *Odes* 3 and argues that the former contains 35 (not 38) poems and the latter 25 (not 30). Griffiths acknowledges that his proposals are not entirely new: indeed the notion that the Roman Odes are a single poem is at least as old as Porphyrio. Yet the very fact that the views expressed (albeit in piecemeal fashion) by previous commentators have had little impact is eloquent testimony to the genuine difficulty which we experience when faced with a truly revolutionary re-reading of canonical data. A total of 38 poems does indeed seem anomalous in the light of the multiples of five which constitute the totals of the *Eclogues* and *Satires* 1, but the sceptical will always be able to counter such arguments by pointing to the *Epodes* and *Satires* 2 (17 and 8 poems respectively). And, even if the next 'standard' edition of the *Odes* continues to print the poems in the arrangements sanctified by previous editors, it is nevertheless salutary to be reminded periodically of how precarious the actual evidence is for much of what we think we know about the Horatian corpus.

Much of Griffiths' argument depends upon what constitutes 'closure'. Such a formal matter as closure may be configured in contexts that go beyond the formalist. Oliensis points out that Horace likes to use hair as a closural motif, for example in the very last line of *Odes* 1–3, where, as David West acutely observes,[5] Horace is alluding to the last word of Pindar's *Olympian odes* (14.24); but she also notes that it is a feature of Horace's writing that he continues a sentence when one might have thought that he had concluded, as in *Epod.* 11.25–8 or *Carm.* 2.5.21–4. Oliensis terms this a type of 'feminine ending', and her gendering of the issue brings to light the moral and ethical dimensions of the formalist device: the binding of women's hair stands for more than one kind of control, and her analysis brings out Horace's 'conjunction of "weak" form and effeminate content'. Issues of gender are also encountered in Woodman's contribution, where he suggests that Horace's professed allegiance to Sappho is to be explained by the role which Sappho occupies in the poetry of Catullus and that the dualism of gender found in Catullus has been imitated but transformed by Horace in his claims on Sappho and Alcaeus. Such a suggestion attributes to Horace a distinctly unusual interpretation of his models, yet Barchiesi observes that the singing of the *Carmen saeculare* by paired choruses of boys and girls was also highly unusual and that the participation of female voices in paeanic performance is quite anomalous.

If Horace was to continue, and depart from, a particular form of paean, he was obliged to construct an appropriate literary history, as Barchiesi shows. The Greek tradition in general, and especially the part played in it by Pindar, constitute an essential precondition for this most Roman of poetic productions: the whole of the *Carmen saeculare* is a meditation on the unique status of Rome *vis-à-vis* Greek culture. Pindar is important for other contributors too. Griffiths defends his 'unitarian' view of the Roman Odes by invoking Horace's Pindaric ambitions, while Freudenburg sees Horace in *Epistles* I as portraying himself as a second Pindar, with similar sources of inspiration and a similar responsibility for pleasing great men. Pindar in fact provided an excellent paradigm for the Augustan poet, as Feeney points out, whereas Zetzel argues that in the 30s Callimacheanism raised moral and ideological problems: this explains the more ambivalent attitude to Callimachus which is shown by Horace, who even deploys the imitation of Callimachus to make anti-Callimachean points.

Zetzel reminds us of how much evidence is missing from the 30s to contextualise Horace's attitudes to neotericism; but it seems clear that Horace was anxious that his own generation not be seen as merely an epilogue to the previous generation. Hence Horace both admired and criticised the *Eclogues*. His friend's bucolics lack the social commitment of his own *sermones*, which play an influential role in forming the kind of poetry which we know as 'Augustan'. It is not without significance that, as Feeney notes, the central section of Horace's letter to Augustus is devoted to the social function of choral lyric and glances obliquely at the poet's own *Carmen saeculare*.

Epistles 2.1 raises directly the question to which numerous contributors advert, namely, the poet's relationship with the *princeps*. If Augustus was *solus* at the time when the epistle was written (2.1.1), so too was Horace, as Feeney points out; Horace exchanges places with the *princeps* at the end of the letter (2.2.264–70), while Freudenburg draws attention to the fact that the poet, calling himself *princeps*, describes himself as *triumphator* in the final ode of Book 3. According to Freudenburg, Horace in *Epist.* 1.19 appears as both leader and follower (lines 23–4), thus strikingly resembling Augustus himself: Lowrie observes that in the *Res gestae* (8.5) Augustus portrays himself in precisely these terms, while Barchiesi notes that both poet and *princeps* are innovators and antiquarians.

If there were so many similarities between the two men, what was the relationship between them? Nisbet, following the approach which he pioneered more than forty years ago,[6] embarks on some extraordinarily intricate detective work to recover the social world of Messalla, giving a thicker description than ever before of this aristocrat's circle. He shows how the ode for Messalla is accommodated to the tastes, career and temperament of its addressee, while at the same time managing to honour his patron, Maecenas, as well. Du Quesnay, likewise developing his own earlier work,[7] explores the relationship between Maecenas and Horace in the first epode. Given the sensitivity shown by Horace to Messalla and Maecenas, it would seem to follow *a fortiori* that Augustus would be handled with at least equal tact and discretion; yet Feeney detects major differences in taste between Horace and Augustus in *Epist.* 2.1, with Horace taking on the role of preceptor to correct those differences; while Moles, who agrees that the poems of *Epistles* Book 1 are no less well matched to their addressees, nevertheless detects tensions, ambiguities and reservations in Horace's attitudes to Maecenas and Augustus alike. It is no mere formal philosophical question that is being thrashed out in the *Epistles* but an urgent contemporary issue: how far to be engaged or disengaged? The social and political backdrop to Horace's exploration of the range of philosophical choices is in no way inert. Again, Lowrie, Freudenburg, Barchiesi and Feeney in different ways address the question of the social and political backdrop to Horace's poetry. These chapters do not treat the poetry as a transcription of an already existing and codified reality or ideology, as is seen most clearly in Barchiesi's discussion of the 'real' performance of the *Carmen saeculare*. Here we see once more the important ideological consequences of a nuanced formalist approach. Barchiesi shows that the ideological dimension of the *Carmen saeculare* depends to a great extent on its generic choices, and that the odd underestimation of the *Carmen saeculare* is a result of the fact that it is, uniquely, the record of a real performance.

Du Quesnay finds Cicero a useful guide to the ways in which Greek philosophical thinking is adapted to and blended with Roman values, while Moles supports his view of the profoundly philosophical nature of *Epistles* Book 1 by appealing to parallels with Cicero. Feeney too sees Cicero as heavily influential for Horace's discussion of literary history, while Lowrie makes Cicero form one apex of a triangle whose other corners are represented by Horace and Augustus: poet and statesman are united in the figure of Cicero, who therefore serves as an *exemplum* for each. This is not to say that Horace did not criticise Cicero, and the change in literary taste which this criticism implies goes hand in hand with the change which took place in political life between the late republic and the age of Augustus. The case of Cicero shows how questions of 'literary' taste are always implicated in other legacies, political and moral. Horace was uniquely sensitive to the interconnectedness of human experience, in all its aspects, and only a criticism that responds to interconnectedness can hope to begin to do him anything like justice.

NOTES

I HORACE'S BIRTHDAY AND DEATHDAY

This chapter was developed from a paper given to the AGM of the Classical Association at Durham in 1993. I am grateful to questioners at the meeting and subsequently to the editors and Professor Niall Rudd and Professor David West for helpful criticism. The faults which remain are mine.

1 See Schmidt (1908); Argetsinger (1992) 175–93.
2 Cicero, Virgil, Horace, Persius, Lucan.
3 Rostagni (1944) 122–3; see Borzsák (1984) x–xi for literature.
4 E.g. Fraenkel (1957) 65.
5 Criticism 1937–72 is reviewed by Setaioli (1981). For later treatments see Lowrie (1992) and commentary in Cavarzere (1992) and Mankin (1995).
6 Fragments of Alcaeus, Anacreon, Archilochus, and Bacchylides have been adduced, but Horace was vastly better read in early lyric than any modern critic and less dependent on chance excerpts. Suggested dates range from 43 to 31.
7 Bentley's objection to plural (3 *amici*) followed by singular (6 *tu*) continues to worry some. Housman's *Amici*, given spurious currency in the Stuttgart Teubner (1985), ignores the fact that Latin poetry was meant to be heard, not read silently from modern print. But see Lowrie (1992) 417.
8 Davis (1991) 14 uses *puer* (12) to support his claim that Horace deliberately diminishes the heroic.
9 A military reference has been denied, e.g. by Carrubba (1969) 26–7; that the interpretation is ancient is suggested by *contubernales* (Porph. ad loc.).
10 *Sat.* 1.7.18–19, *Carm.* 2.7.9ff., *Carm.* 3.4.26, *Epist.* 2.2.46ff.
11 Since the posthumous (1608) edition of Torrentius (L. Vanderbeken, d. 1595). The most detailed case has been made by Kilpatrick (1970), but his over-eagerness has encouraged doubt.
12 Pelorus (variously spelt), the most Easterly point of Sicily and Hannibal's helmsman (Val. Max. 9.8; Serv. on Virg. *Aen.* 3.411). Cape Palinurus was notorious since the naval disaster of 253 (Oros. 4.9.10–11).
13 Possibly based on dubious etymology of Palinurus as 'return wind'. But Horace must have travelled from Greece to Italy at least once somehow, so the scholium may contain truth. It is accepted by C. Koch in *RE* 18.3. Syndikus (1973) 60 n. 59 dismisses all suggestions as pure guesswork.

14 App. *B Civ.* 5.98–9. Cf. *Eleg. Maec.* 1.41–2. See N–H (1978) on *Carm.* 2.17.20.

15 Fraenkel (1957) 71–5 insisted that Maecenas was in Rome. Woodman (1983a) 238 agrees, as does Schoonhoven (1980) 62–3. Against this: Kraggerud (1984), esp. 118–19; Mankin (1995) 161. Du Quesnay in this volume (Chap. 2) argues strongly that Maecenas and Horace were both present at Actium.

16 N–H (1978) 100; Nisbet (1984) 16.

17 See Mayer (1994) and N–H (1978) ad loc.

18 Wistrand (1958) 35–6.

19 See Norden (1913) 143–63. For further discussion see Nisbet (Chap. 6) in the present volume.

20 Horace seems to have set a trap for the critics who for centuries have debated which Cato is meant, for the Censor was named Priscus and Uticensis was a toper. Ps.-Acro chose the former and that view is still the popular one.

21 Cf. Cairns (1982) 243; Santirocco (1986) 136–8.

22 I do not imagine that Horace charged fees, but I am sure he expected rewards.

23 Syme (1986) 201.

24 Messalla's personal account appears to have been used by Plutarch in his life of Brutus.

25 In *Carm.* 2.7, to another fellow-veteran of Philippi with whom the poet partied (6–8), the Massic is *obliuiosum* (21).

26 See Bradshaw (1970) 143. It is unfortunate that Fraenkel supported the dubious theory that Horace gave up writing lyric because he was disappointed with the reception of *Odes* 1–3 (Fraenkel (1957) 308, 339–50).

27 Cf. Santirocco (1986) 144–7; on closure in general see Fowler (1989a) and (1997).

28 Pöschl (1970) 180–96. Aristotle uses this metaphor as a prime example in the *Poetics* (1457b 22–5).

29 Unqualified *nenia* in Horace means a 'dirge' (as explained by Cicero: *Leg.* 2.62), but critics persist in translating it here as 'coda' or simply as 'song' (*OLD* 2). This passage is judged 'obscure' by Heller (1943) in a lexicographical study.

30 *Epod.* 9.1, 36; *Carm.* 1.37.5.

31 Cf. Alc. 347(a), 352 L–P.

32 Cf. K–H (1964) ad loc.

33 Sacrifices to Neptune were made on 2 Sept. (Actium), 23 Sept. (Birthday of Augustus) and 1 Dec., as well as on 23 July.

34 Mikalson (1975) 89.

35 See Boll (1950) 156–224; Eyben (1973) 150–71.

36 Contemporary interest is suggested by Varro's lost *De Hebdomadis*; see Gell. 3.10 for a description of this work.

37 Censorinus, *De die natali* 33. The same scheme is given in a scholium at the end of Pollux Book 1 but a different Hippocratic scheme of sevens is given by Philo (*De opificio* 105) after quoting Solon's poem (27) listing ten periods of seven years.

38 See Censorinus 36–7; Bouché-Leclerq (1899) 526–32.

39 Wickham (1891) ad loc.

40 We do not know how Horace weathered his earlier great climacteric – his 21st year – but it was an eventful one in Rome after the Ides of March.
41 See N–H (1970) xxxv–vii.
42 For a basic introduction see Barton (1994a).
43 See Dicks (1963) 72–3; Cramer (1954) 248–51.
44 Dilke (1973) 108–9.
45 Cf. N–H (1970) on *Carm.* 1.7.13; Lyne (1995) 9–11.
46 Rudd (1982) 404.
47 West (1991) 48–52.
48 See Brind' Amour (1983) 70–4.
49 See Barton (1994b) 40–7.
50 Syndikus (1972) 460 n. 24.
51 Vahlen (1898) 245–6; cf. Fraenkel (1957) 22–3.
52 Cf. Seneca, *Dial.* 10.20.3, Pliny, *Ep.* 3.1.10, Tac. *Ann.* 12.27.3. See Goodyear (1981) 99 on Tac. *Ann.* 1.62.1.
53 See Dreizehnter (1978) 70–81.
54 Dio Cass. 55.7. As it is the last item for the year, it has been assumed that the death occurred towards the end of 8 BC.
55 Numerologists may note that Maecenas in Greek letters when converted into numbers (a common astrological practice) = 330. After 330 days of an ordinary year the next day is 27 November.
56 In consular years; by the astronomical calendar he was somewhat older.

2 *AMICVS CERTVS IN RE INCERTA CERNITVR*

1 Suet. *Aug.* 17.2 *nec multo post nauali proelio apud Actium uicit in serum dimicatione protracta, ut in naue uictor pernoctauerit.* Throughout this essay Caesar refers to Imperator Caesar Divi filius, more usually called Octavian in modern accounts. On the importance of the name, see Millar (1999) 1–3.
2 Dio 50.4.4–5 with Reinhold (1988) ad loc.; Plut. *Ant.* 60.1 with Pelling (1988) 264.
3 Dio 50.21–2; 50.26–7. This is not of course evidence for what was said but it is evidence for what Dio, with a much fuller range of contemporary sources available than we have, thought the situation was on the day of the battle.
4 App. *B Civ.* 4.38.161; 4.45.193; Suet. *Aug.* 17.2.
5 The timing of this declaration is still controversial: for the position adopted here, see Fadinger (1969) 245–52 as against Woodman (1983a) 211–13; Pelling (1988) 264; (1996) 54 n. 294.
6 I assume that the triumph was voted as soon as the senators with Caesar at Actium had returned to Rome. The fact that so many senators had participated made it in some sense their war, their victory and their triumph as well. Dio (51.19.1) indicates only that it was voted before the fall of Alexandria. Horace's phrase also implicitly mocks the claim imputed to Antony by Caesar to be πάσης μὲν τῆς γῆς πάσης δὲ θαλάσσης κυριεύοντα (Dio 50.25.4) and points to the fulfilment of the *coniuratio totius Italiae.* Cf. Setaioli (1981) 1729–30.
7 The text as printed is from Murray and Petsas (1989) 76. It is heavily restored and much disputed. See also Carter (1977).

8 Together with *Sat.* 2: see, e.g., *EO* 1.220 (Nisbet); 259; 262 (D'Anna); 267 (Setaioli). They are wrongly dated by Du Quesnay (1995) 134, though the general point being made there still stands. *Carm.* 2.17 may belong to the same period: N–H (1970) xxix; 244 (but contrast N–H (1978) 4).

9 See Pelling (1988) on Plut. *Ant.* 58.2 and Reinhold (1988) 101; 127–8.

10 Dio (51.4.3) is explicit about the year (30 BC): contrast Pelling (1988) 300; (1996) 61, who puts it at the end of 31 BC.

11 Suet. *Aug.* 17.3 *ab Actio cum Samum in hiberna se recepisset, turbatus nuntiis de seditione praemia et missionem poscentium, quos ex omni numero confecta uictoria Brundisium praemiserat, repetita Italia tempestate in traiectu bis conflictatus, primo inter promuntoria Peloponnesi atque Aetoliae, rursus circa montes Ceraunios utrubique parte liburnicarum demersa, simul eius, in qua uehebatur, fusis armamentis et gubernaculo diffracto; nec amplius quam septem et uiginti dies, donec ad desideria militum ordinarentur, Brundisii commoratus.* See Casson (1995) 270–3; de Saint Denis (1947) 201–3.

12 See also Augustus, *Res gestae* 25.2–3 *iurauit in mea uerba tota Italia sponte sua, et me belli quo uici ad Actium ducem depoposcit.... qui sub signis meis tum militauerint fuerunt senatores plures quam DCC, in iis qui uel antea uel postea consules facti sunt ad eum diem quo scripta sunt haec LXXXIII, sacerdotes circiter CLXX.* Cf. Virg. *Aen.* 8.678–9 *hinc Augustus agens Italos in proelia Caesar | cum patribus populoque, penatibus et magnis dis.*

13 Compare Kraggerud (1984) 21–43; *EO* 1.414–15 (Kraggerud).

14 The senators and leading equestrians who had accompanied Caesar might have left immediately after the sea battle (3 or 4 September). There was certainly no reason for them to stay after the surrender of Antony's land forces, which happened about 9 or 10 September (Plut. *Ant.* 68.3). The crossing will have taken perhaps two or three days: Casson (1995) 281–96. On 14 September *secura nauigatio* gave way to *incerta nauigatio* (Veg. *Mil.* 4.39) and it is likely that Caesar will have wanted to have the senators home by then.

15 Epode 1, at the head of a collection that appeared after Actium, can only refer to Actium, as Watson (1983) 66 and Nisbet (1984) 198 n. 34 rightly insist against Thompson (1970) 332, who refers the poem to the earlier war against Sextus Pompeius.

16 Macrob. *Sat.* 2.4.29.

17 The issues are fully discussed by Wistrand (1958). See Hanslik (1962) 338–9 and the decisive comments of N–H (1978) 99–100; Nisbet (1984) 9–10 with 198 nn. 29 and 30 as against Fraenkel (1957) 71–5. Nisbet's arguments are accepted by Cavarzere (1992) 117–18: compare Mankin (1995) 161 and see also *EO* 1.220 (Nisbet); 269 (Setaioli); 415 (Kraggerud). There is also the explicit evidence of *Elegiae ad Maecenatem* 1.45–8 (*cum freta Niliacae texerunt laeta carinae, | fortis erat circa, fortis et ante ducem, | militis Eoi fugientis terga secutus, | territus ad Nili dum fugit ille caput*), which there seems no good reason to reject (in spite of Schoonhoven (1980) 62–4). For continuing caution, see *EV* 3.413; *EO* 1.796 (La Penna); Reinhold (1988) 126; and Pelling (1996) 61 n. 324, who prefers to follow both Syme (1939) 292 and Woodman (1983a) 238 in taking the view that Maecenas remained in Rome, although he allows that it is just possible that Maecenas was at Actium and returned very soon

afterwards, as argued by Wistrand (1958) 6–19 (which is the view adopted here). See also above, pp. 00–0.

18 Dio 49.16.2 τά τε ἄλλα τὰ ἐν τῇ πόλει τῇ τε λοιπῇ Ἰταλίᾳ Γάιος τις Μαικήνας, ἀνὴρ ἱππεύς, καὶ τότε καὶ ἔπειτα ἐπὶ πολὺ διῴκησεν (with the note of Reinhold (1988)); 51.3.5 (referring to late 31 BC) ᾧ καὶ τότε ἥ τε Ῥώμη καὶ ἡ λοιπὴ Ἰταλία προσετέτακτο (with Reinhold's note); Vell. Pat. 2.88.2 with Woodman (1983a) ad loc. That is to say that the arrangements were similar to those made during the war with Sextus Pompeius: see Dio 49.16.2 (with Reinhold ad loc.), but for that period there is Appian, B Civ. 5.99 and 5.112 to provide a corrective.

19 The conspiracy of M. Lepidus, son of the former triumvir, was once thought to belong to 31 BC (see Syme (1939) 298) and so to be an obstacle to supposing Maecenas was at Actium. But this episode must in fact belong to the end of 30 BC, if the consul Balbinus (Appian, B Civ. 4.50) is to be identified with L. Saenius cos. suff. 30 BC, as argued by Wistrand (1958) 15: see Kienast (1982) 66; MRR 3.184; Syme (1986) 35; Pelling (1996) 62. See also Vell. Pat. 2.88 with Woodman (1983a) 237–8.

20 Cf. Kraggerud (1984) 26–7.

21 See Cairns (1972) 141; 248 n. 28. Compare especially Tib. 1.3.1 Ibitis Aegaeas sine me, Messalla, per undas; Ov. Tr. 1.1.1 sine me, liber, ibis in urbem. Cairns' generic identification is accepted in different degrees by Cavarzere (1992) 119; Mankin (1995) 49 and, especially, EO 2.732–3 (Fedeli). The metrically unified group Epodes 1–10 is thus framed by two variations on the propemptikon. On the propemptikon, see especially Cairns (1972) index s.v.; McKeown (1998) 222 and Kerkhecker (1999) 172–4 for examples and bibliography.

22 The dangers of the journey are a standard topic of the propemptikon: see Cairns (1972) 252 n. 17; Ov. Am. 2.11.9–32 with McKeown.

23 For Liburnis see App. Ill. 7.4 καὶ ναυτικοὶ μὲν ἐπὶ τοῖς Ἀρδιαίοις ἐγένοντο Λιβυρνοί, γένος ἕτερον Ἰλλυριῶν, οἳ τὸν Ἰόνιον καὶ τὰς νήσους ἐλῄστευον ναυσὶν ὠκείαις τε καὶ κούφαις, ὅθεν ἔτι νῦν Ῥωμαῖοι τὰ κοῦφα καὶ ὀξέα δίκροτα Λιβυρνίδας προσαγορεύουσιν. The best account is provided by Panciera (1956).

24 As at Hor. Carm. 1.37.30; Prop. 3.11.44. Murray and Petsas (1989) 150 point out that the conceptualisation of Actium as a battle between Antony's heavy fleet and Caesar's light fleet is clear in the design of the campsite memorial at Actium within a year of the battle.

25 For propugnacula, see Plin. HN 32.3 sed armatae classes imponunt sibi turrium propugnacula, ut in mari quoque pugnetur uelut e muris; Veg. Mil. 4.8.3 saxa . . . maxima uero pondere formaque uolubili in propugnaculis digeruntur, ut demissa per praeceps . . . hostes obruant subeuntes; 4.44.6 in maioribus etiam liburnis propugnacula turresque constituunt, ut tamquam de muro ita de excelsioribus tabulatis facilius uulnerent uel perimant inimicos. propugnacula, then, are not purely or even mainly defensive, as claimed by Kraggerud (1984) 39 n. 9.

26 For the sense 'go right into the midst of', 'charge right in among', compare Sen. Ep. 59.8 [an extended military metaphor] sapiens autem, ad omnem incursum munitus, intentus, non si paupertas, non si luctus, non si ignominia, non si dolor impetum faciat, pedem referet interritus et contra illa ibit et inter illa; Stat. Theb. 4.318–21 unde haec furibunda cupido, | nate, tibi? teneroque unde improba

pectore uirtus? | *tu bellis aptare uiros, tu pondera ferre* | *Martis et ensiferas inter potes ire cateruas?*; Sil. *Pun.* 14.384–6; 393–4 [on the clash of the Carthaginian and Roman fleets] *medias* [sc. *naues*] *inter sublimior ibat* | *terribilis uisu puppis, qua nulla per omne* | *egressa est Libycis maior naualibus aeuum.* | . . . *procurrunt leuitate agili docilesque regentis* | *audiuisse manum Latio cum milite puppes.* Another possible example is *B Afr.* 83.2 (*equo admisso in hostem inter principes ire contendit*) if Klotz' conjecture *inter* is accepted in place of *contra* of the MSS. For examples where the danger is of a non-military kind, see Scipio Aemilianus apud Macrob. *Sat.* 3.14.6 (= *ORF* 30.1) *eunt, inquam, in ludum saltatorium inter cinaedos uirgines puerique ingenui*; Claud. *In Gildonem* 184–6 *crinitos inter famulos pubemque canoram* | *orbatas iubet ire nurus nuperque peremptis* | *adridere uiris.* These examples were located using *BTL-1*; for an earlier attempt relying on *TLL* see Watson (1983) 66–7.

   The phrase *ire inter* is of itself ambiguous. It can be used of either someone or something moving within and as part of a pack or group and in the same direction. The nearest parallels for this sense would seem to be: Hor. *Sat.* 1.1.115–16 *instat equis auriga suos uincentibus, illum* | *praeteritum temnens extremos inter euntem*; Ov. *Tr.* 5.12.25–6 *male currit et inter* | *carceribus missos ultimus ibit equus*; Mart. 7.8.7–8 *festa coronatus ludet conuicia miles,* | *inter laurigeros cum comes ibit equos*; *Pervigilium Veneris* 41–3 *iam tribus choros uideres feriatis noctibus* | *congreges inter cateruas ire per saltus tuos* | *floreas inter coronas, myrteas inter casas.* If that is how it is used here then the *alta nauium . . . propugnacula* are those of Caesar's fleet, as is assumed by Ps.-Acro (*hi autem qui proelium nauale ordinant, cum his nauiculis discurrunt inter maiores naues*); Nisbet (1984) 10; Kraggerud (1984) 24. Panciera (1956) 135 n. 1 is more hesitant. There seems to me some truth in the remark of Nisbet (1984) 10 that '*ibis* suits the whole enterprise better than the moment of attack (the same is true of the plural *Liburnis*)'. But for his assertion, or the similar view of Kraggerud (1984) 24, that '*inter* suggests comradeship and loyalty . . . sooner than hostility' there seems to be no justification.

27 See Hor. *Carm.* 1.37.30 with N–H (1970) 420; Prop. 3.11.44; 4.6.47–54; Virg. *Aen.* 8.689–92; Liv. *Per.* 132; Woodman (1983a) 222 on Vell. Pat. 2.84.1 (*nauium haec magnitudo modica nec celeritati aduersa, illa specie et terribilior*); Dio 50.18.4–5; 23.2–3; 32.2–3 and 51.1.2 (with Reinhold (1988) ad locc.); Plut. *Ant.* 61.1; 62.2–6; 66.1–3 (with Pelling (1988) ad locc.); Flor. 2.21.5–6; Veg. *Mil.* 4.33 *sed Augusto dimicante Actiaco proelio, cum Liburnorum auxiliis praecipue uictus fuisset Antonius* (with Milner (1996) 142). See also Casson (1971) 97–140; Pelling (1996) 55 n. 257. The argument of Murray and Petsas (1989) 143–51 that the tradition originates with Augustus' own *Memoirs* (c.24/23 BC) is unpersuasive, not least because of their unsatisfactory treatment of Epode 1 (144–5 n. 57) and their own argument that this way of conceptualising the battle is evident in the campsite memorial immediately after the battle.

28 For *paratus omne . . . periculum subire* in declarations of friendship, see Catull. 11.13–14 *omnia haec, quaecumque feret uoluntas* | *caelitum, temptare simul parati*; Cic. *Fam.* 15.4.12 *mitto quod . . . pericula . . . subieris et multo etiam magis, si per me licuisset, subire paratissumus fueris, quod denique inimicum meum tuum inimicum putaris.*

29 For the taking of the oath, see Dio 50.6.6. Those who had sworn the oath did not vow allegiance in perpetuity (as happened in later imperial oaths) but only for the war against Cleopatra, and the *coniurati* served strictly not as *milites* but *pro milite*: see Linderski (1984) 79–80. The texts are assembled and discussed by Herrmann (1968), esp. 78–89; 118–20. For further bibliography, see Linderski (1984) 79 n. 30; Reinhold (1988) 98 and add González (1988).

30 Compare, for example, *eosdem amicos sociosque quos eis esse intellexero habebo, eosdem inimicos meos esse statuam quos eorum partibus animaduertero* (González (1988) 113, lines 12–16).

31 *Si quis periculum ei salutique eius infert inferetque, armis bello interneciuo terra marique persequi non desinam* (*ILS* 190.3–5); cf. González (1988) 113, lines 17–18 *terra marique usque ad internicionem persequar*.

32 Cf. *ILS* 190.10–11 *neque me neque liberos meos eius salute cariores habebo* and compare Suet. *Calig.* 15.3; E–J 315.

33 Cf. *ILS* 8781.16–17 παντὶ τρόπῳ ὑπὲρ τῶν ἐκείνοις ἀνηκόντων πάντα κίνδυνον ὑπομενεῖν. For *paratus omne . . . periculum subire* in the *coniuratio*, compare Caes. *B Gall.* 1.5.3 *paratiores ad omnia pericula subeunda*; Cic. *Red. sen.* 14 *qui* [sc. *magistri*] *ad laborem, ad industriam, ad pericula pro patria subeunda adhortantur;* Livy 34.34.3 *quae mora si laborem tantum ac periculum haberet, ut et animis et corporibus ad sustinenda ea parati essetis hortarer uos*; Curt. 5.13.5 *omnes pariter conclamant paratos ipsos sequi: nec labori nec periculo parceret.*

34 For Philippi see Plin. *HN* 7.148; for the war with Sextus, see App. *B Civ.* 5.99 and 112. *periculum* might also carry a further contemporary resonance as the the fall of Alexandria is celebrated, according to the calendars (E–J p. 49), *quod eo die imperator Caesar rem publicam tristissimo periculo liberauit.*

35 Sherk (1969) No. 58.81–3 (late 31 BC) Σέλευκον τὸν ναύαρχόν μου . . . συνεστρατευμένον μοι πάντα τὸν πολέμου χρόνον καὶ διὰ παντὸς ἡριστευκότα καὶ πᾶσαν ἀποδείξιν εὐνοίας τε καὶ πίστεως. Compare 58.87–91 (30 BC) Σέλευκος . . . ἐμὸς ναύαρχος ἐμ πᾶσι πολέμοις συνεστρατευμένος μοι καὶ πολλὰς ἀποδείξεις καὶ τῆς εὐνοίας καὶ τῆς πίστεως καὶ τῆς ἀνδρείας δεδωκώς; and, from earlier in the decade, before the *coniuratio*, 58.12–18 (below).

36 For Caesar's tactics at Actium, see Florus 2.21 *Caesaris naues a binis remigum in senos nec amplius ordines creuerant; itaque habiles in omnia quae usus posceret, ad impetus et recursus flexusque capiendos, illas grauis et ad omnia praepeditas singulas plures adortae missilibus, simul rostris, ad hoc ignibus iactis ad arbitrium dissipauere*; Dio 50.23.1–3; 29.4; 32.2–8 and compare Panciera (1956) 144–7.

37 See, e.g., Veg. *Mil.* 4.8.3.

38 See *OLD* s.v. *periculum* 4b. Brink (1982b) 34 has argued that *tuo* is redundant as one cannot undergo a danger, which faces another, other than at risk to oneself. He prefers either (as does Delz (1988) 497) *Caesari*, which he takes with *tuo* to mean *pro Caesare tuo*, or Wakefield's conjecture *tui*. Either would put the emphasis more heavily on Maecenas' friendship with Caesar and would fit well with the general theme of the poem. However, neither emendation is necessary. The genitive is regularly used to define the person who faces the danger (see *OLD* s.v. *periculum* 2b). The logically redundant *tuo* serves to shift the emphasis to the danger faced by Maecenas and so leads naturally into Horace's concern for his survival expressed in the next couplet.

39 Menander Rhetor recommends that the propemptic speaker should say of his departing friend (397.28) ὅτι βασιλεῦσι χρήσιμος ἔσται γνωσθεὶς διὰ τὴν ἀρετήν.

40 Sherk (1969) 58.12–18 Σέλευκος ... συνεστρατεύσατο ἡμεῖν ... ὄντων αὐτοκρατόρων ἡμῶν, πολλὰ καὶ μεγάλα ἐκακοπάθησεν ἐκινδύνευσέν τε, οὐδενὸς φεισάμενος τῶν πρὸς ὑπομονὴν δεινῶν καὶ πᾶσαν προαίρεσιν πίστιν τε παρέσχετο τοῖς δημοσίοις πράγμασιν, τούς τε ἰδίους καιροὺς τῇ ἡμετέραι σωτηρίαι συνέζευξεν πᾶσάν τε βλάβην περὶ τῶν δημοσίων πραγμάτων τοῦ δήμου Ῥωμαίων ὑπέμεινε, παροῦσιν καὶ ἀποῦσίν τε ἡμεῖν χρηστὸς ἐγένετο.

For the contemporary resonance compare the language attributed to Herod when, in Caesar's presence later in the spring of 30 BC, he successfully both defends his loyalty to Antony and convinces Caesar of the kind of friend he will be to him (Caesar) in the future (Joseph. *AJ* 15.189–94, esp. 190).

41 For Maecenas' Epicureanism, see Du Quesnay (1984) 51–2; André (1967) 15–61; Castner (1988) 87–8; Evenepoel (1990) 106–7. See also the important discussion of Maecenas' self-presentation by Woodman (1983a) 239–44.

42 Epicurus, *Sent. Vat.* 28 (= Long–Sedley 22F2) δεῖ δὲ καὶ παρακινδυνεῦσαι χάριν φιλίας; Diog. Laert. 10.117–20 (= Long–Sedley 22Q6) καὶ ὑπὲρ φίλου ποτὲ τεθνήξεσθαι.

43 For the request of the departing traveller that the speaker should accompany him, see e.g. Tib. 1.1; Prop. 1.6; Stat. *Silv.* 3.2.

44 See Cairns (1972) 56–7.

45 See Sherk (1969) 58 (the Seleukos dossier) and Millar (1999) 18–30.

46 Possibly the play by Accius: see Powell (1990) 112.

47 For requests to accompany the departing traveller, see e.g. Ov. *Her.* 3.67–9; *Met.* 11.441–3; *Tr.* 1.3.79–88. Normally such requests are declined or there would logically be no farewell.

48 Compare Prop. 1.8, where the speaker exceptionally succeeds in dissuading the departing traveller from leaving.

49 Most editors follow the manuscripts and retain *si* for *sit*. At first sight Ov. *Her.* 13.164 *siue – quod heu! timeo – siue superstes eris* seems to provide support. But other instances of *si . . . si* only serve to reveal that the omission of any verb is problematic: Publ. *Sent.* A 8 *ames parentem, si aequus est, si aliter, feras*; Hor. *Epist.* 1.1.65–6 *rem facias, rem | si possis, recte, si non, quocumque modo, rem*; 1.6.67–8 *si quid nouisti rectius istis | candidus imperti; si nil, his utere mecum*; 1.10.41–2 *calceus . . . | si pede maior erit, subuertet, si minor, uret*. Porphyrion simply believed *si* to be redundant (*bis posuit particulam 'si', sed semel abundat. melius enim sic loqueretur: quibus te superstite uita iucunda est, si contra sit, grauis est. ergo uerbum extrinsecus hic accipiendum 'sit', ut plena fiat elocutio*). *si* is not required to give an ablative absolute a conditional sense: see, e.g., Woodman–Martin (1996) 443–4. As a result Aldus Manutius conjectured *sit* and this has recently been supported by Kraggerud (1984) 40 n. 13 (with further arguments); Delz (1988) 497; and Nisbet (1995a) 199. Decisive for *sit* is the fact that *si* with an ablative absolute seems to be unparalleled in Classical Latin (Lease (1928) 350; Hofmann–Szantyr (1965) 140.4; Keydana (1997) 272).

50 So Hanslik (1962) 336–7. At *Sat.* 1.6.1–6; *Carm.* 1.1.1; 3.29.1, Horace emphasises Maecenas' social superiority. For the importance of friendship as a theme in the propemptikon, see Men. Rhet. 395.26–31; 397.9–12.

51 Noted by Ableitinger-Grünberger (1971) 102. For similar effects in Ovid's *Metamorphoses*, see Lateiner (1990).

52 Cf. Cic. *Att.* 10.11.1; *Red. pop.* 2; Ov. *Met.* 8.405; *Tr.* 5.14.2; [Quint.] *Decl. maior.* 9.14. For the *coniuratio*, see n. 33. It is closely related to other notions such as calling one's friend *mea uita* or one's other self or a half of one's soul: see Hor. *Carm.* 1.3.8 and 2.17.5–6 (with N–H ad locc.); McKeown (1998) 286; 325. Maecenas (fr. 2.1 Courtney) addresses Horace as *mea uita*.

53 Cf. Plaut. *Merc.* 741–3: *cur ego uiuo? cur non morior? quid mihist in uita boni? | certumst, ibo ad medicum atque ibi me toxico morti dabo, | quando id mi adimitur, qua causa uitam cupio uiuere.*

54 For the idea that life without friends is intolerable, see Arist. *Eth. Nic.* 1155a3; Cic. *Planc.* 80 *quae potest esse uitae iucunditas sublatis amicitiis; Amic.* 47; 55; 86; 102 *sed quoniam res humanae fragiles caducaeque sunt, semper aliqui anquirendi sunt, quos diligamus et a quibus diligamur; caritate enim beniuolentiaque sublata omnis est e uita sublata iucunditas; Fin.* 1.66 *cum solitudo et uita sine amicis insidiarum et metus plena sit, ratio ipsa monet amicitias comparare.* While the language is similar, Horace is not generalising about the human condition, but concerned to express the dependence of his own happiness on the existence of a particular friend.

55 Cf. Tac. *Ann.* 1.61.4 *cladis eius superstites; Ann.* 2.71.2 *tot bellorum superstites; Germ.* 6.4; Flor. 1.39 *superstites poenae suae.* The source of the threat is not always made explicit: Ter. *An.* 487 *deos quaeso ut sit superstes* (i.e. of the dangers which threaten a new born child); Ov. *Her.* 13.164; Luc. 3.747; Flor. 2.32. Contrast Mankin (1995) ad loc. who wrongly insists on narrowing the meaning in line with *superstites dicimus qui supersint mortuis* and then proceeds to draw an unwarranted and utterly implausible inference about what Horace supposedly implies about indifference to the death of others, even of Caesar.

56 For the contrast of *iucunda ~ grauis*, see Sen. *Ep.* 73.3; Quint. *Inst.* 4.1.17 *prout asperi lenes, iucundi graues, duri remissi fuerint*; 10.1.46; Rutilius Lupus 2.16; 2.19: cf. Cic. *Fin.* 1.59 *grauioribus morbis uitae iucunditas impeditur. iucundus* is particularly associated with the pleasures of friendship: so, for example, in Catull. 9.9 *iucundum os* (Veranius); 14A.2 *iucundissime Calue*; 50.16 *iucunde* (Calvus); compare for other close relationships, 64.215 *ante mihi longe iucundior unice uita*; 67.1 *o dulci iucunda uiro, iucunda parenti*; 68.93 *ei misero fratri iucundum lumen ademptum*; 109.1 *iucundum, mea uita, mihi proponis amorem.* For *grauis* cf. Sallust, *Iug.* 14.15 *morte grauiorem uitam exigent*; Sen. *Suas.* 6.8 *uita . . . morte grauior detracta libertate.*

57 For the euphemistic *si contra*, compare Plin. *Pan.* 67.5 *egit cum dis ipso te auctore, Caesar, res publica, ut te sospitem incolumemque praestarent, si tu ceteros praestitisses; si contra, illi quoque a custodia tui capitis oculos dimouerent teque relinquerent uotis, quae non palam susciperentur.* Had similar prayers been uttered before Actium?

58 For the idea, compare Laelius speaking of the death of Scipio (Cic. *Amic.* 104).

59 Contrast Mankin (1995) 51 who thinks it might be a genuine plural; Babcock (1974) 23, who thinks the plural might 'create here a slightly exaggerated tone of importance'. For competing loyalties in the propemptikon, see Prop. 1.6, Tib. 1.3. The theme was perhaps established by Gallus (2.2–5 Courtney).

60 The text here follows Nauck's punctuation (see Mankin (1995) ad loc.) against Housman (1972) 5, who carried the question right through to 14 on the grounds that 'it is absurd to make Horace say "shall I continue to stay at home or continue to go to the wars"'. But the slight syllepsis, if there is one, does not seem to me to be intolerable. But rather than taking *persequemur otium* as meaning 'continue in' (*OLD* s.v. *persequor* 10), it is better to take it to mean 'seek out' (*OLD* s.v. *persequor* 4; 5), as it does at Cic. *Off.* 3.1.1 *nam et a re publica forensibusque negotiis armis impiis uique prohibiti otium persequimur et ob eam causam urbe relicta rura peragrantes saepe soli sumus*. In any event, it seems better to avoid the awkward enjambment of *feremus*, which is not in the manner of the *Epodes*: see Fraenkel (1964) 84–92, *EO* 2.770; 783 (Muecke).

61 For *iubere*, which denotes a request from a friend or patron, see White (1993) 266–8; but he seriously underestimates the force of such requests, principally because he does not recognise fully the obligations imposed by *gratia*: see Hor. *Epist.* 1.18.44–5 *tu cede potentis amici | lenibus imperiis*.

62 Dio makes it clear that senators and equestrians were restricted in the number of οἰκέται they could take with them. The word is usually restricted to slaves but can include what the Romans would call *familiares*. In any event it needs to be noticed that Horace has apparently not himself sworn the oath to follow Caesar. The issue is whether he will follow Maecenas. On the importance of the patron showing consideration to his *amici inferiores*, see Du Quesnay (1984) 43; 207–8 nn. 121–3.

63 See n. 32.

64 Questions of the form *utrumne...an* are rare: a search on *BTL-1* found 53 examples. Apart from Horace, *Sat.* 2.3.250f. and 2.6.70–1, only 8 are in verse (Seneca 4; Martial 2, Ausonius 1 and *Epigr. Bob.* 1). The remaining examples (42) are in (mostly rhetorical) prose and only Cic. *Inv. rhet.* 1.51 and Sisenna 123 (Peter) are earlier than Horace. See Huxley (1966) 60.

65 For *otium dulce*, see Manilius 5.173; Plin. *Ep.* 1.9.6; Claud. *Carm. min.* 30.219–20; Auson. *Ep.* 10.31 and compare *dulcedine otii* at Tac. *Ann.* 1.2.1. For the contrast with *labor*, compare Sen. *Breuit.* 4.2 *omnis eius* [sc. Augustus']*sermo ad hoc semper reuolutus est, ut speraret otium. hoc labores suos, etiam si falso, dulci tamen oblectabat solacio, aliquando se uicturum sibi*; Sall. *Cat.* 10.2; Cic. *Att.* 12.40.2.

66 For life without friends, see Cic. *Amic.* 55; 102; *Fin.* 1.66–70 (the Epicurean view). Horace again narrows the emphasis to Maecenas specifically.

67 Cf. Livy 25.6.19 *laborem et periculum petimus, ut uirorum, ut militum officio fungamur* and, e.g., Caes. *B Gall.* 1.44.3; *B Civ.* 1.64.2; 3.6.1; 3.53.4; 3.82.3; Sall. *Iug.* 28.5; 44.1; 85.7; 85.30; *Cat.* 10.2.

68 For a different view, see *EO* 2.909 (Formicola). For *mollis*, cf. Ov. *Tr.* 3.2.9–10 *quique fugax rerum secura in otia natus | mollis et impatiens ante laboris eram*.

69 Cf. *miles...appellatur...a militia, id est duritia, quam pro nobis sustinent* and contrast *mulier, ut Varro interpretatur, a mollitie*: see Maltby (1991) s.vv. *fortis*,

miles and *mulier*. Note also Sen. *Tranq.* 17.4 *Scipio triumphale illud ac militare corpus mouebat ad numeros, non molliter se infringens, ut nunc mos est etiam incessu ipso ultra muliebrem mollitiam fluentibus, sed ut antiqui illi uiri solebant inter lusum ac festa tempora uirilem in modum tripudiare.* For the etymology of *militia*, see also Cairns (1984), who suggests that the etymology might have been used first in Gallus and does not notice this instance in Horace (220–1). For the contrast between *mollitia* and *ferre laborem*, see Caes. *B Gall.* 4.2.5; 7.20.5.

70 Somewhat comparable is the way in which Horace provides answers to his own questions at *Epod.* 7.14ff. and 16.23ff., although there the question is posed to a group of people rather than to an individual. For such repetitions in responses to a speaker's own question, see Wills (1996) 66–9; 342–6. Although Wills (303) follows Housman's punctuation, his observation on the rarity of the repetition of a future participle by a finite verb still holds: he quotes only Ov. *Her.* 5.59; Tac. *Ann.* 3.16.4. His discussion of 'infinitive combinations' (307–10) does not notice and offers no parallel for *laturi . . . decet ferre.*

71 Cic. *Tusc.* 2.16.38 *aetas tironum plerumque melior, sed ferre laborem, contemnere uulnus consuetudo docet.*

72 See Cic. *Amic.* 15; 51; 103.

73 See Catull. 11.1–14; Hor. *Carm.* 2.6.1–4 (with N–H); Prop. 1.6.1–4; Ov. *Am.* 2.16.19–26 (with McKeown); Stat. *Silv.* 5.1.127–31.

74 See Catull. 11.9; Ov. *Am.* 2.16.19 and compare Virg. *Ecl.* 10.46 (which suggests that Gallus might have referred to the Alps in a propemptic setting).

75 For the Alps, see Vell. Pat. 2.90.1 *Alpes feris incultisque nationibus celebres*; for the Caucasus as *inhospitalis*, see Hor. *Carm.* 1.22.6–7 (with N–H).

76 See Maltby (1991) s.vv. *Alpes*; *Caucasus*. Horace is perhaps making a polemical point against Catullus whose *altas . . . Alpes* (11.9) points to the alternative *de Alpibus quae Gallorum lingua alti montes uocantur* (Maltby (1991) 25; cf. O'Hara (1996a) 281–2 and 91–2 with n. 348 for etymologising in Virgil with languages other than Latin and Greek).

77 For the Caucasus marking the furthest point East, see Cic. *Rep.* 6.12 (20) *ex his ipsis cultis notisque terris num aut tuum aut cuiusquam nostrum nomen uel Caucasum hunc . . . transcendere potuit . . . quis in reliquis orientis aut obeuntis solis ultimis . . . partibus tuum nomen audiet?* Cf. Cic. *Prov. cons.* 31 *mare . . . illud immensum . . . ab Oceano usque ad ultimum Pontum.* For the point of *ultimus* see Maltby (1991) s.v. Hispania Ulterior *ultra uel quod ultima uel quod non sit post hanc ulla, hoc est alia, terra.* Cf. Virg. *G.* 2.122–3 *Oceano propior . . . India . . . | extremi sinus orbis.*

78 For the repetition of compound and simplex with a shift of meaning see Hor. *Carm.* 1.23.10–12 *(persequor ~ sequi)*; *sequemur* here has the sense of *persequemur* 'accompany throughout a journey' (*OLD* s.v. *persequor* 1.b). See Wills (1996) 442 n. 21.

79 See, e.g., Catull. 64.339 (Achilles); Virg. *Aen.* 4.11 (Aeneas); Sen. *HF* 186 (Hercules).

80 See Maltby (1991) s.v. *fortis.* Cf. Hor. *Sat.* 2.2.135.

81 Cf. Kenney *apud* Mankin (1995) 53; *EO* 2.799 (La Penna). For the charge of *mollities* against Maecenas, see *Eleg. Maec.* 2.23–4 *exemplum uixi te*

[sc. Caesar] *propter molle beate* | *unus Maecenas teque ego propter eram*; Vell. Pat.
2.88.2 [Maecenas] *otio ac mollitiis paene ultra feminam fluens*; Sen. *Ep.* 114.8
apparet enim mollem fuisse, non mitem; Macrob. *Sat.* 2.4.12 *Maecenatem... stilo
esse remisso, molli, dissoluto.*

82 As he did previously against Sextus Pompeius: see Wistrand (1958) 16–17;
EO 1.219 (Nisbet).

83 Mankin (1995) 54–5 is probably right to identify these areas as trouble-spots.
There was a triumph for L. Antonius *ex Alpibus* in 41 BC and campaigns against
the Alpine Salassi by Antistius Vetus in 34 (*MRR* 2.411) and by Valerius
Messalla Corvinus shortly afterwards (*OCD*³ [Pelling]; *CAH* 10² [Gruen];
Syme (1986) 204–5). The Caucasus is ill-defined but one can point to a triumph by P. Ventidius *ex Tauro monte* in 38 BC (*MRR* 2.393) and a campaign
by Canidius Crassus against the Iberians and Albanians in 37/36 BC (Dio
49.24.1 with Reinhold (1988) for further bibliography). There were triumphs
for Domitius Calvinus (36 BC), Norbanus Flaccus (34 BC), Marcius Philippus
and Ap. Claudius Pulcher (33 BC) from Spain (*MRR* 2.402; 412; 416; 419)
and there were believed to be plans for the invasion of Britain in 34 BC (Dio
49.38.2 with Reinhold). Gaul, Spain, Syria and Egypt constituted the *Caesaris
prouincia* after 27 BC. There is no reason however to see, as Mankin does, any
implication that the Romans should be going to war against these foreign
people rather than against other Romans.

84 Horace is usually credited with *allapsus* as a coinage: but see Val. Max. 1.6.8
neque allapsus serpentium arceri neque fuga inpediri potuit, and note Serv. on *Aen.*
2.225: *labi proprie serpentum est.*

85 See Maltby (1991) s.v. *iucundus.*

86 For the expression, cf. Cic. *Balb.* 23 *qui nostros duces auxilio laboris, commeatus
periculo suo iuuerit*; Columella, *Rust.* 4.28 *nisi eam* [sc. *naturam*] *labore cum
studio iuueris* and for *iuuare labores* cf. Val. Flacc. 4.420; Sil. *Pun.* 13.519;
15.161; Stat. *Silv.* 1.1.61. Note also the similar word play at Plin. *Ep.* 4.15.13
quaestorem in petendis honoribus omni ope, <u>labore</u>, *gratia simus* <u>iuuaturi</u>, *perquam*
<u>iucundum</u> *nobis erit, si in eundem* <u>iuuenem</u> *studium nostrum et amicitiae meae et
consulatus tui ratio contulerit.*

87 See Cic. *Amic.* 24; *De fin.* 1.68 *quosque labores propter suam uoluptatem
susciperet, eosdem suscipiet propter amici uoluptatem.* Cf. Plut. *Adv. Col.* 1111b
τῆς ἡδονῆς ἕνεκα τὴν φιλίαν αἱρούμενος ὑπὲρ τῶν φίλων τὰς μεγίστας ἀλγηδόνας
ἀναδέχεσθαι.

88 See Hom. *Il.* 2.201; it is tempting to wonder if Archilochus ever used it.

89 Compare [Quint.] *Declam. maior.* 3.1 *fas est uita periclitari, qui natum se meminit
lege pereundi. neque in militiam grauissimo asperrimoque bello ita uenit, ut nesciret
sibi mortem in procinctu habendam, neque est tam imbellis, ut non forti pectore
aduersa, dum non inhonesta, toleret.* For *imbellis* explicitly contrasted with *fortis*,
see Cic. *Amic.* 47; Val. Max. 5.5.1 (L. Scipio). For *imbellis* of individuals,
note Sall. *Iug.* 44.1 *imbellis neque periculi neque laboris patiens*; Stat. *Silv.* 3.2.98
(Phoenix); *Achill.* 1.207 (Lycomedes) and Quint. *Inst.* 12.5.2 *nihil... profuerit
ut si des arma timidis et imbellibus.*

90 See Maltby (1991) s.v. *iuvenis.* Usually *imbellis* is used to describe those too
young or too old to fight, women or unwarlike nations: see e.g. Livy 38.21.14
feminae puerique et alia imbellis aetas; Just. *Epit.* 6.7.3 *senes et cetera imbellis aetas.*

91 For *firmus* of friends and friendship, see *OLD* s.v. 9. For the sense here, cf. Livy 23.34.12 *exercitum . . . ut satis firmum pacatae prouinciae praesidem esse, ita parum bello*; Nep. *Eum.* 11.5 *uiribus ad laborem ferendum firmis.*

92 Cic. *Att.* 2.24.1; cf. *Amic.* 47 *angor iste, qui pro amico saepe capiendus est*; Ov. *Ars am.* 2.350; *Her.* 19.109.

93 Caes. *B Gall.* 7.84.5; Livy 29.1.4 *grauis ea militia procul domo, terra marique multos labores, magna pericula allatura uidebatur; neque ipsos modo sed parentes cognatosque eorum ea cura angebat*; Publ. *Sent.* s 13 [= 655] *semper plus metuit animus ignotum malum*; see further Kenney (1990) on Apul. *Met.* 5.4.2.

94 Cf. Cic. *Tusc.* 5.41 *quae est enim alia fortitudo nisi animi adfectio cum in adeundo periculo et in labore ac dolore patiens, tum procul ab omni metu?*

95 Contrast Cic. *Fam.* 13.17.1 *T. Agusius et comes meus fuit illo miserrimo tempore et omnium itinerum, nauigationum, laborum, periculorum meorum socius; neque hoc tempore discessisset a me nisi ego ei permisissem.*

96 Cf. Cic. *Amic.* 27; 81; Men. Rhet. 396.18–21. In his commentary on the Homeric passage which lies behind this simile, Cicero makes his speaker say (*Div.* 2.65): *cur autem de passerculis coniecturam facit, in quibus nullum erat monstrum?*

97 For similes used to effect closure, see Catull. 2A; 11.22–4; 17.26; 25.12–13; 65.19–24; Virg. *G.* 1.512–14; Hor. *Carm.* 3.5.53–6. For closure of a section of a poem, see *Carm.* 1.12.47–8; 1.22.13–16; Virg. *G.* 1.201–3; 3.89–94; 3.237–41; *Aen.* 1.148–56; 11.492–7; 659–63; 721–4; Prop. 1.3.20; 2.20.5–8; 21.11–14.

98 Hom. *Il.* 2.308–20 (translated by Cicero [*Div.* 2.63: see Pease]); cf. *Il.* 9.323–7; 11.113–17; Aesch. *Sept.* 291–4; 503; Eur. *HF* 71–2; *Heracl.* 1039–41; [Moschus] 4.21–4 (with Vaughn (1976)); Antip. Sid. *Anth. Pal.* 7.210 (= 63 G–P); Ov. *Met.* 12.15–17 (with Bömer); Heliod. *Aeth.* 2.22; Claud. *De rapt.* 3.141–5 (with Gruzelier (1993)). Antipater varies the standard situation with an apparent glance at Aesop, *Fab.* 1 (Perry), usually held to derive from Archilochus 172–81 (West). There is no need to give primacy of allusion to Homer and even less to draw the quite unwarranted inferences that the simile is supposed to put us in mind of the destruction of Troy and, by analogy, of the destruction of Rome, as suggested by Mankin (1995) 56–7.

99 The mother bird feels fear even when she is on the nest: the need for the comma after *timet* is well explained by K–H ad loc.; Fraenkel (1964) 1.87 and Brink (1982b) 34–5: it 'restores the parallelism not otherwise explicit between 15–18 and 19–22'. Although Mankin takes the primary reference to be to Homer, he glosses *auis* as 'hen' (on 14–22). In view of the variety of species deployed in the tradition, it seems better not to be too precise and think broadly of some passerine or other songbird: so Capponi (*EO* 2.281), who also identifies the snakes as belonging to the species *Coluber viridiflavus* (*EO* 2.279). The word *pullis* takes over Cicero's translation of Homer's νεοσσοί (*Il.* 2.311): *recens nati pulli* (Maltby (1991) s.v.); they are not chickens. The adjective *implumis* occurs first here and at Virg. *G.* 4.513 (*nidos*) as a translation of Homer's ἀπτῆσι νεοσσοῖσι (*Il.* 9.323): then Plin. *HN* 10.10 *implumes . . . pullos*; 11.170 *columbarum fetus implumes*. For *adsidens*, cf. *Anth. Pal.* 7.210.1–2 ἄρτι νεηγενέων σε . . . μητέρα τέκνων, ἄρτι σε θάλπουσαν παῖδας ὑπὸ πτέρυγι. *adsidere* is properly used of persons tending the sick: see *OLD* s.v. 1c. This is a standard *beneficium* (e.g. Sen. *Ben.* 3.9.2; 6.14.4; 25.2; 34.1).

100 I take *pullis* ἀπὸ κοινοῦ with both *adsidens* and *timet* and so understand *relictis* as dative: i.e. '[but she fears] more for them when they are left behind'. Mankin (1995) ad loc. misrepresents the argument of Brink (1982b) 34–5.

101 Maltby (1991) s.v. *praesens*. The text I have printed is controversial. Editors are generally unhappy with the pleonasm of *ut adsit* and *praesentibus* as transmitted. Mostly they have suggested emending *praesentibus* to *precantibus* (Shackleton Bailey (1985b) 158), *petentibus* or *poscentibus* (Nisbet (1995a) 199). But Cavarzere (1992) 122 seems right to object that this would be awkward, as Maecenas is not requesting Horace's assistance. I have therefore preferred *uti sit* with Brink (1982b) 35. For *non uti sit auxili latura plus*, compare [Moschus] 4.24–5 μήτηρ, | οὐδ' ἄρ' ἔχει τέκνοισιν ἐπαρκέσαι. There seems to be nothing wrong with *auxilium ferre*...*praesentibus*: compare Ov. *Fast.* 5.136 *sunt praesentes auxiliumque ferunt*; Cic. *Cat.* 2.19 *urbi contra tantam uim sceleris praesentis auxilium esse laturos*; Celsus, *Med.* 3.7 *praesentissimum auxilium*; Fronto, *Ep.* 1.3.5 *eum praesentem accipias*...*et auxilium summum ei*...*feras*.

102 Men. Rhet. 396.3–11.

103 See Kraggerud (1984) 30–1.

104 As it is seen by Cairns (1972) 142. Cf. *EO* 2.733 (Fedeli).

105 For the 'remember me' *topos*, see Cairns (1972) index s.v. *memor sis*. In the syntaktikon it is standard for the departing traveller to emphasise his reasons for going: see Men. Rhet. 432.6–7; 9–14. The final section could be viewed as an 'included syntaktikon', but there seems no advantage in this view.

106 For *spes gratiae*, cf. Livy 35.17.3 *ibi alius alio ferocius, quia quo quisque asperius aduersus Romanos locutus esset, eo spes gratiae maior erat*; Curt. 10.8.17 *simul mementote rem esse cum ciuibus: quibus spem gratiae cito abrumpere ad bellum ciuile properantium est*. Cf. Cic. *Off.* 1.48 *in eos, quos speramus nobis profuturos, non dubitamus officia conferre*.

107 Sen. *Ben.* 2.1.1–2 *inspiciamus*...*quemadmodum dandum sit beneficium*...*ante omnia libenter*.

108 Cic. *Off.* 2.63 *omnes enim immemorem beneficii oderunt*; Sen. *Ben.* 3.1.1 *non referre beneficiis gratiam et est turpe et apud omnes habetur*.

109 Cf. Cic. *Inv. rhet.* 2.66 *gratiam, quae in memoria et remuneratione officiorum et honoris et amicitiarum obseruantiam teneat*. On *gratia* see Hellegouarc'h (1972) 202–8; Saller (1982) 17–21.

110 *Rhet. Her.* 4.25.35 *fortitudo est contemptio laboris et periculi cum ratione utilitatis et conpensatione commodorum*; Livy 9.42.5 *praedae erat largitor et benignitatem per se gratam comitate adiuuabat militemque his artibus fecerat et periculi et laboris auidum*; [Quint.] *Decl. min.* 345.13 *in omnia enim sane lucro trahamur, ducat nos spes ad laborem, ducat ad patientiam: nemo futuri temporis cogitatione ⟨tantum⟩ periculum subit*. Cf. Hor. *Epist.* 2.2.26–40. See Harris (1979) 74–104 for the economic motives of individuals in going to war. Note also that Dio says that at this time (51.3.4) οἵ τε ἐν τῷ τεταγμένῳ ἔτι καὶ τότε ὄντες ... τὸ δὲ δὴ πλεῖστον τῇ τοῦ Αἰγυπτίου πλούτου ἐλπίδι οὐδὲν ἐνεόχμωσαν.

111 Cic. *De or.* 2.346 *gratissima autem laus eorum factorum habetur, quae suscepta uidentur a uiris fortibus sine emolumento ac praemio*; *Inv. rhet.* 2.35 *etiam quae*

magis rara et eximia sunt, si ab eo cum magno aliquid labore aut periculo aut utraque re, cum necesse non esset, officii causa aut in rem publicam aut in parentes aut in aliquos eorum qui modo expositi sunt [sc. *cognatos, amicos, affines, necessarios*] *factum esse dicet; Off.* 1.62 *sed ea animi elatio quae cernitur in periculis et laboribus si iustitia uacat pugnatque non pro salute communi sed pro suis commodis in uitio est: non modo enim id uirtutis non est sed est potius immanitatis omnem humanitatem repellentis.*

112 Compare e.g. Cic. *Balb.* 51 *praemiis digni sunt, qui suo labore et periculo nostram rem publicam defendunt;* Livy 36.40.7 *quorum militum si et in alia prouincia opera uti senatus uelit, utro tandem modo promptiores ad aliud periculum nouumque laborem ituros credat, si persoluta eis sine detractatione prioris periculi laborisque merces sit, an si spem pro re ferentes dimittant, iam semel in prima spe deceptos?* Contrast Cic. *Arch.* 28 *nullam enim uirtus aliam mercedem laborum periculorumque desiderat praeter hanc laudis et gloriae.*

113 For the ingrate, see, e.g., Sen. *Ben.* 1.10.4 *erunt homicidae, tyranni, fures, adulteri, raptores, sacrilegi, proditores; infra omnia ista ingratus est; Ben.* 4.14.1 *quis non ingratum detestetur?*

114 Sen. *Ben.* 2.18.5 *diligentius quaerendus beneficii quam pecuniae creditor. huic enim reddendum est, quantum accepi, et, si reddidi, solutus sum ac liber; at illi et plus soluendum est, et nihilo minus etiam relata gratia cohaeremus; debeo enim, cum reddidi, rursus incipere, manetque amicitia;* 3.14.3–4 *aequissima uox est . . . 'redde quod debes': haec turpissima est in beneficio . . . interituram tantae rei dignitatem, si beneficium mercem facimus;* 3.15.4 *qui dat beneficia, deos imitatur, qui repetit faeneratores;* 4.14.1 *qui beneficium ut reciperet dedit, non dedit;* 4.25.3 *pudeat ullum uenale esse beneficium.* Cf. *gratia uocatur quia gratis datur* (Maltby (1991) s.v. *gratia*).

115 Cf. Sen. *Ben.* 2.17.7 *optimus ille qui facile dedit, numquam exegit, reddi gauisus est, bona fide, quid praestitisset, oblitus, qui accipientis animo recepit;* Gell. *NA* 17.5.4 *quisquis liberaliter et benigne facit, qua mente quoue consilio benignus liberalisque sit: utrum quia mutuam gratiam speret et eum, in quem benignus sit, ad parem curam sui prouocet, quod facere plerique omnes uidentur, an quia natura sit beniuolus benignitasque eum per sese ipsa et liberalitas delectet sine ulla recipiendae gratiae procuratione, quod est omnium ferme rarissimum.*

116 Brink (1982b) 35–6.

117 See Maltby (1991) s.v. *iuvencus* and compare Columella, *Rust.* 6 *praef.* 3 *etiam iumenta et armenta nomina a re traxere, quod nostrum laborem uel onera subuectando uel arando iuuarent.*

118 Hor. *Epist.* 2.2.177–9 *quidue Calabris | saltibus adiecti Lucani, si metit Orcus | grandia cum paruis, non exorabilis auro?* Compare Calp. *Ecl.* 7.16–17.

119 See Maltby (1991) s.v. *fervidus.*

120 Cf. Porphyrion ad loc. *Calabriam manifestissimum* [sc. *est*] *caloratam esse.*

121 See Maltby (1991) s.vv. *Lucani; Lucania; Canis* (ii).

122 I have retained *superni,* which must mean 'lying above something that is stated in the context' (Brink (1982b) 36). Strabo 5.3.12 makes it clear that the luxury villas were on the slopes beneath the town: τὸ Τοῦσκλον ἵδρυται πόλις οὐ φαύλως κατεσκευασμένη· κεκόσμηται δὲ ταῖς κύκλῳ φυτείαις καὶ οἰκοδομίαις, καὶ μάλιστα ταῖς ὑποπιπτούσαις ἐπὶ τὸ κατὰ τὴν Ῥώμην μέρος. τὸ γὰρ Τούσκουλον

ἐνταῦθα ἐστὶ λόφος εὔγεως καὶ εὔυδρος, κορυφούμενος ἠρέμα πολλαχοῦ καὶ δεχόμενος βασιλείων κατασκευὰς ἐκπρεπεστάτας. For *uilla tangat*, see Cic. *Mil.* 51 *ad uillam suam quae uiam tangeret*.

123 Hence *candens*: see *EO* 1.500–1 (Muzzioli). For *Circaea moenia*, cf. Sil. *Pun.* 7.692–3 *Circaeo Tuscula dorso | moenia, Laertae quondam regnata nepoti*; Ov. *Fast.* 4.71–2; *Met.* 14.253. Cf. Prop. 3.32.4 *Aeaei moenia Telegoni*; Sil. *Pun.* 12.535 *Telegoni...muros*; and see Livy 1.49.9 and Dion. Hal. *Ant. Rom.* 4.45.1–2 for an Octavius Mamilius, from Tusculum, who claimed descent from Odysseus and Circe.

124 Dio 51.3.1–5.

125 At *Carm.* 3.29.6–8 Horace urges Maecenas: *ne semper udum Tibur et Aefulae | decliue contempleris aruum et | Telegoni iuga parricidae*. It seems easiest to suppose these are places where Maecenas has villas. For a list of those known to have owned villas near Tusculum, see *RE* s.v. *Tusculum* 1487–8 (McCracken). For a different view of the significance of *Epod.* 1.29–30, see Martina (1989).

126 Dio 51.4.8. For the vast sums distributed by Augustus in 29 BC, see Suet. *Aug.* 41.1 *liberalitatem omnibus ordinibus per occasiones frequenter exhibuit. nam et inuecta urbi Alexandrino triumpho regia gaza tantam copiam nummariae rei effecit, ut faenore deminuto plurimum agrorum pretiis accesserit*; Dio 51.21.3–5 with Reinhold (1988) ad loc.; Millar (1999) 12–14.

127 *Laus Pis.* 230–45; Juv. 7.94; Mart. 1.107.2–3; 8.55; 11.3.10; 12.3.1–2.

128 Shackleton Bailey (1985b) 158 and (1997) 293 has conjectured *perdat* for *perdam* on the basis that 'a man is not likely to pile up riches and then waste them as a dissolute spendthrift. He leaves that to his heir.' The conjecture is supported by Nisbet (1995a) 193, but is rejected by Delz (1988) 497 on the grounds that it would weaken the antithesis of *aut...aut*. It might also be objected that a man with no son, and so no prospect of a grandson, is not likely to decide his course of action out of concern for his *nepos*. Horace's point is that, thanks to Maecenas' earlier generosity, he has no need of material recompense for his *beneficium* and all that he could do with any further riches would be to hoard them or waste them (i.e. spend them on things he neither needs nor really wants). In the context of rejecting riches, wasting them seems neither more nor less illogical than burying them.

129 The only other occurrences of *satis superque* in verse are at *Epod.* 17.19; Catull. 7.2; and *Priapea* 77.11 (25 times in prose). For such phrases marking closure, see Woodman–Martin (1996) on Tac. *Ann.* 3.30.4.

130 This is usually taken to be the gift of the Sabine farm: see *EO* 1.219–20 (Nisbet); 253–8 (Gigli). Horace's lack of explicitness might be intended to be tactful. It would be interesting to know to what extent the gift of the Sabine farm was a reward for writing *Satires* I or for accompanying Maecenas during the Sicilian War, whether it was for either or both.

131 Cic. *Amic.* 30–1 *sed quamquam utilitates multae et magnae consecutae sunt, non sunt tamen ab earum spe causae diligendi profectae. ut enim benefici liberalesque sumus, non ut exigamus gratiam (neque enim beneficium faeneramur, sed natura propensi ad liberalitatem sumus), sic amicitiam non spe mercedis adducti, sed quod omnis eius fructus in ipso amore inest, expetendam putamus.*

132 For *benignitas* as a topic of praise, see Cic. *De or.* 2.343 and compare Curt. 10.5.27.

133 See further Cic. *Off.* 1.44 (with Dyck (1996) ad loc.); 1.42; 2.52–6; Sen. *Ben.* 2.15.1 *dabo egenti sed ut ipse non egeam.* This goes back to the fundamental discussion of *liberalitas* at Arist. *Eth. Nic.* 1119b–1122a.

134 See Maltby (1991) s.v. *auarus.*

135 For the play on the proper name, compare *Sat.* 2.3.142 *pauper Opimius; Carm.* 1.33.2 *immitis Glycerae.*

136 For *nepos,* see Maltby (1991) s.v. *nepos.* Porphyrio ad loc. *nepotem autem ueteres ut prodigum ac luxuriosum dicebant, quia re uera solutioris delicatiorisque uitae soleant esse, qui sub auo nutriantur.* Both vices appear together at Hor. *Sat.* 2.3.82–157; 224–46; *Epist.* 2.2.193–4.

137 See, e.g., Sall. *Cat.* 5.4 (of Catiline) *alieni adpetens, sui profusus;* 5.8 *incitabant praeterea conrupti ciuitatis mores, quos pessuma ac diuorsa inter se mala, luxuria atque auaritia, uexabant.* For prodigality, see Cic. *Off.* 2.54 *multi enim patrimonium effuderunt inconsulte largiendo. quid autem est stultius quam, quod libenter facias, curare, ut id diutius facere non possis? atque etiam sequuntur largitionem rapinae; cum enim dando egere coeperunt, alienis bonis manus afferre coguntur.* For *auaritia,* see [Sall.] *Ad Caes. sen.* 2.8.4 *auaritia belua fera inmanis intoleranda est: quo intendit, oppida agros fana atque domos uastat, diuina cum humanis permiscet, neque exercitus neque moenia obstant, quominus ui sua penetret; fama pudicitia liberis patria atque parentibus cunctos mortalis spoliat.* On *auaritia* and *luxuria* in the discourse on civil war, see Jal (1963) 385–90.

138 Then Ov. *Am.* 1.9.42 *discincta . . . in otia* (see McKeown (1989) ad loc.). Porphyrio (ad loc.) glosses *discinctos pro neglegentibus solemus et nos dicere.* Cf. Servius on *Aen.* 1.210 *accinctos enim industrios dicimus . . . sicut e contra neglegentes discinctos uocamus.* For *industria* as characteristic of those who, unlike Maecenas, sought *dignitas, gloria* and *fama,* see Woodman (1983a) 241.

139 The text of Festus is unfortunately very lacunose at this point. That it referred to an Etruscan etymology is suggested by Ernout–Meillet (1959) s.v. *nepos.* The fullest discussion of *nepos* in the sense 'wastrel' is provided by Heller (1962) 61–70. After detailed discussion, he reconstructs Festus to read (77): *nepotes dicti quia scorpius a Tuscis dicitur nepa, ut apud Graecos luxuriosae uitae homines appellati σκορπισταί, quod non magis his res sua familiaris curae est quam is quibus pater auusque uiuunt.* For the link between *nepos* and *nepa,* see Maltby (1991) s.v. *nepos.* Heller's argument is attractive but the results are inevitably speculative and he surely goes too far in suggesting *nostris* for *Tuscis* (84). Any Etruscan etymology is denied by Bettini (1991) 260 n. 30. But the words *Tuscis dicitur* are clear and it seems that some ancient etymologist tried to establish a link with Etruscan. This would hardly be surprising. Etruscan borrowed *nepos* as *nefts* (Bonfante–Bonfante (1983) 60; 90); and the Etruscans had a reputation for *luxuria* (Heurgon (1964) 98–100). The main problem is that *nepa* is not known to have meant 'scorpion' in Etruscan (see Breyer (1993) 266 n. 295; 267 n. 296).

140 See K–H on *Carm.* 4.11.16, quoting Macrob. *Sat.* 1.15.17. I assume that *iduare* is not a complete invention (*contra* Ernout–Meillet (1959) 306), but

a genuine form assimilated to Latin. Etruscan had no 'd' and the infinitive ending is clearly Latin. See further Pfiffig (1975) 92; Breyer (1993) 295–7. For Maecenas' Etruscan ancestors, see *Sat.* 1.6.1–4; *Carm.* 1.1.1; 3.29.1; Prop. 3.9.1. According to Ps.-Acro (*Carm.* 1.20.5–6) he claimed to be *adfinis* to Porsenna.

141 Cf. Sen. *Ep.* 92.35 *alte cinctum putes dixisse; habuit enim ingenium et grande et uirile, nisi illud secunda discinxissent;* 114.4 *quomodo Maecenas uixerit notius est quam ut narrari nunc debeat quomodo ambulauerit, quam delicatus fuerit, quam cupierit uideri, quam uitia sua latere noluerit. quid ergo? non oratio eius aeque soluta est quam ipse discinctus?* See Schoonhoven (1980) 40–4.

142 *Eleg. Maec.* 1.21–8 *quod discinctus eras, animo quoque, carpitur unum: | diluis hoc nimia simplicitate tua. | sic illi uixere quibus fuit aurea Virgo, | quae bene praecinctos postmodo pulsa fugit. | liuide, quid tandem tunicae nocuere solutae | aut tibi uentosi quid nocuere sinus? | num minus Vrbis erat custos et Caesaris obses, | num tibi non tutas fecit in Vrbe uias?*; Vell. Pat. 2.88.2 *tunc urbis custodiis praepositus C. Maecenas, equestri sed splendido genere natus, uir, ubi res uigiliam exigeret, sane exsomnis, prouidens atque agendi sciens, simul uero aliquid ex negotio remitti posset, otio ac mollitiis paene ultra feminam fluens.* On the significance of Maecenas' behaviour, Woodman (1983a) 242–4 is fundamental.

143 Dio 51.3.5 ὁ Καῖσαρ ... φοβηθεὶς μὴ τοῦ Μαικήνου καταφρονήσωσιν ὅτι ἱππεὺς ἦν.

144 See Babcock (1974) 22.

145 The language is strikingly similar to that used in this poem: *quid faceret?* ∼ *quid nos?; comes* ∼ *comes; miles* ∼ *militabitur; fortiter* ∼ *forti ... pectore.*

146 See Cic. *Leg. agr.* 1.2; 2.48; *Quinct.* 40; *Verr.* 3.184; *Har. resp.* 59; *Cat.* 2.7.

147 Cf. Hor. *Epist.* 2.2.193–4 *scire uolam quantum* simplex *hilarisque* nepoti *| discrepet et quantum discordet parcus* auaro; Quint. *Inst.* 4.2.77 *uerbis eleuare quaedam licebit: luxuria liberalitatis, auaritia parsimoniae, neglegentia* [cf. *discinctus*] *simplicitatis nomine lenietur.*

148 With *perdam*, compare Cic. *Leg. agr.* 1.2 *possessiones ... disperdat ac dissipet ... nepos*; Cic. *Quinct.* 40 *quis tam perditus ac profusus nepos*; and, possibly, Hor. *Epist.* 2.2.195 *spargas tua prodigus* [= *nepos*].

149 Cf. Sen. *Ben.* 1.2.3 *nemo beneficia in calendario scribit nec auarus exactor ad horam et diem appellat.*

150 Dio 51.17.8 τοῖς τε προδανείσασί τι πάντα ἀπηλλάγη, καὶ τοῖς συμμετασχοῦσι τοῦ πολέμου καὶ τῶν βουλευτῶν καὶ τῶν ἱππέων πάμπολλα ἐδόθη.

151 See Powell (1990) 109 for further instances.

152 I would like to express my gratitude to the editors for their understanding and patience, which I have sorely tried, and to Tony Woodman for his perceptive and incisive comments and questions on an earlier draft.

3 DREAMING ABOUT QUIRINUS

This chapter is an elaboration of a suggestion made in the last paragraph of Zetzel (1980). An early version was presented as the Arthur Stocker Lecture at the University of Virginia in 1986; I had returned to the topic for a seminar at Columbia on the literature of the Triumviral period when I received the editors' kind invitation to contribute to this volume. I am indebted to the students in that seminar for their suggestions, and to Susanna Zetzel for her comments. I am very grateful to the editors for their advice and assistance on many points; had I been wise enough to accept it all, this chapter would have been much better. For a survey of recent criticism of the *Liber sermonum*, see Braund (1992) 17–22.

1 Freudenburg (1993) 109–19, 163–73 makes a valiant attempt to give Horace's putative opponents and critics some substance, but his construction of the literary opposition to Horace depends far too much on the untrustworthy evidence of the scholia. If my earlier arguments about the organisation of the book are accepted, there is no possibility of a real (rather than dramatic) chronological interval between 1.4 and 1.10.

2 For a careful analysis of the relationship of Horatian satire to comedy, cf. Freudenburg (1993) 3–51.

3 I am not convinced by the argument of Freudenburg (1993) 168–70 that Hermogenes and the *simius* represent different strands of criticism, but that is not relevant to my own argument.

4 Quirinus' instruction deals with writing Greek poetry, and the previous narrative spoke of mixing Greek and Latin. The two are obviously not the same, but as in context the writing of Greek poetry is clearly an even more offensive activity for a Roman poet than writing macaronic verse, the change is not significant for my argument. K–H (1968) ad loc. suggest that Horace was writing something similar to the Greek epigrams of Roman amateurs preserved in the *Anthology*.

5 The story about the choice of form is clearly ironic, and not to be taken as literal truth; cf. Zetzel (1980) 72. It is taken more seriously (and rebutted) by Du Quesnay (1984) 27–8.

6 It should be noted that in Callimachus the encounter with Apollo is separate from (although adjacent to) the actual dream of his meeting with the Muses who tell him the stories included in the first two books of the *Aetia*; but the scenes of poetic instruction and inspiration are merged in Ennius (and the version of Ennius' dream in Lucretius) as in the introduction to Cicero's *Somnium Scipionis*; in the *Eclogues* the two occur separately in the same poem.

7 Although I am inclined to accept the later date (35) for the *Eclogues*, I do not believe that the case has been, or can be, made conclusively. It is only the undisputed relative chronology of *Eclogues* and *Satires* that concerns me here.

8 Quirinus' second line also, as Denis Feeney points out to me, displays a neoteric concern for word-order in bracketing the verse by a noun–epithet combination, a feature that appears elsewhere in this poem only at line 49, *haerentem . . . coronam*, evocative of Lucretius 1.929.

9 The paradigmatic instance of this technique in Latin is Lucretius' report of Ennius' dream in *Annales* 1, not coincidentally looking back to Callimachus' dream itself. I have argued elsewhere (Zetzel (1998)) that the *Somnium Scipionis* employs the same technique in responding to Lucretius.

10 This paragraph should in no sense be understood as an adequate account of either Callimachus or Callimacheanism in Rome. For a fuller attempt, see Zetzel (1983). The history of Roman Callimacheanism can be constructed as a series of partial adaptations of Callimachus, none of which fully addresses his poetics or even attempts to incorporate the intellectual and political

motivations and contexts of third-century Alexandria. For a (controversial) attempt to interpret Callimachus himself, see now Cameron (1995).

11 For the Callimacheanism of the *Odes*, cf. Ross (1975a) 131–52; there are valuable but incomplete comments on the Callimacheanism of the *Satires* in Freudenburg (1993), particularly at 104–7, 185-211. See also Zetzel (1980) 68.

12 See Freudenburg (1993) 104–7; Zetzel (1980) 68 with earlier bibliography.

13 See most recently Henderson (1993) 70. K–H (1968) aptly cite Porphyrio: *nugae: sic uerecunde poetae nugas solent appellare uersiculos suos.* The Callimachean (or neoteric) context is confirmed by the *molestus'* characterisation of himself as *docti* (7), itself shown to be false by his later emphasis on speed and quantity of composition (23–4).

14 So also at 1.4.22–3, 71–5.

15 On this see Ross (1975a) 132 n. 1 and Cairns (1995) 125 (not citing Ross). There are of course many other sources and contexts for the opening of *Odes* 3.1, exhaustively studied by Cairns, often beyond the limits of plausibility.

16 Lucilius fr. 231 Marx, from *Iliad* 20.443; cf. K–H (1968) ad loc.

17 On Satire 5 see now the important discussion of Gowers (1993). Putnam (1996) 307-10 sees a close connection between this poem and the Fourth Eclogue; for the relationship between the two books, see below.

18 Callimachus fr. 110.61 Pf. On Latin imitations of this technique, see Clausen (1968).

19 See Ross (1975b) 244–6; on this passage 246 n. 31. I note that my understanding of Horace's view of Alexandrianism is greatly indebted to Ross's superb (and too little known) study.

20 On this passage see Gowers (1993) 59. The imitation of this passage by Virgil (*Aen.* 2.310-11), cited by Gowers, following Austin and others, is germane to the argument advanced at the end of this article.

21 Much less likely is the suggestion of K–H (1968) that Horace's word order imitates the scurrying of everyone to save the dinner from combustion.

22 I follow Wickham's OCT in placing the first part of the passage in quotation marks as well as the conclusion.

23 Cf. Freudenburg (1993) 196.

24 'Abschätzig' K–H (1968).

25 See Zetzel (1980). For a full study of the Alexandrian background to Roman poetic books, one awaits Nita Krevans's forthcoming book.

26 See K–H (1968) ad loc.

27 The interpretation of Putnam (1996) 305–6 takes *molle* as unequivocally positive, as do many critics.

28 Both Lucilius and Lucretius themselves (like every other Roman poet) are also Callimachean in some sense, but not in their choice of verbal and metrical styles. Putnam (1996) 310-12 is right to draw attention to the significant juxtaposition of Lucretian and Virgilian echoes; I would modify somewhat (see below) his interpretation of those juxtapositions.

29 Cf. Van Rooy (1973).

30 Cf. Putnam (1996) 311–14.

31 Cf. Ross (1975a).

32 For a clear discussion of some of the peculiarities of the style of the *Eclogues*, cf. Nisbet (1995a) 325–37.

33 The surviving contemporary (or nearly contemporary) strictures on the style of the *Eclogues* involve not Hellenistic affectations but Latinity (*hordea* and *cuium pecus*; on the latter see now Wills (1993)), and the significance and authenticity of Agrippa's (?) criticism of Virgilian *cacozelia* are disputed. At least some of the peculiar Latin, however, is the result of adaptation of Theocritean style: see Nisbet (1995a) 325–37.

34 Cf. Ross (1975a) 76

35 Cf. Zetzel (1996).

36 Cf. Ross (1975b).

37 Seneca, *Ep.* 114.17–19; Quintilian 10.2.18.

38 The allusions are noted but not discussed by Mynors (1990) on *G.* 3.277-9 and 303-4; not noticed by Thomas (1988). Only the use of *Aquarius* at *G.* 3.304 is noted by Putnam (1996) 313.

39 See above, n. 20.

40 For Lucretius' influence on the *Georgics* (strangely minimised by Thomas), cf. Farrell (1991) 169–206.

41 Putnam (1996), an article to which I am greatly indebted, offers a different and perhaps more generous narrative of the development from *Eclogues* to *Satires* to *Georgics*, in which each text retrospectively includes its predecessor in the grand scheme of the development of Roman poetry, e.g. 310: 'Horace's gesture announces that the place of Virgil in the history of literature and in particular of philosophical discourse is equally assured [sc. along with that of Lucretius].' My own reading concentrates on the divergent possibilities of Alexandrianism and the tension among its different elements in Rome.

42 In certain respects, my understanding of Horace's criticism of Roman Callimacheans is similar to that of Brink (1963), esp. 195, except that I do not believe that Horace was ever 'in flagrant disagreement' with Alexandrian principles. Much better is Nisbet's characterization of Horace as hating those who continue 'the affectations of a past generation' (Nisbet (1995b) 397).

4 BIFORMIS VATES

An oral version of this chapter was delivered at Baylor University, the University of Colorado at Boulder, the University of Missouri at Columbia, Penn State University, the University of Texas at Austin, and Washington University, St Louis. I am extremely grateful for these invitations to speak and for the stimulating comments I received in each place; for other help of various kinds I am indebted to D. C. Feeney, J. C. Gibert, B. J. Gibson, S. J. Harrison, C. S. Kraus, D. S. Levene and A. N. E. Tarrant.

References to Sappho and Alcaeus are taken from the edition of Voigt (1971); those to fragmentary Latin poets are taken from the edition of Courtney (1993).

1 Thus e.g. Baxter–Gesner (1806), Doering (1826), Macleane (1881) and Quinn (1980); no comment in K–H (1964).

2 Thus Baxter–Gesner (1806), Doering (1826), Orelli (1850), Macleane (1881), Shorey (1909), Quinn (1980), West (1995). Earlier, Jani (1778) had said the same. Page (1895) added Terpander to Sappho and Alcaeus, while to these three Obbarius (1848) added Pindar, who has no connection with Lesbos at all.

3 K–H (1964) ad loc., N–H (1970) xii (no comment ad loc.).

4 Williams, *OCD²* 528; Syndikus, *OCD³* 725 (thus not mentioning Sappho and privileging Alcaeus). For other minimisations or omissions of Sappho, in addition to those mentioned below, see e.g. Wilkinson (1945) 10 n. 2 ('He did not attempt to *imitate* Sappho' [his italics]), Fraenkel (1957) 167, N–H (1970) xii–xiii, Syndikus (1972) 1, Thill (1979) 115ff. (cf. 128–32), Rudd (1982) 377–8, Conte (1994) 303–5, West (1995) x.

5 Cf. Ath. 4.182f 'the barbitos, which Sappho and Anacreon mention'.

6 Santirocco (1986) 23.

7 Thus e.g. N–H (1970) 15, among numerous others.

8 Not mentioned by N–H (1970) 15.

9 I agree with the argument of Lyne (1995) 98–9 that the Alcaic stanza was so named in Horace's own day. If that is correct, it seems to follow that the Sapphic was so named too: (a) the whole of her first book was written in that metre (see Campbell (1982) 29); (b) Catullus' two 'Sapphic' poems (on which see below, IV) were written in the Sapphic metre; (c) there is an obvious correlation between Horace's very frequent use of each metre and his declared intention of imitating both Sappho and Alcaeus. Cf. also Marius Victorinus (6.161K) in the fourth century AD: *sapphicum metrum . . . sapphicum tamen . . . nuncupatur ideo quod eo frequentius usa sit Sappho quam Alcaeus repertor,* a point no doubt equally valid in the first century BC

10 N–H (1970) ad loc., adding 'but it should be observed that Alcaeus also used this metre'.

11 Quoted on 1.32 by e.g. Keller–Holder (1899) and, though alongside other passages, N–H (1970); also by Richmond (1970) 201. I have adopted the translation of Campbell (1982) 141.

12 So too at 1.37.1 *Nunc* mimics Alc. 332 Νῦν χ-. For various types of sound imitation see e.g. Coleman (1977) on Virg. *Ecl.* 1.1, Levitan (1993), Cairns (1995) 93 and nn. 10–11, Wills (1996) 19.

13 This parallel is mentioned by e.g. Orelli (1850) and Shorey (1909) on Horace and by Voigt (1971) 126 on Sappho.

14 Ferguson (1956) 4.

15 N–H (1970) xii, cf. (1978) 205 'His only overt pronouncement is a literary judgement in favour of Alcaeus' style', La Penna (1972) 208–9 'la palma tocca ad Alceo'.

16 Campbell (1978) 95, cf. Rudd (1982) 387.

17 Mayer (1995a) 292 quotes this line when stressing that public approval is necessary if an author is to be included in a canon, but Brink (1982a) 113–14 sees an 'affectation' on Horace's part.

18 See e.g. N–H (1970) on 1.1.32.

19 Harrison (1988) 474. Cf. also Nicoll (1986) 606, esp. nn. 11–12.

20 See N–H (1978) 271, but not noting Callim. *Aet.* 1.17.

21 N–H (1978) 219 say both that the word *uulgus* suggests 'unimportance' and, quoting La Penna (1972), that 'Horace is reacting against the tastes of the neoterics and their Augustan successors . . .; at the same time he is making a manifesto about his own poetry, which purported to imitate the practical outlook and masculine style of Alcaeus'.

22 References in Campbell (1982) 5, 9, 11.

23 References in Campbell (1982) 3, 35, 37, 39; also last n.

24 *ARV* 385/228 = Munich 2416.

25 See esp. Rosenmeyer (1985) 81–2 'The ancients practiced model criticism. Their allegiances and affiliations connect, not with a mode or a kind, but with a father, a personal guide' (I am grateful to A. Orlebeke for this reference). I am not, of course, denying the practice of *contaminatio* or 'window references' and the like, for which see below, n. 50.

26 Cf. also Sen. *Controv.* 9.1.13, Quint. 10.1.101.

27 See Courtney (1993) 153–5.

28 Williams (1969) 151, Quinn (1980) 296–7; cf. also Ferguson (1956) 4, Syndikus (1972) 1.

29 'Roman poets rarely touch on the subject of female writers' (Knox (1995) 310). Sappho's gender seems to attract little comment from Horatian scholars but note Feeney (1993) 62 n. 48; also below, p. 58.

30 See e.g. Wilkinson (1945) 13 'His pride at having introduced Aeolian lyric to Italy is very likely due, not to the phrases or ideas, nor even to the small amount of spirit, which he derived from Alcaeus and Sappho, but to his success in mastering and adapting their metres', N–H (1970) xii, Woodman (1974) 156 n. 51.

31 Macleod (1979b) 89 and 93 = (1983) 245 and 249 (also 101–2 = 257–8).

32 See Russell (1964) ad loc. (translation from Russell and Winterbottom (1972) 476).

33 See Fairweather (1974) 259–75; also relevant is Griffin (1985) 32–47 and esp. 183–97 on 'the creation of characters in the *Aeneid*'.

34 See Horsfall (1995) 1–25.

35 N–H (1970) xxvi; cf. also Syndikus (1972) 6–7.

36 Since Horace at *Sat.* 2.1.30–1 has just explained that Lucilius treated his books as his friends (*sodalibus*), it is interesting that, according to Porphyrio ad loc., Aristoxenus *ostendit Sapphonem et Alcaeum uolumina sua loco sodalium habuisse.*

37 Cf. Prop. 1.7.13 *me legat assidue post haec neglectus amator*, Ov. *Tr.* 2.5 *carmina fecerunt ut me cognoscere uellet, Rem. am.* 765 *lecto . . . Gallo*; and note Woodman (1974) 121. Any unwanted associations of Horace's verb *uulgaui* are headed off by the sentence which follows (33–4 *iuuat immemorata ferentem | ingenuis oculisque legi*).

38 Brink (1982a) 324.

39 Enn. *Ann.* 2–11 and Skutsch (1985) ad loc.; note also Brink (1982a) 93 'Homer's "essence", not just his subject-matter or style, is "passed on" to later writers, who as it were "incorporate" it, to make it part of themselves.'

40 *Epist.* 2.2.99 is rather different, since Horace's portrayal as 'Alcaeus' is there focalised by his adversary (*puncto illius*). N–H (1970) xii, who say that Horace's imitation of Alcaeus concerns 'technique rather than attitude of mind' and that 'the differences between the two poets are in fact more illuminating than the resemblances', interpret the line of the epistle as evidence that readers of the *Odes* were in fact misled by Horace's claims therein to imitate Alcaeus.

41 Thill (1979) 130, quoting Wilamowitz (1913) 308.
42 Diog. Laert. 8.77, and note also the cases of Atalanta and Epeius at Pl. *Resp.*
   620b–c. Servius on *Aen.* 6.448 refers to the 'Platonic or Aristotelian tenet' that
   animas per μετεμψύχωσιν *sexum plerumque mutare*: see O'Hara (1996) 182, and
   also below, n. 56.
43 According to Thomson (1997) 327, 'No certainty has yet been attained' on
   the question whether the fourth stanza is in its right place; but I believe that
   it is.
44 But Sappho has delayed the reader's realisation of this until line 14 (Edwards
   (1989) 594).
45 Note also the various epigrams in the *Greek Anthology* (6.269, 7.489, 505)
   which purport to have been written by Sappho but were in fact written by
   someone else (Page (1981) 127–8). An early example of such personification
   is Alcaeus 10 (see Dover (1964) 207), which provides the 'motto' for *Carm.*
   3.12 (see e.g. Richmond (1970) 199). Porphyrio assumed that Horace has
   transformed the speaker into a man, viz. himself (so too Quinn (1980) ad
   loc.); but Williams (1969) 86 believes that the allusion to Alcaeus proves that
   Neobule is the speaker (so too Fraenkel (1957) 178).
46 Zetzel (1992) 52 has acutely noted that Catullus' expression *gemina teguntur |
   lumina nocte* (51.11–12) is paralleled only at Callim. *Hymn* 5.82 and 92 with
   reference to the blinding of Teiresias, who, according to another myth, was
   celebrated for his changes of sex.
47 See e.g. Macleod (1983) 160–1, Adler (1981) 130ff., Wiseman (1985) 121–2,
   146, 176, 178, Miller (1994) 103–13, Skinner (1997) 131–47.
48 So Rosati (1996) 215.
49 So Knox (1995) 305 and Rosati (1996) 215.
50 For 'window references' see e.g. Thomas (1986) 188, 193, Wills (1996) 239.
51 Respectively Sappho 136 and Campbell (1982) 3 n. 5.
52 See Foley (1984). At *Carm.* 1.17.20 'Horace implicitly compares himself with
   Penelope' (Macleod (1983) 17 n. 1).
53 Zeitlin (1985).
54 It may be that self-address was itself associated with Sappho: see fr. 133(b)
   (frs. 1.20 and – probably – 65.5 are different but perhaps illustrate a related
   phenomenon).
55 See e.g. Skinner (1997) 133 and n. 5.
56 See esp. O'Hara (1996a), particularly 212–14, on the (now lost) poem by
   Sostratus (probably a contemporary of Catullus) which dealt with Teiresias'
   changes of sex. Note too the case of Caeneus at Virg. *Aen.* 6.448–9, where
   Austin (1977) refers to some other cases of sex-change at Plin. *HN* 7.36, and
   Laevius' poem entitled *Protesilaodamia*.
57 E.g. *Anth. Pal.* 4.1.5 (Meleager), 5.132.7 (Philodemus), 7.17 (Laurea).
58 See Courtney (1993), 70, 72; there is a lacuna in line 5 which is usually sup-
   plemented with a masc. adj. (*subido*) agreeing with *mihi*. It is likely that *dum
   pudeo* in line 4 alludes also to Sappho 137.
59 Jenkyns (1982) 49. For Sappho's *Nachleben* see e.g. Stark (1957), Malcovati
   (1966), La Penna (1972) and some of the numerous recent books on Sappho.
60 See Adams (1984) 73–4.
61 *qui* is printed by Ellis and Kroll.

62 Gleason (1995) 161, whose whole discussion is concerned principally with physical gestures and the like. For the effeminate style see e.g. Bramble (1974) 41–5.

63 Indeed Horace in his *Odes* has often seemed to his readers to be a particularly 'masculine' poet: see e.g. N–H (1970) xxv, (1978) 219 (above, n. 20), Macleod (1983) 223.

64 See e.g. Brown (1993) ad loc.; and also above, p. 38.

65 Coburn–Christensen (1990) 4.4705. See Jackson (1993), esp. 593–600.

66 There is a vast bibliography on this subject: see e.g. Hoeveler (1990), esp. 1–23, Nattiez (1993), e.g. 111ff. For Blake, a particularly noteworthy case, see Fuller (1988), index 'sexuality'. The notion is fundamental to Jungian psychology and, as the Chinese conception of Yang and Yin illustrates, is not restricted to one particular culture or period.

67 Nattiez (1993) 37.

68 See Courtney (1993) 66–7 and 139 for discussion, noting that the notion is associated esp. with Orphic literature. (The text of Laevius 26.2 is corrupt.) See also Delcourt (1961) and, on the symbol of the androgyne in early Christianity, Meeks (1974), a reference I owe to J. Barclay.

69 *Anon. Lat.* 10 *nec aliter ingenium bonum constat nisi uirtutem ex masculina, sapientiam ex feminina specie conceperit* (= André (1981) 57). This passage, which is generally assumed to derive from Loxus, has recently appeared in the almost simultaneous publications of Barton (1994b) 115 and Gleason (1995) 59. For Sappho as a representation of wisdom see Ael. *VH* 12.19 (Campbell (1982) 7), but Aelian's appeal to Plato (*Phdr.* 235b–c) is based on misremembering.

70 See Dillon (1977) 175; Boyarin (1993) 35–43. For the view that wisdom is both masculine and feminine cf. Philo, *De fuga et inventione* 51; compare also Diogenes of Babylon fr. 33 (*SVF*) (see Obbink (1996) 19–20).

71 Perhaps related is the philosophical theme 'the virtue of man and woman is the same', which ultimately goes back to Plato: see Dillon (1995).

72 The standard text is that of Winnington-Ingram (1963). Part of Book 2 is translated in Russell–Winterbottom (1972) 552–8, from which my translated excerpts are taken, the whole work by Mathiesen (1983), who discusses the problems of the author's dates (10–14), and Barker (1989) 2.392–535.

73 For a very different application of Aristides to Horace's *Odes* see the formidable paper of Cucchiarelli (1999).

74 See Mathiesen (1983) 27–33.

75 Rudd (1982) 385–404.

76 Courtney (1993) 277 has only two parallels, from Cicero and Apuleius, for this phrase applied by men to men. The phrase is of course frequently used of women (*OLD uita* 5).

77 Courtney (1993) 277.

78 See Woodman (1983b); also Fraenkel (1957) 341–2. For a recent study see Moralejo (1995).

79 Cf. Stat. *Silv.* 5.3.154–5 *saltusque ingressa uiriles* | ... *Sappho.* It might be objected that Sappho's reputation as lesbian argues against her representing idealised female qualities; but her femaleness seems adequately attested by

e.g. the description of her poems as her 'daughters' (*Anth. Pal.* 7.407.9–10)
and the story of her love for Phaon, the subject of the *Epistula Sapphus*, where
she is described as *poetria Sappho* ([Ov.] *Her.* 15.183), as in Galen (4.771
Kühn 'We hear . . . Sappho described as poetess [*poiētrian*]') and Terentianus
Maurus (6.390K).

80 It is the argument of Cucchiarelli (1999) that *mascula* is to be taken with *pede*
and that the whole phrase is an almost technical reference to metre.

81 Fraenkel (1957) 339.

82 Fraenkel (1957) 424.

5 JUST WHERE DO YOU DRAW THE LINE?

I gratefully acknowledge friendly help and discussion on the issues put forward here from David West and (as further acknowledged below) Michael
Reeve.

1 For lectional signs in Latin texts of Horace's time see Wingo (1972), esp.
54–61 on the use of *paragraphoi* to mark section-boundaries in the *Carmen de
bello Actiaco*; Parsons in Anderson et al. (1979) 129–31, publishing the 'Gallus'
elegiacs from Qaṣr Ibrîm; and Heyworth (1995) 121–2.

2 Thus the end of Propertius '3.25' echoes the beginning of '3.24'. Combine
this observation with the fact that the two together constitute a re-run of the
themes and structure of 1.1, and it becomes clear that '3.24 + 25', last poem in
Book 3, was designed to round off the Cynthia experience which the opening
poem of the *Monobiblos* – also 38 lines, with a break-point in the centre – had
introduced. See in general Schrijvers (1973) and Esser (1976).

3 See Roberts et al. (1997), especially Rutherford's paper on the Greek lyric poets, highlighting features like prayers, sphragistic passages in which the poet
'signs off', 'natural end points' like crownings and arrivals, as well as less
expected markers like the mention of 'hair' (Rutherford (1997); also this
volume, Ch. 7). On ring-composition, see pp. 75–6. For idiosyncratic habits,
one might think of Horace's predilection for ending poems with 'hanging'
speeches (1.7, 1.15, 3.11, 3.27) or quasi-photographic images frozen in words
for all time (1.9, 1.17, 2.13, 3.5, 4.2) or scenes in Hades (2.13, 2.18, 2.19,
4.7; see Schrijvers (1973) 150–1, who extends this category to include 'une
mention ou une allusion concernant le terme de la vie humaine'). Hanging
similes, which leave the poem as it were suspended before the reader's eye,
make an especially elegant and sophisticated ending, as Keats (*On First Looking into Chapman's Homer*) and Matthew Arnold (*The Scholar Gypsy*) saw;
cf. Catullus 11; 17 and 65, Virgil, *Georgics* 1; also this volume, p. 27 and
n. 97.

4 Similarly, anyone who started by reading Propertius 1.1, 2.14, 2.32, 3.6 and
3.14 might incautiously conclude that *quod si* was a reliable indicator that
we had reached the final couplet, but that impression would not be borne
out by a study of the whole corpus. The same applies to Catullus: contrast 15 and – accepting Westphal's transposition – 42 with 14.8. This makes
quod si at *Carm.* 3.1.41 nicely ambiguous; I argue below that it does *not* signal
poem-end.

5 See Heyworth (1995).

6 The same exercise (but excluding the Roman Odes) was carried out briefly, and rather superficially, for all four books by Sturtevant (1912). Sturtevant was concerned to justify the *status quo* rather than engage in the more radically subversive enterprise which I am here undertaking. But he made some shrewd hits, to which I shall refer below.

7 The compositional balance of Book 2 is so peculiar – twelve poems in alcaics, six in sapphics, one hipponactean, and only a single asclepiadic, compared with fifteen in Book 1 and eleven in Book 3 – that I leave it out of account here. It may be that when he came to distribute the poems into books, Horace gave priority to the elegant arrangement of the first and third, and did his best to dispose what was left in the second; with such a narrow metrical range available, however, there was a limit to the amount of variation he could achieve. If that speculation is right, readers would have been more reliant on *paragraphoi* here than elsewhere.

8 See Port (1926) 456.

9 See Cameron (1968) 330 n. 1.

10 Omitting 3.5, widely regarded as spurious. I may add that Charles Murgia, with whom I spent six months in Berkeley having any number of stimulating disagreements, said something to my liking for once when I asked him in a neutral, offhand tone of voice how many of the much-disputed *Heroides* had actually been composed by Ovid. 'Ten', he replied instantly.

11 Skutsch (1963), at 239 n. 6. During the same years, Livy was organising his history in *pentads* and *decades* of books: see Walsh (1974) 8–9. And in at least one ancient library Euripides' plays seem to have been stored in boxes of five: see Snell (1935), offering an elegant explanation of the survival of the 'alphabetic' plays.

12 The book of epodes, seventeen in all, begins with a sequence of ten iambic poems before moving on to an iambo-dactylic set. As for the eight which make up *Satires* 2, Fraenkel (1957) 137 thought he had 'run short of suitable subjects and settings'.

13 So Port (1926) 297.

14 Fraenkel (1957) 112 n. 1. Fraenkel dealt only in decimal currency ('the ideal number of ten', *ibid.* 137); that three books added up to fifteen, he thought, 'may be accidental'.

15 N–H (1970), introducing 1.38, record ironically: 'Sometimes it was felt that Horace could not have rounded off the book with so slight a poem; two odes must surely have been lost, to make the number up to forty.'

16 Cf. Prop. 1.13.29–30 *cum sit Ioue digna et proxima Ledae | et Ledae partu gratior, una tribus.*

17 Cf. Sturtevant (1912) 122, hunting for reasons to justify the juxtaposition of what he thought two alcaic poems: 'No ... motive is apparent for putting the Tyndaris ode immediately after the palinode *unless this too is addressed to her*' (my italics). See also Hahn (1939) 223–7 (describing the two poems as 'pendants'), and Collinge (1961) 46 ('No doubt *O matre pulchra filia pulchrior* would forge a mental link in the reader's mind with Helen of the previous ode and Tyndaris (*of all names*) of the following.' Again, my italics). The treatment

in Santirocco (1986) 49–52 is excellent. Syndikus (1972) 1.180 n. 1 rejects the linkage: 'Die milderen Töne aber sind die unserer Palinodie'.

18 Fraenkel (1957) 208 n. 2.

19 See Evans (1971).

20 Further evidence that 15 and 16/17 were composed as a diptych is provided by what seem to be deliberate verbal echoes: *uitabis* used in contrasting senses of both Paris (15.18) and 'Tyndaris' (17.18); and a stanza placing each character in a valley (eighth stanza of 15; fifth stanza of 17).

21 Campbell (1988) ad loc.; cf. Terpander testimonium 19.

22 Compare 3.1.1–4 *Odi profanum uulgus et arceo; fauete linguis*, etc.; the similarity suggests that this first stanza of the Roman Odes was also intended to stand apart as a proem.

23 Cf. *igitur* in Prop. 1.8 and 2.13b; see Fedeli (1980) on Prop. 1.8a.1.

24 As editors conventionally print it – but see pp. 74–5

25 Commager (1962) 327–8.

26 E.g. *Carm.* 1.21 and 1.32. See Schrijvers (1973) 149.

27 The explanation of Wilkinson (1951) 143 was a chronological one: 'it is interesting to note that the earliest specimen (1, 26, *Musis amicus*) is a light poem of only three stanzas, whereas those written later are nearly all much longer'. See pp. 11ff. for his alleged sequential scheme.

28 Sturtevant (1912) 122 was foxed by this pair: 'No connection between them can be detected.'

29 The poem's *sensus sumptus est ab Anacreonte ex libro tertio.*

30 Already known in Rome in Lucilius' day (fr. 484 Marx).

31 Athenaeus 4.128b, 14.615a.

32 Kilpatrick (1969).

33 Indeed, he was prepared to see the sapphic poem 1.32 as a similar preface to the following piece dedicated to Tibullus, even though that is in asclepiads; but quite apart from the question of metre, in what sense is 1.33 a *Latinum carmen*, as promised in 1.32.3–4? Textual difficulties in 1.32 obscure its interpretation: *cumque* in line 15, if sound, seems to refer to *general* appeals for help, rather than to a specific occasion; and it is a circular argument for Kilpatrick (1969) 239 to claim that the problem of *Poscimur / Poscimus* in line 1 'would be neatly solved by the context'.

34 See, for example, Santirocco (1986) 74–8, esp. his view (78) that at this point in the book Horace is setting the scene for 'his return to politics and political poetry which is *announced in C. 1.34 and accomplished in C. 1.35*' (my italics).

35 Compare the appearance of 'Pudor' in both preface and 'body' of 1.24 (lines 1, 6).

36 Mindful of the wrath meted out by Anderson (1988) to 'numerologists and diagram-artists' ('simplistic', 'impatient', 'implausible', 'irritating', 'explosive', 'acrimonious', 'fantastic', 'fanatic', 'intolerable', 'outrages', 'indignities', 'enormities', 'rage', 'fury' are some of the words employed), I am hesitant even to raise the question of book structure here. But it does look rather as if Horace was aiming at a quadripartite scheme: (1) nine poems opening with a general dedication to Horace's patron Maecenas (these are already recognised by scholars as a set – the so-called 'Parade Odes'); (2) nine poems

(sapphics first and third) opening with an invocation to Mercury; (3) nine poems (sapphics first and third) opening with a renewed appeal to Maecenas; (4) eight poems (sapphics first and third) opening with an invocation to Venus. That is: he wanted as far as possible to divide the book into four quarters, but since fours into 35 won't quite go, 9–9–9–8 is the best available fit. Those who wish to venture further into this strange universe where rival symmetries vie for supremacy may consult the works of (e.g.) Salat (1969), Mutschler (1974) and Dettmer (1983).

37 If I express my warm gratitude to Michael Reeve for help with this section, it is not because he is responsible in any way for its arguments (he has not seen it in this form), but because his acute but kindly criticism persuaded me to demolish a previous and even more imperfect formulation.

38 On 3.1.1 he notes *haec autem ode multiplex per uarios deducta est sensus*; then no mention of any kind of break until 3.7.1. See Heyworth (1995) 141.

39 Where they agree: see Heyworth (1995) 147–8.

40 To avoid confusion with the *paragraphos* which marked unambiguous poem-end, on the other hand, perhaps a modicum of vertical white space is a better typographical device.

41 A standard type: cf. e.g. *Carm.* 1.8 and 29, Catullus 9, 29, 45, etc., Pindar, *Ol.* 2.

42 See below, n. 51.

43 On the ambivalence of *quod si* (3.1.41) as a closural marker see above, n. 4.

44 This kind of pious declaration is itself a closure-marker in the hymn genre: cf. Catullus 63.91 *procul a mea tuos sit furor omnis, era, domo*, Callimachus, *Hymn to Demeter* 116–17 (the conclusion of the narration). And if 3.2.26ff. echoes the end of Callimachus' sixth and last hymn, so too 3.1.5ff. recalls the beginning of his first, to Zeus.

45 See Collinge (1961) 47: 'Odes 1–3 of the third book scarcely admit of a pause between them . . . as if each ode ended with a μέν clause, to be picked up with an antithetical δέ clause in the next. And the Muse, reproached for the grandeur of her song at the close of iii.3, is invited to embark on lengthy choric melody at the next ode's very outset.'

46 The heavenly duo thus themselves respond in a further ring-compositional bridge; as, over a wider span, do the *uirgines puerique* of 3.1.4 with the *progenies uitiosior* at the very end.

47 Note that Calliope is asked for a *longum melos* (3.4.2).

48 Compare the break at 3.2.48, which I argued above was marked because of the parallel with the end of 2.12. I am of course acutely aware of the method-ological impropriety of relegating one class of similar passages to the status of 'false parallels' while simultaneously resting my own case on another set which are thereby implicitly labelled 'true parallels'. The crux of the issue is not whether, in trying to find a path through such difficult terrain, one can incorporate *all* the data without contradiction, but whether one can construct a convincing 'best fit' of as much of it as possible.

49 Fraenkel (1957) 285.

50 Compare *Pythians* 5, where the opening *gnōmē* is similar: not, as here, 'x with-out y is no good', but 'Wealth is great as long as it is accompanied by virtue' (i.e., x is good as long as y comes with it; same pattern at *Pythians* 11.55–7.).

The thought which launches *Isthmians* 3 provides another variant: 'Luck is all right provided that you avoid getting above yourself'; that is, *x* is good as long as it is not accompanied by *y*.

51 Thus the following early themes are further developed in the 'first block': the just man receiving possibly unjust treatment from Jupiter; the boat in a storm at sea; and *uirtus* gaining its heavenly reward.

52 Compare the end of *Pythians* 9, which perhaps influenced the closing sentence of the Regulus ode.

53 See Miller (1998) 550–1.

54 The closing paragraph of Miller (1998) makes this point, even if he is not concerned to mark a strong break after the Apollo stanza.

55 Lohmann (1991) also emphasises the importance of through-composition, though for him the 'große Ode' comprises poems 1–4.

6 A WINE–JAR FOR MESSALLA

1 *lectum*, the transmitted reading, would refer to a select sub-category of Massic wine, but it does not combine easily with *quocumque nomine*. I have therefore conjectured *laetum*, an easy change; phrases like 'in whatever name you rejoice' are common in liturgical contexts such as we have here (n. 10).

2 *pia* suits the religious language best if it is taken as 'kindly'. *pietas* is occasionally ascribed to gods even in the classical period (Pease (1935) on Virg. *Aen.* 4.382); the word lies behind English 'pity' as well as 'piety' (cf. 'pie Jesu').

3 Syme (1986) 382–95.

4 Hammer (1925); Syme (1986) 201–10.

5 Tac. *Ann.* 6.11.3 *quasi nescius exercendi*; Jer. *Chron.* 164 Helm *inciuilem esse potestatem contestans*; Syme (1986) 211–12.

6 Horace may reflect this controversy in his remarks about an ambitious Laevinus (*Sat.* 1.6.11–15), though the point there is that the man is unworthy of his ancestors.

7 Unlike Fraenkel (1957) 132 n. 2 I take *ambitione relegata* with the following list of important supporters; as the ablative absolute forms an independent clause, the following *te* is still emphatic.

8 *fratre* is usually thought to refer to Messalla's half-brother, L. Gellius Poplicola (*cos.* 36), but Potitus Messalla (*cos.* 29) would make a better pair than an older man with a different name. Gordon (1957) 44–5 and Syme (1979) 264 regarded Potitus as a second cousin of our Messalla, Hanslik (*RE* 8A.133, 165) as an older half-brother; he might even have been a younger brother who obtained the consulship early through family influence. Jerome (n. 9) implies that Messalla had an important brother of the same name; he may have used a reliable list of *exempla*.

9 Jer. *Adv. Iovinian.* 1.46 *Valeria, Messallarum soror, amisso Seruio uiro, nulli uolebat nubere*; Syme (1984) 1419.

10 Norden (1913) 143–63; Pulleyn (1994) 19–20.

11 Syme (1979) 414 'it is reasonable to postulate 64 BC or thereabouts'; (1986) 201, 218–20.

12 Cf. *Carm.* 2.7.1–2 *O saepe mecum tempus in ultimum | deducte Bruto militiae duce.* See also Bradshaw in this volume, pp. 6–7.

13 Feeney (1993) 58–9.

14 *CIL* 6.32338.11; Syme (1986) 46.

15 Tib. 2.5; *CIL* 6.32323 (= *ILS* 5050).152 (on the *ludi saeculares*); Syme (1986) 48–9.

16 *CIL* 6.32338.4; Syme (1986) 46–7.

17 Syme (1979) 263–4. Perhaps 'Corvinus' was thought a good family name for the son of 'Niger', as ravens were proverbially black (Petron. *Sat.* 43.7 *niger tamquam coruus*; Apul. *Met.* 2.9.2 *coruina nigredine*).

18 *CIL* 6.3826 (= *ILS* 46); Cic. *Har. resp.* 12.

19 *CIL* 6.32323 (= *ILS* 5050).50; Syme (1986) 48.

20 Dio 51.21.2; Syme (1979) 261.

21 Pease (1920) on Cic. *Div.* 1.12; Thompson (1936) 161. Manilius says that Corvus got his name 'by the help of the winged creature that carries Phoebus in the form of a bird' (1.782–3 *at commilitio uolucris Coruinus adeptus | et spolia et nomen qui gestat in alite Phoebum*). Silius invents an eloquent Corvinus with the bird of Phoebus on his helmet to prophesy the disaster at Lake Trasimene (5.77–9).

22 Livy 8.11.13 *Falernus [ager] qui populi Campani fuerat usque ad Vulturnum flumen plebi Romanae diuiditur.* Sometimes Massic wine was regarded as a kind of Falernian; cf. Sil. 7.207–11; *ILS* 8579 *Fal. Mas.*

23 *MRR* 1.135–6; Salmon (1967) 207–8; Frederiksen (1984) 185 (with map 3). Livy 8.8.19 and Val. Max. 1.7.3 put the battle near Vesuvius, which is accepted by Oakley (1998) ad loc., but this seems too far south; Livy himself says that the defeated Latins retreated to Vescia (8.11.5), which was near the Mons Massicus (*RE* 8A.1693).

24 Nisbet (1959) 73–4 = (1995a) 1–2.

25 Mart. 3.111.1 *de Sinuessanis uenerunt Massica prelis.*

26 Wiseman (1979) 113–17.

27 *Sat.* 1.10.28–9 *cum Pedius causas exsudet Publicola atque | Coruinus*; Pedius was married to a sister of Messalla Corvinus (Plin. *HN* 35.21). Wiseman (1974) rightly attaches *Publicola* to *Coruinus* (citing *Catalepton* 9.40); the family professed popular leanings.

28 Perhaps the punctilious Messalla was himself associated with *pietas*; cf. Vell. 2.71.1 *nec ... maius exemplum hominis grati ac pii quam Coruinus in Caesarem fuit*; Ov. *Pont.* 2.2.21 (to his son Messalinus) *quaeque tua est pietas in totum nomen Iuli.*

29 Livy 7.26.2; 9.17.12 (Torquatus and Corvus a match for Alexander the Great); Ov. *Fast.* 1.601–2 *quidam celebres aut torquis adempti | aut corui titulos auxiliaris habent*; Gell. 9.11 and 13; Amm. Marc. 24.4.5.

30 D'Arms (1990) 308–19; Murray (1993) 91 and 96–7. They point out the more genuine equality of the Greek symposium.

31 Wiseman (1979) 113; cf. above, n. 27.

32 Cic. *Mur.* 70; Lyne (1995) 107–8, quoting Philodemus, *Anth. Pal.* 11.44 (his famous invitation to Piso). For friendships with the great see White (1993) 3–34.

33 For absolute comparatives applied to wine cf. *Epod.* 9.33 *capaciores . . . scyphos*, *Carm.* 1.9.6 *benignius*.

34 Sen. (?) *Anth. Lat.* 405.8 *cuius Cecropio pectora melle madent*; Citroni (1975) on Mart. 1.39.3.

35 Quint. *Inst.* 1.7.35; 10.1.113 *at Messalla nitidus et candidus et quodam modo praeferens in dicendo nobilitatem suam*; Ov. *Pont.* 2.2.49 (to Messalla's son) *nitor ille domesticus.*

36 Cic. *Sen.* 46. Powell (1988) ad loc. compares Quint. *Inst.* 6.3.105; Plut. *Cat. Mai.* 21.3, 25.2.

37 Feeney (1986); Henderson (1997).

38 Plin. *Ep.* 3.12.3 (on Caesar and Cato) *describit enim eos quibus obuius fuerit, cum caput ebrii retexissent, erubuisse.* As Pliny has just imitated Horace's ode (3.12.1 *Socraticis tantum sermonibus abundet*), he seems to have associated our passage with the younger Cato.

39 Plut. *Cat. Min.* 6.1 προϊόντι δὲ τῷ χρόνῳ μάλιστα προσίετο τὸ πίνειν ὥστε πολλάκις ἐν οἴνῳ διάγειν εἰς ὄρθρον (cf. 6.2, 44.1); Mart. 2.89.1–2 *quod nimio gaudes noctem producere uino,* | *ignosco: uitium, Gaure, Catonis habes.*

40 Cic. *Mur.* 60–6, *Sest.* 60; Plut. *Cat. Min.* 4.1, 10.1, 16.1, 54.5.

41 Plut. *Cat. Mai.* 23.1 λάλον; Astin (1978) 163.

42 Syme (1978) 119–21; (1986) 231–2.

43 Syme (1991) 198–201. L. Calpurnius Bibulus studied with Messalla at Athens in 45, fought with him at Philippi, and joined with him in negotiating the surrender (App. *B Civ.* 4.17.136). He is mentioned at *Sat.* 1.10.86 in conjunction with Messalla and other members of the family (above, p. 82).

44 Syme (1991) 201 corrects his earlier statement that this Calpurnia was the actual granddaughter of Cato.

45 Cichorius (1922) 233–7; Syme (1986) 385 n. 15.

46 Cichorius regarded Maecenas and Messalla as rival patrons of letters, but their circles were not mutually exclusive; cf. White (1993) 35–45.

47 Plut. *Quaest. conv.* 715e ἔνιοι γὰρ εὑρετικὴν φύσιν ἔχοντες ἐν δὲ τῷ νήφειν ἀτολμοτέραν καὶ πεπηγυῖαν, ὅταν εἰς τὸ πίνειν ἔλθωσιν ὥσπερ ὁ λιβανωτὸς ὑπὸ θερμότητος ἀναθυμιῶνται.

48 Quint. *Inst.* 4.1.8 *quaedam in his quoque commendatio tacita si nos infirmos imparatos impares agentium contra ingeniis dixerimus qualia sunt pleraque Messallae prooemia*; Tac. *Dial.* 20.1 *quis nunc feret oratorem de infirmitate ualetudinis suae praefantem qualia sunt fere principia Coruini?* Here *ualetudinis* may be due to a misunderstanding of Quintilian's *infirmos*, which need not refer to health.

49 Wind (1958) 31–56, 103–6. But see also Oliensis in this volume, p. 95.

50 The raven from which Corvinus derived his name lived even longer than the crow; cf. Hes. fr. 304.3 M–W.

51 Hom. *Il.* 1.248–9 λιγὺς Πυλίων ἀγορητής, | τοῦ καὶ ἀπὸ γλώσσης μέλιτος γλυκίων ῥέεν αὐδή.

52 Rostagni (1960) 2.809–33 = (1961) 405–27.

53 Lyne (1978) 39–45.

54 Presumably Messalla attached himself to Phoebus because of his association with augury as well as poetry; see n. 21 above, Tib. 2.5.11–12 (addressing the

god) *tu procul euentura uides, tibi deditus augur | scit bene quid fati prouida cantet auis* (the poem on Messalla's son).

55 *Paroemiogr.* 2.148 ἀρχαιότερος Κόδρου ἐπὶ ὑπερβολῇ ἀρχαιότητος καὶ εὐγενείας. So Eust. *Od.* 1.58 ἐποίησε Κόδρους καλεῖσθαι τοὺς δι᾽ ἀρχαιότητα εὐήθεις.

56 Hor. *Carm.* 3.19.2 *Codrus pro patria non timidus mori* (two poems earlier than Messalla's ode); Pease (1958) on Cic. *Nat. D.* 3.49.

57 See Livy 8.9.4 *in hac trepidatione Decius consul M. Valerium magna uoce inclamat*; this suggests that Valerius is already familiar to the reader (similarly at 8.3.5 the interrex described simply as 'M. Valerius' is surely Corvus). *MRR* 1.137 distinguishes the pontifex from Corvus (as apparently does *De uiris illustribus* 26.5); but in *MRR* 2.630 (index) Broughton records the possibility that they are identical.

58 The Pithoeanus reads *Cordi*, which is accepted by Housman and more recent editors; but there is point in the association of 'Codrus' with a poem about another king of Athens (cf. Reggiani (1976) 133–4).

59 For the identity of the recipient of the *Ars poetica* see Syme (1984) 1230–2; (1986) 379–81.

7 FEMININE ENDINGS, LYRIC SEDUCTIONS

I would like to thank Denis Feeney, John Shoptaw, Humphrey Tonkin, Tony Woodman, and especially Michael Putnam for their help with this essay. My text for Horace is that of Klingner (1959).

1 As remarked by Axelson (1945) 51, Horace prefers the ordinary term *capillus* in his hexameter poetry, the more elevated *coma* and *crinis* in the *Odes*.

2 This attribute of hair as of nails (body parts often paired in medical texts) was well recognised in antiquity; cf. Arist. *Gen. an.* 745a, *Hist. an.* 518b. The detachability of hair and nails makes them ideal candidates for magical manipulation, in which setting they function as synecdoches for the human whole. On the meanings of hair in antiquity see the wide-ranging and suggestive discussion of Levine (1995).

3 This *corona* also evokes the *coronis*, an Alexandrian punctuation marking the ends of poems and collections. It may be pressing the allegory too far to remark that the lyric 'flowers' of *Odes* 1 are, as per the poet's instructions, all gathered from Horace's own garden.

4 With some misgivings, I here retain the text of Klingner (1959). Though Brink (1971) 25–7 makes a strong case for reading *incomptam Lacaenae | more comam religata nodo*, the advocacy of dishevelment, even tempered by a *nodus*, strikes me as fundamentally un-Horatian.

5 On the false endings of *Carm.* 4.1 and 3.14, see Oliensis (1998) 119–20, 145–9. There are good overviews, from different perspectives, of Horatian closure in Schrijvers (1973) and Esser (1976), a useful survey of closure in Greek lyric in Rutherford (1997), and much of interest on closure as an interpretive category in the two articles by Fowler (1989a, 1997). Smith (1968) remains essential reading.

6 Reckford (1969) 96–7.

7 Cf. *Carm.* 2.13.35–6, where lyric song uncurls the snakes twisted into the Furies' hair (*intorti capillis | Eumenidum recreantur angues*); *Carm.* 2.19.19–20, where Bacchus 'bind[s] his Bacchants' hair in an innocuous viper knot' (*nodo coerces uiperino | Bistonidum sine fraude crinis*).

8 So, e.g., mourning women and Bacchants loosen their hair.

9 West (1967) 106 proposes translating *religas* as 'you unbind'. But this translation, while justified by the verb's inherent ambiguity, accords ill with the immediately following phrase *simplex munditiis* – a phrase which suits Pyrrha's coiffure better than its undoing.

10 For the association of hair and sea, cf. the *uiridis Nereidum comas* at *Carm.* 3.28.10.

11 'Unknotting' can also figure the closural consummation of death. Cf. Virgil's account of the death of Dido at the end of *Aen.* 4, a death that lingers until Iris cuts a lock of Dido's hair, thereby 'releas[ing]' her (*soluo*, 703) from her body.

12 On the erotic poetics of delay, see above all Owen (1989), esp. 24–31 (with a reading of Hor. *Carm.* 4.11); my essay as a whole is much indebted to Owen's meditations on the lyric mode.

13 For an account of the temporal dynamics of this ode, see Ancona (1994) 31–6.

14 I have borrowed this last phrasing ('soon Lalage...') from the translation of Macleod (1979b) 95.

15 I have skirted the much-discussed problem of this ode's addressee (whom I take, following Macleod (1979b) 96, to be Horace); see further Fantham (1979); Jocelyn (1980); Jones (1983).

16 Cf. Jones (1983) 34; Commager (1962) 253.

17 If we follow Brink (1971) 22–3 and exchange *ferox* for *fugax* (which appears in the identical position in the next stanza, attached to *Pholoe*), we get a simpler but also less interesting poem. For a similarly enriching (mis)distribution of adjectives, cf. the lurking arbutes and green snakes of *Carm.* 1.17.5–8, with the comments of Putnam (1994) 360–1.

18 Cf. Jocelyn (1980) 199.

19 With line 16, Horace completes not only an argument but a tricolon (marked by the reiteration of *iam* at 10, 13, and 15), a sentence, and a stanza.

20 *discrimen* is a noun and the subject of its clause; I have sacrificed syntactical accuracy here in order to preserve Horace's word order.

21 See N–H (1970) ad loc.

22 For this meaning of *discrimen*, see *OLD* s.v. 1b; the word play is remarked by N–H (1978) ad loc.

23 See Levine (1995) 100 with n. 47.

24 Cf. the loose end of *Carm.* 1.17 (with *crinibus* identically placed).

25 See Esser (1976) 76.

26 *socii nostri cum belligerare nobiscum uellent, profecto ratiocinati essent etiam atque etiam quid possent facere, si quidem sua sponte facerent et non haberent hinc adiutores multos, malos homines et audaces* (*Auct. ad Her.* 4.16) .

27 Cf. Velleius Paterculus, who describes Maecenas as *otio ac mollitiis paene ultra feminam fluens* (2.88.2). As Michael Putnam has remarked to me, Maecenas'

attachment to the soft style may have helped to motivate Horace's loose endings; we may be witnessing the effects of a kind of group aesthetic.

28 For Roman attacks on 'effeminate' style, see Freudenburg (1990) 198–9 (citing, e.g., Tac. *Dial.* 18, Quint. *Inst.* 12.10.12); on the rich postclassical tradition of the 'virile style', see Parker (1996). On the circularity of the period, see the references and discussion in Wilkinson (1963) 173–4. Aristotle's description of periodic style – 'speech which contains its own beginning and ending and which is no longer than what can be readily taken in' (λέξιν ἔχουσαν ἀρχὴν καὶ τελευτὴν αὐτὴν καθ' αὐτὴν καὶ μέγεθος εὐσύνοπτον, *Rh.* 1409a) – precisely matches his description of the well-ordered tragic plot (*Poet.* 1450b–1451a); one set of principles regulates both small-scale and large-scale compositions. The anticlosural tendency of the 'lax' style is clearly set forth in Aristotle's critique (morally neutral by contrast with the treatise *Ad Herennium* and Seneca's epistle) of λέξις εἰρομένη, 'strung-together' or 'continuous' style, as 'lack[ing] a *telos* within itself' (οὐδὲν ἔχει τέλος καθ' αὐτήν) and 'displeasing because of its unboundedness' (ἀηδὲς διὰ τὸ ἄπειρον, *Rh.* 1409a).

29 See, e.g., Fraenkel (1957) 239 (on the 'gentle finale' of *Carm.* 2.1); Commager (1962) 117 (on Horace's predilection for the 'dying close').

30 Cf. Sappho fr. 1, where Aphrodite voices the perspective I am calling comic (the perspective that recognises that desire is multiple and serial), while Sappho speaks out of the 'tragic' present.

31 Horace thus produces, as if by accident, a tricolon crescendo (*non . . . nec . . . sed*), though the closural effect is muted by the balanced alternatives of the final dicolon (*aut . . . aut*). The anticlosural tendency of the dicolon is suggested by the fact that, when Cicero mangles his own sentences to demonstrate the importance of word order, the mangled versions all end with pairs (*Orat.* 232): *mercatores venaliciique, e Syrio Aegyptoque, ab aliquo Syro aut Deliaco*.

32 At line 8 Klingner prints Peerlkamp's conjecture *illa* where most other editors retain the transmitted *illi* (i.e., 'whether the greater prize fall to you or to her'). Though I retain Klingner's text here, the textual question does not affect my argument.

33 It may be relevant that a *tergum Gaetuli immane leonis* is a prize at Virg. *Aen.* 5.351 and that a victorious athlete is compared to Ganymede at the end of Pind. *Ol.* 10 (99–105); inverted allusions to games, with contestants and prize exchanging places, would then frame the struggle over Nearchus, as the poem moves dialectically away from the very model of competition.

34 Cf. Commager (1962) 144.

35 For the unwarlike Paris, see *Il.* 3.30–7; Hor. *Carm.* 1.15. The angry lion is also Iliadic; see *Il.* 18.318–22, where Achilles is compared to a lion enraged at the loss of its cubs (plural, as in Horace's imitation here). This Pyrrhus is a minor and derivative son of Achilles.

36 Cf. the confluence of 'effeminate' form and content in Catull. 11, which likewise closes with the vehicle of a simile, likening Catullus' dead love for Lesbia to a 'flower at the field's edge touched by a passing plough' (*uelut prati | ultimi flos, praetereunte postquam | tactus aratro est*, 22–4). A more unexpected

resemblance links the end of *Carm.* 3.20 to that of the sombre 3.5; compare *posuisse...fertur* (3.20.11–13), *fertur...remouisse* (3.5.41, 43), in each case followed by a simile, with the tenor preceding the vehicle. Although the syntax of the Regulus ode is tighter (*non aliter* [50] requires *quam* [53] to complete its sense), the ode does finally elude the syntactical bond: *tendens Venafranos in agros | aut Lacedaemonium Tarentum* (where the participle, a free addition to an already completed sense, offers alternatives joined, like the alternative paradigms which close the ode on Nearchus, by *aut*). Like the *arbiter* Nearchus, Regulus functions as a mediator, standing between the Senate and the disgraced Roman soldiers to resolve the oppositions which govern the beginning of the poem.

37 Putnam (1995a) 127–30.

38 See below, n. 43, for a similar recuperation in *Carm.* 1.6.

39 As often, Horace plays the tangent off the circle.

40 The sexism is actually something of a side effect; the term is of course grammatical in origin.

41 I do not mean to propose effeminacy as the universal content or effect of Horace's errant closural syntax, of course. See, e.g., *Carm.* 3.5 (discussed above, n. 36), where the levity of the centrifugal close is an index not of weakness but of the moral strength of Regulus, who can take his impending death thus lightly (though one might argue that this close functions simultaneously as consolation for the weak-willed, escapist poet, who cannot keep his gaze firmly fixed on Regulus' horrible end).

42 In *Epist.* 2.2, the first thing the seller draws attention to is the slave's good looks (*et | candidus et talos a uertice pulcher ad imos*, 3–4). For the poet/poem as erotic object, cf. *Epist.* 1.7.25–8 and *Epod.* 14 (poems I have discussed elsewhere: see Oliensis (1998) 89–90, 180–1).

43 The two attributes are scornfully conjoined by Nereus in *Carm.* 1.15.13–15: *nequiquam Veneris praesidio ferox | pectes caesariem grataque feminis | inbelli cithara carmina diuides.* Only a few poems earlier, in 1.6, Horace was himself declining to engage in battle (poetry) and describing his Muse as *inbellis...lyrae potens.* In light of the allusion at 1.6.15–16 to Diomedes' Iliadic *aristeia* (in the course of which Diomedes, with Athena's help, wounds both Ares and Aphrodite), the final stanza, with its celebration of erotic battles, reads as a polemical appropriation, in the interests of a lyric manifesto, of Athena's mockery of the wounded Aphrodite (Hom. *Il.* 5.421–5). It is this rehabilitation of the Venusian model of which *Carm.* 1.15 offers its critical (epic) (p)review. For illuminating readings of the relation of *Carm.* 1.6 to 1.15, see Davis (1991) 27; Lowrie (1997) 133–4.

44 Cf. *Carm.* 3.25, where *deuius* conveys Horace's Callimachean distaste for the much-trodden path.

45 On the force of *amanda*, cf. Putnam (1986) 197.

46 On abundant hair as a sign of virility, see Levine (1995).

47 These flourishing closes are to be contrasted with the last of the *Epodes*, where the poet's hair is represented as prematurely blighted by Canidia's poisons (*tuis capillus albus est odoribus*, 17.23).

8 THE UNIQUENESS OF THE *CARMEN SAECVLARE* AND
ITS TRADITION

1 The reference work for historical and epigraphic evidence is still Pighi
(1965).

2 Augustus lists India, Scythae, Albani and Medi, and the Horatian text at
53–6 has the same names in reverse order: *Ad me ex In[dia regum legationes
saepe missae sunt non uisae ante id tempus] apud qu[em]q[uam] R[omanorum
du]cem. Nostram am[icitiam appetiuerunt] per legato[s] B[a]starn[ae Scythae]que
et Sarmatarum, q[ui sunt citra flu]men Tanaim [et]ultra, reg[es, Alba]norumque
rex et Hiber[orum et Medorum]*. Interestingly, the Eastern Albani are sometimes identified as stray descendants of the Italian Albani, via the wanderings
of Heracles' band across the Mediterranean (cf. Just. *Epit.* 42.3.4: I owe the
reference to Matthew Leigh); Medi and Albani are mentioned together again
in Vell. 2.40.1.

3 Cf. Virg. *Ecl.* 1.44, where a similar ambivalence, related to a different speaking
persona, has been analysed by Du Quesnay (1981) 134.

4 Cf. White (1993) 125. Note also lines 70–2, where Diana is propitious to the
prayer of the *XVuiri* but friendly, and so slightly warmer, to the song of the
pueri.

5 I owe most of this point to Denis Feeney.

6 Anchises is not a model of victory and power, but he is regularly represented in
Roman epic as a sacrificer and keeper of religious traditions, and he is also the
one who voices the idea of *parcere/debellare* in the *Aeneid*. Putnam (2000) 164
n. 60 interestingly notes that the use of *sanguis* as a personal apposition and
of *prior* in adjacent lines could be reminiscent of a passage in Virgil, *Aen.* 6.
852–3, where Anchises is the speaker and the message is an attempt to stop
civil wars, with reference to the divine lineage of Julius Caesar. The prominent mention of Anchises in the strophe, so untypical of official language about
Augustus, has the interesting effect of displacing Julius Caesar, the expected
link between Augustus and the Olympic world in imperial propaganda, and
the *Diuus Caesar* and his comet had been showcased in the preparations of the
Ludi. So the entire quatrain could be described as a renegotiation of the civil
wars legacy. On the evolving role of the deceased Caesar in Augustan Rome
see White (1988).

7 For the effect of implied colour opposition, note Virg. *Aen.* 1.469–71 *Rhesi
niueis tentoria uelis . . . caede cruentus*.

8 As Feeney (1998) 33 has explained.

9 Pointed out by Putnam (2000) 60. For a historically based approach to 'para-
grams' in Augustan poetry see Armstrong (1995) 229–32 and Oberhelman–
Armstrong (1995) 239–41.

10 Cf. the text in Pighi (1965) 113–16.

11 Similarly, the Parcae at 25 are *ueraces cecinisse*, and guarantee the future of
Roman *cantus* (22), while the Moerae of the ritual proceedings show no connection with song,

12 In this sense, in extant Latin poetry, since Acc. *Praetext.* 27. For a similar
ambiguity in the old cliché *solis rota* see Lunelli (1975).

13 Just as, in the following lines, 'day' precedes 'night': Pascoli (1921) 293–4 notes that in chronological sequence 'games' and 'night' are expected to return before, respectively, 'song' and 'day'.

14 The poem wittily exploits a time-warp effect created by the official programme: the (re)invention of the 'old' prophecy is validated by the language of Roman dominance 'over the Latins'. The prayer by the emperor responds to the oracle: *uos quaeso precorque, uti imperium maiestatemque p.R. Quiritium duelli domique auxitis, utique semper Latinus obtemperassit* (Augustus to the Moerae: II4.92–4 Pighi), the oracle dictates the rules of engagement: 'never forget this oracle, and the entire land of Italy and the entire land of the Latins will carry the yoke of Roman rule forever' (the Sibyl: 57.37–8 Pighi), so that the song is the only verbal medium in the festival that shifts the language of past imperialism to distant eastern enemies in the present and future (51–6) and conversely includes *Latium* (66) in the prayer for prosperity. Since the prophecy needs an early Republican tone to be empowered as prophecy, and the ritual prayers depend on the prophecy, the song validates *ab euentu* the prophecy but receives in exchange the important allowance to refer to the world of 17 BCE and (para-prophetically) beyond.

15 Wilamowitz (1913) 316 (cf. 320 on *Carm.* 4.6) briefly commented that it is not surprising if a Roman song for choral performance turns to Pindar's processional anthems as a model (he was typically impatient about generic discussions, and presumably wanted to gesture towards the more interesting problem of modes of performance (processional or static?), a hot question for *Carmen* scholarship in his time, and suggest a link with the problematic distinction between prosodia and paeans in Pindaric performance). Pasquali (1964) 736 n. I (originally publ. 1920) was untypically vague in his reference to the Pindaric invocation of Apollo in an epinician passage, a curious choice since he had contributed an important analysis of the influence of *Pae.* 6 on Horace, *Carm.* 4.6 (Pasquali (1964) 752–5).

16 So respectively Barchiesi (2000) 179 (from a paper presented to a 1997 conference; the present chapter profits from a reading of Rutherford's edition in the galleys, and I thank the author for this anticipation); Hardie (1998) 260–1; Rutherford (2001) 33.

17 Point (i) is independently, though briefly, argued in a couple of papers of mine, Barchiesi (1996) and (2000); cf. Wilamowitz (1913) 320, and space forbids a discussion of (ii) here. My approach to the uniqueness of the *Carmen* and to the metaliterary – but not performative – function of 4.6 can now be usefully combined with the strong metrical points argued by Rossi (1998).

18 My information is mostly dependent on Bona (1988); Kaeppel (1992); Stehle (1997); Schroeder (1999); Rutherford (2001), and for reasons of space I cannot offer detailed discussions of specific problems and different approaches in this field. The references to the Pindaric fragments are based on Rutherford (2001).

19 Turner (1984) 118 points out that the papyrological record shows that Pindar's religious poetry was more widely read than the epinicia that we automatically identify with the quintessential Pindar. Even if this is taken to be slightly

exaggerated (for it seems likely that papyrologists have been less active in publishing scraps of previously known epinician poems than brand new fragments of lost genres), the survival in papyri is a significant testimony.

20 The three interpretations given in the text for *horiai* are very close to each other, and it makes no difference for my purposes which one is preferred, while, for reasons that I have no space to discuss here, I am reluctant to accept the translation 'are appropriate' given by Cannatà Fera (1980) and (1990) 136ff. For the importance of time in the Pindaric understanding of the genre see below, p. 123.

21 On the link between the *incipit* and Delian paeans cf. Kaeppel (1992) 147.

22 Cf. Rutherford (2001) 285.

23 Rutherford (2001) 277–8.

24 The enormous role of assonance, etymology and alliteration in the song can be seen as a sophisticated link with early Rome, as a response to the artistry of Pindaric and Simonidean models, and also as a counterbalance for the simplification of lexical choices.

25 Pointed out in Putnam (2000) 131.

26 Fraenkel (1957) 391 simply interprets the passage as a self-reference to the *Carmen* (cf. Ov. *Tr.* 2.25) but the link is well illustrated by Norden (1939) 249 n. 3.

27 Stehle (1997) focuses on gender difference in performance. On female choruses appropriating paeans as challenges to convention and self-conscious experiments in generic impurity see Rutherford (2001) 59; on Soph. *Trach.* 205–22 as a case in point see Rutherford (2001) 113–14, and Easterling (1982) 104. Hardie (1998) 274–7 does not convince me that the anomaly should be explained away by pointing to Greek models where a male chorus invites support from female performers, or imagines a vocal unison with a chorus of virgins.

28 White (1993) 303 n. 21, with Fraenkel (1957) 380 n. 3.

29 On Italy as a central problem in the *Aeneid* see e.g. Toll (1997); Suerbaum (1999) 192–7.

30 This strategy imparts poetic coherence to the hymn but also creates a spatial interplay with the rituals in the Campus: on the character of the Terentum ('valenza ctonia e catactonia insieme') see Coarelli (1997) 83; on the subterranean altar to Dis and Proserpina, 20 ft below the Campus, Coarelli (1997) 87.

31 Scheid (1995).

32 Pingiatoglou (1981); Bettini (1998) 97.

33 Fraenkel (1957) 379.

34 Mommsen (1912) 356.

35 My position here is particularly close to the discussion of Coarelli (1997) 102: the Augustan Games are neither a fake nor a sign of continuity with a traditional matrix; the 'normalizzazione' promoted by Augustus is always innovative and tied to contemporary agendas, yet precisely for this reason the process uses a maximum of traditional elements and creates a new context for them.

36 Feeney (1998) 36.

37 Powell (1925) 174 (note the address to Brutus at Hor. *Sat.* 1.7.24). An interesting assessment of Horace's position is Cameron (1995) 295.
38 On the sun and Augustus cf. e.g. Barton (1995); Hardie (1993) 126.
39 Mommsen (1912) 357–8.
40 Night is present in the poem only in the auspicious expression *grata nocte* at 23–4.
41 Coarelli (1997) 116; Beard–North–Price (1998) 1.71.
42 On the intertwining of personal voice and choral expression and the instability of the poet's position in the text of Pindar as an influence on Horace and a mirage for the Roman literary tradition see Barchiesi (2000).
43 See above, p. 115, on Pindar's generic self-definition.
44 This line of argument finds independent support in the metrical observations of Rossi (1998).
45 I am grateful to Mary Depew, Matthew Leigh, Nicholas Purcell for suggestions, to the editors for their revision, and to Michael Putnam and Ian Rutherford for sharing their unpublished texts with me.

9 SOLVS SAPIENS LIBER EST

1 For the metaphors, see Lundström (1976) 178–84, and Thomas (1998) 105–7.
2 Regularly a criminal, the gladiator is marked as an *infamis*. He is forced to exhibit his *infamia* every time he takes up arms in the arena. On the *infamia* of actors and performers in the *ludi*, see Edwards (1993) 123–6.
3 Traina (1991) 301.
4 Cima in Pascoli (1921) lxxx, and Gigon (1977) 477.
5 Traina (1991) 300–1.
6 For *flectere* as equine metaphor, and *durum* meaning 'stiff with age', see Quinn (1980) 298–9. Hardie (1993) 128–9 suggests that the poet's return in *Carm.* 4.1.1–7 has a close parallel in Ennius' return to the writing of panegyric epic at the beginning of *Annales* 16, where he seems to compare himself to a superannuated racehorse. He goes on to note (p. 138, n. 38) that 'Horace may have had the lines in mind (as well as Ibycus 7.5ff.D) at the beginning of *E.* 1 when he justifies his refusal to write further lyric by comparing himself to an ageing horse.'
7 Though he cannot help dreaming of Ligurinus at the end of *Carm.* 4.1 . Thus he signals the divided nature of the book, which features frequent 'drifts' into erotic song.
8 The book is commonly dated to late 20 or early 19 BC. See Mayer (1994) 10–11.
9 Williams (1995) argues that Horace's father was, in all likelihood, not the freed-slave his poems regularly claim he was.
10 *Epist.* 1.13, on which see below pp. 138–9.
11 For *uates* designating 'the poet in his inspired aspect', see N–H (1970) on *Carm.* 1.1.35. Garn (1954) 33 detects a 'leichte Ironie' in the deliberate balancing of a term so formal against the familiar *amicus*.
12 The lyric poet of 1.1 and the guest of 1.7 both object to having had 'enough', with *spectatum satis* of 1.1.2 matching *iam satis est* in 1.7.16.

13 Garn (1954) 37 finds in lines 26–8 at least three clear references to the erotic odes of *Carm.* Book 1, though the most obvious and telling allusion is certainly to *Carm.* 3.2.13: *dulce et decorum est pro patria mori.* Inside the plea for 'sweet talk' and 'an attractive laugh' (*dulce . . . decorum . . . et*) resonate the remembered sounds of Horace at his most vatic and morally responsible. As if to say, 'that's what I want back, Maecenas; the chance to use my lyric voice – now so famously pegged as engaged and *pro patria* – irresponsibly!' i.e. for seducing rather than preaching.

14 *inspice, si possum donata reponere laetus.*

15 For *spatiis* as 'ground for racing' see Mayer (1994) on 1.7.42.

16 E.g. *Epist.* 2.1.257–8 *sed neque paruum | carmen maiestas recipit tua*; *Carm.* 3.3.72 *magna modis tenuare paruis*; *Carm.* 4.2.31–2 *operosa paruus | carmina fingo.* Fraenkel (1957) 335–6 makes a strong case for the literary colouring of this refusal only to conclude: 'In those cases it is the writing of lofty poetry to which Horace's *paruitas* is alleged to be an insurmountable hindrance; in the case of the letter to Maecenas it is life on a grand scale.' I believe the two go hand-in-hand here, as they so often do in a Roman setting where big martial projects (esp. *res gestae*) commonly reap hefty rewards. For the aphorism recalling Callimachus, *Aetia* 2, see Mayer (1994) on *Epist.* 1.7.44. Moles (in the current volume) rightly adds a Panaetian background.

17 The designation *regia Roma* is telling. It implies that Rome is the poet's land of opportunity. A land of Pindaric *reges* ('kings' = 'patrons') to be praised in song, 'used' (cf. *regibus uti*, 1.17.13–14, discussed below) and profited from. This sense was activated just seven lines earlier with *rexque paterque | audisti coram* (37–8).

18 Garn (1954) 38: 'Dieser ganze Abschnitt (v. 34–45) . . . ist reich an Anklängen an die Oden.' The majority of the references Garn cites are to the moral/exhortatory poems of Book 3, with the last Pindaric stanza of *Carm.* 3.1 showing the strongest impact.

19 For the pros and cons of assuming an actual 'rift' between Maecenas and Horace, see Kissel (1994).

20 Fraenkel (1957) 328 points to an unsettling mismatch early in the poem, between lines 8–9 and their recalled counterpart at *Sat.* 2.1.18–19: 'I do not know whether the similarity is intentional, but it is conceivable that Horace meant to remind his friend of that other *sermo* in which, many years ago, he had described what Maecenas' friendship meant to him.'

21 For details of the cure, see Ps.-Acron's notes on *Epist.* 1.15.3.

22 To prove there were no hard feelings on Augustus' part for being turned down, Suetonius cites a subsequent letter wherein Augustus invites the poet to enjoy the privileges of his house *tamquam si conuictor mihi fueris. recte enim et non temere feceris, quoniam id usus mihi tecum esse uolui, si per ualitudinem tuam fieri possit.*

23 Quint. *Inst.* 10.1.109 (*Cicero*) *non enim pluuias, ut ait Pindarus, aquas colligit, sed uiuo gurgite exundat, dono quodam prouidentiae genitus.*

24 For the poet as fountain of song, see Pind. *Pyth.* 4.299.

25 Hubbard (1995) makes an excellent case for the Pindaric shaping of much of the book's water imagery. Her analysis of *Epist.* 1.3.25–7 connecting *frigida*

curarum fomenta to θερμὸν ὕδωρ of *Nem.* 4.4 leads me to suspect that Pindaric memories are cued in the notions of Musa as healer, and the rival water-regimes considered in the first lines of *Epist.* 1.15.

26 *uerba ministret* puts the wine in the wine-steward's role.

27 For example, the conclusion of *Epist.* 1.17 offers what looks to be a lesson taught from the poet's fictional misadventures in *Sat.* 1.5.

28 Much is gained by connecting *male sanos* of line 3 to *Epist.* 1.1.101–2, where the poet chides Maecenas for being too enamoured of the dishevelled, madly inspired poet: 'you assume that I am solemnly raging (*insanire...sollemnia*), and you neither laugh at me nor think I am in need of a doctor.'

29 The *triumphator*, while at the head of his troops, typically drove the conquered, and all the spoils of battle, ahead of him. See Scullard (1981) 95–6.

30 Porphyrion explains *temperat Alcaeus* in line 29 with: <u>*miscemus, inquit, et Alcaei*</u> *metrum, sed neque eodem ordine utimur uersuum.* For the vexed history of the interpretation of lines 28–9, see Fraenkel (1957) 341–6. I have sided with Fraenkel against Lejay, Mayer and others by taking the genitive *Archilochi* with *musam* rather than *pede.* My reasoning, leaving aside obvious grammatical advantages, is twofold: (1) Horace can (as the Scholiasts suggest) be thought to have 'tempered' the verse of his models not by altering their schemes within individual poems, but by *blending* them in various ways over the course of his three books, most obviously in the Parade Odes which feature, among other metrical schemes, Archilocheans, Alcaics, and Sapphics, the very models Horace mentions here; and (2) Horace innovates with his *pede* in line 22, by putting it where no one else has set foot before. So Sappho, likewise, must be thought to innovate with *her pede* in line 29.

31 Lucretian allusions here also include Lucr. 1.117–19, 927–8; 5.9, 55.

32 Clearly behind both the Lucretian and Horatian passages stands Apollo's warning to Callimachus at *Aetia* 1.23–30, especially lines 26–7 'don't drive your chariot *in the common tracks of others*' (ἑτέρων δ' ἴχνια μὴ καθ' ὁμὰ δίφρον ἐλᾶν), itself a remake of Pind. *Pyth.* 4.247 and *Pae.* 7b.11–14. For a brief intertextual history of the metaphor, see Thomas (1998) 108–10.

33 Cf. *Carm.* 3.25 where Dionysian inspiration puts the poet off in a grove, or a cave, then on a Thracian hillside, wreathed in grape-vines, following the god.

34 The second of these options has a clear counterpart in the water-inspired *sacerdos* of Propertius 3.1.3–4, lines that deliberately recall and recast the triumphal vaunt of *Carm.* 3.30: *primus ego ingredior puro de fonte sacerdos | Itala per Graios* <u>*orgia ferre*</u> *choros.*

35 The freedom to be groped, buggered, and tossed aside. Ironically, this *liber* ('book'), because set free, is not truly *liber* ('a free man'), but a mere *libertus* ('a freedman'). Hinds (1985) 13–14 demonstrates that the same *liber/liber* pun is at the heart of Ovid's studied imitation of *Epist.* 1.20 in *Tristia* 1.1.

36 Elsewhere in less obvious ways, but especially here in treating the theme of the poet's pipe-dream of freedom, I am deeply indebted to the complex and remarkable study of W. R. Johnson (1993).

37 Lowrie (1997) 324 remarks on the clear connection established in *Odes* Book 3 between Bacchic inspiration and the poet's *panegyrical* high: 'The poems

taken together create a story that we as readers must put together. *C.* 3.25 gives the story's conclusion after the fact: Bacchus, the god of wine and the symposium, enables Horace to cross his own boundaries, and to praise Caesar.'

38 The interlocutor mocks the poet's Dionysiac pretensions with the 'honey-oozing' remark in line 44.

39 For the load's several designations as epistolary terms, see Clarke (1972) 158. For *reddere* as epistolary term, see *OLD* s.v. *reddo* 12, Cic. *Att.* 1.15.2 and 11.22.1 <u>*fasciculum reddidit*</u> *Balbi tabellarius.*

40 Mayer (1994) 205 suggests that the letter tactfully handles the problem of addressing Augustus directly. I prefer to see it as emphasising and performing the problem. Clearly Augustus was struck by the letter's failure to address him directly as a friend, and he let Horace know, in a subsequent letter, that he was not pleased. Thus, in opening his separate (by request) *Epistle to Augustus*, Horace reminds us of that earlier indirect attempt, with <u>*morer tua tempora*</u>, <u>*Caesar*</u> (line 4) recalling *Epist.* 1.13.17–18 *carmina quae possint oculos auresque* <u>*morari*</u> | <u>*Caesaris*</u>.

41 The parting lyric / ludic comparison rounds off the last letter to Maecenas with the figure that began the first.

10 POETRY, PHILOSOPHY, POLITICS AND PLAY

I thank: helpful seminarians at LILS (16/2/1996) and NECROS (23/11/1998); David West for oral sparrings; and Francis Cairns and the editors for criticism of written versions.

1 K–H (1970) 370; Courbaud (1914) 36; Fraenkel (1957) 308; Macleod (1979a); Kilpatrick (1986); Ferri (1993); Williams (1968) 1–6; Mayer (1986), endorsed by Galinsky (1996) 253, 419; Mayer (1994), esp. 39–47; Rudd (1993b).

2 Williams (1968) 14, 19–22; Mayer (1994) 143, 174, 205; Seager (1993) 34–5; Lyne (1995) 144–57; Oliensis (1998) 154–65, 168–81.

3 Inchoate earlier treatments on which I draw: Moles (1986); (1995).

4 Freudenburg (1993) 29 reverses the argument, as do those who see 16–17 and 18–19 as glossing Horace's Stoic and Epicurean odes.

5 Mayer (1994) 90.

6 Mayer (1994) 92 and cf. (e.g.) the sparkling exploration of this complex of ideas in Sen. *Ep.* 33.

7 Not discussed by the sceptical Rudd (1993b) 67–71.

8 Excepting the interpretation of 5 (confirmed by 16.15 *latebrae dulces*: p. 153 below), this material is garnered from Préaux (1968), K–H (1970) and Mayer (1994).

9 Denied by Rudd (1993b) 67.

10 E.g. the influence of the philosophical letter (Dilke (1981) 1844, 1846) and other philosophical modes (Harrison (1995b) 48–57); Lucretian influence (Ferri (1993)); the *Epistles'* status as *sermones*, with debatable links to *Bionei sermones* (*satura*) and 'diatribe': cf. variously Horsfall (1979); Rudd (1979); Brink (1982a) 254, 299–300; Braund (1992) 25, 31 n. 61; Muecke (1993) 2–4.

11 Culled from Williams (1968) 1–7; Mayer (1986); (1994) 39–47; Rudd (1993b) 64–5, 67, 77, 82–3.
12 Williams (1968) 1–30 vs Fraenkel (1957) 308–63; De Pretis (1998) (sophisticated reformulation).
13 Kilpatrick (1986) 2–6; Braund (1992) 25; Freudenburg (1993) 28–9; Johnson (1993) 4–5, 114–15; Lyne (1995) 186–7; n. 10 above.
14 Nisbet (1959); McGann (1963); Allen (1970); Harrison (1992); Jones (1993); Johnson (1993) 11 n. 4 and 11–17; Lyne (1995) 146–7.
15 So I believe: Suet. *Vita Hor.*, Loeb ed. 2.486.
16 Moles (1995) 168.
17 Putnam (1995b).
18 Thus e.g. McGann (1969) 35; Macleod (1977) 360 and (1979a) 16; Harrison (1995b) 49–50; Moles (1995) 162.
19 Cf. Maltby (1991) 406 for *nauus*' association with ships.
20 *Pace* Mayer (1994) 124; cf. also 1.37 ~ 2.1–2 (p. 147); 18.96ff. (p. 156).
21 Macleod (1977) 360, 363ff.
22 Macleod (1979a) 21; Mayer (1986) 72; Johnson (1993) 88–9.
23 McGann (1969) 10–12, 22–3.
24 Maltby (1991) 506.
25 Kindstrand (1976) 47–8, 192.
26 E.g. Pl. *Leg.* 2.656c; Dio Chrys. 4.30; Chris Rowe cites also Heraclitus fr. 52 αἰὼν παῖς ἐστι παίζων, πεσσεύων· παιδὸς ἡ βασιληίη ('Time is a child playing a game of draughts; the kingship is in the hands of a child').
27 Kindstrand (1976) 47–8.
28 Cf. *OLD* s.v. *ludo* 6b.
29 I suspect that, especially after the anagrammatic play with 'Maecenas' (1–3), 7 *purgatam ... personet aurem* also recalls *Flaccus* (as also 4.15–16 *me pinguem et nitidum bene curata cute uises|cum ridere uoles Epicuri de grege porcum* (Moles (1995) 167)), cf. *Epod.* 15.12; *Sat.* 1.9.20; 2.1.19), Horace's improved aural status not so much *glossing* his existing cognomen as 'renaming' him Q. Horatius Socrates. The humour of 4.16 will be enhanced by Horace's relapse into his customary 'flaccidity'.
30 E.g. Lucian, *Demon.* 5.
31 Cic. *Off.* 1.148; 3.116.
32 Moles (1995) 163.
33 Traina (1991); Rudd (1993b) 82–3; Mayer (1994) 44.
34 Where *pituita* presumably includes an allusion to Horace's *lippitudo* (~ 29; cf. *Sat.* 1.5.30–1), i.e., dramatically speaking, Horace himself is still (unsuccessfully) aspiring to orthodox Stoicism (~ 16–17).
35 1.16: p. 155 below; Horace's ultimate Epicureanism: p. 157 below.
36 Heinze (1889); Fiske (1920); Muecke (1993) 2–8.
37 Johnson (1993) 42; 1.68–9 also ~ 16.73–9 and 1.17 ~ 16.67 (p. 153).
38 McGann (1969) 10–12 (quotation from 10); Moles (1986) 37–8.
39 Maurach (1968); McGann (1969) 33–87; Johnson (1993) 66–71.
40 Detail in Moles (1986) 36–9, cf. (1995) 164, also Eidinow (1990) 566.
41 As he probably was: Cairns (1995) 124.
42 Moles (1995) 164–6.

43 Moles (1995) 167; for Jones (1993) 8, Albius is 'not looking at things philosophically': rather, his philosophy is criticised.
44 For the Epicureanism see McGann (1969) 44–6; Moles (1995) 167; Eidinow (1995).
45 Lyne (1995) 72–3, 139, 155.
46 Similarly: McGann (1969) 34–7; Johnson (1993) 9, 55–6; Lyne (1995) 144–50.
47 Ahl (1984).
48 Fowler (1989b) 129ff.
49 Broadly 'anti-Maecenas' readings of 7: Johnson (1993) 9, 43–4; Seager (1993) 34; Lyne (1995) 150–5; Oliensis (1998) 157–65; above, pp. 128–31.
50 Macleod (1979a) 27; Ferri (1993) 112–13.
51 Note also Oliensis' gloss ((1998) 182) on Augustus' failure to secure Horace's secretarial help: 'Horace chose to write letters on his own account [i.e. the *Epistles*] and not on the emperor's.'
52 I intend fuller treatment elsewhere.
53 Cf. e.g. *Carm.* 2.7.28 (Moles (1987) 70); 3.2.13 (Pinsent (1976)).
54 Support from 33–5 ∼ 18.111–12 (of Jupiter).
55 Thus Mayer (1994) 229.
56 1.1.22–4; 29.5–8.
57 Hardie (1990); Hubbard (1995).
58 E.g. Cic. *Rep.* 2.51.1; Ov. *Tr.* 2.39.
59 Millar (1973).
60 McGann (1969) 74; Lyne (1995) 147.
61 Armstrong (1989) 129–31 (important).
62 'Stoic': Moles (1987) 64–5; 'last words': Plut. *Brut.* 51.1 with Moles (1983) 773.
63 E.g. Du Quesnay (1995).
64 Epistles 17 and 18: Moles (1986) 43–6 (rather misrepresented by Rudd (1993b) 69 and 86 n. 20).
65 Bowditch (1994).
66 McGann (1969) 80; Jones (1993) 10.
67 Moles (1995) 170 (controverting Mayer (1994) 254), adapted.
68 Johnson (1993) 69.
69 Suet. *Vita Hor.* Loeb ed. 2.486–8.

II HORACE, CICERO AND AUGUSTUS

My thanks to Alessandro Barchiesi, Seth Benardete, Denis Feeney, Nicholas Horsfall, Mary Jaeger, Phillip Mitsis, and Tony Woodman for their generous criticism.
1 Both claim to have saved citizens, Augustus as a *priuatus*, with language very much like Cicero's, see Galinsky (1996) 49–51. Augustus admittedly only won the title *pater patriae* in 2 BCE after Horace's death, but Horace anticipates the designation with *pater* (*Carm.* 3.24.27) hinting toward Augustus. Pseudo-Sallust pricks Cicero's bubble by addressing him as *Romule Arpinas* in the invective against Cicero (7). Weinstock (1971) records numerous instances

where Ciceronian innovations for himself or others eventually resulted in formal honours for Augustus (*corona ciuica*, 163–6; founder imagery, 178–80, 189–93; *parens patriae*, 201–5; claims to virtues and *clupeus uirtutis*, 228–30; emphasis on *concordia* and *Concordia Augusta*, 261–6; on *pax* and *Ara pacis*, 269); also Wallace-Hadrill (1990) 149, 160ff.

Shared genres between Augustus and Cicero include protreptic (Augustus' *hortatio ad philosophiam*, Cicero's *Hortensius*), didactic poetry (Augustus on Sicily, Cicero's *Aratea* and perhaps the *Nilus*), light verse (Augustus' epigrams composed in the bath, Cicero's epigrams, *Pontius Glaucus*, *Uxorius*, *Alcyones*), accounts of accomplishments (*Res gestae diui Augusti* and thirteen books of memoirs up to the Cantabrian war, Cicero's various accounts of his consulship and exile in prose and verse): see Suetonius, *Aug.* 85.2 and Soubiran (1972) intro. In addition, Augustus started a tragedy, *Ajax*, but, in accord with Horace's views on the eraser, remarked to friends who inquired, *Aiacem suum in spongiam incubuisse*. Despite Cicero's incessant self-promotion (Plutarch, *Cic.* 24), his autobiography had to wait until Suringar's (1854) ingenious cento: *M. Tulli Ciceronis commentarii rerum suarum sive de vita sua*.

2 For a history of Cicero's line, see Allen (1956), Malcovati (1943) 261. Conte–Barchiesi (1989) 101–3 and Barchiesi (1993) 155–8 prove the allusion's rhetorical point in context. See also Wills (1996) 32.

3 Cicero poetic fragments from Courtney (1993) unless otherwise stated.

4 Given the problems of dating the original draft of the *Res gestae* (Brunt and Moore (1967) 6, Ramage (1987) 13, Nicolet (1991) 19, 27 n. 12, 42 n. 51), we cannot tell whether, when, or what Horace knew of it; on resemblances to Horace, see Santirocco (1995) 231.

5 Santirocco (1995): Horace manipulates Augustus as a figure who serves now as analogue for the poet, now for his audience, now as subject of poetry. The intervention of Cicero multiplies these relations.

6 Griffin (1993) 5: 'Horace never names Cicero; whether because he was betrayed by Octavian and proscribed by the Triumvirs, or because he was *vieux jeu*, part of the last generation and its tastes, Horace leaves it for us to decide.' See also Griffin (1985) 201.

7 Allen (1956) 143 would have greater confidence in Horace's allusion if he 'imitated Cicero frequently and conspicuously'. May (1990) adds *Epist.* 2.1.34–9 and Cic. *Brut.* 285–9, but suggests both may derive from 'rhetorical models' (180). Compare *Tusc.* 1.5 to *Ars P.* 325ff. Cicero clearly matters as Horace's predecessor *qua* literary historian: Grant–Fiske (1924) and (1929); Hinds (1998) 63–74; Feeney in this volume; though Brink (1971) 132, 338, 373 is sceptical. Barchiesi (1962), who fully understands the historical and rhetorical reasons underlying their antithetical tastes (41–3), asserts: 'tra Cicerone e Orazio esiste una fondamentale identità di vedute sulla natura dell'arte e sulla funzione dell'artista' (40).

8 E.g. Grant–Fiske (1929) and (1924), Wili (1948) passim, Treggiari (1973), Mayer (1985) and (1986), Oliensis (1998) chapter 5.

9 Fraenkel (1957) 391, 393. Similar are the parallels of K–H (1970) at *Epist.* 2.1.5–22 to *Nat. D.*

10 On allusion's passion, see Conte–Barchiesi (1989) 81.

11 Pasquali (1950) posits Ennius as the shared reference of Horace, *Epist.* 2.1.256 and Cicero fr. 8. Hendry (1993) 143–6 derives *fatale monstrum* (*Carm.* 1.37.21) from a lost work of early Roman drama via *Div.* 1.98.

12 We, like the ancients, characterise people by their strengths: *Ciceronem eloquentia sua in carminibus destituit*, Seneca, *Contr.* 3, preface 8; *carmina quod scribis Musis et Apolline nullo | laudari debes: hoc Ciceronis habes*, Martial 2.89. It was, however, common for political figures to write literary works in Cicero's day and the paradox is a modern preconception, see Townend (1965) 109. Silk (1952) 147 repeats Zielinski's 1912 call for a thorough study of the influence of Cicero's philosophical essays on Horace as a direct literary relationship. See also Hubbard (1975) 57.

13 Barchiesi (1993) 150–1 categorically rejects a separation between politics and aesthetics, literary and social function – but Horace imposes this separation on us, along with the obligation to resist it.

14 Some of the parallels traced below between the *Pro Archia* and *Epist.* 2.1 are in Brink (1982a) and Murley (1925).

15 Augustus erected statues of exemplary predecessors in the exedrae of the Forum Augusti as models to which he himself was to be held (Suet. *Aug.* 31.5). Cicero elsewhere sets himself up as an example both literary and political (implied at *De or.* 1.79, 1.95; explicitly at *Leg.* 3.14, *Rep.* 1.5–6; he even excerpts himself – the poem on his consulship – at *Div.* 1.11).

16 Klingner (1950) 21–2 compares *Serm.* 2.1: Trebatius means slander by *mala carmina* (82), while Horace turns the issue toward aesthetics with *bona* (83).

17 For *pinguis* as 'stupid' as opposed to Callimachean, see *Catalepton* 9.61–4.

18 Literature surpasses statuary as a mirror of the soul: correspondences are *expressi / expressam*, *signa / statuas et imagines*, *animi / animorum*, *uirorum clarorum / summi homines* (*Epist.* 2.1.248–50, *Arch.* 30). This *topos* extends earlier: see Fraenkel (1957) 396, whose parallels lack the verbal similarities here. Archias was encored (*reuocatum*, *Arch.* 18); Horace warns against unsolicited encores (*loca iam recitata reuoluimus irreuocati*, *Epist.* 2.1.223). Horace imitates Cicero's phraseology: *carus fuit Africano superiori noster Ennius, Arch.* 22; *gratus Alexandro regi magno fuit ille | Choerilus, Epist.* 2.1.232–3.

19 Brink (1982a) ad loc.

20 For Tiberius, see Rudd (1989) 12–13; for Lucullus, Cicero says *innumerabilis Armeniorum copias fudit* (*Arch.* 21).

21 Brink (1982a) on lines 26 and 30 suggests a lost section of Sallust's *Histories*.

22 Galinsky (1996) 73–4 denies Cicero as a 'role model' for Augustus (with bibliography), then demonstrates that Augustus basically executed everything Cicero desired for the state, and shows extensive parallels with Cicero's political writings.

23 Thyillos is mentioned along with Archias at *Att.* 1.16.15, Posidonius at *Att.* 2.1.2. For full references to texts discussing the composition (or not) of works on Cicero's consulship, see Harrer (1928); Spaeth (1930/31).

24 Nicolet (1991) 114.

25 Brink (1982a) ad loc.

26 *neque enim Alexander ille gratiae causa ab Apelle potissimum pingi et a Lysippo fingi uolebat, sed quod illorum artem cum ipsis tum etiam sibi gloriae fore putabat* (*Fam.* 5.12.7); *edicto uetuit, nequis se praeter Apellen | pingeret, aut alius Lysippo duceret aera | fortis Alexandri uultum simulantia* (*Epist.* 2.1.239–41).

27 Brink (1982a) 59: 'This argument is humorously overstated; it is perilously close to a smile, however respectful, in the direction of *numen Augusti*.' See Santirocco (1995) 241 for this transition's 'almost syllogistic force'.

28 One who manages, in large part, to avoid Libitina (*Carm.* 3.30.7) must, of course, have first written the praise.

29 Horace's point: *Naeuius in manibus non est et mentibus haeret | paene recens? adeo sanctum est uetus omne poema* (*Epist.* 2.1.53–4).

30 See Ramage (1987) 95 on honours given to Augustus *uiuo me* (*Res gestae*, 9.1).

31 *Carm.* 3.3.9–15 presents the same list. Romulus / Quirinus is included where Augustus is mentioned.

32 Cicero's formulations are relevant to Horace. Both start with the theatre as a medium of social importance and popular appeal, and use Roscius as an *exemplum* (*Arch.* 17; *Epist.* 2.1 *passim* and 82). Cicero's praise of Archias progresses from his skills at improvisation to his more polished work (*Arch.* 18), similarly to Horace, who praises polished poetry (*Epist.* 2.1.71–2) and sets written literature over spectacle at 214–15. Horace, however, would not concur with Cicero's praise of Archias as reaching the *ueterum scriptorum laudem* (*Arch.* 18), and would certainly disapprove of Cicero's producing five hundred lines in a night (Plut. *Cic.* 40.3; Horsfall (1993a) 3 suggests that this method must apply to the *De consulatu* and other such), as he would of Archias' improvising (*Arch.* 18).

33 See Feeney (1998) 114 on the importance of the poets' intervention in the debate which conditioned the terms of Augustus' power: 'Augustus knew that immortality was, in the end, out of his hands.'

34 See Brink (1982a) ad loc. for *sermo* as the epistle's genre. A. Barchiesi suggests to me that *sermones repentes per humum* (2.1.251) goes one better (or worse) than *Musa pedestris* (*Serm.* 2.6.17); see Freudenburg (1993) 183.

35 Lowrie (1997) 108 n. 18. Horace does the inverse at the end of *Epist.* 2.2: he puts comments applicable to himself in the second person.

36 Rudd (1989) 10–11; Barchiesi (1993) 158; Oliensis (1998) 196.

37 Jeffrey Wills suggests *per litteras* that *natam* recalls the most important birth during Cicero's consulship: that of Augustus (see Velleius 2.36), who became *pater patriae* to a greater extent than Cicero.

38 Barchiesi (1993) 157. Although Nisbet (1995b) traces the survivors from Cicero's age to Horace's, he makes the death of Cicero a decisive break 'in literature as well as in history' (390): the triumvirate ushers in a new world Augustus' power cements.

39 I assume the traditional text (with *me*, not *te*) of Cicero's line is correct, and not a parody: see Soubiran (1972) 245 n. 1. Allen (1956) 143 argues that, if we do not think the resemblance accidental, 'we are forced to the conclusion that in Horace's day no one found the Ciceronian verse objectionable'. The Horatian context of citation, however, is bad art, and he changed exactly the things that cause discomfort: a technical flaw, self-praise, civil war.

40 I cannot agree with Griffin (1997) 68 n. 59 that Horace 'deprives the matter of any political substance' – buries it, yes.

41 The social snobs who would keep Horace in his place carp at him with the refrain *libertino patre natus* (*Sat.* 1.6.6, 45–6) in two contexts: his poetic success as a friend of Maecenas, and his military tribunate (*Sat.* 1.6.47–8). Could he have gone as far in the one as he did in the other? See Griffin (1993) 2–3, 11 on Horace's anger over the failure of his 'dazzling career'. The satire shares with the epistle to Florus an assertion of the poet's freedom from avarice, which in turn brings independence.

42 *uacat* as in Soubiran (1972) ad loc.

43 Velleius extols Cicero's *famam uero gloriamque factorum atque dictorum* (2.66.4; see Woodman (1983a) 148–9), but for Horace this picture does not hold together.

44 Horace's argument that we cannot fix a definite dividing line between 'now' and 'then' (*Epist.* 2.1.39–49) pertains well to Cicero, who was more modern than Ennius, but not up to the aesthetic standards of the Alexandrian movement at Rome. Plutarch says as much: Cicero had a reputation as the best poet at Rome, but since many better ones came after, he fell out of fashion (*Cic.* 3–4).

45 This is a less overt 'botching' than in *Carm.* 1.6, as analysed by Ahern (1991). Here the poet intimates through allusion how bad he would be: on the surface nothing offends. Without knowledge of the intertext, the line wins approval: Fraenkel (1957) 398.

46 There was nothing embarrassing about writing up one's own deeds at Rome, see Malcovati (1943) 243–4. Caesar's *commentarii*, Tacitus' comment on how previous generations did so (*Agr.* 1.3), the memoirs of Aemilius Scaurus, Sulla, Rutilius Rufus, and Lutatius Catulus (Allen (1956) 140), may be alleged as support; see Momigliano (1971) 14–15 on this material's autobiographical function, and Marincola (1997) 175–82 on the dangers of self-praise. None of these, however, was in verse. Traglia (1950) 42 states that Cicero's writing such a poem puts him outside the tradition of the genre – at least at Rome: Solon provides a Greek parallel, however inexact. Quintilian finds the poetry, including the line imitated by Horace, over the top. This passage should not be discounted for its post-Republican sensibility precisely because Quintilian is defending Cicero against the charge of boasting: Cicero's self-justifications are defensive and he does not vaunt his eloquence (11.1.17–24; Plutarch, however, begs to differ, *Cic.* 24, *Mor.* (on inoffensive self-praise) 540–1). Cicero, when using himself as an *exemplum* in the dialogues, tends to prosopopoeia or analogous devices that interpose another voice between his and praise, as noted by Quintilian 11.21: Urania, *De cons. suo*, cited above; Atticus, *Leg.* 1.5 and 3.14; a generic third person plural, *Rep.* 1.5–6; Cicero's brother, in apostrophe, *De or.* 3.13. The poem on his consulship is thought to have been written in the third person à la Caesar (Allen (1956) 140 n. 47 with bibliography), though the evidence is slight. When Cicero, in a letter to Atticus (2.3.4), cites Calliope's praise, from his own poem, as reason to adhere to the path of *uirtus* and win the *laudes bonorum* (*De cons. suo*, fr. 11), each layer of distancing turns out to

242   Notes to pages 167–171

be a further level of Cicero's own voice. The effect is not self-involution, but wit.

47 Allen (1956) 144 notes that Juvenal is not entirely condemnatory.

48 Conte–Barchiesi (1989) 103, Barchiesi (1993) 157. K–H (1970) ad loc. call attention to a Ciceronian parallel with more points of contact than they pursue: *nihil est enim tam insigne nec tam ad diuturnitatem memoriae stabile, quam id, in quo aliquid offenderis* (*De or.* 1.129). The issue is perfection in various arts, including drama, for which Roscius is adduced both as the exemplary figure and the expert who cannot stand flaws. The moral fits Horace's argument about his abilities here: *nam qui non potest, qui uitiose facit, quem denique non decet, hunc, ut Apollonius iubebat, ad id, quod facere possit, detrudendum puto* (130).

49 Pasquali (1950) 128 assumes that allusion implies some form of admiration.

50 The two mentions of Parthians in this poem occur when Horace does what he disclaims doing, here in the disavowed sample, earlier when he admits to lying about not writing poetry (*Epist.* 2.1.111–13). Is Augustus lying like a Parthian in casting his diplomatic recovery of the standards as military?

51 Gurval (1995) 33 downplays the emphasis on Actium in the triple triumph, but see Pelling (1997) 290.

52 Cicero's other most ridiculed verse (*Phil.* 2.20).

53 The burden of reference in *Carm.* 4.14.11–12 is primarily literary: to remind that he has in fact written an account of Augustus', or at least his step-sons', *res gestae*. Fraenkel (1957) 398 and Rudd (1989) ad loc. make the reference historical.

54 Except that modern scholars keep making the parallel, and keep disavowing it, see nn. 1 and 21 above.

55 Fraenkel (1957) 383; Rudd (1989) on lines 264–70; Barchiesi (1993) 157–8; Mayer (1985).

56 *The Random House dictionary of the English language* (1966).

57 Rudd (1989) 2.

58 Oliensis (1998) 194–5 shows Horace's disingenuity here: he was no less remunerated than Virgil or Varius.

59 Compare *Sat.* 2.1: Trebatius suggests Horace tell *Caesaris inuicti res* (11), but Horace defends himself as winning praise from Caesar, *iudice laudatus Caesare* (84).

60 On Horace's poetic career as nothing more than an unfortunate episode, see Kilpatrick (1990) 19.

61 Barchiesi (1993) 158. Harrison (1990) 459, on Cicero's representation of his presence at a divine council (Ps.-Sall. 2.3), 'Even he would have balked at unambiguous self-apotheosis.'

62 Brink (1982a) on line 13.

63 I assume the end does not undo the beginning. Horace handles the analogy between Augustus and the gods more delicately than Choerilus and his ilk (*Herculem . . . et Patrem Liberum et cum Polluce Castorem nouo numini cessuros,* Curt. 8.5.8), so there is nothing to take back.

64 Ps.-Sallust's invective links the proscription to Cicero's line: '*O fortunatam natam me consule Romam!*' '*Te consule fortunatam,*' Cicero? *immo uero infelicem et miseram, quae crudelissimam proscriptionem eam perpessa est* (5).

65 Traglia (1950) 45 remarks on the political motivation for ridiculing Cicero's verse.

12 VNA CVM SCRIPTORE MEO

A number of friends have assisted me in the writing of this chapter. Pride of place goes to my co-editor, who has been as acute and penetrating a reader as ever. It is a pleasure to thank Kirk Freudenburg not only for his comments on this piece, but for many years' conversation about Horace, and for making it possible for me to read his illuminating forthcoming work, including a book on Roman satire. I thank also Alessandro Barchiesi, Joe Farrell, and Stephen Hinds for their generous correspondence. Finally, Michèle Lowrie gave me searching comments and helped me out of a big impasse at the end; her chapter in this volume comes at many of the same issues from a different, Ciceronian, angle, and my chapter should be read in tandem with hers. Warm thanks to audiences at Cambridge, London, Oxford and Victoria, BC, who heard various versions of these arguments. This chapter is the working out of a paragraph in Feeney (1992), my first attempt at exploring the relationship between the politics of Augustan poets and the poetics of Augustus. There I commented on Horace's 'acute sensitivity to the transformations of *libertas* under the triumvirate and Principate' (9), and asked why Horace's Epistle to Augustus represented the history of literature and of censorship as coextensive at Rome.

1 Dio 47.43.1.
2 Plut. *Brut.* 41.2.
3 Briefly, Fitzgerald (1988) on the *Epodes*; Henderson (1998) Ch. 3, and especially Freudenburg's forthcoming book, on the *Satires*; for a different interpretation, see Du Quesnay (1984), Galinsky (1996) 57. We return to this theme below.
4 Henderson (1999) 102–3; cf. Nisbet (1995b) 390 on Horace as one of the 'three great literary innovators' of the 30s (along with Virgil and Sallust).
5 'Gravitational pull' is the phrase of Freudenburg (forthcoming), capturing the energy created by the relationship between Horace and his addressees. Cf. Oliensis (1998) for the different 'faces' Horace assumes with different readers, esp. 7–13 on the complementary ways of addressing Augustus in *Epist.* 2.1 and Florus in *Epist.* 2.2; and Henderson (1999) 206–7 on language in Horace's *Sat.* 1.9 'in its contemporary ("Bakhtinian") understanding as a saturated dialogism ... – a matter beyond individualizing "characterization" or ethopoeia; rather, the valorization of a topology of social/political relations'.
6 Williams (1968) 73.
7 Barchiesi (1993) 150. My debts to Barchiesi's analysis of the interplay between the realms of 'poet and *Princeps*' will be evident (Barchiesi (1993) and (1994)). Habinek (1998) 9 promises that his methodology will be an advance on Barchiesi's, but I do not think he delivers: as will emerge in this chapter, I agree rather with, e.g., Felperin (1990) and Perkins (1992) in being unpersuaded that it is possible to 'relate the ideology of the text to the material circumstances of ancient society', as Habinek professes to be able to do (loc. cit.).

8 Cf. Brink (1982a) 566, to which we return below. Although I disagree with much of the analysis of Habinek (1998) 93–102, I concur strongly in wanting to take seriously 'the very form of literary chronology that structures the body of the letter' (93).

9 For Augustus' angle, see the fragment of his *Epistle to Horace* preserved by Suetonius' *Life of Horace*, in which Augustus wonders why Horace hasn't yet addressed an Epistle to him, asking 'Are you afraid that it will be a black mark against you with posterity that you look like a friend of mine?' (*an uereris ne apud posteros infame tibi sit, quod uidearis familiaris nobis esse?*).

10 Feeney (1998) 114, on *Epist.* 2.1.6 and 229–31; Augustus is unique in being honoured as divine while he is still present here on earth (*praesenti tibi maturos largimur honores*, 15), but what will guarantee his divinity when he is no longer *praesens*?

11 On 'the ruler as artist', see Fowler (1995) 252, 254; Alessandro Barchiesi and Tony Woodman both remind me that the phrase *res Italas* can refer to subject-matter (as that of the shield of Aeneas, Virg. *Aen.* 8.626). The Epistle, then, is an extreme case of Horace's typical adaptation of his poetry to the qualities of his addressees, on which see Nisbet (1995a) 1–5, and in this volume; Armstrong (1993) on the importance of the Pisones as the addressees of the *Ars poetica*.

12 Brink (1982a) 552–4. In connecting Horace's description of Augustus as *solus* with the death of Agrippa, I follow Syme (1939) 392 and (1978) 173, despite Brink (1982a) 554 n. 3 and Rudd (1989) ad loc.; cf. Habinek (1998) 92–3.

13 *Res gestae* 10.2.

14 Dio Cass. 54.28.2–3; on Agrippa as Augustus' virtual co-regent at the time of his death, see Reinhold (1933) 98–105, *CAH*² 10.97. I follow the edict of Barnes (1998) 144 in eschewing the phrase *maius imperium*.

15 Wili (1948) 341, Klingner (1950) 32, Brink (1982a) 559; on the 'watershed' in Roman literary history represented by this year, see Brink (1982a) 546.

16 Brink (1963) 208–9.

17 Apart from this note, I am as silent as Horace is about (i) Propertius, who may have been no more than eight or nine years younger, and (ii) the great figure of the next generation, Ovid. Does Horace's awareness of these (and other) figures lie behind the frequent first person plurals of the poem, as Michèle Lowrie suggests to me (89, 117, 214, 219)?

18 Oliensis (1998) 12 brings out very clearly how, within *Epistles* 2 as a book, 'Horace's only "patron" is Augustus'.

19 Cf. the valuable observations of Horsfall (1993b) 60–3 on *Epist.* 2.1.216–18, together with Oliensis (1998) 193. Note how earlier in the poem the people, if they agree with Horace about the ancients, are 'using their head, siding with me, and giving a *iudicium* with the favour of Jupiter' (*et sapit et mecum facit et Ioue iudicat aequo*, 68). For a minor-key anticipation of this theme, note *Sat.* 2.1.82–4. Tony Woodman points out that there is a big shift from the end of *Odes* 1.1, with its important stress on the *iudicium* of Maecenas (*quodsi... inseres*, 35).

20 As Kirk Freudenburg puts it to me, Horace's solitude is partly historical 'fact', partly self-construction as he is 'sucked into the imperial vortex'.

21 *Inst.* 10.1.54; cf. 1.4.3 and 10.1.59 for other mentions of canonical procedure, with 2.5.25–6 on contemporary models; on the canons, Pfeiffer (1968) 203–8, Jocelyn (1979) 74–5, Scotti (1982). At *Tr.* 2.467–8 Ovid alludes to the canonical suppression of living authors' names; cf. Vell. Pat. 2.36.3. As Kirk Freudenburg points out to me, the clearest example of Quintilian's self-denying ordinance is at *Inst.* 10.1.96, where he mentions the recently deceased Caesius Bassus as a prominent lyricist, adding that he is surpassed by living talents, whom he leaves anonymous.

22 Douglas (1966) ix.

23 Nisbet (1995b) 403; also as a compliment to the original plan of Pollio's leader, Julius Caesar, who had charged Varro with the task of organising a library (Horsfall (1993b) 59).

24 Already in the fourth century, the prominent tragedian Astydamas had enviously observed of his three great predecessors that 'they have the advantage of time, for envy does not touch them': Astydamas 60 *TrGF*, T 2a. Here, of course, is a cardinal point of difference which Horace identifies between himself and Augustus, whom he represents as uniquely beyond envy even before his death (5–17).

25 Bloomer (1997) 67.

26 Suet. *Gram.* 16.3, with the important discussion of Kaster (1995) 188–9.

27 Oliensis (1995) and (1998) 174–5 on Horace's 'conflicting impulses toward elitism and popularization'. This interest in Horace's simultaneous lust for and dread of popularity is more valuable than the monocular focus on his elitism in Habinek (1998), esp. 99–102.

28 Feeney (1993) 45; to the references there, add Syme (1939) 255 and Brink (1963) 166–70, 195, 214, which I should have cited; compare Farrell (1991), esp. Ch. 7, Nisbet (1995b) 395–6, and Zetzel in this volume. The pan-Callimachean tendency that Horace consistently skewers persists strongly in modern criticism.

29 See Catull. 10.5–12 and 28.9–10 for the rapacity and cynicism of the operation.

30 Catull. 68.97–100, 101.1–2.

31 Catullus is leaving the plains of Phrygia and the fertile land of Nicaea to see the famous cities of Asia (*linquantur Phrygii, Catulle, campi | Nicaeaeque ager uber aestuosae: | ad claras Asiae uolemus urbes*, 46.4–6); Horace suppresses Phrygia and transfers the fertility and plains to Asia (*an pingues Asiae campi collesque morantur?*, 5). Tony Woodman suggests another Catullan touch, in the link between *Epist.* 1.3.2 (*scire laboro*) and Catull. 67.17 (*scire laborat*).

32 In *Epist.* 1.13, addressing Tiberius, he will give us an object lesson in how to talk to the leader of the *cohors* – very differently from the way Catullus talked to Memmius (28.9–10).

33 Hubbard (1995) 220–1: 'he is . . . teasingly showing how to make use of Pindar, and by no means in Titius' way'.

34 Hubbard (1995) 220.

35 West (1967) 30–9. In a forthcoming paper on *Epist.* 2.2, Kirk Freudenburg comes to analogous conclusions, arguing that in both Epistles Florus'

status as a lawyer is a focus for the themes of legitimate ownership of poetic property.

36 Horace describes the divine honours paid to the living Augustus as *maturos* (15): is that 'occurring at the proper time, timely' (*OLD* s.v.7) or 'occurring before the proper or usual time, premature, early' (*OLD* s.v.9)?

37 Brink (1982a) 566.

38 Russell (1981) 159; cf. Williams (1978) 270–1.

39 Leo (1901) 99–107, Podlecki (1969), Russell (1981) 159–68. The masterpiece of Pfeiffer (1968) scandalously skips straight from Aristotle to Alexandria: Richardson (1994).

40 Rawson (1985) 267–81, Kaster (1995) xxiv–xxviii (both Greek and Roman).

41 Williams (1978) 270.

42 Williams (1978) 271.

43 See Fantham (1996) 18, 45–7, for the importance of Cicero and Tacitus in this regard.

44 Brink (1982a) 59.

45 Cf. Norden (1927) 376–8 on Virgil as the first transposer of periodic prose style to verse. Horace has a very similar moment at *Sat.* 1.10.56–64, illustrating the gap between his technique and Lucilius'.

46 Brink (1982a) ad loc: '*criticus*, in place of Latin *iudex*, occurs twice only in Republican and Augustan Latin – in this passage and at Cic. *Fam.* IX.10.1' (the Cicero passage is also highly ironic and tongue-in-cheek: Brink (1982a) 418–19).

47 Conveniently in Courtney (1993) 93–4.

48 Pope's Note at this point in his *Imitation* is wonderful: 'The whole paragraph has a mixture of Irony, and must not altogether be taken for Horace's own Judgment, only the common Chat of the pretenders to Criticism'; cf. Brink (1982a) 104.

49 Not the least of the problems in these very difficult lines on Ennius is that it was not just the critics who claimed Ennius as *alter Homerus*, but Ennius himself (despite Brink (1982a) 95–6).

50 Leo (1901) 149–50; Focke (1923); Petrochilos (1974) 144–62; Vardi (1996).

51 At least, so far as taste is concerned, as Michèle Lowrie reminds me: for Augustus' *imitatio Alexandri*, see n. 93 below.

52 I realise that these claims about Horace's attitude to cross-cultural comparison will seem odd to those who believe that he regularly casts himself as another Alcaeus, for example; but I plan to justify these claims about Horace's attitudes to σύγκρισις, and his debt to Cicero's literary histories, in a paper for a collection edited by Michael Paschalis (although the subject of Horace's debts to Cicero deserves a book).

53 Klingner (1950) 22–3.

54 Perkins (1992) 179; cf. Barchiesi (1962) 43, Hinds (1998) Ch. 3, esp. 63.

55 Perkins (1992); an important discussion of these issues in Hinds (1998) Ch. 3, with focus on Hor. *Epist.* 2.1.50–75 at 69–71; cf. Goldberg (1995) 5–12. Of course, at some level, the teleological interestedness described by Perkins is true of any history: Martindale (1993) 17–23.

56 Brink (1982a) 566.

57 Klingner (1950) 18, Hinds (1998) 55.
58 White (1987) 233–4, Hinds (1998) 69–70.
59 Cf. Cicero on Thucydides (*Brut.* 288); for Horace's Ciceronian apprehension of such matters, see Barchiesi (1962) 66 n. 300.
60 For a devastating general attack on history's claims to explain causes, see Veyne (1984) 87–105, 144–72.
61 For the inadequacies of literary historical contextualisation, see Perkins (1992) Ch. 6, esp. 128: 'How can an essay or book adequately display the intricate, manifold involvement of a particular text in the hugely diverse context that is thought to determine it? Moreover, any context we use for interpretation or explanation must itself be interpreted. In other words, the context must be put in a wider context, which itself must be interpreted contextually, and so on in a recession that can only be halted arbitrarily.' Cf. Felperin (1990), esp. 142–69 (a critique of New Historicist contextualisation in particular); Martindale (1993) 13; Goldberg (1995) 19–26; Fowler (2000) x–xi, 174. Naturally, it is in practice impossible to write about literature without one kind of contextualisation or another, as my own essay shows (Martindale (1993) 14–15): the question is how much weight to put on their explanatory or causal value.
62 Veyne (1988) 178.
63 Brink (1982a) 142–3.
64 The anomalous nature of this single performance's social function, however, emerges clearly from Barchiesi's chapter in this volume.
65 As Michèle Lowrie put it to me.
66 Brink (1982a) 184–5; Porcius Licinus, e.g., could be more specific: *Poenico bello secundo* ... (fr. 1, Courtney (1993)). Alessandro Barchiesi points out to me that *Graecia capta* is a particular tease because it resembles so closely triumphal labels that are chronologically specific (*Achaia capta, Corintho capta*).
67 Hinds (1998) 63 with 82; cf. Brink (1962) 192, on *Epist.* 2.1.161–3: 'a tendency rather than a date'; Rudd (1989) on 156–7.
68 On the *Epodes*, see Schmidt (1977), Fitzgerald (1988) and Oliensis (1991), with Watson (1995), who professes to take issue with these scholars' conclusions about Horace's impotence, but who to my mind actually ends up confirming and taking even further their picture of Horace's inversion of the epodic voice. On the *Satires*, see Du Quesnay (1984), Kennedy (1992) 29–34, Freudenburg (1993) 86–92, 102, 209, Muecke (1995), Henderson (1998) Ch. 3 and (1999) Ch. 8, and especially Freudenburg (2001) 15–124.
69 Hunter (1985); cf. Freudenburg (1993) 86–92 on the influence of Philodemus' concept of παρρησία in the *Satires*, and Armstrong (1993) 192–9 for the *Ars*; on παρρησία in general, see Scarpat (1964). See Johnson (1993) for *libertas* as the dominant theme of *Epistles* I.
70 We should remind ourselves that Horace had never addressed a poem to Augustus until the Fourth Book of *Odes*, published only the year before: Brink (1982a) 536, Feeney (1993) 54, on the oddity of the sole apparent exception, *Odes* I.2.
71 Barchiesi (1993) 155–8.

72 Williams (1968) 73. In connection with Williams' point about the heavy emphasis on drama in the post-Aristotelian critical tradition, note Horace's play on two key Aristotelian concepts, ὄψις, 'spectacle', and μίμησις, 'imitation/representation'. Following Aristotle in seeing ὄψις as the least artistic of all the aspects of drama (Poet. 1450b16–18, 1453b1–8; cf. Edwards (1993) 105), Horace says that the pleasure in contemporary drama has all gone from the ear to the uncertain eyes (ab aure... ad incertos oculos, 187–8; remember that his own poetry will engage both the ears and eyes of the Princeps, Epist. 1.13.17). In line 195, with his description of a giraffe (diuersum confusa genus panthera camelo), Horace acts out for us just how uncertain the eyes can be: you really cannot tell what you are looking at when you are looking at a giraffe, and the intricate and ultimately uncategorisable grammar mimics this visual uncertainty, as is shown by the intricate grammatical exegeses of Brink (1982a) and Rudd (1989) ad loc. (Rudd: 'one cannot be sure'). At the end of this section the key Aristotelian concept of μίμησις receives attention (205–7): 'Everyone is clapping. Has the actor said anything yet? Of course not. What is making them clap, then? lana Tarentino uiolas imitata ueneno.' But this too is mere ὄψις; the only μίμησις taking place on the Roman stage is a dyed cloak imitating the colour of violets.

73 Habinek (1998) 99. This binarism leads him also to say some very strange things about the 'vulgar' and 'nonelite' nature of the imagines alluded to at the end of the poem (264–5): 99, 102.

74 So, very clearly, Brink (1982a) 220: 'Even the equites share the prevailing grossness of taste.'

75 Though he misplaces the reason for Horace's difference with the Emperor ('who had conceived them [i.e., Horace and his contemporaries] of little Use to the Government'). For varying accounts of Horace's differences with Augustus' taste for spectacle and theatre, attested in Suet. Aug. 43–5 and 89.1, see Klingner (1950) 32, Fraenkel (1957) 395–6, La Penna (1963) 148–62, Brink (1982a) 562–5.

76 Barchiesi (1993) 152: 'insieme discente e maestro'.

77 Hopkins (1983) 14–20, Edwards (1993) 110–19, Bartsch (1994); cf. Fowler (1995) on Augustus' aestheticising of politics.

78 Cf. Cic. Ad Brut. 1.9.2 tibi nunc populo et scaenae, ut dicitur, seruiendum est, and Cic. Amic. 97 in scaena, id est in contione, with the note of Powell (1990) ad loc. for material on 'the comparison of a public meeting with a theatrical performance'.

79 On the sack of Corinth in 146 BCE as an event that the Romans consciously constructed as a major turning-point in Greek–Roman relations, see Purcell (1995), esp. 143.

80 Sat. 1.10.39, 72–7; Epist. 1.19.41–5.

81 Schnurr (1992) 156.

82 Rawson (1991) 509, 543. On the implications of the seating arrangements, cf. Kolendo (1981) and Schnurr (1992): Horace alludes to the separate seating of people and knights in 186–7, and in Epod. 4.15–16 he had used the violation of the Lex Roscia as an emblem of the dissolution of order. The relationship between the poet's art and the performances staged by the Princeps is likewise

fundamental to Ovid's argument in his Epistle to Augustus (*Tr.* 2.279–84, 497–520): Barchiesi (1993) 167.

83 This is part of the problem with the performance genres of drama or oratory– as Cicero says repeatedly in his oratorical works (e.g., *Brut.* 183–9), and, as Horace says in the *Ars* (153), if the people do not respond properly to performance, it is bound to flop: Mayer (1995b) 291–4. The political and the critical traditions both say you have to pay attention to the *uulgus* but both have serious qualms about it. Livy's rather similar reservations about contemporary theatre are an interesting comparandum: Feldherr (1998) 165–87.

84 Discussions of the evidence (Suet. *Aug.* 44.2, *CIL* 6.32323.56–7, Mart. 5.41.8, Dio 54.30.5) in Rawson (1991) 525–6, canvassing various dates between 22 and 18, and Schnurr (1992) 159, suggesting the *Lex Iulia de maritandis ordinibus* of 18. Nicholas Purcell has kindly discussed with me the pitfalls of any secure reconstruction of the scope of any such ban, and the problems of whether Horace would have qualified as an *eques* of the right status to be covered. His caution has been salutary.

85 See Muecke (1993) ad loc., and on *Sat.* 2.7.53; cf. Wiseman (1971) 71–2 on Horace's equestrian status.

86 A modification of the Lucretian formula *nunc age* + imperative (Brink (1982a) ad loc.); cf. Barchiesi (1993) on Horace's didacticism in the Epistle.

87 Again, 'gravitational pull' is the phrase of Freudenburg (forthcoming), a powerful study of this effect in the correspondence of Horace and Florus.

88 Brink (1982a) 567, 571; cf. La Penna (1963) 171 n. 1; White (1993) 132.

89 Oliensis (1998) 2–3; cf. Kennedy (1992) 40–2, Santirocco (1995), Feeney (1994) 347: 'The poets are not mirroring something that is a given, but participating in a social praxis as they make their constructions.'

90 Santirocco (1995) 243.

91 Hunter (1996) 105, 97; cf. Lowrie in this volume, and for Horace's use of this Pindaric trope in the *Odes*, see Lowrie (1997) 107–8. Theocritus 16 is as important to Horace at the end of this Epistle as it is in *Odes* 4 (on which see Barchiesi (1996) 13–17, 25–9). I am not concentrating on the problems of remuneration; briefly, it is instructive to juxtapose Oliensis (1998) 194–7 on the different kinds of 'gifts' in this closing section with Hunter (1996) 105 on the ambiguities of χάριτες ('both "poems" and the "favour" or "pay" which those poems bring') and τιμή ('as well as "honour", [the term] can also mean "pay" or "public office"'). Note how Horace's *Musarum dona* (243) modulates into the loaded word *munera* (246, 267), a word which carries all of the meanings listed by Hunter for his key Greek terms, except for 'poems' – plus, in addition, 'funeral rites', with which his poem ends.

92 Cicero is the focus for the anxieties of ridicule here (256, and 262–3): see Barchiesi (1993) 157 and Lowrie in this volume.

93 Such I take to be part of the point of 241–4, where Horace says that Alexander was such a bad judge of contemporary poetry that you would swear he had been born in Boeotia: apart from the allusion to the proverbial stupidity of Boeotians, we should note that Boeotia was the home of Pindar, and when Alexander sacked Thebes in 335 he killed or enslaved everybody except for priests, *xenoi* of the Macedonians, and the descendants of Pindar,

and destroyed every building except for the house of Pindar (Plut. *Alex.* 11.6; Arr. *Anab.* 1.9.10). As Alessandro Barchiesi reminds me, Augustus had his own problems of how to imitate models correctly: on his imitation of Alexander, see Galinsky (1996) 48, 167–8, 199–200.

94 Barchiesi (1993) 158.

95 *est operae pretium* looks to Enn. *Ann.* 494–5 and *op. inc. fr.* ii Skutsch; cf. Barchiesi (1962) 66, 69–70 for Horace's admiration for Ennius, and Hinds (1998) 15 for the way Ovid acknowledges the canonising power of Ennius' apotheosis of Romulus. Even in the earlier denunciation of the craze for the archaic, Horace had been careful to close his demolition of the *critici* by saying that the *ueteres* are not to be condemned altogether just because their defenders are idiots: see Hinds (1998) 70–1 on Horace's tribute to Livius Andronicus in 2.1.69–75.

96 Space forbids detailed exemplification: besides the commentaries, see n. 91 for Pindar, Simonides, and Theocritus as models for the problems of praise and patronage; n. 95 for Ennius; n. 92 for Cicero; n. 94 for Catullus.

97 Important discussions in Hardie (1993), esp. 121–2, 133–5, and Barchiesi (1996) 12–13, 21 (on *Carm.* 4.8). Note how *uidendis artibus* (242) picks up all the Aristotelian objections to the pleasure gained by the uncertain eyes in the section on spectacle (187–8).

98 Exactly as in Anchises' speech in Virgil's Underworld (*excudent alii spirantia mollius aera | . . . uiuos ducent de marmore uultus*, *Aen.* 6.847–8).

99 Barchiesi (1996) 21, on this theme in *Carm.* 4.8, where Parrhasius and Scopas are the paradigms.

100 If sculpture is what it is: Brink (1982a) 431–2.

101 Cf. Wallace-Hadrill (1988) 232: 'Greek παιδεία, as far as we can see, was socially undifferentiated, belonging to, even defining, the world of the leisured. It was part of the Roman response to a threat to introduce sharp differentiation.' It is very poignant to see a Roman lyricist including the playing of the cithara as one of the things one cannot imagine a Roman doing properly (*psallimus*, 33).

102 Even when the Romans do have a natural affinity (for tragedy, 165–6), it keeps getting overridden by their lack of capacity for *ars* (167). It is instructive to compare Roman historians' defence of their writing in a political and martial society: Kraus–Woodman (1997) 17.

103 The untethered memory of the public performance of the *Carmen saeculare* stands out as the exception (132–8): again, see Barchiesi in this volume for the significance of that exception.

104 Cf. Brink (1982a) 522, 559–61, on the options facing the later Horace, either 'to continue the political motif' (559), or else 'the three long literary epistles' (560).

EPILOGUE

1 Horsfall (1995) 24.

2 Wilkinson (1945) 1 (a similar remark in N–H (1970) xxv–xxvi); for Wilkinson's own account of his time at Bletchley Park see F. H. Hinsley and A. Stripp

(ed.), *Code breakers: the inside story of Bletchley Park* (1993) 61–7 (with a photo of him in plate 10).

3 Fraenkel (1957) vii.
4 Williams in Harrison (1995a) 296–313.
5 In his forthcoming commentary on *Odes* 3.
6 Nisbet (1959) = (1995a) 1–5.
7 Du Quesnay (1984) 19–58.

ABBREVIATIONS AND BIBLIOGRAPHY

Note. Scholarly discussions and the like are generally listed under B, and through-out the book are referred to by author's name, date and page-number. Periodical abbreviations generally follow the system used in *L'année philologique*.

A ABBREVIATIONS

BTL-1	*Bibliotheca Teubneriana Latina*, Stuttgart–Leipzig–Turnhout, 1999
CAH² 10	*Cambridge ancient history*, Vol. 10, 2nd edn, ed. A. K. Bowman, E. Champlin and A. Lintott, Cambridge, 1996
CIL	*Corpus inscriptionum Latinarum*, Berlin, 1863–
E–J	V. Ehrenberg and A. H. M. Jones, *Documents illustrating the reigns of Augustus and Tiberius*, 2nd edn, Oxford, 1976
EO	*Enciclopedia Oraziana*, dir. S. Mariotti, Vols. 1–3, Rome, 1996–98
EV	*Enciclopedia Virgiliana*, dir. F. Della Corte, Vols. 1–5, Rome, 1984–91
ILS	*Inscriptiones Latinae selectae*, ed. H. Dessau, Berlin, 1892–1916
K–H	A. Kiessling and R. Heinze, *Q. Horatius Flaccus*, Vol. 1 *Oden und Epoden*, repr. Zurich–Berlin, 1964; Vol. 2 *Satiren*, repr. Dublin–Zurich, 1968; Vol. 3 *Briefe*, repr. Dublin–Zurich, 1970
MRR	T. R. S. Broughton, *The magistrates of the Roman republic*, Vols. 1–3, New York–Atlanta, 1951–86
N–H	R. G. M. Nisbet and M. Hubbard, *A commentary on Horace: Odes*, Vols. 1–2, Oxford, 1970–8
OCD	*Oxford classical dictionary*
OCT	Oxford classical text(s)
OLD	*Oxford Latin dictionary*, ed. P. G. W. Glare, Oxford, 1968–82
ORF	*Oratorum Romanorum fragmenta*, ed. H. Malcovati, 4th edn, Turin, 1967
PMG	*Poetae melici Graeci*, ed. D. L. Page, Oxford, 1962
RE	*Paulys Real-Encyclopädie der klassischen Altertumswissenschaft*, ed. G. Wissowa et al., Stuttgart, 1893–1978
SVF	*Stoicorum veterum fragmenta*, ed. H. von Arnim, Vols. 1–4, Leipzig, 1905–24
TrGF	*Tragicorum Graecorum fragmenta*, ed. B. Snell, R. Kannicht and S. L. Radt, Vol. 1², Göttingen, 1986
TLL	*Thesaurus linguae Latinae*

B BIBLIOGRAPHY

Ableitinger-Grünberger, D. (1971). *Der junge Horaz und die Politik: Studien zur 7. und 16. Epode.* Heidelberg
Adams, J. N. (1984). 'Female speech in Roman comedy', *Antichthon* 18.43–77
Adler, E. (1981). *Catullan self-revelation.* New York
Ahern, C. F., Jr (1991). 'Horace's rewriting of Homer in *Carmen* 1.6', *CP* 86.301–14
Ahl, F. (1984). 'The art of safe criticism in Greece and Rome', *AJP* 105.174–208
Allen, W., Jr (1956). 'O fortunatam natam...', *TAPA* 87.130–46
   (1970). 'The addressees in Horace's first Book of Epistles', *Studies in Philology* 67. 255–66
Ancona, R. (1994). *Time and the erotic in Horace's Odes.* Durham, NC–London
Anderson, R. D. et al. (1979). 'Elegiacs by Gallus from Qaṣr Ibrîm', *JRS* 69.125–55
Anderson, W. S. (1988). Review of Santirocco (1986), *CP* 83.165–7
André, J.-M. (1967). *Mécène: essai de biographie spirituelle.* Paris
   (1981). *Anonyme Latin: traité de physiognomonie.* (Budé.) Paris
Argetsinger, K. (1992). 'Birthday rituals: friends and patrons in Roman poetry and cult', *CA* 11.175–93
Armstrong, D. (1989). *Horace.* New Haven–London
   (1993). 'The addressees of the *Ars poetica*: Herculaneum, the Pisones and Epicurean protreptic', *MD* 31.185–230
   (1995). 'The impossibility of metathesis', in D. Obbink (ed.), *Philodemus and poetry* 210–32. New York–Oxford.
Astin, A. E. (1978). *Cato the Censor.* Oxford
Austin, R. G. (1977). *P. Vergili Maronis Aeneidos Liber sextus.* Oxford
Axelson, B. (1945). *Unpoetische Wörter.* Lund
Babcock, C. L. (1974). '*omne militabitur bellum*. The language of commitment in Epode 1', *CJ* 70.14–31
Barchiesi, A. (1993). 'Insegnare ad Augusto: Orazio, Epistole 2,1 e Ovidio, Tristia II', *MD* 31.149–84 (= *Speaking volumes* (London, 2001) 79–103)
   (1994). *Il poeta e il principe. Ovidio e il discorso augusteo.* Rome
   (1996). 'Poetry, praise and patronage: Simonides in Book 4 of Horace's *Odes*', *CA* 15.5–47
   (2000). 'Rituals in ink. Horace on the Greek lyric tradition', in M. Depew and D. Obbink (edd.), *Matrices of genre* 167–82, 290–4. Cambridge, MA
Barchiesi, M. (1962). *Nevio epico.* Padua
Barker, A. (1989). *Greek musical writings.* Vol. 2 *Harmonic and acoustic theory.* Cambridge
Barnes, T. D. (1998). 'Tacitus and the *Senatus consultum de Cn. Pisone patre*', *Phoenix* 52.125–48
Barton, T. S. (1994a). *Ancient astrology.* London
   (1994b). *Power and knowledge: astrology, physiognomics, and medicine under the Roman empire.* Ann Arbor
   (1995). 'Augustus and Capricorn', *JRS* 85.33–51
Bartsch, S. (1994). *Actors in the audience: theatricality and doublespeak from Nero to Hadrian.* Cambridge, MA

Baxter, W., and Gesner, J. M. (1806). *Q. Horatii Flacci opera*. Edinburgh

Beard, M., North, J. and Price, S. R. (1998). *Religions of Rome*. Vols. 1–2. Cambridge.

Bettini, M. (1991). *Anthropology and Roman culture: kinship, time, images of the soul*. Eng. trans. Baltimore–London

(1998). *Nascere*. Turin

Bloomer, M. (1997). *Latinity and literary society at Rome*. Philadelphia

Boll, F. (1950). *Kleine Schriften zur Sternkunde des Altertums*. Leipzig

Bömer, F. (1982). *P. Ovidius Naso, Metamorphosen: Kommentar Buch XII–XIII*. Heidelberg

Bona, G. (1988). *Pindaro. I Peani*. Cuneo

Bonfante, G., and Bonfante, L. (1983). *The Etruscan language: an introduction*. Manchester

Borzsák, S. (1984). *Q. Horati Flacci opera*. Leipzig

Bouché-Leclerq, A. (1899). *L'Astrologie grecque*. Paris

Bowditch, L. (1994). 'Horace's poetics of political integrity: *Epistle* 1.18', *AJP* 115.409–26

Boyarin, D. (1993). *Carnal Israel. Reading sex in Talmudic culture*. Berkeley–Los Angeles–Oxford

Bradshaw, A. (1970). 'Horace, *Odes* 4.1', *CQ* 20.142–53

Bramble, J. C. (1974). *Persius and the programmatic satire*. Cambridge

Braund, S. H. (1992). *Roman verse satire*. (*Greece & Rome* New Surveys in the Classics No. 23.) Oxford

Breyer, G. (1993). *Etruskisches Sprachgut im Lateinischen unter Ausschluss des spezifisch onomastischen Bereiches*. Leuven

Brind' Amour, P. (1983). *Le Calendrier romain*. Ottawa

Brink, C. O. (1962). 'Horace and Varro', *Varron* (Fondation Hardt Entretiens 9) 175–206. Vandoeuvres–Geneva

(1963). *Horace on poetry: prolegomena to the literary Epistles*. Cambridge

(1971). 'Horatian notes II: despised readings in the manuscripts of the *Odes*, Book II', *PCPS* 17.17–29

(1982a). *Horace on poetry: Epistles Book II*. Cambridge

(1982b). 'Horatian notes III: despised readings in the manuscripts of the *Epodes* and a passage of *Odes* Book 3', *PCPS* 28.30–56

Brown, P. M. (1993). *Horace: Satires I*. Warminster

Brunt, P. A. and Moore, J. M. (1967). *Res Gestae Divi Augusti*. Oxford

Cairns, F. (1972). *Generic composition in Greek and Roman poetry*. Edinburgh

(1982). 'Horace *Odes* 3, 22: genre and sources', *Philologus* 126.227–46

(1984). 'The etymology of *militia* in Roman elegy', in L. Gil and R. M. Aguilar (edd.), *Apophoreta Philologica Emmanueli Fernandez-Galiano oblata* 2.211–22. Madrid

(1995). 'Horace's first Roman Ode', *PLLS* 8.91–142

Cameron, A. (1968). 'The first edition of Ovid's *Amores*', *CQ* 18.320–33

(1995). *Callimachus and his critics*. Princeton

Campbell, D. A. (1978). 'Aeolium carmen: Horace's allusions to Sappho and Alcaeus', *EMC* 22.94–8

(1982–93). *Greek lyric*. Vols. 1–5. (Loeb.) Cambridge, MA–London

Cannatà Fera, M. (1980). 'Peani, ditirambi, treni in Pind. fr. 128 c Sn.-M.', *GIF* NS 11.181–8

(1990). *Pindarus: Threnorum fragmenta*. Rome

Carrubba, R. W. (1969). *The Epodes of Horace*. The Hague

Carter, J. M. (1977). 'A new fragment of Octavian's inscription at Nicopolis', *ZPE* 24.227–30

Casson, L. (1995). *Ships and seamanship in the ancient world*. 2nd edn. Baltimore–London

Castner, C. J. (1988). *Prosopography of Roman Epicureans from the second century BC to the second century AD*. (Studien zur Klassischen Philologie 34.) Frankfurt am Main–Bern–New York–Paris

Cavarzere, A. (1992). *Orazio: il libro degli Epodi*. Venice

Cichorius, C. (1922). *Römische Studien*. Leipzig (reprinted 1961)

Citroni, M. (1975). *M. Valerii Martialis Epigrammaton liber primus*. Florence

Clarke, M. L. (1972). 'Horace, *Epistles* i.13', *CR* 22.157–9.

Clausen, W. (1968). 'Catullus and Callimachus', *HSCP* 74.85–94

Coarelli, F. (1997). *Il Campo Marzio*. Rome

Coburn, K., and Christensen, M. (1990). *The notebooks of Samuel Taylor Coleridge*. Vol. 4. London

Coleman, R. (1977). *Vergil: Eclogues*. Cambridge

Collinge, N. E. (1961). *The structure of Horace's Odes*. Oxford

Commager, S. (1962). *The Odes of Horace: a critical study*. New Haven

Conte, G. B. (1994). *Latin literature: a history*. Eng. trans. Baltimore–London

Conte, G. B., and Barchiesi, A. (1989). 'Imitazione e arte allusiva: modi e funzioni dell'intertestualità', in G. Cavallo, P. Fedeli, and A. Giardina (edd.), *Lo spazio letterario di Roma antica* 1.81–114. Rome

Courbaud, E. (1914). *Horace, sa vie et sa pensée à l'époque des épîtres: étude sur le premier livre*. Paris

Courtney, E. (1993). *The fragmentary Latin poets*. Oxford

Cramer, F. H. (1954). *Astrology in Roman law and politics*. Philadelphia

Cucchiarelli, A. (1999). 'Hor. *epist.* 1, 19, 28: *pede mascula Sappho*', *Hermes* 127.328–44

D'Arms, J. (1990). 'The Roman convivium and the idea of equality', in O. Murray (ed.), *Sympotica* 308–20. Oxford

Davis, G. (1991). *Polyhymnia: the rhetoric of Horatian discourse*. Berkeley–Los Angeles–Oxford

De Pretis, A. (1998). '"Epistolarity" in the First Book of Horace's *Epistles*'. (Unpublished PhD dissertation.) Bristol

de Saint Denis, E. (1947). '*mare clausum*', *REL* 25.196–214

Delcourt, M. (1961). *Hermaphrodite. Myths and rites of the bisexual figure in classical antiquity*. Eng. trans. London

Delz, J. (1988). Review of Shackleton Bailey (1985a), *Gnomon* 60.495–501

Dettmer, H. D. (1983). *Horace: a study in structure*. Hildesheim

Dicks, D. R. (1963). 'Astrology and astronomy in Horace', *Hermes* 91.60–73

Dilke, O. A. W. (1973). 'Horace and the verse letter', in C. D. N. Costa (ed.), *Horace* 94–112. London

(1981). 'The interpretation of Horace's *Epistles*', *ANRW* 2.31.3.1837–65

Dillon, J. (1977). *The middle Platonists*. London
  (1995). 'The equality of the sexes – variations on a rhetorical theme in the
    fourth century AD', *Hermathena* 158.27–35
Doering, F. G. (1826). *Q. Horatii Flacci opera omnia*. London
Douglas, A. E. (1966). *M. Tulli Ciceronis Brutus*. Oxford
Dover, K. J. (1964). 'The poetry of Archilochus', *Archiloque* (Fondation Hardt
    Entretiens 10) 183–222. Vandoeuvres–Geneva
Dreizehnter, A. (1978). *Die rhetorische Zahl*. Munich
Du Quesnay, I. M. Le M. (1981). 'Vergil's First *Eclogue*', *PLLS* 3.29–182
  (1984). 'Horace and Maecenas. The propaganda value of *Sermones* I', in
    Woodman–West (1984) 19–58, 200–11
  (1995). 'Horace, *Odes* 4.5: *Pro reditu Imperatoris Caesaris divi filii Augusti*', in
    Harrison (1995a) 128–87
Dyck, A. R. (1996). *A commentary on Cicero, De Officiis*. Ann Arbor
Easterling, P. E. (1982). *Sophocles. Trachiniae*. Cambridge
Edwards, C. (1993). *The politics of immorality in ancient Rome*. Cambridge
Edwards, M. J. (1989). 'Greek into Latin: a note on Catullus and Sappho',
    Latomus 48.590–600
Eidinow, J. S. C. (1990). 'A note on Horace, *Epistles* 1.1.26 and 2.2.75', *CQ*
    40.566–8
  (1995). 'Horace's Epistle to Torquatus (*Ep.* 1.5)', *CQ* 45.191–9
Ernout, A., and Meillet, A. (1959). *Dictionnaire étymologique de la langue latine*.
    Paris
Esser, D. (1976). *Untersuchungen zu den Odenschlüssen bei Horaz*. Meisenheim am
    Glan
Evans, S. (1971). 'Odyssean echoes in Propertius 4.8', *G&R* 18.51–3
Evenepoel, W. (1990). 'Maecenas: a survey of recent literature', *Anc. Soc.*
    21.99–117
Eyben, E. (1973). 'Die Einteilung des menschlichen Lebens im römischen
    Altertum', *RhM* 116.151–90
Fadinger, V. (1969). *Die Begründung des Prinzipats. Quellenkritische und
    staatsrechtliche Untersuchungen zu Cassius Dio und der Parallelüberlieferung*.
    Berlin
Fairweather, J. (1974). 'Fiction in the biographies of ancient writers', *Anc. Soc.*
    5.231–75
Fantham, E. (1979). 'The mating of Lalage: Horace, *Odes* 2.5', *LCM* 4.47–52
  (1996). *Roman literary culture: from Cicero to Apuleius*. Baltimore–London
Farrell, J. (1991). *Vergil's Georgics and the traditions of ancient epic*. Oxford
Fedeli, P. (1980). *Sesto Properzio. Il primo libro delle Elegie*. Florence
Feeney, D. C. (1986). 'History and revelation in Vergil's Underworld', *PCPS*
    32.1–24
  (1992). '*Si licet et fas est*: Ovid's *Fasti* and the problem of free speech under the
    Principate', in Powell (1992) 1–25
  (1993). 'Horace and the Greek lyric poets', in Rudd (1993a) 41–63
  (1994). Review of White (1993), *BMCR* 5.346–9
  (1998). *Literature and religion at Rome: cultures, contexts, and beliefs*. Cambridge
Feldherr, A. (1998). *Spectacle and society in Livy's History*. Berkeley–Los Angeles–
    London

Felperin, H. (1990). *The uses of the canon: Elizabethan literature and contemporary theory.* Oxford

Ferguson, J. (1956). 'Catullus and Horace', *AJP* 77.1–18

Ferri, R. (1993). *I dispiaceri di un epicureo: Uno studio sulla poetica oraziana delle Epistole (con un capitolo su Persio).* Pisa

Fiske, G. C. (1920). *Lucilius and Horace: a study in the classical theory of imitation.* Madison

Fitzgerald, W. (1988). 'Power and impotence in Horace's *Epodes*', *Ramus* 17.176–91

Focke, F. (1923). 'Synkrisis', *Hermes* 58.327–68

Foley, H. P. (1984). '"Reverse similes" and sex roles in the *Odyssey*', in J. Peradotto and J. P. Sullivan (edd.), *Women in the ancient world: the Arethusa papers* 59–78. Albany

Fowler, D. P. (1989a). 'First thoughts on closure', *MD* 22.75–122

(1989b). 'Lucretius and politics', in M. T. Griffin and J. Barnes (edd.), *Philosophia togata: essays on philosophy and Roman society* 120–50. Oxford

(1995). 'Horace and the aesthetics of politics', in Harrison (1995a) 248–66

(1997). 'Second thoughts on closure', in Roberts et al. (1997) 3–22

(2000). *Roman constructions: readings in postmodern Latin.* Oxford

Fraenkel, E. (1957). *Horace.* Oxford

(1964). *Kleine Beiträge zur klassischen Philologie.* Vols. 1–2. Rome

Frederiksen, M. (1984). *Campania.* Rome

Freudenburg, K. (1990). 'Horace's satiric program and the language of contemporary criticism in *Satires* 2.1', *AJP* 111.187–203

(1993). *The walking Muse: Horace on the theory of satire.* Princeton

(2001). *Satires of Rome.* Cambridge

(forthcoming). 'Writing to/through Florus: sampling the addressee in Horace *Epistles* 2.2'

Fuller, D. (1988). *Blake's heroic argument.* London–New York–Sydney

Galinsky, K. (1996). *Augustan culture: an interpretive introduction.* Princeton

Garn, E. (1954). *Odenelemente im 1. Epistelbuch des Horaz.* Diss. Potsdam

Gigon, O. (1977).'Horaz und die Philosophie', in L. Straume-Zimmermann (ed.), *Die antike Philosophie als Maßstab und Realität* 437–508. Zurich–Munich

Gleason, M. W. (1995). *Making men. Sophists and self-presentation in ancient Rome.* Princeton

Goldberg, S. M. (1995). *Epic in republican Rome.* Oxford

González, J. (1988). 'The first oath *pro salute Augusti* found in Baetica', *ZPE* 72. 113–27

Goodyear, F. R. D. (1981). *The Annals of Tacitus: Books 1–6.* Vol. 2. Cambridge

Gordon, A. E. (1957). 'Potitus Valerius Messalla, Consul Suffect 29 BC', *University of California Publications in Classical Archaeology* 3.2.31–64

Gowers, E. (1993). 'Horace, *Satires* 1.5: an inconsequential journey', *PCPS* 39.48–66

Grant, M. A., and Fiske, G. C. (1924). 'Cicero's "Orator" and Horace's "Ars Poetica"', *HSCP* 35.1–74

(1929). *Cicero's De oratore and Horace's Ars poetica.* Madison

Griffin, J. (1985). *Latin poets and Roman life*. London
    (1993). 'Horace in the thirties', in Rudd (1993a) 1–22
    (1997). 'Cult and personality in Horace', *JRS* 87.54–69
Gruzelier, C. (1993). *Claudian. De raptu Proserpinae*. Oxford
Gurval, R. A. (1995). *Actium and Augustus: the politics and emotions of civil war*.
    Ann Arbor
Habinek, T. (1998). *The politics of Latin literature: writing, identity, and empire in
    ancient Rome*. Princeton
Hahn, E. A. (1939). '*Epodes* 5 and 17, *Carmina* 1.16 and 1.17', *TAPA* 70.213–30
Hammer, J. (1925). *Prolegomena to an edition of the Panegyricus Messallae*.
    New York
Hanslik, R. (1962). 'Horaz und Aktium', *Serta philologica Aenipontana/Innsbrucker
    Beiträge zur Kulturwissenschaft* 7–8.335–42
Hardie, A. (1998). 'Horace, the Paean and Roman choreia (Odes 4, 6)', *PLLS*
    10.251–93
Hardie, P. (1990). 'Ovid's Theban history: the first "anti-*Aeneid*"?', *CQ*
    40.224–35
    (1993). '*Ut pictura poesis*? Horace and the visual arts', in Rudd (1993a) 120–39
Harrer, G. A. (1928). 'Some verses of Cicero', *Studies in Philology* 25.70–91
Harris, W. V. (1979). *War and imperialism in Republican Rome 327–70 BC*. Oxford
Harrison, S. J. (1988). 'Deflating the *Odes*: Horace, *Epistles* 1.20', *CQ* 38.473–6
    (1990). 'Cicero's "De temporibus suis": the evidence reconsidered', *Hermes*
    118.455–63
    (1992). 'Fuscus the Stoic: Horace *Odes* 1.22 and *Epistles* 1.10', *CQ* 42.543–7
    (1995a). *Homage to Horace: a bimillenary celebration*. Oxford
    (1995b). 'Poetry, philosophy and letter-writing in Horace *Epistles* 1', in D. Innes,
    H. Hine and C. Pelling (edd.), *Ethics and rhetoric: classical essays for Donald
    Russell* 47–62. Oxford
Heinze, R. (1889). *De Horatio Bionis imitatore*. Bonn
Hellegouarc'h, J. (1972). *Le Vocabulaire latin des relations et des partis politiques sous
    la république*. 2nd edn. Paris
Heller, J. L. (1943). 'Nenia παίγνιον' *TAPA* 74.215–68
    (1962). 'Nepos σκορπιστής and Philoxenus', *TAPA* 93.61–89
Henderson, J. (1993). 'Be alert (your country needs lerts): Horace, *Satires* 1.9',
    PCPS 39.67–93
    (1997). *Figuring out Roman nobility: Juvenal's eighth satire*. Exeter
    (1998). *Fighting for Rome: poets and Caesars, history and civil war*. Cambridge
    (1999). *Writing down Rome: satire, comedy, and other offences in Latin poetry*.
    Oxford
Hendry, M. (1993). 'Three problems in the Cleopatra Ode', *CJ* 88.137–46
Herrmann, P. (1968). *Der römische Kaisereid. Untersuchungen zu seiner Herkunft
    und Entwicklung*. Göttingen
Heurgon, J. (1964). *The daily life of the Etruscans*. New York
Heyworth, S. J. (1995). 'Dividing poems', in O. Pecere and M. D. Reeve
    (edd.), *Formative stages of classical traditions: Latin texts from antiquity to the
    Renaissance* 117–48. Spoleto
Hinds, S. (1985). 'Booking the return trip: Ovid and *Tristia* 1', *PCPS* 31.13–32
    (1998). *Allusion and intertext: dynamics of appropriation in Roman poetry*.
    Cambridge

Hoeveler, D. L. (1990). *Romantic androgyny. The women within.* University Park–London

Hofmann, J. B., and Szantyr, A. (1965). *Lateinische Grammatik 2.2: Lateinische Syntax und Stilistik.* Munich

Hopkins, K. (1983). *Death and renewal.* Cambridge

Horsfall, N. (1979). 'Horace, *Sermones* 3', *LCM* 4.117–19

(1993a). 'Cicero and poetry: the place of prejudice in literary history', *PLLS* 7.1–7

(1993b). 'Empty shelves on the Palatine', *G&R* 40.58–67

(1995). *A companion to the study of Virgil.* Leiden–New York–Cologne

Housman, A. E. (1972). *The classical papers of A. E. Housman* (ed. J. Diggle and F. R. D. Goodyear). Vols. 1–3. Cambridge

Hubbard, M. (1975). 'The capture of Silenus', *PCPS* 21.53–62

(1995). '*Pindarici fontis qui non expalluit haustus*: Horace, *Epistles* 1.3', in Harrison (1995a) 219–27

Hunter, R. (1985). 'Horace on friendship and free speech: *Epistles* 1.18 and *Satires* 1.4', *Hermes* 113.480–90

(1996). *Theocritus and the archaeology of Greek poetry.* Cambridge

Huxley, H. H. (1966). 'Horace *Epode* 1.7–10 and the superfluous interrogative enclitic', *PACA* 9.60

Jackson, H. J. (1993). 'Coleridge's women, or Girls, girls, girls are made to love', *Studies in Romanticism* 32.577–600

Jal, P. (1963). *La Guerre civile à Rome: étude littéraire et morale.* Paris

Jani, C. D. (1778). *Q. Horatii Flacci opera.* Leipzig

Jenkyns, R. (1982). *Three classical poets.* London

Jocelyn, H. D. (1979). '*Vergilius cacozelus* (Donatus *Vita Vergilii* 44)', *PLLS* 2.67–142

(1980). 'Horace, *Odes* 2.5,' *LCM* 5.197–200

Johnson, W. R. (1993). *Horace and the dialectic of freedom: readings in Epistles 1.* Ithaca

Jones, F. (1983). 'Horace, four girls and the other man (*Odes* 2.5)', *LCM* 8.34–7

(1993). 'The role of the addressees in Horace, *Epistles*', *LCM* 18.7–11

Kaeppel, L. (1992). *Paian.* Berlin

Kaster, R. A. (1995). *Suetonius: De grammaticis et rhetoribus.* Oxford

Keller, O., and Holder, A. (1899). *Q. Horatii Flacci opera.* Leipzig

Kennedy, D. F. (1992). '"Augustan" and "anti-Augustan": reflections on terms of reference', in Powell (1992) 26–58

Kenney, E. J. (1990). *Apuleius: Cupid and Psyche.* Cambridge

Kerkhecker, A. (1999). *Callimachus' Book of Iambi.* Oxford

Keydana, G. (1997). *Absolute Konstruktionen in altindogermanischen Sprachen.* Göttingen

Kienast, D. (1982). *Augustus: Prinzeps und Monarch.* Darmstadt

Kilpatrick, R. S. (1969). 'Two Horatian proems: *Carm.* 1.26 and 1.32', *YCS* 21.215–39

(1970). 'An interpretation of Horace's *Epode* 13', *CQ* 20.135–41

(1986). *The poetry of friendship: Horace, Epistles 1.* Edmonton

(1990). *The poetry of criticism: Horace, Epistles 11 and Ars Poetica.* Edmonton

Kindstrand, J. F. (1976). *Bion of Borysthenes.* Uppsala

Kissel, W. (1994). 'Krise einer Freundschaft? (Hor. epist. 1,7)', in S. Koster (ed.), *Horaz-Studien* 79–102. Erlangen

Klingner, F. (1950). 'Horazens Brief an Augustus', *SBAW* 5.1–32. Munich

(1959). *Horatius. Opera.* (Teubner) Leipzig

Knox, P. E. (1995). *Ovid: Heroides. Select epistles.* Cambridge

Kolendo, J. (1981). 'La Répartition des places aux spectacles et la stratification sociale dans l'Empire Romain: à propos des inscriptions sur les gradins des amphithéâtres et théâtres', *Ktèma* 6. 301–15

Kraggerud, E. (1984). *Horaz und Aktium.* Oslo

Kraus, C. S., and Woodman, A. J. (1997). *Latin historians. (Greece & Rome* New Surveys in the Classics No. 27.) Oxford

La Penna, A. (1963). *Orazio e l'ideologia del principato.* Turin

(1972). 'Sunt qui Sappho malint: note sulla σύγκρισις di Saffo e Alceo nell' antichità', *Maia* 24.208–15

Lateiner, D. (1990). 'Mimetic syntax: metaphor from word order, especially in Ovid', *AJP* 111.204–37

Lease, E. B. (1928). 'The ablative absolute limited by conjunctions', *AJP* 49.348–53

Leo, F. (1901). *Die griechisch-römische Biographie nach ihrer literarischen Form.* Leipzig

Levine, M. M. (1995). 'The gendered grammar of Mediterranean hair', in H. Eilberg-Schwartz and W. Doniger (edd.), *Off with her head! The denial of women's identity in myth, religion, and culture* 76–130. Berkeley

Levitan, W. (1993). 'Give up the beginning?: Juno's mindful wrath (*Aeneid* 1.37)', *LCM* 18.14

Linderski, J. (1984). 'Rome, Aphrodisias and the *Res Gestae*: the *genera militiae* and the status of Octavian', *JRS* 74.74–80

Lohmann, D. (1991). 'Horaz Carmen III 2 und der Zyklus der "Römer-Oden"', *Der Altspr. Unt.* 3/91.62–75

Long, A. A., and Sedley, D. N. (1987). *The Hellenistic philosophers.* Vols. 1–2. Cambridge

Lowrie, M. (1992). 'A sympotic Achilles, Horace *Epode* 13', *AJP* 113.413–33

(1997). *Horace's narrative Odes.* Oxford

Lundström, S. (1976). 'Der Eingang des Proömiums zum dritten Buche der Georgica', *Hermes* 104.163–91

Lunelli, A. (1975). 'Solis rota', in *Scritti in onore di C. Diano* 201–16. Bologna

Lyne, R. O. A. M. (1978). *Ciris.* Cambridge

(1995). *Horace: behind the public poetry.* New Haven–London

Macleane, A. J. (1881). *Q. Horatii Flacci opera omnia.* London

Macleod, C. (1977). 'The poet, the critic, and the moralist: Horace, *Epistles 1,* 19', *CQ* 27.359–76 (= Macleod (1983) 262–79)

(1979a). 'The poetry of ethics: Horace, *Epistles* 1', *JRS* 69.16–27 (= Macleod (1983) 280–91)

(1979b). 'Horatian *imitatio* and *Odes* 2.5', in D. West and T. Woodman (edd.), *Creative imitation and Latin literature* 89–102, 222–4. Cambridge (= Macleod (1983) 245–61)

(1983). *Collected essays.* Oxford

Malcovati, E. (1943). *Cicerone e la poesia.* Pavia

(1966). 'La fortuna di Saffo nella letteratura latina', *Athenaeum* 44.3–31

Maltby, R. (1991). *A lexicon of ancient Latin etymologies.* Leeds

Mankin, D. (1995). *Horace: Epodes.* Cambridge

Marincola, J. (1997). *Authority and tradition in ancient historiography*. Cambridge

Martina, M. (1989). 'A proposito di *Hor. Epod. 1.29*', *B. Stud. Lat.* 19.49–53

Martindale, C. (1993). *Redeeming the text: Latin poetry and the hermeneutics of reception*. Cambridge

Mathiesen, T. J. (1983). *Aristides Quintilianus. On music*. New Haven–London

Maurach, G. (1968). 'Der Grundriss von Horazens erstem Epistelbuch', *AC* 11.73–124

May, J. M. (1990). 'The monologistic dialogue as a method of literary criticism: Cicero, *Brutus* 285–289 and Horace, *Epistles* 2.1.34–39', *Athenaeum* 68.177–80

Mayer, R. (1985). 'Horace on good manners', *PCPS* 31.33–46
   (1986). 'Horace's *Epistles* I and philosophy', *AJP* 107.55–73
   (1994). *Horace: Epistles Book I*. Cambridge
   (1995a). 'Horace's *Moyen de Parvenir*', in Harrison (1995a) 279–95
   (1995b). '*Graecia capta*: the Roman reception of Greek literature', *PLLS* 8.289–307

McGann, M. J. (1963). 'Vinnius Valens, son of Vinnius Asina?', *CQ* 13.258–9
   (1969). *Studies in Horace's first book of Epistles*. Brussels

McKeown, J. C. (1989, 1998). *Ovid: Amores*. Vols. 2–3. Leeds

Meeks, W. A. (1974). 'The image of the androgyne: some uses of a symbol in earliest Christianity', *History of Religions* 13.165–208

Michie, J. (1964). *The Odes of Horace*. London

Mikalson, J. D. (1975). *The sacred and civil calendar of the Athenian Year*. Princeton

Millar, F. (1973).'Triumvirate and Principate', *JRS* 63.50–69
   (1999). 'The first revolution: Imperator Caesar, 36–28 BC', *La Révolution romaine après Ronald Syme: bilans et perspectives* (Fondation Hardt Entretiens 46) 1–38. Vandoeuvres–Geneva

Miller, J. F. (1998). 'Horace's Pindaric Apollo (*Odes* 3.4.60–4)', *CQ* 48.445–52

Miller, P. A. (1994). *Lyric texts and lyric consciousness*. London

Milner, N. P. (1996). *Vegetius: Epitome of military science*. 2nd rev. edn. Liverpool

Moles, J. (1983). 'Some "last words" of M. Iunius Brutus', *Latomus* 42.763–79
   (1986). 'Cynicism in Horace *Epistles* I', *PLLS* 5.33–60
   (1987). 'Politics, philosophy and friendship in Horace *Odes* 2, 7', *QUCC* 25.59–72
   (1995). Review of Mayer (1994), *BMCR* 6.2.160–70

Momigliano, A. (1971). *The development of Greek biography*. Cambridge, MA

Mommsen, Th. (1912). *Reden und Aufsätze*. Berlin

Moralejo, J. L. (1995). 'Horacio y sus modelos griegos. (En torno a *Epi.* I 19, 21–34)', in E. Falque and F. Gascó (edd.), *Graecia capta: de la conquista de Grecia a la helenización de Roma* 45–81. Huelva

Muecke, F. (1993). *Horace: Satires II*. Warminster
   (1995). 'Law, rhetoric, and genre in Horace, *Satires* 2.1', in Harrison (1995a) 203–18

Murley, C. (1925). 'Cicero, *Pro Archia* and Horace, *Epistles* II, 1, 223ff.', *CJ* 21.533–4

Murray, O. (1993). 'Symposium and genre in the poetry of Horace', in Rudd (1993a) 89–105

Murray, W. M. and Petsas, P. M. (1989). *Octavian's campsite memorial for the Actian War.* Philadelphia

Mutschler, F.-H. (1974). 'Beobachtungen zur Gedichtanordnung in der ersten Odensammlung des Horaz', *RhM* 117.109–33

Mynors, R. A. B. (1990). *Virgil: Georgics.* Oxford

Nattiez, J.-J. (1993). *Wagner androgyne.* Eng. trans. Princeton

Nicolet, C. (1991). *Space, geography, and politics in the early Roman Empire.* Eng. trans. Ann Arbor

Nicoll, W. S. M. (1986). 'Horace's judgement on Sappho and Alcaeus', *Latomus* 45.603–8

Nisbet, R. G. M. (1959). 'Notes on Horace, *Epistles* 1', *CQ* 9.73–6 (= Nisbet (1995a) 1–5)

  (1984). 'Horace's *Epodes* and history', in Woodman–West (1984) 1–18 (= Nisbet (1995a) 161–81)

  (1995a). *Collected papers on Latin literature* (ed. S. J. Harrison). Oxford

  (1995b). 'The survivors: old-style literary men in the triumviral period', in Nisbet (1995a) 390–413

Nisbet, R. G. M., and Hubbard, M. (1970, 1978). *A commentary on Horace: Odes Book 1* and *Odes Book 11.* Oxford

Norden, E. (1913). *Agnostos Theos.* Leipzig–Berlin (reprinted Darmstadt, 1956)

  (1927). *P. Vergilius Maro: Aeneis Buch VI.* 3rd edn. Leipzig

  (1939). *Aus altrömischen Priesterbüchern.* Lund

Oakley, S. P. (1998). *A commentary on Livy books VI–X.* Vol. 2. Oxford

Obbarius, T. (1848). *Q. Horatii Flacci carmina.* Jena

Obbink, D. (1996). *Philodemus On piety: critical text with commentary.* Oxford

Oberhelman, S., and Armstrong, D. (1995). 'Satire as poetry and the impossibility of metathesis', in D. Obbink (ed.), *Philodemus and poetry* 233–54. New York–Oxford

O'Hara, J. (1996a). *True names: Vergil and the Alexandrian tradition of etymological wordplay.* Michigan

  (1996b). 'Sostratus *Suppl. Hell.* 733: a lost, possibly Catullan-era elegy on the six sex changes of Tiresias', *TAPA* 126.173–219

Oliensis, E. (1991). 'Canidia, Canicula, and the decorum of Horace's *Epodes*', *Arethusa* 24. 107–38

  (1995). 'Life after publication: Horace, *Epistles* 1.20', *Arethusa* 28.209–24

  (1998). *Horace and the rhetoric of authority.* Cambridge

Orelli, J. G. (1850). *Q. Horatius Flaccus.* Zurich

Owen, S. (1989). *Mi-Lou: poetry and the labyrinth of desire.* Cambridge, MA

Page, D. L. (1981). *Further Greek epigrams.* Cambridge

Page, T. E. (1895). *Q. Horatii Flacci Carminum Libri IV. Epodon Liber.* London

Panciera, S. (1956). 'Liburna', *Epigraphica* 18.130–56

Parker, P. (1996). 'Virile style', in L. Fradenburg and C. Freccero (edd.), *Premodern sexualities* 199–222. New York–London

Pascoli, G. (1921). *Lyra.* Livorno

Pasquali, G. (1950). 'Un verso oraziano, Cicerone ed Ennio', *SIFC* 24.127–8

  (1964). *Orazio Lirico.* Rev. repr. (Orig. publ. 1920.) Florence

Pease, A. S. (1920). *M. Tulli Ciceronis de divinatione.* Urbana

  (1935). *Publi Vergili Maronis liber quartus.* Cambridge, MA

  (1958). *M. Tulli Ciceronis de natura deorum.* Vol. 2. Cambridge, MA

Pelling, C. B. R. (1988). *Plutarch: Life of Antony.* Cambridge
  (1996). 'The triumviral period', in *CAH* ² 10.1–69
  (1997). Review of Gurval (1995), *JRS* 87.289–90
Perkins, D. (1992). *Is literary history possible?* Baltimore–London
Petrochilos, N. K. (1974). *Roman attitudes to the Greeks.* Athens
Pfeiffer, R. (1968). *History of classical scholarship: from the beginnings to the end of the Hellenistic age.* Oxford
Pfiffig, A. J. (1975). *Religio Etrusca.* Graz
Pighi, G. B. (1965). *De ludis saecularibus populi Romani Quiritium.* 2nd edn. Amsterdam
Pingiatoglou, S. (1981). *Eileithyia.* Würzburg
Pinsent, J. (1976). 'Horace, *Odes* 3.2.13', *LCM* 1.84
Podlecki, A. J. (1969). 'The Peripatetics as literary critics', *Phoenix* 23.114–37
Port, W. (1926). 'Die Anordnung in Gedichtbüchern augusteischer Zeit', *Philol.* 81.280–308; 427–68
Pöschl, V. (1970). *Horazische Lyrik: Interpretationen.* Heidelberg
Powell, A. (1992). *Roman poetry and propaganda in the age of Augustus.* Bristol
Powell, J. G. F. (1988). *Cicero: Cato Maior de senectute.* Cambridge
  (1990). *Cicero: On friendship and the Dream of Scipio.* Warminster
Powell, J. U. (1925). *Collectanea Alexandrina.* Oxford
Préaux, J. (1968). *Horace. Epîtres, livre I.* Paris
Pulleyn, S. (1994). 'The power of names in classical Greek religion', *CQ* 44.17–25
Purcell, N. (1995). 'On the sacking of Carthage and Corinth', in D. Innes, H. Hine and C. Pelling (edd.), *Ethics and rhetoric: classical essays for Donald Russell* 133–48. Oxford
Putnam, M. C. J. (1986). *Artifices of eternity: Horace's fourth book of Odes.* Ithaca–London
  (1994). 'Structure and design in Horace *Odes* 1.17', *CW* 87.357–75
  (1995a). *Virgil's Aeneid: interpretation and influence.* Chapel Hill–London
  (1995b). 'From lyric to letter: Iccius in Horace *Odes* 1.29 and *Epistles* 1.12', *Arethusa* 28.193–208
  (1996). 'Pastoral satire', *Arion* 3.303–16
  (2000). *Horace's Carmen Saeculare. Ritual magic and the poet's art.* New Haven
Quinn, K. (1980). *Horace: the Odes.* Basingstoke–London
Ramage, E. S. (1987). *The nature and purpose of Augustus' 'Res Gestae'.* Stuttgart
Rawson, E. (1985). *Intellectual life in the late Roman republic.* London
  (1991). '*Discrimina ordinum*: the *lex Julia theatralis*', in *Roman culture and society: collected papers* 508–45. Oxford
Reckford, K. J. (1969). *Horace.* New York
Reggiani, R. (1976). 'Varianti testuali e "funzionalità" semiologica: Cordo e Codro in Giovenale', *QUCC* 21.125–36
Reinhold, M. (1933). *M. Agrippa.* Geneva, NY
  (1988). *From Republic to Principate: an historical commentary on Cassius Dio's Roman History Books 49–52 (36–29 BC).* Atlanta
Richardson, N. J. (1994). 'Aristotle and Hellenistic scholarship', in *La Philologie grecque à l'époque hellénistique et romaine* (Fondation Hardt Entretiens 40) 7–28. Vandoeuvres–Geneva

Richmond, J. A. (1970). 'Horace's "mottoes" and Catullus 51', *RhM* 113.197–204

Roberts, D. H., Dunn, F. M., and Fowler, D. (1997). *Classical closure: reading the end in Greek and Latin literature*. Princeton

Rosati, G. (1996). 'Sabinus, the *Heroides* and the poet-nightingale. Some observations on the authenticity of the *Epistula Sapphus*', *CQ* 46.207–16

Rosenmeyer, T. G. (1985). 'Ancient literary genres: a mirage?', *Yearbook of Comp. and Gen. Lit.* 34.74–84

Ross, D. O. (1975a). *Backgrounds to Augustan poetry*. Oxford

(1975b). 'The *Culex* and *Moretum* as post-Augustan literary parodies', *HSCP* 79.235–63

Rossi, L. E. (1998). 'Orazio, un lirico greco senza musica', *Seminari Romani di Cultura Greca* 1.163–81

Rostagni, A. (1944). *Suetonio: De poetis*. Turin

(1960). 'Virgilio, Valgio e ... Codro. Chi era costui?', *Studi in onore di Luigi Castiglioni* 2.809–33. Florence (= *Virgilio minore* (2nd edn, Rome, 1961) 405–27)

Rudd, N. (1979). '*Epistles* and *Sermones*', *LCM* 4.149

(1982). 'Horace', in E. J. Kenney and W. V. Clausen (edd.), *The Cambridge history of classical literature* 2.371–404. Cambridge

(1989). *Horace: Epistles Book II and Epistle to the Pisones ('Ars Poetica')*. Cambridge

(1993a). *Horace 2000: a celebration. Essays for the bimillennium*. Bristol

(1993b). 'Horace as a moralist', in Rudd (1993a) 64–88

Russell, D. A. (1964). '*Longinus': On the sublime*. Oxford

(1981). *Criticism in antiquity*. London

Russell, D. A. and Winterbottom, M. (1972). *Ancient literary criticism*. Oxford

Rutherford, I. (1997). 'Odes and ends: closure in Greek lyric', in Roberts et al. (1997) 43–61

(2001). *Pindar's Paeans. A reading of the fragments with a survey of the genre*. Oxford

Salat, P. (1969). 'La Composition du livre I des Odes d'Horace', *Latomus* 28.554–74

Saller, R. P. (1982). *Personal patronage under the early Empire*. Cambridge

Salmon, E. T. (1967). *Samnium and the Samnites*. Cambridge

Santirocco, M. S. (1986). *Unity and design in Horace's Odes*. Chapel Hill–London

(1995). 'Horace and Augustan ideology', *Arethusa* 28.225–43

Scarpat, G. (1964). *Parrhesia. Storia del termine e delle sue traduzioni in latino*. Brescia

Scheid, J. (1995). 'Graeco ritu. A typically Roman way of honoring the gods', *HCSP* 97.15–31

Schmidt, E. A. (1977). '*Amica uis pastoribus*: der Iambiker Horaz in seinem Epodenbuch', *Gymnasium* 84.401–23

Schmidt, W. (1908). *Geburtstag im Altertum*. Giessen

Schnurr, C. (1992). 'The *lex Julia theatralis* of Augustus: some remarks on seating problems in theatre, amphitheatre and circus', *LCM* 17.147–60

Schoonhoven, H. (1980). *Elegiae in Maecenatem: prolegomena, text and commentary*. Groningen

Schrijvers, P. H. (1973). 'Comment terminer une ode?', *Mnem.* 26.140–59
Schroeder, S. (1999). *Geschichte und Theorie der Gattung Paian.* Stuttgart–Leipzig
Scotti, M. (1982). 'I "canoni" degli autori greci', *Esperienze letterarie* 7.74–91
Scullard, H. H. (1981). *Festivals and ceremonies of the Roman Republic.* London
Seager, R. (1993). 'Horace and Augustus: poetry and policy', in Rudd (1993a) 23–40
Setaioli, A. (1981). 'Gli Epodi di Orazio nella critica dal 1937–72 (con un' appendice fine al 1978)', *ANRW* 2.31.3.1674–1788
Shackleton Bailey, D. R. (1985a). *Horatius. Opera.* (Teubner.) Stuttgart
    (1985b). '*Vindiciae Horatianae*', *HSCP* 89.153–70
    (1997). *Selected classical papers.* Ann Arbor
Sherk, R. K. (1969). *Roman documents from the Greek East: senatus consulta and epistulae to the age of Augustus.* Baltimore
Shorey, P. (1909). *Horace: Odes and Epodes.* Boston
Silk, E. T. (1952). 'Notes on Cicero and the Odes of Horace', *YCS* 13.145–58
Skinner, M. B. (1997). '*Ego mulier*: the construction of male sexuality in Catullus', in J. P. Hallett and M. B. Skinner (edd.), *Roman sexualities* 129–50. Princeton
Skutsch, O. (1963). 'The structure of the Propertian Monobiblos', *CP* 58.238–9
    (1985). *The Annals of Ennius.* Oxford
Smith, B. H. (1968). *Poetic closure.* Chicago
Snell, B. (1935). 'Zwei Töpfe mit Euripides-Papyri', *Hermes* 70.119–20
Soubiran, J. (1972). *Cicéron: Aratea, fragments poétiques.* Paris
Spaeth, J. W. (1930/31). 'Cicero the poet', *CJ* 26.500–12
Stark, R. (1957). 'Sapphoreminiszenzen', *Hermes* 85.325–35
Stehle, E. (1997). *Performance and gender in ancient Greece.* Princeton
Sturtevant, E. H. (1912). 'O matre pulchra filia pulchrior', *CR* 26.119–22
Suerbaum, W. (1999). *Vergils 'Aeneis'.* Stuttgart
Suringar, W. H. D. (1854). *M. Tulli Ciceronis commentarii rerum suarum sive de vita sua.* Leiden
Syme, R. (1939). *The Roman revolution.* Oxford
    (1978). *History in Ovid.* Oxford
    (1979). *Roman papers.* Vol. 1. Oxford
    (1984). *Roman papers.* Vol. 3. Oxford
    (1986). *The Augustan aristocracy.* Oxford
    (1991). *Roman papers.* Vol. 6. Oxford
Syndikus, H. P. (1972, 1973). *Die Lyrik des Horaz.* 2 vols. Darmstadt
Thill, A. (1979). *Alter ab illo. Recherches sur l'imitation dans la poésie personelle à l'époque augustéenne.* Paris
Thomas, R. F. (1986). 'Virgil's *Georgics* and the art of reference', *HSCP* 90.171–98
    (1988). *Virgil: Georgics Books III–IV.* Cambridge
    (1998). 'Virgil's Pindar?', in P. Knox and C. Foss (edd.), *Style and tradition: studies in honor of Wendell Clausen* 99–120. Stuttgart–Leipzig
Thompson, D. W. (1936). *A glossary of Greek birds.* Oxford (reprinted Hildesheim, 1966)
Thompson, M. W. (1970). 'The date of Horace's First *Epode*', *CQ* 20.328–34
Thomson, D. F. S. (1997). *Catullus: edited with a textual and interpretative commentary.* Toronto–Buffalo–London

Toll, K. (1997). 'Making Roman-ness and the *Aeneid*', *CA* 16.34–56

Townend, G. B. (1965). 'The poems', in T. A. Dorey (ed.), *Cicero* 109–34. London

Traglia, A. (1950). *La lingua di Cicerone poeta*. Bari

Traina, A. (1991). 'Orazio e Aristippo. Le *Epistole* e l'arte di convivere', *RDF* 119
    285–305

Treggiari, S. (1973). 'Cicero, Horace, and mutual friends: Lamiae and Varrones
    Murenae', *Phoenix* 27.245–61

Turner, E. G. (1984). *Papiri greci.* (Ed. by M. Manfredi.) Rome

Vahlen, J. (1898). 'Varia', *Hermes* 33.245–61

Van Rooy, C. A. (1973). '"Imitatio" of Vergil, *Eclogues* in Horace, *Satires*, Book
    I', *AC* 16.69–88

Vardi, A. D. (1996). '*Diiudicatio locorum*: Gellius and the history of a mode in
    ancient comparative criticism', *CQ* 46.492–514

Vaughn, J. W. (1976). *The Megara (Moschus IV): Text, translation and commentary.*
    (*Noctes Romanae* 14.) Bern–Stuttgart

Veyne, P. (1984). *Writing history. Essay on epistemology.* Eng. trans. Manchester
    (1988). *Roman erotic elegy: love, poetry, and the West.* Eng. trans. Chicago

Voigt, E.-M. (1971). *Sappho et Alcaeus. Fragmenta.* Amsterdam

Wallace-Hadrill, A. (1988). 'Greek knowledge, Roman power', *CP* 83.
    224–33
    (1990). 'Roman arches and Greek honours: the language of power at Rome',
    PCPS 36.143–81

Walsh, P. G. (1974). *Livy.* (*Greece & Rome* New Surveys in the Classics No. 8.)
    Oxford

Watson, L. C. (1983). 'Two nautical points: 1. Horace *Epode* 1.1–2; 2. Catullus
    4.20–21', *LCM* 8.66–9
    (1995). 'Horace's *Epodes*: the impotence of *iambos*?', in Harrison (1995a)
    188–202

Weinstock, S. (1971). *Divus Julius.* Oxford

West, D. (1967). *Reading Horace.* Edinburgh
    (1991). '*Cur me querelis* (Horace, *Odes* 2.17)', *AJP* 112.45–52
    (1995). *Horace Odes I: Carpe diem.* Oxford

White, P. (1987). 'Horace, *Epistles* 2.1.50–54', *TAPA* 117.227–34
    (1988). 'Julius Caesar in Augustan Rome', *Phoenix* 42.334–56
    (1993). *Promised verse: poets in the society of Augustan Rome.* Cambridge, MA

Wickham, E. C. (1891). *The works of Horace.* Vol. 2. Oxford

Wilamowitz-Moellendorff, U. von (1913). *Sappho und Simonides.* Berlin

Wili, W. (1948). *Horaz und die augusteische Kultur.* Basel

Wilkinson, L. P. (1945). *Horace and his lyric poetry.* (2nd edn 1951.) Cambridge
    (1963). *Golden Latin artistry.* Cambridge

Williams, G. (1968). *Tradition and originality in Roman poetry.* Oxford
    (1969). *The third book of Horace's Odes.* Oxford
    (1978). *Change and decline: Roman literature in the early empire.* Berkeley–Los
    Angeles
    (1995). '*Libertino patre natus*: true or false?', in Harrison (1995a) 296–313

Wills, J. (1993). 'Virgil's *Cuium*', *Vergilius* 39.3–11
    (1996). *Repetition in Latin poetry: figures of allusion.* Oxford

Wind, E. (1958). *Pagan mysteries in the Renaissance*. London
Wingo, E. O. (1972). *Latin punctuation in the classical age*. The Hague–Paris
Winnington-Ingram, R. P. (1963). *Aristidis Quintiliani de musica libri tres*. (Teubner.) Leipzig
Wiseman, T. P. (1971). *New men in the Roman senate: 139 BC – AD 14*. Oxford
    (1974). *Cinna the poet*. Leicester
    (1979). *Clio's cosmetics*. Leicester
    (1985). *Catullus and his world*. Cambridge
Wistrand, E. (1958). *Horace's Ninth Epode and its historical background*. Göteborg
Woodman, A. J. (1974). 'Exegi monumentum', in T. Woodman and D. West (edd.), *Quality and pleasure in Latin poetry* 115–28, 151–6. Cambridge
    (1983a). *Velleius Paterculus: the Caesarian and Augustan narrative*. Cambridge
    (1983b). 'Horace, Epistles 1, 19, 23–40', *MH* 40.75–81
Woodman, A. J., and Martin, R. H. (1996). *The Annals of Tacitus Book 3*. Cambridge
Woodman, T., and West, D. (1984). *Poetry and politics in the age of Augustus*. Cambridge
Zeitlin, F. (1985). 'Playing the other: theater, theatricality, and the feminine in Greek drama', *Representations* 11.63–94
Zetzel, J. (1980). 'Horace's *Liber sermonum*: the structure of ambiguity', *Arethusa* 13.59–77
    (1983). 'Re-creating the canon: Augustan literature and the Alexandrian past', *Critical Inquiry* 10.83–105
    (1992). 'Roman romanticism and other fables', in K. Galinsky (ed.), *The interpretation of Roman poetry: empiricism or hermeneutics?* 41–57. Frankfurt–Bern–New York–Paris
    (1996). 'Poetic baldness and its cure', *MD* 36.73–100
    (1998). '*De re publica* and De rerum natura', in P. Knox and C. Foss (edd.), *Style and tradition: studies in honor of Wendell Clausen* 230–47. Stuttgart–Leipzig
Zielinski, T. S. (1912). *Cicero im Wandel der Jahrhunderte*. Leipzig

INDEXES

B INDEX LOCORUM